Assessing Young Children in Inclusive Settings

The Blended Practices Approach

Second Edition

by

Kristie Pretti-Frontczak, Ph.D.
Inclusion Thought Leader • Educators' Educator • Fierce Play Advocate
Inclusive Schooling
B2K Solutions, Ltd. and Inclusive Schooling, LLC
Hinckley, Ohio

and

Jennifer Grisham, Ed.D.
Passionate Teacher Educator • Prolific Author • Administrative Sage
University of Kentucky
University of Kentucky, Lexington

with

Lynn D. Sullivan, M.Ed.
Systems Thinker • Strategic Connector • Path Finder
LDS Consulting
Fort Worth, Texas

with invited contributors

·P·A·U·L·H·
BROOKES
PUBLISHING CO.®

Baltimore • London • Sydney

Paul H. Brookes Publishing Co.
Post Office Box 10624
Baltimore, Maryland 21285-0624
USA

www.brookespublishing.com

Typeset by Progressive Publishing Services, York, Pennsylvania.
Manufactured in the United States of America by Sheridan Books, Inc.

All examples in this book are composites. Any similarity to actual individuals or circumstances is coincidental, and no implications should be inferred.

Stock art © iStockphoto.

Library of Congress Cataloging-in-Publication Data

Names: Pretti-Frontczak, Kristie, author. | Grisham, Jennifer, author. |
 Sullivan, Lynn, author.
Title: Assessing young children in inclusive settings: the blended practices approach/by Kristie
 Pretti-Frontczak, Ph.D., Inclusion Thought Leader, Educators' Educator, Fierce Play Advocate
 Inclusive Schooling, B2K Solutions, Ltd. and Inclusive Schooling, LLC, Hinckley, OH, and Jennifer
 Grisham, Ed.D., Teacher Educator, Author, Sage University of Kentucky, University of Kentucky,
 Lexington, with Lynn D. Sullivan, M.Ed., Systems Thinker, Strategic Connector, Path Finder, LDS
 Consulting, Fort Worth, Texas, with invited contributors.
Description: Second Edition. | Baltimore, Maryland: Paul H. Brookes Publishing Co., 2023 |
 Previous edition copyright 2011 | Includes bibliographical references and index.
Identifiers: LCCN 2022019997 (print) | LCCN 2022019998 (ebook) | ISBN 9781681255996 (Paperback) |
 ISBN 9781681256009 (epub) | ISBN 9781681256016 (pdf)
Subjects: LCSH: Educational tests and measurements. | Early childhood education. |
 Inclusive education.
Classification: LCC LB3051 .A76646 2023 (print) | LCC LB3051 (ebook) |
 DDC 372.126/2—dc23/eng/20220520
LC record available at https://lccn.loc.gov/2022019997
LC ebook record available at https://lccn.loc.gov/2022019998

British Library Cataloguing in Publication data are available from the British Library.

· 2026   2025   2024   2023   2022

10   9   8   7   6   5   4   3   2   1

Contents

Chapter 5   Critical Decision-Making Practices 83

Lynn D. Sullivan, Kristie Pretti-Frontczak,
and Jennifer Grisham

Section II   **Reasons for Conducting Assessment (Assessment Purposes)**

Kristie Pretti-Frontczak, Jennifer Grisham, Lynn D. Sullivan,
and Sarah Hawkins-Lear

Chapter 7   Assessment for Progress Monitoring Purposes 137
*Jennifer Grisham, Kristie Pretti-Frontczak, Ashley Lyons-Picard,
Sarah Hawkins-Lear, and Lynn D. Sullivan*

**Chapter 8   Recommended Practices in Identifying
Children for Special Services** 163
Kristie Pretti-Frontczak and Jennifer Grisham

Chapter 9   Program Evaluation 197
Jennifer Grisham and Kristie Pretti-Frontczak

About the Downloads and Online Companion Materials

Purchasers of this book may download, print, and/or photocopy appendices for professional or educational use.

To access the materials that come with this book:

1. Go to the Brookes Publishing Download Hub: http://downloads.brookes publishing.com

2. Register to create an account (or log in with an existing account).

3. Filter or search for the book title *Assessing Young Children in Inclusive Settings: The Blended Practices Approach, Second Edition*.

The **downloads** include the following:

Appendix A   Lists of Recommended Practices for the Decision-Making Process

Appendix B   Revised Curriculum-Based Assessment Rating Rubric and Glossary

The **Online Companion Materials** include PowerPoints for each book chapter. Each PowerPoint includes slides, additional resources, and suggested application activities.

About the Authors

Kristie Pretti-Frontczak, Ph.D., President of B2K Solutions, Ltd., and Partner at Inclusive Schooling, LLC, Hinckley, Ohio

Dr. Pretti-Frontczak, is a highly sought-after speaker, accomplished author, and educators' educator. She began her career as an early interventionist and then spent 16 years as a tenured professor at Kent State University. While at Kent State, she directed 13 federal grants, mentored hundreds of graduate students, and authored many articles, chapters, and books related to supporting young children in inclusive settings. Dr. Pretti-Frontczak was one of the original co-creators of the Assessment, Evaluation, and Programming System for Infants and Children and, alongside her mentor Dr. Diane Bricker, pioneered research related to embedding instruction into daily activities. She also played a primary role in conducting one of the first treatment validity studies on authentic assessment and worked extensively to validate standards for rating the quality of early childhood assessments. She is a past president of the International Division for Early Childhood and a recipient of the Merle B. Karnes Award for Service to the Division. She has conducted research and written extensively on the topics of tiered interventions and how to support systems change in early care and education. Over the past decade, her work has centered on raising the emotional intelligence of educational leaders, including those forging a bridge between preschool and kindergarten. By raising the emotional intelligence of educational leaders, kinder, more inclusive, and more creative schools are built. Since 2013, she has followed her true passion for designing and delivering transformative professional development as a social entrepreneur. She currently partners with Dr. Julie Causton from Inclusive Schooling to create schools where all students flourish and educational systems, practices, and spaces are reimagined. To date, she has accumulated over 50,000 hours of helping educators and leaders work from a place of compassion, hope, and love in locations from Cincinnati to Singapore.

Jennifer Grisham, Ed.D., Professor, University of Kentucky, Lexington

Dr. Grisham is Professor in the Interdisciplinary Early Childhood Education program at the University of Kentucky, Lexington. She received her doctorate in education from the University of Kentucky. She is also Faculty Director of the Early Childhood Laboratory at the University of Kentucky, an inclusive early childhood program for children from birth to 5 years of age. Dr. Grisham has directed research projects on topics including linking assessment and instruction, early care and education program quality, and individualizing instruction for young children with disabilities. In addition, she has conducted research on the effectiveness of instructional procedures that are embedded into developmentally appropriate activities, the application of multitiered systems of support in early childhood settings, and coaching teachers and caregivers to implement evidence-based instructional strategies with fidelity. In addition, Dr. Grisham is Project Director for the Kentucky Deaf-Blind Project, which provides technical assistance to families and service providers of infants, toddlers, children, and youth with deaf-blindness. She coauthored a book titled *Reach for the Stars: Planning for the Future* (2013), which is used to support families of young children to plan for their children's future and articulate their priorities to educational team members, as well as *Blended Practices for Teaching Young Children in Inclusive Settings* (2017) and *Blended Assessment Practices in Early Childhood Education* (2011). Finally, Dr. Grisham directed the nationwide field test for the AEPS®-3 and is a member of the Early Intervention Management Research Group that oversees research and development of the AEPS-3. Dr. Grisham is frequently asked to provide professional development to state departments of education, universities, and local education agencies on topics on which she conducts research throughout the country. Dr. Grisham is cofounder of a children's home and preschool program in Guatemala City called Hope for Tomorrow, where she accompanies students on the education abroad program. Dr. Grisham also works internationally in other locations to promote inclusion of young children with disabilities and collaborates with colleagues around the world on issues that support the development of early intervention services.

Lynn D. Sullivan, M.Ed., Private Consultant, LDS Consulting, Fort Worth, Texas

Lynn D. Sullivan is currently a private consultant in the areas of special education, early childhood, and interagency collaboration. After a first career in social work, she spent 35 years as the early childhood consultant for one of 20 regional technical assistance centers in Texas. In that career with Education Service Center (ESC), Region 11, Ms. Sullivan provided consultative and technical assistance to local school districts, charter schools, and community agencies in the development and improvement of instructional programs and services for students with disabilities ages 3, 4, and 5. She planned, facilitated, presented, and coordinated regional training for educators (including pre-K and kindergarten teachers), speech-language pathologists, diagnosticians, and campus and district leaders of preschoolers with disabilities. These were based on federal, state, regional, and local data sources along with anecdotal patterns, trend lines in longitudinal data analysis, and school district priorities. In conjunction with Drs. Pretti-Frontczak and Grisham, Ms. Sullivan developed a multi-year, data-driven project to support and sustain best practices in meeting the needs of young children with disabilities in small and rural communities. This collaboration involved ESC staff, campus and district leadership, and a national research team. The national research team incorporated design and lessons learned in several published materials. It was during that project that the curriculum framework elements of the ASAP acronym (assessment, scope and sequence, activities, and progress monitoring) and umbrella visual were created. Ms. Sullivan also co-developed with Dr. Grisham a multiyear project to inform, support, and sustain research-based Tier 3 strategies on targeted campuses. This project involved the use of face-to-face sessions, asynchronous resources, and online conferencing platforms. The project coordinated efforts across ESC staff, university researchers, and campus teams in several counties who provided services for young learners with IEPs. Ms. Sullivan served as the Part B representative on the Texas Interagency Coordinating Council for Early Childhood Intervention for 18 years and is currently a member of CEC and DEC, having served as Texas DEC president from 1994 to 1996. In 2007, she was honored to be a Curriculum Section co-author for the DEC resource *Promoting Positive Outcomes for Children with Disabilities: Recommendations for Curriculum, Assessment, and Program Evaluation*. More recently, she co-edited the 2014 DEC publication *Blending Practices for All Children* (Young Exceptional Children Monograph Series No. 16).

About the Contributors

Rebecca V. Crawford, Ph.D., Clinical Faculty, Eastern Kentucky University, Richmond

Dr. Rebecca Crawford is clinical faculty in Applied Human Sciences at Eastern Kentucky University. Dr. Crawford has experience as a preschool teacher, as well as director of a child care center. She advocates for early intervention and inclusion of all children.

Sarah Hawkins-Lear, Ed.D., Clinical Associate Professor, University of Kentucky, Lexington

Dr. Sarah Hawkins-Lear is a clinical associate professor in the Department of Early Childhood, Special Education, and Rehabilitation Counseling at the University of Kentucky. Prior to higher education, Dr. Hawkins-Lear provided services to young children with high-intensity needs within the home, child care centers, inclusive preschool classrooms, and clinical settings. Dr. Hawkins-Lear teaches courses that focus on authentic assessment, embedded instruction, intervention planning, and assistive technology in early childhood settings. Her research interests include designing interventions for early childhood educators to implement when working with young children who have high-intensity needs.

Ashley Lyons-Picard, M.Ed., Adjunct, Kent State University, Kent, Ohio

As an academic, adjunct, consultant, coach, parent of children with special needs, and advocate, Ashley Lyons-Picard is dedicated to exploring and identifying solutions to the complex issues that face the field of special education, particularly that of early intervention and early childhood special education (EI/ECSE). Having benefited from an education and work experience in the field, and subsequently raising children who are twice exceptional, Ashley has a strong and unique perspective that she brings to her research, writing, delivery of preservice and in-service professional development, and advocacy. Ashley previously served as the Division for Early Childhood Children's Action Network Coordinator, Chair of the DEC Policy and Advocacy Council, and CAN Coordinator for the Ohio subdivision of DEC. She is an adjunct at Kent State University and a consultant for a variety of education-related projects and initiatives, with a focus on assessment, IEPs, inclusion, parent–professional development, advocacy, and educational leadership. Ashley is passionate about advocating for young children with exceptionalities and their families, with a focus on systems-level changes that will improve the funding, implementation, accessibility, and effectiveness of services for all young children.

Julie Harp Rutland, Ph.D., Associate Professor, Eastern Kentucky University, Richmond

Julie Harp Rutland, Ph.D., is Associate Professor in the College of Education and Applied Human Sciences at Eastern Kentucky University. Julie has experience in many roles, including that of a teacher, administrator, researcher, and early interventionist working directly with young children and their families. Julie has authored chapters and articles, and presents at both state and international conferences annually, with a focus on early intervention, sibling intervention, and working with families. Currently, she serves the Division for Early Childhood of the Council for Exceptional Children at both the state and national level. In addition to her professional roles, Julie is a parent of four children, with one having multiple disabilities. The combination of these experiences has provided a unique lens with which Julie views early childhood education.

Lin Zhu, Ph.D., Assistant Professor, Eastern Washington University, Cheney

Lin Zhu is Assistant Professor of Early Childhood Education at Eastern Washington University. She earned her doctoral degree in special education from the University of Kentucky.

Foreword

I am honored that the authors asked me to write this foreword for *Assessing Young Children in Inclusive Settings: The Blended Practices Approach, Second Edition*. I have had the privilege to study under Dr. Pretti-Frontczak as a graduate student and the opportunity to collaborate and learn from Dr. Grisham for many years. As an early childhood consultant in Iowa, where many teachers were transitioning from traditionally segregated classrooms to those utilizing a blended model, the first edition of this book was crucial in supporting my work as a consultant and coach. The contribution these authors have made and their ability to make space for open and honest conversations about these complex topics has allowed practitioners to be vulnerable and open to learning new skills. As a teacher, consultant, and coach of adults, I am thankful for their research, passion, collaboration, and friendship.

My own understanding and implementation of inclusive practices has been transformed by *Blended Practices for Teaching Young Children in Inclusive Settings* (Grisham-Brown, Hemmeter, & Pretti-Frontczak, 2005). During the transition of moving to blended classrooms, the difficulties have been evident. Teachers have struggled to know how to provide instruction, assess all students with differing needs, and meet various program requirements based on funding. The first edition of this book came at a time when teachers needed support and a path to follow. Authentic assessment resonated with many teachers, as the message of play and simultaneously providing instruction was a strength. The ability for teachers to play, instruct, and observe using authentic assessment concurrently changed their world. Teachers were previously completing several standardized assessments because they were required; however, they rarely afforded teachers information on child strengths or how to plan developmentally appropriate activities for the children. Authentic assessment allows teachers to observe children during play while also documenting what they know and what they still need to learn. Authentic assessment allows teachers to focus on functional skills that young children need to navigate their daily routines and activities.

It is the responsibility of all who support young children to be consumers of research to ensure the assessments they are using with young children are appropriate and useful in developing goals, guiding instruction, and increasing the positive outcomes for children and their families. Readers will find Pretti-Frontczak and colleagues have provided early care and education providers a tool to support them in developing their understanding of the technical adequacy of assessments they use. Teachers can now feel empowered to ask questions about the purpose of the assessments to ensure they are validated for their stated purpose.

Assessment practices in early childhood once looked very similar to the K-12 system; however, authentic assessment has played a key role in reshaping the assessment landscape. Observing children to make instructional decisions and using curriculum-based assessment in early childhood have given teachers the information they need to make curricular decisions, plan for groups and individual children, and confidently embed new learning into the daily activities and routines of the children. Young children learn through repetition; the more opportunities teachers can provide throughout the day for a child to practice functional skills in meaningful ways, the quicker the child will learn.

This book should be required for every new teacher working in early care and education environments. It supports them in navigating the complexities of teaching and assessment in a blended classroom while also providing real-life examples and solutions to situations that arise across many programs. I am grateful for the opportunity to learn from these transformational authors.

Melanie Reese
Education Program Consultant
Iowa Department of Education

REFERENCE

Grisham-Brown, J., Hemmeter, M. L., & Pretti-Frontczak, K. (2005). *Blended practices for teaching young children in inclusive settings*. Paul H. Brookes Publishing Co.

Foreword

Assessment Equity in Inclusive Settings

What does equity mean within assessment in inclusive early childhood special education? Imagine that inclusion and equity are birth rights, that assessment is truly about highlighting strengths and determining what is needed to provide access, supports, and participation. With grounding in these areas, equity should be a concept we embrace *before* considerations about assessment. Through focusing on systems, we can address each layer related to assessment to consider how it can be more equity centered. My colleagues and I assert that equity-empowered systems take an asset-based focus on disability in young children (Blanchard et al., 2021). This means that there are ways to prepare for assessing (within systems and individuals) and ways to interpret and use assessment information that focus on assets, access, participation, and supports while also acknowledging the ways racism and bias impact systems and institutions (Iruka, 2022). Here are a few decision points that can support equity in assessment:

1. Policies around eligibility: How is information gathered to determine eligibility? Which instruments are used? Settings of assessment? How is the family/caregiver voice elevated? When and where does assessment occur? What languages are included or available? Based on the answers to these questions, how are these decisions made and how often are they reviewed or revised? Is there equitable access for young children and families?

2. Beyond policies and system-level decisions, individuals should start with their own positionality around assessment and the focus of assessment to support equity. In other words, what are your biases around assessment, the child or setting? How do those on the team acknowledge and minimize the impact of their biases?

   a. When interpreting results and/or making diagnoses, how is family voice and perspective represented? How are potential diagnoses viewed through a cultural lens to understand the microcultural differences in development and consider alternative understandings of development?

3. For child progress monitoring, when, where, how, and by whom is child data collected? How is progress determined and data interpreted? What are the ways that individualized instruction is planned to support progress? How are different ways of expression and knowing documented to acknowledge progress?

4. When assessing for program planning, what measures or assessments are used and how are these decisions made? Are there areas you feel are not capturing through the selected measure(s) and, if so, how will you gather this information from a wide range of children? How is the information gathered used for individual and group planning? What accountability strategies and methods are used and how does this inform a feedback loop and programmatic, classroom, or other changes?

Equity within assessment is not a passive pursuit. It is an important step in advancing equity for all young children, their families, and society, especially for children with disabilities. Without intentional awareness, effort and action, we decidedly reinforce entrenched practices that may pathologize certain children and underserve others. We have a responsibility to make equity a priority for all our children.

Sheresa Blanchard, Ph.D.
Assistant Professor
East Carolina University

REFERENCES

Blanchard, S. B., Newton, J. R., Didericksen, K. W., Daniels, M., & Glosson, K. (2021). Confronting racism and bias within early intervention: The responsibility of systems and individuals to influence change and advance equity. *Topics in Early Childhood Special Education, 41*(1), 6–17.

Iruka, I. U., Sheridan, S., Koziol, N., Schumacher, R., Kerby, H., Prokasky, A., & Choi, D. H. (2022). Examining malleable factors that explain the end-of-kindergarten racial/ethnic Gaps. *The Elementary School Journal, 122*(3), 378–410.

Liberman, A. (n.d.). *Working towards more equitable childhood assessments: A conversation with Dr. Iheoma Iruka.* https://www.newamerica.org/education-policy/edcentral/a-conversation-with-dr-iheoma-iruka/

Foreword

Like the first edition, this new edition of *Assessing Young Children in Inclusive Settings: The Blended Practices Approach* is a must-read for professionals who want to develop their practices according to current scientific evidence. The implementation of authentic evaluation practices in early childhood programs is a complex process due to the trajectory that has existed for decades of evaluating children's deficits through the application of standardized tests. Thanks to the teachings that this book gives us, professionals feel accompanied during the process. From the description of the concept of authentic evaluation practices to each of the recommendations presented, the authors make the reader feel motivated to apply the proposals in their professional practices.

With the first edition of this book, many of us professionals learned what authentic assessment means and, above all, how to develop new skills to be able to carry it out in our daily practice. *Assessing Young Children in Inclusive Settings: The Blended Practices Approach, Second Edition*, will help professionals not only further improve the quality of their assessment practices but also provide service delivery models to support all young children in inclusive early education settings.

I want to express my gratitude to the authors for introducing "Recommended Practices for Assessing Children Who Are Dual Language Learners or Multilanguage Learners" as Chapter 10 in this edition. In my professional experience in Spain and many Latin American countries, professionals are making efforts to improve their practices toward an approach focused on the strengths of children and their families and with interventions in their natural environments. However, early childhood educators need support to assess and meet the needs of children from diverse cultural and linguistic backgrounds. Diversity enriches us, and the evaluation cannot adhere to the standardized patterns of child, family, and environment with which professionals feel identified. Chapter 10 provides strategies for focusing on language skills and cultural practices of families and for allowing children alternative responses.

Thanks to the generosity of the authors, I learned the true meaning of authentic evaluation and, above all, how to make it a reality in different countries, regardless of our culture and the country we come from. *Assessing Young Children in Inclusive Settings: The Blended Practices Approach, Second Edition*, invites us to continue reflecting on the quality of practices and motivates all of us who yearn for authentic assessment practices to become a reality that allows all children and their families to continue advancing.

Margarita Cañadas, Ph.D.
Director of the Early Childhood Center and Professor of Occupational Therapy
at the Catholic University of Valencia, Spain
Director of the Iberoamerican Observatory of Early Intervention Capacitas-UCV

Acknowledgments

Working on a second edition, by some measures, is a rather straightforward process. For us, however, most things are never straightforward. We started working on the second edition in 2019, and for at least the first year, the work that was accomplished was by a group of graduate students from the University of Kentucky, including Cameron Tyrrell, Chen Quinquin, Lindsay Johns, and Ndaru Prapti. Without their help, we wouldn't have been able to update all of the research and assessments covered in this book. We would also like to express a special note of gratitude to Toni-Ann Rusiana, who worked across chapters to fix APA citations, located key evidence to support recommended practices, and wrote a number of sections to ensure practical application. We would also like to express our gratitude to Ashley Lyons-Picard, who contributed to several chapters in the book, helped to edit across the book, and helped us to bring this book to completion. Last, we wish to acknowledge the long-term impact Lynn Sullivan has had on our work around blended practices. We've worked directly with Lynn for more decades than we wish to count, and because of her leadership, her wisdom, and her passion for inclusive and authentic assessment, we have honed practices around the curriculum framework described in this book and other publications. We have also come to better understand what teams need by way of support and have grown in our own knowledge around supporting systems to implement blended practices in early childhood settings. We are forever grateful for her friendship and her contributions to this book.

To all educators and leaders who work
tirelessly to achieve inclusive educational systems for all.

—*Kristie Pretti-Frontczak*

To my husband Daniel Halbert and son Kendall Brown, who
sustained me during the time I was writing this book, and to the memory
of my mother, Nancy Grisham, who motivated me more than I ever realized.

—*Jennifer Grisham*

To my husband Mark, who has always had faith
in me and has been there for almost all of the journey.

—*Lynn D. Sullivan*

Recommended Practices (Assessment Processes)

CHAPTER 1

Introduction

Jennifer Grisham and Kristie Pretti-Frontczak

WHY A SECOND EDITION

Assessing Young Children in Inclusive Settings: The Blended Practices Approach, Second Edition is intended to once again provide practical guidance to teams on how to engage in authentic assessment practices for all young children. The specific purpose of this book is to provide detailed information on the reasons for, and structures associated with, performing assessment for young children and their families. As is the case with most educational practices, the purposes for which assessments are conducted expand with time, recommended assessment practices are refined, and the contexts for conducting assessment continue to evolve. As such, the second edition of *Assessing Young Children in Inclusive Settings: The Blended Practices Approach* aims to include the most up-to-date recommendations for how to assess young children as established by research, our professional organizations, and governing bodies and through our collective experiences. This edition dives deeply into the most common reasons assessment is conducted with young children (e.g., program planning, progress monitoring), while acknowledging that teams need strategies and support as they engage in other assessment purposes such as identifying children for special education services, tiering instructional and behavioral supports, and assessing children's readiness for kindergarten. The focus of this book continues to be on blending assessment practices and service delivery models to support all young children in inclusive early education settings. In this edition, we also intentionally name system-level policies and practices that continue to marginalize families and children and cause harm by using outdated models of disability. The issues related to system-level inequities, from how we identify children for services to how we monitor performance over time, are deep and wide. We, the authors of this edition, also recognize that we have much to learn and much more work to do. We recognize that the existing systems of power and privilege associated with several of our key identities (i.e., we are all Caucasian, English is our primary language, we live in affluent neighborhoods, we are considered neurotypical, and we have advanced education) afford us many advantages and benefits. We must do more than identify inequities; we must work together with families, early educators, institutions of higher education, and policy makers to change how we support young children and their families. In writing this book, we are advocating for a systemwide change when it comes to assessment practices and young children.

In *Blended Practices for Teaching Young Children in Inclusive Settings* (Grisham-Brown & Hemmeter, 2017), the companion to the present book, a curriculum framework is described for conceptualizing how to support young children in inclusive early childhood settings. The curriculum framework is designed to: 1) link assessment to instructional practices, 2) serve as a foundation for curriculum design in blended early childhood programs, and 3) provide a process for decision making for teachers who teach diverse groups of children. The curriculum framework consists of four elements: 1) assessment, 2) scope and sequence, 3) activities and instruction, and 4) progress monitoring. Whereas Grisham-Brown and Hemmeter place emphasis on Elements 2 and 3, *Assessing Young Children in Inclusive Settings: The Blended Practices Approach, Second Edition* focuses on Elements 1 and 4, with an expanded conceptualization of the term *assessment*. Together, the two books provide teachers in blended classrooms with information on how to plan, implement, and evaluate instruction and programs for young children with and without disabilities.

MAJOR THEMES OF THIS BOOK

In preparation of the second edition of *Assessing Young Children in Inclusive Settings: The Blended Practices Approach*, we conducted a thorough review of current early childhood recommended practices (i.e., Copple & Bredekamp, 2009; Division for Early Childhood, 2014), legislative initiatives (e.g., Preschool Development Grants, 2014), and accreditation and practice standards (e.g., National Association for the Education of Young Children [NAEYC], 2018; Head Start). From this review, two important findings emerged. First, early childhood educators are required to address multiple mandates, standards, and processes that blended programs must address related to assessing young children. Those are summarized in Table 1.1. Second, our review yielded

Table 1.1. Early childhood standards for various early childhood programs and associated accountability mandates

Program standards	Child care	Head Start	State-funded pre-K	Special education
Program quality standards	State licensing standards (49 states)	Federal program performance standards	State program standards (39 states)	Federal Individuals with Disabilities Education Act (IDEA) regulations
	Stat Quality Rating & Improvement Systems (QRIS) (14 states + 29 pilots)			State program standards
Assessing local program quality	State licensing visits	Federal Program Review Instrument for Systems Monitoring (PRISM)	State program monitoring (30 states)	State program reviews
Standards for children's learning	State early learning guidelines (49 states)	Federal child outcomes framework	State early learning guidelines (49 states)	Three functional goals (federal)
Child assessments	No current requirements	Progress toward Head Start outcomes reported three times per year	State pre-K assessments (13 states)	States report percent of children in five categories

From Schultz, T., Kagan, S. L., & Shore, R. (2007). *Taking stock: Assessing and improving early childhood learning and program quality* (p. 18). National Early Childhood Accountability Task Force; adapted by permission.
Key: IDEA, Individuals with Disabilities Education Act of 1990 (PL 101-476).

four major themes: 1) authenticity, 2) collaborative partnerships, 3) utility, and 4) educational equity. These themes are highlighted in a number of ways throughout the book, by being either featured as a chapter or embedded across chapters. Below are descriptions of each theme.

Authenticity

Authenticity refers to the way in which early childhood assessments are conducted. Assessments should be conducted within the context of a child's daily activities and routines by adults with whom the child is familiar, keeping in mind that even if we conduct assessments in early care and education classrooms, these settings are not authentic for all children's experiences; there is often a cultural mismatch between the child and the context. This mismatch needs to be part of the consideration as assessments are conducted, data are analyzed, and the information is used to make important decisions. Authenticity also refers to the skills that are assessed. Functional skills that children need in order to participate in daily activities and routines should be the focus of the assessment and should be assessed using materials that are part of the child's environment. In addition, the skills that are assessed should encompass the totality of what young children need to learn, representing a comprehensive assessment that examines the whole child. Due to the fact that early development is interrelated, gathering information about young children in their natural environment is preferable to assessing skills in isolation, as is done when conventional assessment practices are implemented. In addition, conventional assessment often results in a deficit approach for describing young children, rather than a supportive approach that is characteristic of authentic assessment practices. As evidenced by a large-scale study by Bagnato et al. (2014), authentic assessment is highly valued by early childhood providers and preferred over conventional assessment practices.

Collaborative Partnerships

Collaborative partnerships, consisting of professionals, paraprofessionals, and nonprofessionals, should gather assessment information and make decisions about the children with whom they work. These teams may include a teacher, an assistant, an administrator, and volunteers who support the entire class. For individual children, team members may include medical personnel (e.g., neurologist, nurse), therapists (e.g., physical, occupational, speech), and itinerant teachers (e.g., vision, hearing). Regardless of the team's composition, each member should be involved in the assessment process, and the child's family and other familiar caregivers should guide each team. Throughout the book, team roles and models of assessing children are discussed. Central to each discussion is the notion that team members need to cooperate (i.e., create collaborative partnerships) with each other by sharing information, being willing to step outside of their traditional roles, and making meaningful contributions to the decision-making process. Although the teacher is recognized as the professional instructional leader in early childhood settings, it is essential for all who work with young children to participate in the assessment process. The value for collaborative partnerships is one shared by those who identify recommended practices for the field (i.e., Division for Early Childhood (DEC), 2014; NAEYC, 2018).

Utility

Conducting any assessment with young children should have a purpose. In particular, the assessment information gathered should be useful in developing goals and guiding the development of instruction that results in positive outcomes for children. The process of learning how to use data that are collected to guide instructional decisions is a major focus of this book. Although state and federal agencies require data collection for data reporting and accountability, the data collected for those purposes are secondary to the need to know how to use assessment information to improve outcomes for young children. No purposes are ignored in this text, but they are not the central focus. As authors and advocates of reducing testing requirements so that teachers can collect assessment data needed to make sound instructional decisions, we offer ideas for how to use assessment information to answer multiple assessment questions. When assessments provide information on what to teach, where to teach, with what to teach, and how to teach, they have good utility, which is a recommended practice valued by all (DEC, 2014; Copple & Bredecamp, 2009; Thum & Kuhfeld, 2020).

Educational Equity

When assessment practices aid in ensuring "every child is seen for who they truly are and their unique interests and gifts are surfaced and cultivated" (Bright Morning, n.d., para. 5), we are working on educational equity. When assessment practices allow some children to succeed or fail based upon social or cultural factors (e.g., ability, race, gender, socioeconomic status, geographic location, citizenship status), we are not. Instead, systemic inequities are perpetuated, particularly for children and families from traditionally marginalized groups and identities. Currently, most educational assessment practices are steeped in inequity, where ability in particular is seen through a medical lens, as described by Causton and Pretti-Frontczak (2021). As depicted in Figure 1.1, a medical lens focuses on individual child deficits, sees "normal" as something that is true or real, seeks to fix or remediate the individual, and largely ignores systemic inequities and societal barriers that disable children and marginalize families. Throughout this book, intentional efforts are taken to notice, name, and then alter practices away from a medical lens and transition assessment practices to an equity lens. It is up to each and every early educator to examine and change "practices, policies and approaches to ensure every child gets what they need every day" (Cohen, 2020, para. 3).

TRANSITION TO AN EQUITY LENS OF DISABILITY

MEDICAL LENS

- Disability resides within the individual
- Focus on individual pathology or impairment
- Aim is to fix or remediate
- Disability Labels are seen as deficits
- Focus on the label as a problem, not the systems
- Ignore systemic inequities

EQUITY LENS

- Disability is a socially constructed identity
- Focus on societal barriers that disable people
- Aim is to provide "just right" supports
- Disability is a natural difference
- Focus on the systems as a problem, not disability
- Name and address systemic inequities

Figure 1.1. Depiction of the medical lens of disability as well as the mindset and practice shifts that are needed to transition to an equity lens. (From Causton, J., & Pretti-Frontczak, K. [2020]. *Transition to an equity lens of disability*. Inclusive Schooling; reprinted by permission.)

OVERVIEW OF MAJOR BOOK SECTIONS

The overarching definition of *assessment* used throughout the book is that it is a process of gathering information for purposes of making decisions. This definition provides the foundation for the organization of much of the book. Because the first part of the definition refers to a process and the second part to a purpose, the first two sections of the book correspond with those themes: Section I: Recommended Practices (Assessment Processes) and Section II: Reasons for Conducting Assessment (Assessment Purposes). In addition, there are important contemporary issues associated with assessing young children that bear special attention. For that reason, the revised edition of this book includes Section III: Special Topics in the Assessment of Young Children. Below, we describe each section.

Section I: Recommended Practices (Assessment Processes)

Section I describes the **process** for conducting assessment of young children in blended classrooms. The process is guided by recommended practices described by professional organizations that represent young children, expert committees that direct policy related to early childhood issues, and/or legislation enacted to oversee programs for young children. Recommended practices are highlighted in Chapters 2 through 5. Chapter 2 defines authentic assessment and differentiates it from conventional assessment. The chapter describes the advantages of authentic assessment, as well as its evidence base. Chapter 3 focuses on the importance of family involvement in the assessment process. The chapter describes the legal mandates for involving families in assessment, approaches for involving families in assessment, and considerations for doing so. Chapter 4 highlights the importance of determining the technical adequacy of assessment instruments. The chapter defines terminology associated with technical adequacy, describes differences between various types of early childhood assessments, and explains strategies for interpreting conventional assessment instruments. Chapter 5 describes the elements of a critical decision-making process for using assessment information. Details on the five steps of the process—gathering, documenting, summarizing, analyzing, and interpreting—are discussed and examples are provided.

Section II: Reasons for Conducting Assessment (Assessment Purposes)

Section II, Chapters 6 through 9, focuses on the **purposes** for conducting assessments with young children. Chapter 6 includes information on how to collect assessment information to plan programs for young children in blended classrooms. Information on how to select curriculum-based assessments as well as specific information on commonly used assessment tools for program planning are described. In Chapter 7, how to gather holistic information on children for the purpose of monitoring progress is emphasized. The chapter describes a tiered progress monitoring framework to guide the type, frequency, and amount of data collection teams should consider. Chapter 8 is concerned with the identification of young children who have special needs, emphasizing the processes of Child Find, screening, and diagnostic assessment. Recommended practices for conducting screening and diagnostic assessment are highlighted, and examples of instruments that can be used are provided. Finally, Chapter 9 discusses issues with assessment for the purpose of evaluating early childhood intervention programs. The chapter describes reasons for conducting program evaluations as well as the strategies for doing so. Issues associated with accountability assessments also are discussed.

Section III: Special Topics in the Assessment of Young Children

New to the second edition are Chapters 10 through 12, which address important topics that require special attention. Chapter 10 presents issues associated with assessing children who are dual language learners, including what to assess and how to assess this population. A comprehensive list of assessment tools that might be used with children who are dual language learners is provided. Chapter 11 covers topics associated with assessing young children who have multiple disabilities. Along with guidance on what and how to teach, the transdisciplinary assessment process is highlighted, as well as specific assessment tools for use with the population. Finally, Chapter 12 addresses issues specific to assessing children in kindergarten. While the practices discussed elsewhere in the book are appropriate for this age group, issues associated with kindergarten readiness, curricula focused solely on academic achievement, and response to intervention have impacted how children in kindergarten are assessed. Chapter 12 emphasizes how to use recommended assessment practices in light of these developments.

INTENDED AUDIENCE AND USE

The intended audience for this edition, similar to that for Grisham-Brown and Hemmeter (2017) and the first edition of *Assessing Young Children in Inclusive Settings,* is individuals seeking initial certification to teach young children, primarily in blended certification or licensure programs. Students in blended certification programs take coursework in both early childhood education (ECE) and early childhood special education (ECSE). Their degree allows them to work with children with and without disabilities. Although many states now have some form of blended certification program, others do not. Blended certification may not exist in all states, but all states support inclusive education and early childhood programs that serve children with and without disabilities in the same setting. Therefore, both *Assessing Young Children in Inclusive Settings: The Blended Practices Approach, Second Edition* and *Blended Practices for Teaching Young Children in Inclusive Settings, Second Edition* remain appropriate for licensure programs that offer only ECE or ECSE certifications. The information in *Assessing Young Children in Inclusive Settings: The Blended Practices Approach, Second Edition,* will remain pertinent to future teachers in either certification program.

A second, and equally important, audience includes teachers and other educational professionals who are currently working with young children on a day-to-day basis. The information contained in this book is helpful for those striving toward more inclusive education for all children. For example, teachers with general and/or special education training and responsibilities will learn how to create collaborative partnerships, conduct assessments within the context of daily activities, and plan instruction based upon the strengths and needs of the diverse children they serve. Similarly, consultants, principals, and technical assistance providers will find the book useful in their work to support teachers in inclusive programs. For example, they will find helpful information for designing and delivering professional development, for leading systems change efforts toward inclusive education, and for understanding what inclusive early childhood education looks like in practice.

Previous editions of both blended practices books have been used by teachers, consultants, and administrators for group studies in their school districts and agencies. For example, teachers read one or two chapters each month and met to discuss the implications in their program, or teachers read chapters and discussed implications for practice in threaded discussions and blogs. Although the main focus of the book is children who participate in center-based early childhood programs and who are between the ages of 3 and 5 years, the basic tenets of the book are appropriate for the broader range of young children. In this edition, specific information is provided for how to design an assessment system in kindergarten that adheres to recommended practices for young children. Programs serving children from birth to age 3 and ages 6–8 will find that the principles advocated in *Assessing Young Children in Inclusive Settings: The Blended Practices Approach, Second Edition* are relevant as well. Therefore, universities and programs that emphasize teaching children from birth to age 5 or birth to age 8 will find the book worthwhile.

DEFINITIONS OF KEY TERMS

In an effort to ensure consistency across chapters and between this book and Grisham-Brown and Hemmeter (2017), common terms are defined in the sections that follow. In some cases, an explanation is provided for why one term is used instead of another. In defining key terms, an attempt is made to ensure that early childhood professionals from traditionally ECE or ECSE backgrounds will be comfortable with the terms used.

Assessment

Assessment is defined as a process of gathering information for the purposes of making decisions. Often educators talk about "giving tests," "administering assessments," or "using an assessment tool or measure." Each statement relates to the broader activity or process of gathering information about children (e.g., through direct testing, observations, interviews). These are discussed in Section I. As well, educators may say, "We're collecting portfolio entries," "We're trying to see if _____ can get special education services," or "We've got to test all of the children because Head Start requires it three times a year." These statements relate to the reasons or purposes assessments are conducted (e.g., to monitor progress, determine eligibility, evaluate a program), as discussed in Section II. Recognizing that assessment is a process that happens for various reasons is essential to understanding the tenets of the book. Assessment, defined broadly, is a process of getting to know a child or a group of children for a variety of purposes. This book discusses the major purposes for conducting assessments and associated recommended practices. Within the curriculum framework, however, the term assessment is used as described for engaging in authentic program planning (see Chapters 2 and 7).

Blended Practices

In Grisham-Brown and Hemmeter (2017), blended practices are described as "the integration of practices that can be used to address the needs of all children in inclusive settings" (p. 7). Blended practices imply the merging of theories and philosophies from ECE and ECSE to support diverse groups of young children. Throughout the book, when we refer to groups of children who are diverse, we mean children from a broad age range (birth to 8, with an emphasis on the preschool years) who have multiple and intersecting socially constructed identities including but not limited to ability, race, gender, language, physical health, mental health, ethnicity, geographic location, citizenship, class status, etc. Conversely, when we use the phrase diverse children, it is not shorthand for children who are diverse from the default of White, English speaking, and neurotypical. We mean the full range of children who are served in early childhood programs. The current book emphasizes strategies for gathering information about diverse groups of young children that 1) combine recommendations from professional organizations that represent the broader fields of ECE and ECSE, 2) consider the importance of gathering authentic and meaningful information about all children regardless of ability, and 3) take into account the need for common assessment practices, versus different practices for different groups of children, to better support inclusive programs.

Teacher

Although the strategies presented here are designed for use by all early childhood professionals, there is generally one professional who has primary responsibility for a child's education. That person may be referred to as the provider, educator, or interventionist. In this book, that professional is referred to as the *teacher*, a term that was selected over other commonly used terms in early childhood education for two reasons. First, *teacher* implies a level of professionalism that other terms do not. Given the importance of children's early years, it is imperative that staff who work with young children have the same educational credentials as staff who educate older learners. Using the term teacher, it is hoped, makes a statement about the importance of the work. Second, teacher is used because the focus of the book is on how to assess young children in inclusive educational settings within the context of daily activities and experiences. Whether trained as a general education or special education teacher, or even a related service provider, the term teacher is used throughout in reference to the professional who is most closely associated with planning and revising instruction for young children in a group, center, or district-based early education program.

SUMMARY

This book is intended to guide early childhood teachers in implementing high-quality assessment for children with and without disabilities. A thorough understanding and implementation of the practices discussed in the book should result in improved services for young children and their families.

REFERENCES

Bagnato, S. J., Goins, D. D., & Pretti-Frontczak, K. (2014). Authentic assessment as "best practice" for early childhood intervention: National consumer social validity research. *Topics in Early Childhood Special Education, 34*(2), 116–127.

Bright Morning (n.d.). *Defining "equity": Every child, every day*. https://brightmorning.wpengine.com/2019/12/defining-equity-every-child-every-day/

Causton, J., & Pretti-Frontczak, K. (2021). *Moving from a medical lens to an equity lens*. Inclusive Schooling, LLC.

Cohen, L. (2020). *Looking at your sh** . . . and other ways to sharpen equity tools*. https://brightmorningteam.com/2020/02/looking-at-your-sh-and-other-ways-to-sharpen-equity-tools/

Copple, C., & Bredekamp, S. (Eds.). (2009). *Developmentally appropriate practice in early childhood programs serving children from birth through age 8* (3rd ed.). National Association for the Education of Young Children.

Division for Early Childhood [DEC]. (2014). *DEC recommended practices in early intervention/early childhood special education 2014*. Division for Early Childhood. http://www.dec-sped.org/recommendedpractices

Early Childhood Research Institute on Measuring Growth and Development. (1998). *Theoretical foundations of the Early Childhood Research Institute on measuring growth and development: an early problem-solving model* (Vol. 6). University of Minnesota.

Grisham-Brown, J. L., & Hemmeter, M. L. (2017). *Blended practices for teaching young children in inclusive settings* (2nd ed.). Paul H. Brookes Publishing Co.

Grisham-Brown, J. L., Hemmeter, M. L., & Pretti-Frontczak, K. (2005). *Blended practices for teaching young children in inclusive settings*. Paul H. Brookes Publishing Co.

Marsh, J. A., Pane, J. F., & Hamilton, L. S. (2006). *Making sense of data-driven decision making in education: Evidence from recent RAND research* (OP-170). RAND Corporation.

McLean, M., Bailey, D. B., & Wolery, M. (2004) *Assessing infants and preschoolers with special needs*. Pearson Merrill Prentice Hall.

National Association for the Education of Young Children (2018). *NAEYC early learning program standards* [White paper]. https://www.naeyc.org/sites/default/files/globally-shared /downloads/PDFs/accreditation/early-learning/overview_of_the_standards.pdf

Pretti-Frontczak, K., Bagnato, S., Macy, M., & Sexton, D. (in press). Data driven decision-making to plan programs and promote performance in early childhood intervention: Applying best professional practice standards. In *Early childhood intervention: Programs and policies for special needs children* (Vols. 1–3). Praeger.

Schultz, T., Kagan, S. L., & Shore, R. (2007). *Taking stock: Assessing and improving early childhood learning and program quality*. National Early Childhood Accountability Task Force.

Thum, Y. M., & Kuhfeld, M. (2020). *NWEA 2020 MAP growth achievement status and growth norms for students and schools*. NWEA Research Report. NWEA.

CHAPTER 2

Recommended Practices in Authentic Assessment

Kristie Pretti-Frontczak, Rebecca Crawford, Lynn D. Sullivan, and Jennifer Grisham

Charlotte is a first-year teacher for the Fort Lauderdale Public School System. She teaches in a preschool program that serves 3- and 4-year-old children who are at risk due to economic factors and children who have been diagnosed with disabilities. Charlotte's degree is in preschool special education. She took a class in college on the assessment of young children with special needs. In that class, she was taught to administer several tools commonly used to screen and diagnose children's disabilities, such as the Battelle Developmental Inventory (BDI-3; Newborg, 2020), the Developmental Indicators for the Assessment of Learning (DIAL-4; Mardell-Czudnowski & Goldenberg, 2011), and the Peabody Picture Vocabulary Test (PPVT-5; Dunn, 2019). When she started teaching, she felt prepared to conduct assessments of young children. Once she was in the classroom, however, her supervisor began asking for data on children's performance on individual goals, as well as their performance on curricular outcomes outlined by her state for young children. In fact, her supervisor often asked about how the data Charlotte collected was being used to plan daily activities and lessons. Charlotte soon realized that she could not repeatedly re-administer a test like the BDI as a way of obtaining the type of data expected by her administrator. She also began to understand that such assessments do not necessarily yield information that is useful in selecting teaching goals. In other words, the tests she was using were not aligned with the curriculum. Charlotte needed a new strategy for gathering information about the children in her class.

The dilemma described in the preceding vignette is common for teachers working in blended early childhood settings, particularly after being trained in traditional early childhood special education (ECSE) practices. As mentioned in Chapter 1, traditional ECSE programs tend to focus on the use of conventional assessment practices. *Conventional assessment practices* are those that focus on whether a child can perform specific skills in specific situations. When a conventional assessment is administered, the relationship between the assessor and the child is often unfamiliar, the materials may be unique to the test itself, and the data collection process is often scripted. Furthermore, conventional assessment focuses on a child's ability to recall information and perform on demand and rates a child's response in comparison to a narrowly defined criterion, which is then used to grade, measure, and/or evaluate the child's ability.

As described in the vignette, Charlotte is struggling to use data gathered under rather scripted interactions that take place outside of the daily routines to make decisions about how best to support individuals and groups of children during the daily routine. The conventional assessments Charlotte learned about in her teacher training program are out of alignment with the type of decisions she and her supervisor want to make and are out of alignment with recommended early childhood assessment practices. Charlotte needs training and support for engaging in authentic assessment practices for the purposes of planning and revising instruction.

This chapter highlights the support and actions Charlotte will need to switch from what she knows about assessment to what is most useful for the children and families she serves. In the first section of this chapter, authentic assessment is defined and a comparison to conventional assessment is provided. Chapters 6 and 7 show authentic assessment in action for the key purposes of planning and revising instruction. In the second section of this chapter, the advantages of authentic assessment and the strong evidence base that supports it are explored. The chapter ends with a return to Charlotte and the steps she took to shift her practices to be more authentic and aligned with her instruction.

AUTHENTIC ASSESSMENT

Many early childhood intervention teachers have likely heard the term authentic assessment. In fact, authentic assessment is not new. The practice has appeared in the research for at least 25 years. However, teachers' perceptions and practices related to conducting authentic assessment in the classroom, and the relative value of the information, vary. In this first section, authentic assessment is defined and compared to conventional assessment.

Authentic Assessment Defined

Authentic assessment is the practice of assessing children in their natural environment (e.g., home, school, child care center) on the skills they need throughout their daily routine, using materials that are part of that environment, by people with whom the children are familiar. Authentic assessment is also known as play-based, naturalistic, and performance-based assessment (Grisham-Brown et al., 2008). According to Bagnato and Yeh-Ho, authentic assessment refers "to the systematic recording of developmental observations over time about the naturally occurring behaviors and functional competencies of young children in daily routines by familiar and knowledgeable caregivers in the child's life" (2006, p. 29). According to Meisels and colleagues (1995), "authentic performance assessments are methods of documenting children's skills, knowledge, and behaviors using actual classroom-based experiences, activities, and products" (p. 279). Said simply, authentic assessment is when familiar adults gather information about and with children in familiar settings, playing with familiar toys and objects, and doing familiar everyday activities and actions.

Authentic assessment does not look like how we typically think about testing—conducted in an isolated setting, with scripted delivery; teacher-, timer-, or computer-driven response windows; standardized materials; and isolated, nonlinear, on-demand tasks. Authentic assessment looks like what already happens every day in the classroom: a balance of whole-group instruction, teacher-led small groups, and child-initiated activities with support from adults. Authentic assessment is an intentional part of instruction. It looks like a teacher taking data while watching or playing alongside children during child-selected activities with child-selected materials. To the naive, untrained, or unaware observer, authentic assessment looks like child's play: casual, unstructured, and lacking standardization. The observer will not see a testing area in or outside the room, a testing time identified on the schedule, or dedicated, specific testing materials in a segregated area. However, as the following sections reveal, authentic assessment has the research rigor to meet Charlotte's needs for planning instruction.

Difference Between Authentic Assessment and Conventional Assessment

It might be easier to consider what authentic assessment is not when trying to understand this concept. Authentic assessments are *not* one-time snapshots of a child's knowledge; instead, they are recurring observations or a collection of observations conducted over an extended period of time. Authentic assessments are *not* used to show what a child does not know; rather, these assessments look at what a child does know and can do. Authentic assessments are *not* conducted in rooms unfamiliar to a child using materials they have never seen before. Instead, they are conducted in a location a child is familiar and comfortable with, using materials they have seen before, and performed by individuals a child recognizes.

Whereas authentic assessment "is a form of assessment in which students are asked to perform real-world tasks to demonstrate meaningful application of essential knowledge and skills" (Mueller, 2018), conventional assessment is "the administration of a highly structured array of testing tasks by an examiner in a contrived situation through the use of scripted examiner behaviors and scripted child behaviors in order to determine a normative score for purposes of diagnosis" (Bagnato et al., 2010, p. 5). And whereas conventional assessments "require the same procedures be used for all who are being assessed" (McLean et al., 2004, p. 23), authentic assessment can be used with children with and without disabilities and individual needs are taken into account. See Box 2.1 for additional comparisons between authentic and conventional assessment practices.

Box 2.1.   Authentic Assessment Versus Conventional Assessment

Authentic assessment refers to "the systematic recording of developmental observations over time about the naturally occurring behaviors and functional competencies of young children in daily routines by familiar and knowledgeable caregivers in the child's life" (Bagnato & Yeh-Ho, 2006, p. 29).

Synonyms include play-based, naturalistic, performance-based assessment, can do, competence-based, strength-based, and collaborative.

Conventional assessment and testing refer to "the administration of a highly structured array of testing tasks by an examiner in a contrived situation through the use of scripted examiner behaviors and scripted child behaviors in order to determine a normative score for purposes of diagnosis" (Bagnato et al., 2010, p. 5).

Synonyms include eligibility tests, standardized tests, accountability testing, can't do, deficit model, formal assessment, and isolated.

There are times, however, when rules and/or professional preference may lead to the administration of tools and assessments that are more conventional, which include a "highly structured array of testing tasks by an examiner in a contrived situation through the use of scripted examiner behaviors and scripted child behaviors in order to determine a normative score for purposes of diagnosis" (Bagnato et al., 2010, p. 5). Although conventional assessments may fulfill particular policies or rules (e.g., to determine eligibility for services; program planning at the district, state, or national level; diagnosis of certain disabilities or clinical conditions), authentic assessment is critical for supporting children's ongoing development and learning. Further, there are several advantages and a strong evidence base that indicates whenever possible, policies and practices should incorporate authentic assessment.

ADVANTAGES AND EVIDENCE BASE

Advantages of Authentic Assessment

One of the major advantages of authentic assessment is that the information gathered provides a true measure of what children can do in an environment where they feel comfortable and secure. Unlike conventional assessment, authentic assessment does not rely on whether children correctly respond to questions or activities, but rather provides documentation of numerous components of children's learning. Thus, authentic assessment provides information regarding "the progress children make, their strengths, and the ways they learn and solve problems" (Grubb & Courtney, 1996, p. 5), whereas conventional assessment tests a one-time snapshot of skill mastery. Authentic assessment allows teachers and other professionals to gather needed information about children through observations, portfolios, interviews, and curriculum-based assessments (Diffily & Fleege 1993; Grisham-Brown et al., 2005; McNair et al., 1998). In this way, authentic assessment allows the teacher to understand each child's developmental level and plan a learning environment to meet the needs of every child, regardless of ethnicity, disability, or language. Conventional assessments, on the other hand, only gather information on whether a child can or cannot demonstrate a skill, making planning and individualizing instruction within a group difficult.

Said differently, authentic assessment ensures information is gathered in places where a child commonly spends time, often referred to as the natural environment. The natural environment provides assessors with the opportunity to observe without putting the stresses of unfamiliar adults, places, materials, and activities on children. When children feel comfortable and relaxed, in a familiar setting, a more accurate picture of their development and learning is obtained. Authentic assessment also provides a clear link between information gathered and what is taught. A teacher who knows what skills children need to work on can prepare the environment so the children have planned opportunities to practice those skills. During such planned opportunities, the teacher observes children as they engage in activities and documents the children's skills using written descriptions or counts and tallies. Teachers can also use the information gathered from unplanned moments that occur during the day to document a child's skill level or behavior. For example, a child who is working on verbal communication with peers may spontaneously walk up and greet a peer who has come to school. Although the interaction was not planned, it still provides an opportunity for observing and documenting verbal interactions.

Unlike conventional assessment, authentic assessment also promotes collaboration. In conducting authentic assessment, teachers, families, and other personnel are encouraged to work together to gather information. Collaboration during assessment allows relationships to be built among early childhood professionals and families (Keilty et al., 2009). Positive, trusting relationships among everyone working with a given child foster the opportunity for better understanding of all aspects of a child's life. Once established, these relationships afford the possibility for ongoing, open communication. "Assessment should be a continuing process of parent–professional dialogue because these partners in children's education need to maintain contact, share concerns, report progress and problems, monitor and review events, and jointly celebrate success" (Wolfendale, 1998, p. 357). The various inputs from families and professionals help to ensure that the goals and objectives written for a child, whether the child is typical or has a special need, are accurate and on target.

Support for Authentic Assessment

The shift from conventional assessment practices to authentic assessment practices has extensive support. There are four primary sources of support for authentic assessment in early childhood intervention.

1. The wisdom and recommendations of professional organizations (e.g., American Speech-Language-Hearing Association [ASHA], 2004; Division for Early Childhood of the Council of Exceptional Children [DEC], 2014; National Association for the Education of Young Children [NAEYC], 2020)

2. Committee findings and policies (e.g., National Early Childhood Accountability Task Force, 2007; National Research Council, 2008; Riley-Ayers et al., 2011)

3. Research (e.g., Bagnato et al., 2014; Hallam et al., 2014; Macy et al., 2015)

4. Legislation (e.g., the Individuals with Disabilities Education Improvement Act [IDEIA], 2004; the Every Student Succeeds Act [ESSA], 2015; the Race to the Top—Early Learning Challenge [RTT-ELC], 2011)

For example, from the first source of support, notable early childhood organizations such as the National Association for the Education of Young Children (NAEYC) and the Division for Early Childhood (DEC) have published recommended practices defining what assessment in early childhood education and intervention should encompass; these practices squarely align with authentic assessment. Specifically, NAEYC (2020) states that assessment methods should be ongoing, strategic, reflective, and purposeful; inclusive of multiple methods; and responsive to current developmental accomplishments, language(s), and the cultural experiences of young children. They recommend that assessment focus on children's progress toward developmental and educational goals and reflect families' input in addition to children's background knowledge and experiences. Additional recommended assessment practices from NAEYC include utilizing a system to guide curriculum planning and learning experiences; making decisions such as placement or enrollment in conjunction with families; and administering assessments only for populations and purposes for which they have been demonstrated to produce valid, reliable data.

Similarly, DEC (2014) recommends that when it comes to assessing young children in early childhood special education and intervention contexts, practitioners should work as a team with the family to gather information using multiple developmentally appropriate tools and strategies to identify children's strengths, needs, interests, and preferences across all areas of development; conduct assessments in each language a child uses (dominant and secondary); obtain information about children's routines and activities across different environments; use clinical reasoning in conjunction with assessment data; engage in systematic ongoing assessment to revise instruction as needed; utilize tools with sufficient sensitivity to detect progress; and share assessment results in ways that are understandable and useful to families.

Along with other sources such as policy groups, research, and even legal mandates, there is strong support for authentic assessment as the preferred practice for getting to know children and making instructional decisions regarding their needs for support. Table 2.1 provides direct support from these multiple sources regarding authentic assessment practices in early childhood intervention.

FLIPPING THE SCRIPT

Returning to Charlotte, this section outlines basic steps for flipping from conventional assessment practices to authentic assessment, regardless of the assessment purpose. Given the strong evidence base for authentic assessment, Charlotte was convinced to switch to an authentic assessment approach because it will provide the information she and her supervisor need. In coming to this conclusion, Charlotte took the first necessary step: realizing there is another way to assess children. Next is the more difficult task of changing or flipping her mindset. Instead of acting as the assessor, an evaluator with a test protocol looking for what the child can't do, Charlotte will now need to see herself in the role of a play partner, or a keen detective who is tasked with watching children in their natural habitat. It is the interplay between environmental demands and interactions paired with the interdependence of skills, which develop concurrently, that results in whether a child will struggle (need instructional support).

Table 2.1. Direct support from recommended practices, policies, research, and legal mandates for authentic assessment practices in early childhood intervention

Source	Recommendation
National Association for the Education of Young Children (NAEYC). (2020). *Developmentally appropriate practice: A position statement of the National Association for the Education of Young Children.* Author.	"Methods appropriate to educators' assessment of young children, therefore, include results of their observations of children, clinical interviews, collections of children's work samples, and children's performance on authentic activities." (p. 20)
Division for Early Childhood (DEC). (2014). *DEC recommended practices in early intervention/early childhood special education 2014.* Author. http://www.dec-sped.org/recommendedpractices	RP A7: Practitioners obtain information about the child's skills in daily activities, routines, and environments such as home, center, and community. (p. 8)
American Speech-Language-Hearing Association (ASHA). (2004). *Preferred practice patterns for the profession of speech-language pathology.* Author. http://www.asha.org/policy	Clinical assessment is "sensitive to cultural and linguistic diversity and addresses the components within the WHO's International Classification of Functioning, Disability and Health (2001) framework, including body structures/functions, activities/participation, and contextual factors." (p. 27)
National Research Council (NRC). (2008). *Early childhood assessment: Why, what, and how.* National Academies Press. https://doi.org/10.17226/12446	"Given the challenges of direct assessment with very young children, it is worth first considering less intrusive modes of assessment if they also meet the purposes formulated." (p. 28)
National Early Childhood Accountability Task Force. (2007). *Taking stock: Assessing and improving early childhood learning and program quality.* PEW Charitable Trusts, Foundation for Child Development, & Joyce Foundation.	"Serious concerns remain regarding the appropriate uses of child outcome data given the variance in development, the current state of measures, the shortfall in resources and the multiple factors that affect child well-being, particularly in the early years." (p. 77)
Riley-Ayers, S., Frede, E., Barnett, W. S., & Brenneman, K. (2011). *Improving early education programs through data-based decision-making.* National Institute for Early Education Research (NIEER).	Regardless of the purpose of assessment: "1. Should not make children feel anxious or scared; 2. Information should be obtained over time; 3. An attempt should be made to obtain information on the same content area from multiple and diverse sources, especially when repeated instances of data gathering are not feasible; 4. The length of the assessment should be sensitive to young children's interests and attention spans; 5. Testing for purposes of program accountability should employ appropriate sampling methods whenever feasible." (p. 23)
Hallam, R., Lyons, A., Pretti-Frontczak, K., & Grisham-Brown, J. (2014). Comparing apples and oranges: The mismeasurement of young children through the mismatch of assessment purpose and the interpretation of results. *Topics in Early Childhood Special Education, 34*(2), 106–115.	"Assessments that are designed to measure children against expected standards may be better suited for identifying the need for additional services; the selection of instructional priorities; and the ongoing monitoring and revisions of instruction." (p. 2)
Bagnato, S. J., Goins, D. D., Pretti-Frontczak, K., & Neisworth, J. T. (2014). Authentic assessment as "best practice" for early childhood intervention: National consumer social validity research. *Topics in Early Childhood Special Education, 34*(2), 116–127. https://doi.org/10.1177/0271121414523652	"Simply, the results distinguish authentic assessments as the developmentally appropriate alternative to conventional tests, based on feedback from actual practice-based evidence by consumers." (p. 10)

Table 2.1.   *(continued)*

Source	Recommendation
Macy, M., Bagnato, S. J., Macy, R. S., & Salaway, J. (2015). Conventional tests and testing for early intervention eligibility: Is there an evidence base? *Infants & Young Children, 28*(2), 182–204. https://doi.org /10.1097/IYC.0000000000000032	"The results of our qualitative study and research synthesis raise serious questions about the lack of critical qualities, field validation, and evidence base of conventional tests and testing to fulfill the purpose of early intervention eligibility determination." (Abstract)
Individuals with Disabilities Education Act, 20 U.S.C. § 1400 (2004).	Local education agencies (LEAs) must ensure assessments and evaluations tools "are provided and administered in the language and form most likely to yield accurate information on what the child knows and can do academically, developmentally, and functionally, unless it is not feasible to provide or administer." (Section 1414 [b] [3] [A] [ii])
Every Student Succeeds Act, 20 U.S.C. § 6301 (2015). https://www.congress.gov/bill/114th -congress/senate-bill/1177	"The bill maintains the requirement for a state to administer student assessments in reading, mathematics, and science, according to an established testing schedule. A state may administer either a single assessment or multiple assessments that result in a single, summative score. If specified requirements are met, a state may administer computer adaptive assessments. (Such assessments adapt to the examinee's ability level.)" (Section 1005)
Race to the Top—Early Learning Challenge, 76 Fed. Reg. 53564 (August 26, 2011).	"Comprehensive Assessment System means a coordinated and comprehensive system of multiple assessments—each of which is valid and reliable for its specified purpose and for the population with which it will be used—that organizes information about the process and context of young children's learning and development in order to help Early Childhood Educators make informed instructional and programmatic decisions. A Comprehensive Assessment System includes, at a minimum—(a) Screening Measures; (b) Formative Assessments; (c) Measures of Environmental Quality; and (d) Measures of the Quality of Adult-Child Interactions." (Executive Summary, p. 17)

With a change in mindset, the teacher avoids the temptation to sit the child down to learn what they know or can do and, rather, sits beside the child. By sitting beside the child, the teacher cannot only learn what the child truly knows and can do but also gain a better understanding of why the child may be struggling or why development has stalled.

Charlotte implemented the following sequence. First, she aimed to *connect* with children instead of asking, directing, or telling children what to say or do: she watched for subtle cues that a child is ready to follow directions, share attention, and/or answer questions. Next, she sat with children (i.e., beside children) while they played and interacted with their environment. She was often silent or imitated their motor actions. She avoided assessing by asking questions as if interviewing a guest on a talk show. Instead, she *imitated* what the child was doing. When she found it a challenge to remain quiet, she tried using self-talk. Last, she set the goal of entering a child's play and *matching* her actions to the child's. For example, if the child was using simple motor actions (e.g., dumping, stacking, patting, banging), she also used simple motor actions instead of asking the child to engage in elaborate pretend play. While interacting with the children using these methods, Charlotte repeated to herself the short phrase "connect, imitate, and match." This simple sequence helped her adhere to these authentic assessment methods that will ultimately enable her to better respond to her supervisor's questions about progress within the curriculum.

Charlotte's next challenge was to find the time in her already busy day for this sequence. She realized quickly, however, that because authentic assessment is not about a specific location or time, the entire day was filled with opportunities. Charlotte decided to intentionally plan what she would say, do, and ask when children were lining up, putting on their gear to go outside, putting their snacks away, and walking to the bus or pick up area. These slices of time provided authentic opportunities for her to *connect, imitate,* and *create a match*. As Charlotte gathered information during these intentional times across the day, she began to notice new things about each child. Each child had strengths she had not noticed either when doing conventional assessments or during the busy classroom day. For example, she started seeing when and where children were independent and beautifully interdependent in completing tasks, getting their needs met, and participating in daily activities. She was also able to see the wide variety in the children's abilities to start and stop activities, consistently use skills under changing conditions, and adapt to the demands of different activities. After just a few short weeks of using authentic assessment, she was able to easily take what she had observed and weave it into the design of lesson plans, to share with families how their children were learning and growing, and to bring concerns up at team meetings with her related service providers and paraprofessionals. Charlotte has just begun to implement authentic assessment practices, but she knows she will need a more robust model for systematic authentic assessment.

SUMMARY

This chapter highlighted the support and actions Charlotte will need to switch from what she knows about assessment to what is most useful for the children and families she services. In the first section of this chapter, authentic assessment was defined and a comparison to conventional assessment was provided. In the second section, the advantages of authentic assessment and the strong evidence base behind it were explored. The chapter ended with a return to Charlotte and the steps she took to engage in authentic assessment. In particular, she learned how to connect, imitate, and match children as she flipped her assessment practices from conventional to authentic.

REFERENCES

American Speech-Language-Hearing Association (ASHA). (2004). *Preferred practice patterns for the profession of speech-language pathology.* Author. http://www.asha.org/policy

Bagnato, S. J., Goins, D. D., Pretti-Frontczak, K., & Neisworth, J. T. (2014). Authentic assessment as "best practice" for early childhood intervention: National consumer social validity research. *Topics in Early Childhood Special Education, 34*(2), 116–127. https://doi.org /10.1177/0271121414523652

Bagnato, S. J., Neisworth, J. T., & Pretti-Frontczak, K. (2010). *LINKing authentic assessment and early childhood intervention: Best measures for best practices* (2nd ed.). Paul H. Brookes Publishing Co.

Bagnato, S. J., & Yeh-Ho, H. (2006). High-stakes testing with preschool children: Violation of professional standards for evidence-based practice in early childhood intervention. *KEDI International Journal of Educational Policy, 3*(1), 23–43.

Diffily, D., & Fleege, P. O. (1993). *Sociodramatic play: Assessment through portfolio.* https://eric .ed.gov/?id=ED354079

Division for Early Childhood (DEC). (2014). *DEC recommended practices in early intervention/ early childhood special education 2014.* http://www.dec-sped.org/recommendedpractices

Dunn, D. M. (2019). *Peabody Picture Vocabulary Test* (5th ed.). NCS Pearson.

Every Student Succeeds Act of 2015, PL 114-95, 20 U.S.C. §§ 1001 *et seq.* https://www.congress .gov/bill/114th-congress/senate-bill/1177

Grisham-Brown, J., Hallam, R., & Pretti-Frontczak, K. (2008). Preparing Head Start personnel to use a curriculum-based assessment. *Journal of Early Intervention, 30,* 271–281.

Grisham-Brown, J., Hemmeter, M. L., & Pretti-Frontczak, K. (2005). *Blended practices for teaching young children in inclusive settings.* Paul H. Brookes Publishing Co.

Grubb, D., & Courtney, A. (1996). *Developmentally appropriate assessment of young children: The role of portfolio assessments.* https://eric.ed.gov/?id=ED400114

Hallam, R., Lyons, A., Pretti-Frontczak, K., & Grisham-Brown, J. (2014). Comparing apples and oranges: The mismeasurement of young children through the mismatch of assessment purpose and the interpretation of results. *Topics in Early Childhood Special Education, 34*(2), 106–115.

Individuals with Disabilities Education Improvement Act (IDEA) of 2004, PL 108-446, 20 U.S.C. §§ 1400 *et seq.*

Keilty, B., LaRocco, D. J., & Casell, F. B. (2009). Early interventionists' reports on authentic assessment methods through focus group research. *Topics in Early Childhood Special Education, 28,* 244–256.

Macy, M., Bagnato, S. J., Macy, R. S., & Salaway, J. (2015). Conventional tests and testing for early intervention eligibility: Is there an evidence base? *Infants & Young Children, 28*(2), 182–204. https://doi.org/10.1097/IYC.0000000000000032

Mardell-Czudnowski, C., & Goldenberg, D. S. (2011). *Developmental indicators for the assessment of learning* (4th ed.) (DIAL-4). NCS Pearson.

McLean, M., Wolery, M., & Bailey, D. B., Jr. (2004). *Assessing infants and preschoolers with special needs* (3rd ed.). Pearson.

McNair, S., Thomson, M., & Williams, R. (1998). *Authentic assessment of young children's developing concepts in mathematics and science.* https://eric.ed.gov/?id=ED445922-

Meisels, S. J., Liaw, F., Dorfman, A., & Nelson, R. F. (1995). The work sampling system: Reliability and validity of a performance assessment for young children. *Early Childhood Research Quarterly, 10,* 277–296.

Mueller, J. (2018). *Authentic assessment toolbox.* http://jfmueller.faculty.noctrl.edu/toolbox /whydoit.htm

National Association for the Education of Young Children (NAEYC). (2020). *Developmentally appropriate practice: A position statement of the National Association for the Education of Young Children.* Author.

National Early Childhood Accountability Task Force. (2007). *Taking stock: Assessing and improving early childhood learning and program quality.* PEW Charitable Trusts, Foundation for Child Development, & Joyce Foundation.

National Research Council (NRC). 2008. *Early childhood assessment: Why, what, and how.* National Academies Press. https://doi.org/10.17226/12446

Newborg, J. (2020). *Battelle developmental inventory* (3rd ed.). Riverside.

Race to the Top—Early Learning Challenge, 76 Fed. Reg. 53564 (August 26, 2011).

Riley-Ayers, S., Frede, E., Barnett, W. S., & Brenneman, K. (2011) *Improving early education programs through data-based decision-making.* National Institute for Early Education Research (NIEER).

Wolfendale, S. (1998). Involving parents in child assessments in the United Kingdom. *Childhood Education, 76,* 355–358.

Family Involvement
in the Assessment Process

Julie Harp Rutland, Ashley Lyons-Picard, Jennifer Grisham, and Kristie Pretti-Frontczak

Caroline initially met 4-year-old Eva's parents on a home visit at the beginning of the school year. While on the visit, she learned a little about the types of activities that Eva enjoys, such as playing on the swing set and roughhousing with her daddy. Caroline also found out that there are some times during the day that are difficult for Eva's family. As a member of a young family, Eva has two other siblings, one who is 2 years old and one who is 2 months old. Eva's mom works part time and her dad full time. On days when mom and dad have to be at work at the same time, they have difficulty getting everyone ready and out the door. Although the oldest of the children, Eva requires a great deal of attention while eating breakfast and needs lots of reminders and support while getting dressed in the morning and undressed for baths and bedtime. In fact, when her mom or dad asks her to put on her shoes or coat, Eva will not comply with their requests without a great deal of coaxing.

Now, in the third week of school, Caroline has begun to notice that Eva's mom looks stressed and Eva distressed when they arrive at the Rainbow Early Childhood Development Center, usually 30 minutes later than the official school start time. On two occasions, Eva's mom has shared how difficult the mornings have been. As Caroline completes Eva's classroom-based assessment and prepares for upcoming parent conferences, she reflects on these conversations and considers the importance of incorporating the information as they work together to identify priority goals.

Like many teachers, Caroline is beginning to understand how conversations and interactions with families provide valuable information for planning young children's educational programs. When assessing a child, the teacher must consider the context of the relationships in the many environments in which the child lives and interacts (Bronfenbrenner, 1979; Lee & Walsh, 2001; National Scientific Council on the Developing Child, 2004; Osher et al., 2020). More specifically, teachers must remember that a child's overall development is affected by the interaction between the child's immediate family/community environment and the society in which he or she lives. This makes support and inclusion of families as active participants in the assessment process critical.

Although programs that serve young children emphasize the importance of family involvement in all aspects of the educational program, in reality families' roles in the assessment process are often very narrow. All too often families are involved in the assessment process by simply answering a few questions about their child's developmental history and/or listening while their child's teacher tells them about how their child performed on an assessment. Limiting families' involvement in the assessment process to these simple roles underestimates the importance of the information they can provide and how involvement can benefit families and children.

The purpose of Chapter 3 is to promote family involvement in the assessment process. The chapter is divided into five main sections. First, the theories that support family involvement in the assessment process are discussed, along with how the research has shaped and guided methods for involving families. Second, the legal mandates regarding family involvement are described. Third, the specific roles of the families are listed, and strategies are provided for improving communication with families. Fourth, various tools designed for gathering assessment information from families are reviewed, including structured and unstructured approaches. Fifth, considerations for gathering reliable information from families are provided to help maximize learning outcomes for children.

INVOLVING FAMILIES IN THE ASSESSMENT PROCESS

Better understanding of the importance of family involvement in the assessment process begins with the ideology behind current recommended practices in the early childhood intervention field. Early childhood intervention is grounded by a strong theoretical foundation (Bandura, 1977; Bronfenbrenner, 1979; Bruner, 1986; Gardner, 1977; Knowles, 1984) that focuses on the child not only as the learner, but also as a member of a family and within the systems, cultures, and factors that affect the family members' lives. With an understanding that culture is the most significant system in which children develop (Kaiser & Rasminsky, 2020; Lee & Walsh, 2001), we must also consider foundational theories and philosophies within cultural contexts. The ecological systems theory, the adult learning theory, and family-centered practices will be discussed in this part of the chapter.

Ecological Systems Theory

To understand a child's development, one must consider the different relationships and the many environments that the child experiences as part of his or her everyday life. The ecological systems theory (Bronfenbrenner, 1979) explains the relationships among different social units and the broad impact of these social supports. The theory defines complex layers of the environment, each having an effect on a child's development. Bronfenbrenner depicts these layers as concentric, with the child and family in the innermost circle. The child and family unit is nested in a broader circle of informal social units that consist of relatives, friends, neighbors, child care providers, and other close acquaintances. These units are nested in larger social units, which include neighborhoods, churches, social organizations, and child care centers. Still further, the larger social units are embedded in even larger social systems consisting of governments and other decision-making bodies that could potentially affect the child. A fundamental tenet of the ecological systems theory is that there is interaction both within and between levels so that events occurring in one unit affect what occurs in another unit.

The interaction between factors in the child's immediate family/community/cultural environment and the society in which they live influences their development. As changes or conflicts in any one layer affect the other layers, indirect influences bear upon a child's development as much as more direct influences do. For example, in a poor economy, a child's parent may be forced to work two jobs in order to make ends meet, and the child suffers from lack of parent–child interaction due to a wide-ranging societal problem.

The ecological systems theory is important to consider when working with families during the assessment process because the teacher may need to ask specific questions to learn about a child's different influences and experiences. For example, the teacher may need to ask about the family's support system and the ability of the family to consistently carry out intervention plans in the home setting. To conduct an accurate assessment, teachers must consider not only the child in the immediate environment, but also interactions within and between environments. These environments may include the home, school, child care center, and many other natural environments. Typically, parents, caregivers, teachers, and other professional personnel have played roles in the assessment process. However, when considering the importance of multiple influences on the child, we may also consider including relatives, friends, neighbors, communities, and culture, as well as how interactions among these influences may directly or indirectly affect a child's development.

Adult Learning Theory

Because the focus of early childhood intervention is the broader context of family and not the child, interactions with adults are as important as interactions with children. Designed to better understand the education of adults, adult learning theory (Knowles, 1984) was first introduced by Malcolm Knowles in the 1970s and is based on the following assumptions: Adults are self-directed learners, life experience and knowledge contribute to adult learning, adults learn when they perceive a need to know something, and learning must be relevant. Therefore, the adult learning theory can help teachers understand what may motivate parents and other familiar caregivers to participate in setting individual goals during the assessment process (Marquardt & Waddill, 2004; Mezirow, 1981).

More applicable to early childhood intervention, Knowles suggested that as self-directed learners, adults are resistant to decisions and strategies that are determined without the participation of the adult. In these circumstances, feelings of ill will can result rather than inclusion as part of a team of collaborators. Finally, the adult learning theory assumes that learners are motivated by intrinsic factors (Knowles, 1984). They learn what they want to learn based on what is important to them at any particular time in life. As change and adaptation have become a fact of everyday living, it is extremely important that family priorities be evaluated regularly to address possible changing needs. In response to adult learning theory, early childhood educators should consider what is important to families and try to meet those needs. When planning assessments, teachers need to consider the type of involvement in the assessment process that families would like and the extent to which they would like to be involved. By valuing the information provided, assessment can be designed to be functional within the context of a family's typical daily routines and focus on the family as a whole.

Family-Centered Practices

The field of early childhood intervention has evolved in its view of families, starting with child-centered practices, moving to family-guided practices, and finally arriving at family-centered practices. Family-centered practices involve a set of beliefs, principles, and values for supporting and strengthening the capacity of families to promote and enhance the development of their children (Dunst, 2002). A few of the tenets of family-centered practices include the recognition and respect for 1) the family as the expert on the child, 2) the family as the ultimate decision maker for the child and family, 3) the family as the constant in the child's life, with teachers being a temporary relationship, 4) the family's choice in level of participation, 5) the family's priorities and concerns as the propeller for goals and outcomes, and 6) the family's cultural beliefs and values (Baird & Peterson, 1997).

Family-centered practices use models that conceptualize and implement learning strategies focusing on the child within everyday settings and social relationships. As children may respond differently in environments and with people with whom they are unfamiliar, it is important to use family-centered practices that will result in more reliable measures. Research indicates that using family-centered practices during the assessment process yields higher reported satisfaction and family well-being (Dunst, 1985; Dunst et al., 2006) and better outcomes for children (Dunst, 1985) than the traditional child-centered approach. As the field of early childhood intervention has evolved in its views, so have practices. It is important to implement the tenets of family-centered practices in all aspects of early childhood intervention, including the assessment process. Respect must be given to the family as the expert in providing valuable information about their child and to using family priorities and concerns as the foundation for planning.

The common thread in the aforementioned foundational theories and practices of early childhood intervention (Bronfenbrenner, 1979; Dunst, 1985; Knowles, 1984) is the recognition of the family's role as important and relevant. Theories and practices that are grounded in research contribute to assessment processes that are functional and support the family's ability to promote the child's development because they lead to feelings of empowerment, which in turn lead to better outcomes for children (Hoover-Dempsey et al., 2005). Without careful attention to the important influence of the child's family and culture, the success of early intervention is likely compromised (Dunst, 1985; Lynch & Hanson, 2011).

LEGAL MANDATES

In response to research, and shaped by foundational theories and philosophies, legislative mandates in early childhood intervention that require the involvement of families are now present. These trends include legislation for early childhood special education/early intervention, Head Start, and Early Head

Start. For example, a key component of the federal special education law, the Education for All Handicapped Children Act (PL 94-142), together with its subsequent amendments, references the need for parent involvement. With each reauthorization, Congress has affirmed the commitment to family involvement, leading to what is now known as the Individuals with Disabilities Education Act (IDEA; U.S. Department of Health and Human Services, 2020). See Box 3.1 for examples of how PL 94-142 and subsequent amendments refer to the importance of families.

Early intervention (Part C of IDEA), which serves children from birth through 2 years of age, requires that the family is part of the team that develops the individualized family service plan (IFSP). Families are not only expected to be present, but also expected to describe daily routines, their children's likes and dislikes, the typical interactions that take place within the context of relationships, and how these descriptions affect their parenting and support of their child with disabilities. In fact, one element of the IFSP is a statement of the child's current levels of cognitive, physical, communication, social-emotional, and adaptive development, which can be provided only by or through the family.

As children transition from Part C (early intervention) to part B of IDEA, families of children 3–5 years of age often struggle with the change from family-centered services to child-centered education programs where the school assumes the primary educational responsibility. IDEA requires a 6-month transition period from Part C to Part B to assist families with these changes in services. During the transition, meetings are held with families and evaluations of the child are conducted. Extra time is allowed for conversations

---

Box 3.1.   Examples of the Importance of Family as Stated in IDEA

Sample phrase from PL 94-142, the Education for All Handicapped Children Act: "Parents should be provided training through a not-for-profit agency to enable them to participate more effectively with professionals in meeting educational needs of their child."

Sample phrase from PL 99-457, the Education for All Handicapped Children Act Amendments of 1986: "To enhance the capacity of families to meet the special needs of their infants and toddlers with handicaps."

Sample phrase from PL 105-117, the Individuals with Disabilities Education Act Amendments of 1997: "A family-directed assessment of the resources, priorities, and concerns of the family and the identification of the supports and services necessary to enhance the family's capacity to meet the developmental needs of the infant or toddler . . ."

Sample phrase from PL 108-446, the Individuals with Disabilities Education Improvement Act of 2004: "A written individualized family service plan developed by a multidisciplinary team, including the parents, as required by subsection (e). . . ."

among parents, teachers, and specialists to ensure a positive transition for the child (Johnson, 2001).

Another example of a mandated program that focuses on the family is the Head Start program, which provides grants to local public and private nonprofit and for-profit agencies to provide comprehensive child development services to economically disadvantaged children and their families. Head Start promotes school readiness by supporting the social and cognitive development of children through the provision of educational, health, nutritional, social, and other services to enrolled children and families (U.S. Department of Health and Human Services, 2020). The main focus of Head Start is helping preschoolers develop the early reading and math skills they need to be successful in school. Parents are engaged in their children's learning and help them progress toward their educational, literacy, and employment goals. The Head Start program places a strong emphasis on the involvement of families (U.S. Department of Health and Human Services, 2020). Head Start standards state the need for agencies to maintain regular communication with families, including periodic meetings to discuss assessment results and student progress. Progress reports must be distributed to families in an understandable, uniform format and, if possible, in a language that parents understand. Head Start also encourages direct participation of parents and community members in its implementation. The goal of parent participation is to allow parents to become full partners in the education of their children (U.S. Department of Health and Human Services, 2020).

The Early Head Start program was established to serve children from birth to 3 years of age in recognition of the growing evidence that the earliest years are extremely important to a child's growth and development. Early Head Start promotes healthy prenatal outcomes, enhances infant and toddler development, and empowers the family to function in a healthy manner. One way that Early Head Start promotes family involvement is through home visits. During home visits, Early Head Start workers reinforce the parents' ability to support their child's cognitive, social, emotional, and physical development. Strengths-based parent education is also provided to encourage parents to be their child's first teacher (U.S. Department of Health and Human Services, 2020).

INVOLVING FAMILIES IN THE ASSESSMENT PROCESS

Family involvement in the assessment process is a necessary component of successful early childhood intervention; however, it must be respected as a choice for families. Families may choose to participate in the assessment process at varying levels. One of the tenets of family-centered practices is recognition of and respect for the family as the expert on the child (Baird & Peterson, 1997). In other words, families know their children best; therefore, it is important to welcome their involvement regardless of the level.

There are many ways in which families can be invited to participate in the assessment process. Possible roles families can play include 1) creating opportunities for parents to be *learners* by providing them with important information about their child's development, 2) asking families to share their story or provide their *expert* opinion and information through the process, 3) *teaming* with families as they assist with the assessment process, and/or 4) allowing them to be *advocates* as they describe hopes and dreams for their child. Each of these roles is described in the sections that follow.

Learner

All families have the right to receive important information about their child's education. Teachers should discuss issues with families that relate to curriculum framework design, implementation, and evaluation, such as the underlying philosophy of their teaching. Families should also receive information that will support their child's development when their child is not in school (Grisham-Brown et al., 2005).

Families need information about the school's philosophy of early childhood education in order to understand how children are learning important concepts while engaged in play. Teachers need to share with families how content and individualized goals are being addressed in the classroom. Often, there is a disconnect between home and school, and new strategies are needed to bridge the gap. Visual representations of learning opportunities related to targeted behaviors and/or standards can be used to inform parents about their child's school experiences. These visual representations are referred to as embedding schedules (Grisham-Brown et al., 2005; Hemmeter & Grisham-Brown, 1997; Pretti-Frontczak & Bricker, 2004). Embedding schedules include target behaviors for the child that will be addressed, activities that occur throughout the day, and examples of specific behaviors that the child can demonstrate/practice within a designated activity. By sending embedding schedules home, the teacher is providing another opportunity for families to be learners in the assessment process. Table 3.1 is an example of a classroom embedding schedule.

Table 3.1. Example of a classroom embedding schedule

	Target behaviors		
Activities	Count objects	Use both hands to act upon objects	Interact with peers
Greeting circle	Count friends and days on the calendar	Help teacher place pillows on floor for circle time	Greet peers by name
Small group	Count objects to go to art project	Button shirt prior to art project	Ask peers to pass objects by using appropriate manners
Snack	Count pieces of cereal or snack of the day	Open milk carton	Share important happenings in child's life
Centers/work time	Count objects around the room such as cars in the block area	Make bead necklace to be used in dramatic play	Invite friends to play in a center
Outdoor play	Count butterflies	Button/snap/zip coat before going outside	Join friends in a game of tag

Lesson planning forms are another strategy used by teachers to help families understand how important concepts and standards are being addressed through play in the classroom. The forms include the daily classroom schedule with accompanying activities that will occur throughout the day, standards or broad outcomes for all children that will be the focus of each activity, and suggestions for how the family can promote the identified outcomes at home. Table 3.2 provides an example of a lesson planning form that teachers may send home to families on a weekly basis.

Along with sharing targeted behaviors and daily activities, teachers are required to share assessment information with parents in a variety of settings. A child's progress toward individual goals can be shared formally during parent meetings or informally through notes and phone calls. Teachers need to use multiple ways to communicate with families due to the differences in family schedules, preferences, literacy levels, and primary language. School websites, teacher blogs, e-mail, and texting are all new technologies that can also assist teachers in communicating with families.

If a child has an IFSP or an individualized educational program (IEP) in place, meetings are held to share the child's progress with the parents. During these meetings, parents may be informed that their child has reached

Table 3.2.   Lesson planning form

Schedule/Activities	Learning outcomes	Home
Greeting circle		
• Story: Olivia • Finger play: "This little piggy went to market" • Movement: Parachute	• Enjoy and value reading • Actively participate in conversation • Show rhythm while moving	• Read stories about animal characters • Do finger plays with family members
Small group		
• Farm paintings	• Use tools for writing and drawing • Explore cause and effect	• Go through old magazines and make a farm animal collage
Snack		
• Fruit salad • Milk	• Identify different colors and shapes • Begin to recognize nutritional food choices	• Prepare applewiches 1. Spread peanut butter on two round slices of apple. 2. Put cheese slice in the middle and eat like a sandwich.
Centers/work time		
• Blocks: Farm • Dramatic play: Grocery store • Reading: Animal books	• Take turns with others • Take on pretend roles and situations	• Talk about how food gets to the grocery store from the farm • Build a barn using blocks
Outdoor play		
• Farm animals in the sandbox	• Make believe with objects	• Go to a local farm to see the animals

proficiency for an individualized goal and that it is time to create a new goal. If the child has not yet reached proficiency, plans could also be made to adjust goals or continue work on goals already in place.

Often, parent conferences are held on a regular basis for all children so that the teacher can share assessment results and talk with parents about their child's strengths and weaknesses. At these conferences, for example, teachers may show parents their child's journal, illustrating writing growth over time, or they may explain the results from a formal curriculum-based assessment (CBA). Parent conferences can also serve as a time for parents to inform teachers about their child. Involving families in such bidirectional sharing of information allows further connections to be made between home and school (Cheatham & Ostrosky, 2009).

Sharing information, whether it is in person, through hand-written notes, or through some form of technology, is critical. Teachers also can share valuable information with families by extending learning opportunities to the home. Families are better equipped to help their child when they are provided with in-home learning activities and with suggestions for ways to promote the child's individualized targeted behaviors within their daily routines. For example, if a child is working on fine motor skills as a targeted behavior, the teacher may suggest that the child be given small foods to pick up during mealtimes, such as dry cereal or raisins, or provide the family with developmentally appropriate art activities that will further develop the child's fine motor skills. Teachers should also be well versed in parental concerns such as toilet training, sleep schedules, and sibling relationships (Grisham-Brown et al., 2005; Katz, 1996).

Although it is vital for families to receive information about school policies, curriculum design, and targeted behaviors, teachers should be careful not to limit families' role in the assessment process to that of the learner. Both structured and unstructured approaches to assessment often fail to include the family as an active participant. It is important to remember that families are their child's first teacher and that they know their child best. Therefore, families should play an active role in the assessment process, working together with the teacher and specialists to play additional roles such as expert, team member, and/or advocate.

Expert

Families can provide critical information about their child from their unique perspectives. National Association for the Education of Young Children (NAEYC) guidelines indicate that families feel more like partners when their knowledge and insight about their children are respected (NAEYC, 2009). The Division for Early Childhood (DEC-recommended practices also suggest that families can provide valuable information about their children's interests and abilities (Division for Early Childhood [DEC], 2014). It is important to use families as experts in the assessment process because they have almost constant contact with their child and interact with the child in many different contexts (Vangalder, 1997). These experiences allow families to provide teachers with various types of information that can aid in the design and implementation of valid assessments.

Families can share information about their child's temperament and physical needs, which may help the teacher understand a child's reaction to different assessment situations. For example, a child who tends to be anxious might perform better on CBAs than on structured assessments. A child who has poor fine motor skills may struggle with pen and paper assessments but perform well with oral questioning.

Families also can share information about their child's daily routine. Teachers need to know about these routines in order to have reasonable, culturally sensitive expectations for the child, especially regarding self-help issues. For example, in some cultures mothers assist their child with using utensils for many years, whereas in other cultures mothers encourage independent feeding skills at a young age. When discussing routines, it is helpful to talk with families about how they encourage and limit their child at home. Learning about styles of encouragement and limiting can give insight into the child's behavior and reactions in the classroom (McWilliam et al., 2009). If a child is accustomed to receiving extrinsic rewards for motivation at home, they may have a hard time adjusting to intrinsic rewards used in the classroom. The child may be confused about the different types of encouragement used by parents and teachers and may require some explanation. Limits and consequences will most likely vary between home and school as well. Whereas some homes will use physical punishment, schools are required to use natural consequences, such as removing the child from a troublesome situation.

It is helpful for teachers to learn about the dynamics of a family to better understand the child and his or her behaviors in the classroom. Family relationships and varying types of social-emotional interaction can affect the child's performance on classwork and assessments. Gaining information about the family's history and the child's previous life experiences can help teachers provide more accurate assessment. For example, if the child has recently lost an important family member, they may feel reserved and be more reluctant to answer open-ended questions on an assessment. In contrast, the child may perform well on an assessment that encourages drawing freely and expressing feelings without words.

Information about the family's community involvement and cultural background can help build rapport with the family and child and enable the teacher to provide appropriate resources during the assessment process. (See Chapter 4.) Teachers should consider a child's cultural background in economic, social, and occupational terms instead of focusing solely on ethnicity and race (Westphal, 1989), an idea that will be discussed in detail later in this chapter under Embracing Diversity, Equity, and Inclusion.

Understanding each family's priorities and goals for their child, along with the family's strengths, needs, and resources, allows teachers to plan, implement, and evaluate each child as an individual (Vangalder, 1997), ensuring that the assessment process is accurate and valid. For example, a family's priority may be for the child to improve in the area of language development. Understanding this priority would help the teacher when developing the classroom curriculum and individual goals for the child. More importantly, when teachers acknowledge families' priorities and goals for their child, the families are more likely to feel that their needs are validated and, therefore, will carry out any suggestions regarding teaching the priority in other environments.

Families also can share their child's preferences and tell the teacher what works with their child in order to help teachers develop assessments and interventions that are tailored to students' individual needs. If a student prefers working in a quiet setting, a teacher may allow the child to move to the hallway to be assessed. Students who have strong interests, such as sports or animals, may perform better on assessments that are developed with their interests in mind. As well, children may have preferences about how adults interact with them, the type of environment in which they work best, and the type of materials that motivate them.

Team Member

Families, as collaborative members during the assessment process, can be instrumental in identifying the best assessment strategies and approaches for their children. Therefore, families must be invited to participate in all aspects of the assessment process (Boone & Crais, 1999), including planning the assessment, participating in interviews, helping gather information and testing the child, and helping to determine whether the information collected is representative of their child's actual abilities.

By participating, gathering information, and rating specific behaviors in their children, parents can increase their awareness of their child's development (Dinnebeil & Rule, 1994), thus enhancing their contributions to the development of intervention plans and decision making (Brinckerhoff & Vincent, 1987). The family, along with the teacher and specialists, can develop a more accurate picture of the child by compiling and interpreting their multiple observations of the child (Vangalder, 1997). For example, when teachers use the Assessment, Evaluation, and Programming System for Infants and Children (AEPS®; Bricker et al., 2002, 2022) as an assessment, families are asked to make observations of their child in the home or in other familiar settings and fill out a family report about their children's level of independence on each developmental skill. Family involvement in AEPS may improve program planning or progress monitoring. Figure 3.1 illustrates a portion of the AEPS Family Report II, where parents marked each skill with a "Y" if they feel that their child performs the skill or action described in the question, an "S" if they feel that their child sometimes performs the skill or action, or an "N" if they feel that their child does not perform the skill or action yet.

Cognitive Area

Cognitive skills are those that involve mental processes and reasoning. These skills include problem solving, counting, recalling, imitating categorizing, and pre-reading.

11. Does your child pretend play with other children? (F1) NOTE: Place a "Y," "S," or "N" by items a through c:

    __S__ a. Does your child pretend to be someone else and tell other children who they can pretend to be? For example, your child says, "I'll be the bus driver and you be the kid." (F1.1)

    __S__ b. Does your child act out a pretend story or event? For example, your child says he or she is going fishing and then pretends to catch some fish and cook them. (F1.2)

    __Y__ c. Does your child use pretend objects or motions to play? For example, your child pretends to brush hair without a brush. (F1.3)

12. Does your child play games following rules? (F2)

13. Does your child count at least 20 objects (G1)

Figure 3.1. Completed a portion of the AEPS Family Report II title. (From Bricker, D., Pretti–Frontczak, K., Johnson, J. J., & Strake, E. [2002]. *Assessment, Evaluation, and Programming System for Infants and Children [AEPS®] Second Edition: Volume I. AEPS Administration guide.* Paul H. Brookes Publishing Co.; reprinted by permission.)

Multiple observations, including those from families, can also be collected using the Transdisciplinary Play-Based Assessment and Intervention, Second Edition (TPBA/I2; Linder, 2008). The arena approach to assessment includes families as equal team members along with professionals from various disciplines. One purpose of involving families in this assessment is to determine eligibility for special education services.

TPBA/I2 is a flexible, holistic process that meets the needs of the individual child and the family. In the arena model, one team member is authorized to interact with the child using novel and familiar toys in a natural setting, while the other team members gather information through observation of the child and use of developmental guidelines to help interpret the assessment. Using these guidelines and age tables related to each of the developmental domains, the team interprets their cumulative information to determine the ability level of the child. Results from the assessment help develop effective individualized goals. The results also help teachers determine strategies for promoting higher levels of skills or more functional behaviors (Adrienne & McCollum, 1992; Linder, 2008).

Active family involvement does not mean that professionals abdicate their responsibilities. It is still the responsibility of teachers and specialists to help families choose a reasonable course of action for achieving targeted behaviors. All team members should be actively involved in suggesting and providing appropriate options for individualized goals (Berman & Shaw, 1995). Families are the most familiar with their child, but they are not always familiar with appropriate interventions or developmentally appropriate practices. It is the job of the teachers and specialists to share their expertise and to help guide families and facilitate teamwork when working together. Involving families in the TPBA/I2 assessment process as team members leads to a report that seems honest to those families and, ultimately, leads them toward appropriate solutions and resources (Berman & Shaw, 1995).

Advocate

Although professionals in the field of early childhood intervention have a great interest in the children they serve and teach, families have the greatest vested interest in their children. They must live with the results and strategies that are developed from the assessment. Therefore, families may confirm or refute assessment information, based on their knowledge and understanding of their child's abilities and characteristics. Their advocacy may be achieved through gathering information and commenting on their child's behaviors and performance during assessment, asking questions about the methods used during the evaluation, and making sure they clearly understand the process (Berman & Shaw, 1995). To provide support, families must be advocates for their children throughout each step of the assessment process, including planning the evaluation, gathering information, and analyzing the results. Family advocacy at times may be as simple as ensuring that the time of day and the length of observations are appropriate and in the best interest of the child. Families can provide a fresh perspective on how services should be delivered (Thegan & Weber, 2002) and must be supported in their efforts to develop skills to communicate concerns, goals, placement options, and many other types of key information that is relevant to the assessment process.

Benefits to Families and Children

When families are fully involved in the assessment process, there are improved outcomes for both children and families. The term *outcomes* refers to the end result of services. It is important that outcomes be functional or meaningful to children and families in their everyday lives and routines across a variety of settings. In addition to the outcomes that are directly related to core content, parent involvement also contributes to better attitudes about school (Epstein, 2000).

Another result of family involvement in the assessment process is increased family satisfaction. Using family-centered practices, such as including families in assessment, leads to feelings of empowerment (Hanft & Pilkington, 2000) and a higher level of parents' well-being (Dunst et al., 2006). In addition, involving families in the assessment process increases the likelihood of learning outcomes that are meaningful to the family, which increases the likelihood of the family addressing targeted skills within typical routines using strategies developed from information gained during the assessment.

APPROACHES FOR GATHERING
ASSESSMENT INFORMATION FROM FAMILIES

Information can be gathered from families with unstructured and structured approaches. Using a combination of these approaches, teachers can gather valuable information about children's strengths and weaknesses as well as monitor their progress toward important learning outcomes. Unstructured approaches involve asking open-ended questions that allow families the opportunity to provide as little or as much information as they desire. Structured approaches include those that are linked to the use of CBA tools in planning instruction.

Unstructured Approaches

Interviews, informal observations, and open-ended questioning are examples of unstructured approaches to gather information. Formal measurement tools may not provide all of the necessary information to clearly depict the strengths and concerns of each child and family, thereby hindering the development of strategies that are functional (Dunst & McWilliam, 1988).

On the other hand, formal measurement tools that take an unstructured approach, such as the Routines-Based Interview (RBI; McWilliam et al., 2009) or the Asset-Based Context Matrix (Wilson et al., 2004), provide a framework for gathering information on family routines, interests, interactions, and participation in everyday activities. Although these tools are typically used in early intervention (birth to 3) contexts, they could easily be adjusted to fit the information collection needs of practitioners working with children in other early childhood settings.

An RBI focuses on discussing the family's daily routines and asking parents to share their satisfaction with each routine. The interview is often conducted using an open form that does not specify the routine being discussed and a structured form that lists the specific routine and questions to ask the family. While discussing daily routines with parents, the teacher records the family's level of satisfaction with their child's engagement during each of the routines. Routines that may be discussed during an RBI include waking up, diapering/dressing, feeding/meals, getting ready to go/traveling, hanging out/watching TV, bath time, outdoors, and nap/bedtime. If adjusting the format of the RBI to collect information for families or preschoolers/kindergarteners, teachers could explore some of the same family routines while also asking questions about routines such as planned instructional time at home or free time.

Similarly, the Asset-Based Context Matrix focuses on the context of natural environments or routines in which the child interacts and lives. The model focuses on using the child's interests and assets within daily activities to promote new opportunities for growth. Information about the child is gathered through observations, interactions, and conversations with the family. Once the information is gathered, teachers and families enter the information into a matrix that can be easily used to develop goals and interventions. Information obtained through these less formal measures can provide a clearer picture of each unique child and assist in developing strategies that will be functional (Wilson & Mott, 2006).

Another tool that has been used in early intervention and mental health contexts—and could be effectively applied to many more educational situations—is the eco-map. An eco-map is a graphic or visual representation of the informal and formal support a child and/or family identifies as available (Baumgartner et al., 2012; McCormick et al., 2008). In the early intervention context, it is sometimes discussed as a means by which teams can examine the emotional, material, and informational resources a family has and then work together to identify how to obtain support and/or resources that are lacking (Jung, 2010). No two eco-maps are the same and there is individualization in terms of implementation, but all eco-maps provide an at-a-glance picture of the support a child currently has within and across systems (such as family, community, medical, school, and so on). Use of the eco-map in educational contexts, including those where it is not widely used such as for preschool or elementary child assessment, can help teams better understand what resources families currently have and therefore can be useful in program planning when considering the school and home connection.

Different techniques are used by teachers when communicating with families. Some use a conversational approach, whereas others use direct questioning or forms for interviewing. Research suggests that the conversational approach, which gives parents conversational control, better reflects actual family goals (Cheatham & Ostrosky, 2009), and the use of open-ended questions helps to create mutual trust and free-flowing communication (Reedy & Walls, 1996).

The use of open-ended questions is important when unstructured approaches are employed to gather limitless information from families. Open-ended questions are those that cannot be answered by a simple yes or no or other one-word answer, but instead invite the family to expand on their answers in order to share more information about their child. Table 3.3 contains examples of closed-ended questions and how they can be converted into open-ended questions.

Table 3.3. Using open-ended questions versus closed-ended questions

Topic	Closed-ended	Open-ended
Self-help	Does your child bathe themself?	How is your child involved with bath time?
Literacy	Does your child identify letters?	How does your child interact with printed materials such as magazines, books, and menus?
Numeracy	Does your child know how to count?	How does your child use numbers in their daily routines?
Communication	How many words does your child say?	How does your child get their wants and needs met?

Structured Approaches

Structured approaches for gathering assessment information from families are associated with curriculum-based assessments (CBAs). CBAs are designed to measure specific skills for families and teachers to determine the child's current level of development. Some CBAs have specific forms and/or processes for involving families in their children's assessment. Active family involvement in the assessment process is built into CBAs through the use of reports, interviews, family albums, developmental record books, profiles, narrative family reports, and conferencing. Table 3.4 describes how selected CBAs involve families in the assessment process. For more comprehensive information regarding key

Table 3.4. Description of how select curriculum-based assessments involve families in the assessment process

CBA	Description
Assessment, Evaluation, and Programming System for Infants and Children, Third Edition (AEPS®-3) (Bricker et al., 2022)	The Family Report has two sections: Family Routines and Family Observations. A process for involving families in the development of individualized goals is provided.
BRIGANCE Inventory for Early Development-II (Brigance, 2004)	A developmental record book with a color coding system is used to inform families of their children's progress. The recording system helps families and teachers identify individualized goals.
Carolina Curriculum for Preschoolers with Special Needs (CCPSN), Second Edition (Johnson-Martin et al., 2004)	Regular conferences are held to maintain family participation. Families are included in discussions about their child's intervention program and planned activities.
Creative Curriculum Developmental Continuum Assessment (Trister-Dodge et al., 2002)	Suggestions for gathering information about child and family are provided (e.g., routines, culture). The Child Progress and Summary form is provided to families to demonstrate their child's progress.
Hawaii Early Learning Profile (HELP) (Furano et al., 2006)	The Help Chart and HELP Family Participation format facilitate parent involvement by letting the family choose how much they want to be involved in their child's assessment and planning.
The Ounce Scale (Meisels et al., 2003)	Albums serve to gather information from the family, including photographs, drawings, and written information. Developmental Profiles and Standards help teachers work with families during conferences to evaluate children's progress and identify goals.
Transdisciplinary Play-Based Assessment and Intervention, Second Edition (TPBA/I2) (Linder, 2008)	Information is gathered from families through the Child and Family History Questionnaire and the Family Assessment of Child Functioning Daily Routines Rating form.
Work Sampling System, Fourth Edition (WSS) (Meisels et al., 2001)	Ongoing assessment is summarized three times per year (fall, winter, spring) for each child. An easy-to-read report is given to families to share the results. An optional narrative family report is provided, but no specific role is assigned to the parent to help gather information to use as part of the process.
Teaching Strategies GOLD (Heroman et al., 2010)	Information about children's development and learning is gathered from the family through the Family Conference Form.

Source: Kansas University Center on Developmental Disabilities (2010).

CBAs, please see the Kansas Inservice Training System's resource *Curriculum-Based Assessments for Measuring Early Childhood Outcomes* (https://kskits.ku.edu/ta/ECOOutcomes/documents/ECO_CBA_matrix_8_18_15.pdf).

Across unstructured and structured approaches, a key way to gather information from families is through interviews. Table 3.5 offers basic DOs and

Table 3.5. Interviewing DOs and DON'Ts

Strategy	DOs	DON'Ts
Body language	DO respect preferences for space and eye contact (may be cultural differences). DO keep your notes visible.	If taking notes, DON'T keep your head down the entire time. DON'T hide notes behind a clipboard or hide behind a computer screen.
Silence/waiting	DO be comfortable with some silence to let the speaker know you want to hear what they have to say.	DON'T restate the question right away if the speaker is taking some time to respond. DON'T interrupt.
Listening/ attending	DO clear your head of competing thoughts. DO direct your full attention to the speaker. DO attend to the tone of voice and facial expressions.	DON'T focus exclusively on what was said; also focus on HOW it was said.
Encouraging and affirming	DO simple verbalizations to encourage the speaker to continue (e.g., "Go on," "Can you tell me more about that?"). DO validate strengths.	DON'T reassure yourself by minimizing the speaker's feelings or experience (e.g., "You're strong; you'll get over it").
Reflecting content and feelings	DO use your own words to point out either the content or feelings behind the message (e.g., reflecting content: "What I'm hearing you say is that since her baby brother was born, bedtime has been a challenge again for Anna").	DON'T be a "mind-reader" (e.g., "I know just how you feel"). DON'T invalidate the speaker's experience by finding the silver lining (e.g., "At least the child wasn't seriously hurt"). DON'T divert the focus of the conversation (e.g., "If you think that's bad, let me tell you about what I went through").
Questioning	DO ask one question at a time. DO use open-ended questions (what, how) to gather more detailed information.	DON'T disguise a directive as a question (e.g., "You're giving him a lot of tummy time, aren't you?").
Clarifying and validating	DO restate what was said to check for your understanding.	DON'T make assumptions (e.g., "You know what I mean, right?"). DON'T use logical arguments (e.g., "If you don't go to your scheduled appointments, you can't expect progress").
Summarizing	DO restate the main points of the conversation, which can be done halfway through and at the end (e.g., "So far we've identified two concerns . . .").	DON'T advise prematurely, especially if unsolicited (e.g., "If I were you, this is what I would do . . ." or "You really ought to . . .").

From Pretti-Frontczak, K., Lyons, A., & Travers, K. (2015). *Five steps to functional assessment: Evaluation and assessment base training and coaching content* [PowerPoint]. B2K Solutions^SM, Ltd.; adapted by permission.
Sources: CONNECT (n.d.), Foster (n.d.), and Friend (2010).

DON'Ts when it comes to interviewing families and other important caregivers. Recommendations and practical strategies are summarized.

CONSIDERATIONS FOR GATHERING RELIABLE INFORMATION FROM FAMILIES

There are many issues teachers must consider when gathering information from families. How will the information be gathered? How will the teacher get families to be open and forthcoming with information? How is information about the family best used to help the child? Understanding family involvement in the assessment process and how to use effective communication skills can help teachers answer these questions. It is also important that teachers have knowledge of scheduling needs and unique needs of diverse groups in order to collect reliable information. Finally, it is important for teachers to understand how to define family priorities, set individual goals, and plan programs with families in mind.

Understanding Levels of Family Involvement

As previously discussed, one of the tenets of family-centered philosophy is the recognition and respect for a family's choice in how they want to be involved in the assessment process. Assessment practices should encourage and support varying levels of family involvement (i.e., from involving the family as receivers of information to using the family as important experts, team members, and advocates).

Effective Communication Strategies

Regardless of whether structured or unstructured assessment approaches are utilized, the assessment information gathered will be most useful if teachers use effective communication strategies. It is important to maintain a very clear and open level of communication with families in order to maximize the amount of information collected. "Communication is noticeably enhanced when the following indicators are observed: (a) warmth, (b) empathy, (c) respect, (d) genuineness, (e) listening, and (f) concrete practicality" (Maring & Magelky, 1990, p. 606). Warmth and empathy may be achieved by signaling openness through body language, such as keeping one's arms uncrossed and sitting close to the family members instead of across from them. It also may increase the family's comfort level if the teacher reflects on what families say and restate their concerns to show understanding. Finally, asking questions that encourage families to speak their minds and share their concerns will help teachers learn valuable information about the child (Topping & Hoffman, 2002). Trained assessment providers know that by using effective communication strategies, more opportunities to gain new information will be created.

In gathering information, it is important that teachers use a variety of communication methods with families. Teachers can communicate with families informally through phone calls, e-mails, or written notes or more formally through home visits, conferences, or team meetings (Grisham-Brown et al., 2005). Teachers often use anecdotal records to record a child's developmental milestones. For example, if the teacher notices Sandy tying her shoe independently for the first time, she may note her achievement with the date and time so she can share the information with Sandy's family during a conference and record her fine motor skill development.

Formal and informal communications with families are opportunities to demonstrate a belief in the value of a successful partnership between home and school (Studer, 1993). When teachers communicate effectively with families, a level of intimacy and understanding develops that allows teachers to obtain more accurate and useful information during the assessment process (Reedy & Walls, 1996). Mutual give and take in the parent–teacher relationship leads to a sharing of trust as well as information (Reedy & Walls, 1996).

Considerate Scheduling

In making family involvement in the assessment process a priority, teachers must consider the unique scheduling needs of each family. Many families have work schedules and transportation needs that can make attending meetings during the school day a hardship. Therefore, teachers should evaluate each family's scheduling needs on an individual basis and consider alternative options for communicating with families who cannot attend meetings during school hours. This is especially true if young children have to be assessed remotely, particularly if a child requires more one-on-one support from a family member to meaningfully engage in the assessment.

The first consideration for involving families should be giving plenty of advance notice and sending reminders so that they can make arrangements to attend. It may be helpful for some families to hold meetings in the evening or at a time when a babysitter can be provided at the school. Home visits work well for families with transportation needs, and conference calls can replace face-to-face meetings when not all parties involved can arrange a suitable meeting time.

Embracing Diversity, Equity, and Inclusion

Another tenet of the family-centered approach is respecting differences in beliefs and values (Baird & Peterson, 1997). Families cannot be treated as if they are all the same because they will vary in their ideas about strategies, treatment, causes of illness, independence, discipline, and child rearing. Families also differ in their cultural values and the amount of support that they receive from their relatives and communities. Understanding how a family is organized, structured, and defined can help teachers become sensitive to the unique needs of the child during the assessment process. Developing a relationship with families before engaging in formal assessment practices can help teachers plan and carry out a more accurate assessment based on each child's individual goals.

Cultural values and experiences influence children's lives and unique identities, which in turn influence behavior, emotions, and thinking (Gollnick &

Chinn, 2005). Teachers must extend their cultural awareness beyond racial, ethnic, and linguistic diversity, while also recognizing the importance of racial and ethnic identities. As of 2019, for the first time more than half of the U.S. population under the age of 16 identified as being an ethnic or racial minority. Further, nearly 40% of this group identifies as either Hispanic, Latino, or Black (Frey, 2020). In addition, critical calls to embrace antiracist education practices have reached a crescendo in recent years, and the start of the COVID-19 pandemic put the issue of inequity directly into the public eye as school closings and online learning demanded a rethinking of education in the United States. Addressing systemic racism and our own biases in education begins with teachers acknowledging how Black, Indigenous, and children and families of color have been both intentionally and unintentionally harmed by the existing education system. It also requires taking the initiative to fight for equity by doing the personal and emotional work of confronting biases to effectively work to support children and partner with families (Love, 2020). With the majority of teachers being Caucasian, it is critical that these teachers confront their biases and consider the impact of their assumptions. Further, teachers must consider the primary language of the family, their reading abilities, and cultural factors (e.g., sharing personal family information may be taboo in some cultures) when selecting strategies for gathering information (Lo, 2008). When families share information with teachers about their culture and traditions, teachers can use the information to enrich their curriculum and make families feel involved. The teacher becomes a co-learner with the students as they share about the special parts of their culture.

Families from other cultures may be less familiar with the U.S. educational system (De Feyter & Winsler, 2009) and parental responsibility in the learning process (Pelletier & Corter, 2005). Language barriers (Hernandez et al., 2009) and the fact that dual language learner families are more likely to live in a lower socioeconomic environment (Hernandez et al., 2009) place the family at risk for discrimination (Sattin-Bajaj, 2009). Furthermore, children of such families may have experienced trauma directly and/or indirectly related to the above challenges. If the teacher is aware of a language barrier, one way he or she can help is to make sure to have an interpreter available for the family and child during the assessment process.

Just as culture can determine the definition of family structure and authority within the family, it also may affect who is included on the intervention team. Families often extend beyond parents and siblings and can include grandparents, aunts, uncles, and many other people who have an important role in the child's life (Berman & Shaw, 1995).

Defining Priorities

Family priorities, or the ways in which families prefer practices in early childhood education, and family concerns, areas that family members identify as problems, are key elements to the development of the goals and curriculum

for all children (McGonigel et al., 1994). Furthermore, recommended practice suggests that goals be derived from the priorities and concerns of families (Sandall et al., 2005). Family priorities and concerns that are directly and
indirectly related to the child's development should be documented so that
the family is viewed as a whole. Then strategies that occur within the context
of everyday routines (classroom activities, family activities, and community)
should be developed to reflect these priorities and concerns. A curriculum that
is designed in response to the priorities and concerns of families empowers
families to enhance the development of their child (Hanft & Pilkington, 2000).
Assessment should be based on the family's priorities and concerns and should
reflect what the family wants to gain from the assessments.

Setting Individual Goals

Taking into consideration the priorities and concerns of families and their children, it is clear that each child is a unique individual with distinctive needs
and interests. Recommended practice suggests that all children need individualized goals and instruction (Grisham-Brown et al., 2005). Strategies must be
implemented in developmentally appropriate environments and include activities and experiences that are based on the child's interests.

Program Planning

Assessment should be used to make decisions about program planning. As part
of the assessment process, families may share information about their child's
hobbies and interests, which may be helpful in determining themes of study
in the classroom. Children are much more engaged in the program when it
revolves around their areas of interest. For example, if many families share that
their children enjoy taking care of their pets at home, inviting a veterinarian
to speak to the class may be an exciting opportunity for the children to extend
their learning. If other families share their children's interest in cars and trucks,
then transportation may be an obvious focus of study.

When teachers consider field trip opportunities, knowledge about the
students' families is important. Families can be wonderful learning resources
when teaching students about the communities in which they live. Families
also can offer inexpensive learning experiences by inviting children to their
farms, offices, or other places of employment. Finally, families can offer helpful
information when planning celebrations in the classroom. It is important to
be respectful of family traditions and cultural values when planning celebrations, especially those that revolve around traditional holidays. Family traditions within the classroom can help children experience multiculturalism in a
unique way.

SUMMARY

Chapter 3 provided suggestions and strategies on how teachers can fully
involve families in the assessment process. First, teachers need to understand

the theories and philosophies that support family involvement as well as the laws that mandate the inclusion of families in the assessment process. Theories and philosophies discussed in the chapter include the ecological systems theory, the adult learning theory, and family-centered philosophy.

The chapter also described four different ways that families can be involved in the assessment process. Although the role of parent as learner is important, the roles of expert, team member, and advocate must also be considered. The benefits families receive from being fully involved in the assessment process include better outcomes for children and families and feelings of empowerment for parents.

A discussion of unstructured and structured approaches for gathering assessment information from families was provided. Unstructured approaches use less formal methods, such as interviews, informal observations, and open-ended questioning, to obtain information. Structured approaches are associated with existing assessment tools and include formal methods for gathering information from families about their children's development and/or otherwise involving families in the assessment process. Considerations for gathering reliable information from families were also discussed. These considerations include understanding levels of family involvement, using effective communication strategies, being considerate of scheduling issues, showing sensitivity toward diversity, defining priorities, setting individual goals, and developing the curriculum.

REFERENCES

Adrienne, F., & McCollum, J. (1992). *Transdisciplinary arena assessment process viewing guide. A resource for teams* (Report No. EC 302 429). Child Development Resources.

Baird, S., & Peterson, J. (1997). Seeking a comfortable fit between family-centered philosophy and infant–parent interaction in early intervention: Time for a paradigm shift? *Topics in Early Childhood Special Education, 17*(2), 139–165.

Bandura, A. (1977). *Social learning theory.* Prentice-Hall.

Baumgartner, J., Burnett, L., DiCarlo, C. F., & Buchanan, T. (2012). An inquiry of children's social support networks using eco-maps. *Child Youth Care Forum, 41,* 357–369. http://doi.org/10.1007/s10566-011-9166-2

Berman, C., & Shaw, E. (1995). *Family directed child evaluation and assessment under IDEA: Lessons from families and programs* (Report No. ES 308 439). National Early Childhood Technical Assistance System.

Boone, H., & Crais, E. (1999). Strategies for family-driven assessment and intervention planning. *Young Exceptional Children, 3*(1), 2–12.

Bricker, D., et al. (2002). *Assessment, Evaluation, and Programming System for Infants and Children (AEPS®), Second Edition.* Paul H. Brookes Publishing Co.

Bricker, D., Dionne, C., Grisham, J., Johnson, J. J., Macy, M., Slentz, K., & Waddell, M. (2022). *Assessment, Evaluation, and Programming System for Infants and Children, Third Edition (AEPS®-3).* Paul H. Brookes Publishing Co.

Brigance, A. (2004). *BRIGANCE Inventory for Early Development-II (IED-II, 0–7 yrs).* Curriculum Associates, Inc.

Brinckerhoff, J., & Vincent, L. (1987). Increasing parental decision-making at the individualized educational program meeting. *Journal of the Division for Early Childhood, 11*(1), 46–58.

Bronfenbrenner, U. (1979). *The ecology of human development.* Harvard University Press.

Bruner, J. (1986). *Actual minds, possible worlds.* Harvard University Press.

Cheatham, G. A., & Ostrosky, M. M. (2009). Listening for details of talk: Early childhood parent–teacher conference communication facilitators. *Young Exceptional Children, 13*(1), 36–49.

CONNECT: The Center to Mobilize Early Childhood Knowledge (n.d.). *Communication strategies to build collaboration.* http://community.fpg.unc.edu/sites/community.fpg.unc.edu /files/resources/Handout/CONNECT-Handout-3-1.pdf

DeFeyter, J. J., & Winsler, A. (2009). The early developmental competencies and school readiness of low-income immigrant children: Influences of generation, race/ethnicity, and national origins. *Early Childhood Research Quarterly, 24,* 411–431.

Dinnebeil, L. A., & Rule, S. (1994). Congruence between parents' and professionals' judgments about the development of young children with disabilities: A review of the literature. *Topics in Early Childhood Special Education; 14*(1), 1–25.

Division for Early Childhood (DEC). (2014). *DEC recommended practices in early intervention/ early childhood special education 2014.* http://www.dec-sped.org/recommendedpractices

Dunst, C. J. (1985). Rethinking early intervention. *Analysis and Intervention in Developmental Disabilities, 5,* 165–201.

Dunst, C. J. (2002). Family-centered practices: Birth through high school. *Journal of Special Education, 36,* 139–147.

Dunst, C. J., Bruder, M. B., Trivette, C. M., & Hamby, D. W. (2006). Everyday activity settings, natural learning environments, and early intervention practices. *Journal of Policy and Practice in Intellectual Disabilities, 3*(1), 3–10.

Dunst, C. J., & McWilliam, R. A. (1988). Cognitive assessment of multiply handicapped young children. In T. Wachs & R. Sheehan (Eds.), *Assessment of developmentally disabled children.* Plenum Press.

Epstein, J. (2000). *School and family partnerships: Preparing educators and improving schools.* Westview.

Foster, N.J. (n.d.). *Barriers to everyday communication.* http://www.directionservice.org/cadre /pdf/Barriers.pdf

Frey, W. H. (2020). *The nation is diversifying even faster than predicted, according to new census data.* Brookings Institution Metropolitan Policy Program Report. Brookings Institution.

Friend, M., & Cook, L. (2010). *Interactions: Collaboration skills for school professionals* (6th ed.). Pearson.

Furuno, S., O'Reilly, K. A., Hosaka, C. M., Inatsuka, T., Zeisloft-Falbey, B., & Allman, T. (1985–2014). *Hawaii Early Learning Profile (HELP).* Vort Corporation.

Gardner, H. (1977). The first seven . . . and the eighth. *Educational Leadership, 55,* 12–15.

Gollnick, D. M., & Chinn, P. C. (2005). *Multicultural education in a pluralistic society* (7th ed.). Pearson.

Grisham-Brown, J., Hemmeter, M. L., & Pretti-Frontczak, K. (2005). *Blended practices for teaching young children in inclusive settings.* Paul H. Brookes Publishing Co.

Hanft, B. E., & Pilkington, P. E. (2000). Therapy in natural environments: The means or end goal for early intervention? *Infants & Young Children, 12*(4), 1–13.

Hemmeter, M. L., & Grisham-Brown, J. (1997). Developing children's language skills in inclusive early childhood classrooms. *Dimensions of Early Childhood, 25*(3), 6–13.

Hernandez, D. J., Takanishi, R., & Marotz, K. G. (2009). Life circumstances and public policies for young children in immigrant families. *Early Childhood Research Quarterly, 24*(4), 487–501.

Heroman, C., Burts, D. C., Berke, K. L., & Bickart, T. S. (2010). *Teaching Strategies GOLD® objectives for development and learning.* Teaching Strategies.

Hoover-Dempsey, K. V., Walker, J. M., Sandler, H. M., Whetsel, D., Green, C. L., Wilkins, A. S., & Closson, K. (2005). Why do parents become involved? Research findings and implications. *The Elementary School Journal, 106*(2), 105–130.

Johnson, C. D. (2001). Transition: Making it a process rather than an event. *Educational Audiology Review, 18*(3), 5–11.

Johnson-Martin, N., Attermeier, S., & Hacker, B. (2004). *Carolina Curriculum for Preschoolers with Special Needs* (2nd ed.). Paul H. Brookes Publishing Co.

Jung, L. A. (2010). Identifying families' supports and other resources. In R. A. McWilliam (Ed.), *Working with families of young children with special needs.* Guilford Press.

Kaiser, B., & Rasminsky, J. S. (2020). Valuing diversity: Developing a deeper understanding of all young children's behavior. *Teaching Young Children, 13*(2). https://www.naeyc.org /resources/pubs/tyc/dec2019/valuing-diversity-developing-understanding-behavior

Kansas Inservice Training System. (2015). *Curriculum-based assessments for measuring early childhood outcomes*. Kansas University Center on Developmental Disabilities. https://kskits .ku.edu/ta/ECOOutcomes/documents/ECO_CBA_matrix_8_18_15.pdf

Katz, L. G. (1996). Child development knowledge and teacher preparation: Confronting assumptions. *Early Childhood Research Quarterly, 11*(2), 135–146.

Knowles, M. S. (1984). *Andragogy in action: Applying modern principles of adult learning.* Jossey-Bass Publishers.

Lee, K., & Walsh, D. J. (2001). Extending developmentalism: Cultural psychology and early childhood education. *International Journal of Early Childhood Education, 7,* 71–91.

Linder, T. (2008). *Transdisciplinary Play-Based Assessment and Intervention, Second Edition (TPBA/I2).* Paul H. Brookes Publishing Co.

Lo, L. (2008). Expectations of Chinese families of children with disabilities towards American schools. *The School Community Journal, 18*(2), 73–90.

Love, B. (2020, February 6). White teachers need anti-racist therapy. *Education Week.* https:// www.edweek.org/teaching-learning/opinion-white-teachers-need-anti-racist-therapy/2020/02

Lynch, E. W., & Hanson, J. J. (2011). *Developing cross-cultural competence: A guide for working with children and their families* (4th ed.). Paul H. Brookes Publishing Co.

Maring, G. H., & Magelky, J. (1990). Effective communication: Key to parent/community. *Reading Teacher, 43*(8), 606–607.

Marquardt, M., & Waddill, D. (2004). The power of learning in action learning: A conceptual analysis of how the five schools of adult learning theories are incorporated within the practice of action learning. *Action Learning: Research and Practice, 1*(2), 185–202.

McCormick, K., Stricklin, S., Nowak, T., & Rous, B. (2008). Using eco-mapping to understand family strengths and resources. *Young Exceptional Children, 11*(1), 17–28.

McGonigel, M. J., Woodruff, G., & Roszmann-Millican, M. (1994). The transdisciplinary team: A model for family-centered early intervention. In L. J. Johnson, R. J. Gallagher, M. J. LaMontagne, J. B. Jordan, J. J. Gallagher, P. L. Hutinger, & M. B. Karnes (Eds.), *Meeting early intervention challenges: Issues from birth to three* (2nd ed.). Paul H. Brookes Publishing Co.

McWilliam, R., Casey, A. M., & Sims, J. (2009). The routines-based interview: A method for gathering information and assessing needs. *Infants & Young Children, 22*(3), 224–233.

Meisels, S. B., Marsden, D. B., Dichtelmiller, M. K., & Jablon, J. R. (2001). *Work Sampling System (WSS).* Pearson Assessments.

Meisels, S. B., Marsden, D. B., Dombro, A. L., Weston, D. R., & Jewkes, A. M. (2003). *The Ounce Scale.* Pearson Early Learning.

Mezirow, J. (1981). A critical theory of adult learning and education. *Adult Education, 32*(1), 3–24.

National Scientific Council on the Developing Child. (2004). *Young children develop in an environment of relationships.* Working Paper No. 1. http://www.developingchild.net

Osher, D., Cantor, P., Berg, J., Steyer, L., & Rose, T. (2020). Drivers of human development: How relationships and context shape learning and development. *Applied Developmental Science, 24*(1), 6–36. https://doi.org/10.1080/10888691.2017.1398650

Pelletier, J., & Corter, C. (2005). Toronto First Duty: Integrating kindergarten, childcare, and parenting support to help diverse families connect to schools. *Multicultural Education, 13*(2), 30–37.

Pretti-Frontczak, K., & Bricker, D. (2004). *An activity-based approach to early intervention* (3rd ed.). Paul H. Brookes Publishing Co.

Reedy, Y. B., & Walls, R. (1996). *Obtaining information through basic communication.* (Report No. PS 024 884). Head Start Association's 23rd Annual Training Conference.

Sandall, S., Hemmeter, M. L., Smith, B. J., & McLean, M. (2005). *DEC recommended practices: A comprehensive guide.* Sopris West.

Sattin-Bajaj, C. (2009). *Informing immigrant families about high school choice in New York City: Challenges and possibilities.* National Center on School Choice. Vanderbilt University (NJ1).

Studer, J. (1993). Listen so that parents will speak. *Childhood Education, 70*(2), 74–76.

Thegan, K., & Weber, L. (2002). *Family support: A solid foundation for children (more than a nice thing to do!)* (Report No. PS 030 871). North Carolina Partnership for Children.

Trister-Dodge, D., Colker, L. J., & Heroman, C. (2002). *Creative Curriculum for Preschool* (4th ed.). Gryphon House.

Topping, D. J., & Hoffman, S. J. (2002). Helping teachers become teacher researchers. *Journal of Reading Education, 27*(3), 20–29.

U.S. Department of Health and Human Services. (2020). *Head Start*. https://www.acf.hhs.gov/ohs/about/head-start

Vangalder, C. J. (1997). *CARE: Caregiver assistance, resources and education. A case study of a family-centered assessment and intervention model* (Report No. EC 305 546). Holland Public School District.

Westphal, S. (1989). Notes on the first National ICC Parents' Meeting. *Early Childhood Bulletin*, 3–4.

Wilson, L. L., & Mott, D. W. (2006). Asset-based context matrix: An assessment tool for developing contextually-based child outcomes. *CASEtools, 2*(4), 1–12.

Wilson L. L., Mott, D. W., & Battman, D. (2004). The asset-based context matrix: A tool for assessing children's learning opportunities and participation in natural environments. *Topics in Early Childhood Special Education, 24*(2), 110–120.

CHAPTER 4

Recommended Practices for Determining Technical Adequacy

Kristie Pretti-Frontczak and Jennifer Grisham

Leah has taught early childhood intervention (ECI) for 8 years. Recently she relocated to a new school district in a different state. She is very happy with her new position because she is using her expertise to work with young children in an inclusive setting. However, Leah is very concerned by the assessment practices used in the school district. One common practice in the district is to administer a norm-referenced and standardized test to 3-year-olds suspected of having developmental delays. If a child qualifies for early childhood special education services and supports, the results of that test are used heavily to develop an individualized educational program (IEP). This concerns Leah because it starts the conversation from a deficit model where the goal is to fix and remediate versus building upon the child's strengths and determining the supports and services that will give them the best opportunity to learn and develop. The administration of a norm-referenced and standardized test also concerns Leah because these types of tests are rarely validated for the purpose of determining eligibility for ECI and are biased for many of the populations of children being tested. In addition, Leah is bothered by the fact that the school district requires every preschool teacher to use a developmental screening instrument twice a year to assess every child in the program. Leah understands that there are many accountability mandates in ECI; however, she is troubled by how her new district meets these requirements. In her former district, the educational team carefully selected instruments for determining eligibility based on each child's unique characteristics and sought to discover their strengths, not how far from the norm they performed. When developing IEPs and demonstrating children's progress from the beginning to the end of the year, the classroom staff utilized curriculum-based assessments, which looked at all areas of development and learning. Leah knows that although she is new, it is her responsibility to bring these concerns to the rest of the team.

Using the right tool for the job is a logical recommendation for any profession or identified task. For example, if one wants to stir a pot, using a spoon is helpful, or if one wants to measure a temperature, a thermometer is handy. As highlighted in the chapter vignette, however, ECI teachers face a couple of key challenges in using assessment instruments for their intended and validated purposes. First, local, state, or federal agencies may develop policies or mandate practices that are impractical, invalid, and arguably harmful and unethical. For example, many times assessments are used or required without documented technical adequacy and lead to biased decisions. Further, assessments are often used for purposes other than those intended or scores/procedures validated. Second, ECI teachers may lack the training and ongoing support needed to administer assessments with fidelity, to be aware of their implicit bias, and to interpret and use assessment information to better serve young children and their families. In general, teachers may find navigating the world of ECI assessment practices frustrating, with many policies conflicting with recommended practice.

The purpose of this chapter is to help teachers be critical consumers of assessments and use assessments for the purposes for which they were intended and validated. It is also intended to highlight practices and policies that perpetuate inequity within the education system and offer steps teachers can take to question and disrupt harmful practices. The chapter is divided into three main sections. First, basic terms related to the technical adequacy of assessments are discussed. Second, the different types or classifications of ECI assessments are reviewed. Third, basic skills needed to administer and interpret conventional assessments are described, including calculating chronological age, adjusting for prematurity, establishing basals and ceilings, and interpreting reports.

TECHNICAL ADEQUACY

Throughout the book, we discuss how teachers use assessments to make a wide array of decisions (e.g., eligibility for services, planning instructional efforts, program evaluation) that often have a significant impact on the lives of young children and their families. Thus, it is imperative that teachers understand how to select and use assessment instruments for their intended purposes (e.g., screening, program evaluation) and populations (e.g., 4-year-olds, children who are at risk), and to minimize both implicit and systemic bias.

The first rule for selecting and using an assessment instrument (regardless of reason or population) is to ensure its technical adequacy (American Educational Research Council, American Psychological Association, & National Council on Measurement in Education, 1999). Technical adequacy relates to documented evidence of an assessment instrument's unbiased, reliable, and valid scores or procedures that are used in making sound decisions for a given population.

Teachers need to be aware, however, that not all assessment instruments sold, mandated, or selected have established technical adequacy. In fact, since the 1960s, expert and consumer reviews of ECI assessment practices have found a paucity of evidence that scores produced and inferences made are valid or reliable for the purposes or populations for which they are used (see Box 4.1). For example, Clifford et al. (2018) found that there are only a few user-friendly assessment tools with psychometric integrity to monitor the developmental progress and goals of children. Grisham et al. (2021) found that additional research should be conducted on test–retest reliability, internal consistency, and other psychometric properties. This lack of technical adequacy is found across types of measures from conventional to authentic. Even many of the ECI assessments, which are rated as authentic and suggest a strong link to instruction, lack basic evidence of technical adequacy. Further, many have not been validated for their marketed purposes (e.g., progress monitoring, accountability) or for use with young children from diverse backgrounds and with a variety of abilities (Bagnato et al., 2010; Brown & Hubbell, 2009). For example, Chieh et al. (2020) found that various factors, such as social-emotional learning can prevent achieving effective assessments without taking cultural diversity into consideration.

Teachers must have the knowledge and confidence to select and use assessment instruments with established technical adequacy. All too often, individuals in leadership or administrative positions lack a background or expertise

---

Box 4.1.   Examples of Reviews Documenting How Assessment Instruments Lack Technical Adequacy

1970s—Salvia and Ysseldyke (1978) found that common assessments used by special educators were lacking in technical adequacy and did not meet recommended assessment practices.

1980s—Bracken (1987) found that of the hundreds of early childhood intervention assessments, many did not meet any standard set forth regarding technical adequacy. Of the 10 reviewed, all had limitations in the areas of reliability and validity.

1990s—Bracken et al. (1998) found that 13 preschool measures of social-emotional functioning lacked or had low reliability and validity and had issues with the standardization samples, as well as issues with item structure as related to basals, ceilings, and gradation.

2000s—Macy et al. (2007) found no research to support the common assessments used for early intervention eligibility, and Brown and Hubbell (2009) found many common assessments to be lacking in documented technical adequacy and a notable discrepancy between publishers' defined intended uses and research to validate those uses.

---

in working with young children or are unaware of recommended early childhood assessment practices. In such instances, assessment instruments may be used inappropriately for a given purpose or population (e.g., using a screening instrument for reporting accountability data). The next section defines common measurement terms related to technical adequacy and provides suggestions that will allow teachers to serve as critical consumers of assessment instruments (see Box 4.2). Specifically, validity, reliability, and bias are discussed.

Validity

As defined by the American Educational Research Association, American Psychological Association, and National Council on Measurement in Education, *validity* is "the degree to which evidence and theory support the

---

Box 4.2.   Consumer Tip

Use the Rabinowitz et al. (2007) worksheet to examine the technical adequacy of a given assessment instrument. Although the worksheet was developed for examining assessments used for dual language learners, it can easily be used to examine assessments for any population, including young children who are neurodiverse and/or who meet criteria to qualify for early childhood special education services.

interpretations of test scores entailed by proposed uses of tests" (1999, p. 9). As stated by McCloskey,

> Validity is not an inherent characteristic; it is a function of how and with whom the scale is used. If a scale is seen as having many uses (e.g., to determine eligibility; plan children's programs), then it must be validated for each use. Also, if the scale is to be used with one or more rater groups, its use must be validated for each rater group. (1990, p. 54)

The basic tenet of validity is that an assessment instrument correctly and accurately measures what it was intended to measure (i.e., the overall degree of justification for test interpretation and use). For instance, a teacher interested in measuring a child's ability to read would use an assessment instrument known to measure characteristics or indicators of reading capabilities (e.g., vocabulary, fluency, picture naming, rhyming). Using a test that measured the child's problem-solving skills or ability to count objects in order would not be a valid way to assess a child's reading ability. Although the preceding example is obvious in terms of validity, it gets at the heart of the matter; that is, if a child is being assessed with an instrument not meant for that purpose, it is difficult to obtain an accurate measure of what the child is truly able to accomplish.

There are many forms of validity, but all relate or contribute to the appropriateness, meaningfulness, and usefulness of the specific inferences made from test scores. Some common terms related to validity include criterion, concurrent, construct, content, convergent, discriminant, face, and predictive. The terms social validity and treatment validity have been increasingly referenced and are critical to the examination of technical adequacy. Table 4.1 defines and lists characteristics of common types of validity. Further, McCloskey (1990) provides teachers with suggestions about how to determine the validity of an assessment's scores or procedures (see Box 4.3).

Reliability

Reliability, an issue closely related to validity, refers to the stability and consistency of assessment results (Sattler, 2001). Within the assessment process, some form of error is anticipated; however, the higher the reliability of an assessment's scores or procedures, the more confidence users can have in its accuracy. Reliability results are reported most often in the form of correlation coefficients (e.g., $r = .80$, $r = .93$). Reliability correlation coefficients range from -1.00 to $+1.00$. A negative correlation means there is an inverse relationship: As one score or attribute goes up, the other goes down. A positive correlation means that as one score or attribute goes up, the other goes up, or as one goes down, the other goes down. Stated differently, a correlation of 0 indicates no consistency, and a correlation of $+1.00$ or -1.00 indicates perfect consistency (i.e., a perfect positive linear relationship or a perfect decreasing linear relationship exists). Scores from well-constructed assessments with many items should produce correlations in the .80 to .95 range, whereas the scores of assessments with fewer items or fewer scoring options are typically in the .70 to .85 range. Correlations for questionnaires often fall around .5.

Table 4.1. Common types of validity and basic definitions and associated characteristics

Type	Definitions/characteristics
Content	"Refers to whether the items on a test represent the domain that the test is supposed to measure" (Sattler, 2001, p. 115) • Consumers should consider the appropriateness and completeness of items (e.g., does the test contain enough items related to the domain of interest) as well as how the items assess the domain of interest (e.g., what is the level of mastery being assessed). • Asks the question as to whether the domain of interest (e.g., reading, expressive communication, motor skills) is actually being assessed • Example: Strong and convincing rationale by test developers in terms of the process by which content was selected and clear evidence that the content is theoretically sound and/or supported by experts for inclusion
Criterion	"Refers to the relationship between test scores and some type of criterion or outcome . . ." (Sattler, 2001, p. 115) • One thing (e.g., test, variable) corresponds to something else. • Two types—*concurrent* and *predictive* • Example: Each item on the *Assessment, Evaluation, and Programming System for Infants and Children, Third Edition (AEPS®-3)* (Bricker et al., 2022) includes a criterion to which a child's performance is compared prior to a judgment being made in terms of whether the child can perform the skill, how well the child performs the skill, how often they perform the skill, and so forth. For example, the criterion for the AEPS item of "responds to established social routines" is "When given general verbal and/or contextual cues, the child performs a single response associated with established social routines such as mealtime, toileting, dressing/undressing, bathing/washing, naptime/bedtime, and/or classroom events."
Concurrent	"Refers to whether test scores are related to some currently available criterion measure" (Sattler, 2001, p. 115) • "Extent to which a test correlates with another measure administered close in time to the first" (McLean et al., 2004, p. 39). • Type of *criterion* validity • Example: Findings from administering the gross motor area of the Hawaii Early Learning Profile (Holt et al., 2004) and the gross motor area of The Carolina Curriculum for Preschoolers with Special Needs, Second Edition (Johnson-Martin et al., 2004) at similar points in time produce related findings.
Predictive	"Refers to the correlation between test scores and future performance on a relevant criterion" (Sattler, 2001, p. 115) • Answers the following question: Is the score obtained on the test an accurate predictor of future performance on the criterion? • Type of *criterion* validity • Example: A relationship between a child's performance on picture naming and rhyming as measured by Individual Growth and Development Indicators during preschool and the child's future performance in reading as measured by Dynamic Indicators of Basic Early Literacy Skills (DIBELS), Eighth Edition (University of Oregon, 2018) during first grade.
Construct	"Refers to how well performances on different measures of the same domain in different formats correlate positively" (Sattler, 2001, p. 116) • Not established in a single study but rather based upon an aggregate of evidence over time • Two types—*convergent* and *discriminant* • Example: Results of a factor analysis confirm that findings are similar for more than one population, that responses by different people are similar, or that test items cluster as expected.

Table 4.1.   *(continued)*

Type	Definitions/characteristics
Convergent	"Refers to how well performances on different measures of the same domain in different format . . . correlate positively" (Sattler, 2001, p. 116) • Measures that should be related are in reality related • Form of *construct* validity • Example: Positive correlations are found between a curriculum-based assessment and a parent report regarding a child's current abilities.
Discriminant	Refers to the "extent to which a given scale differs from other scales designed to measure a different conceptual variable" (Eisert et al., 1991, p. 45) • Measures that should not be related are in reality not related (i.e., tests designed to measure unrelated constructs should not correlate). • Form of *construct* validity and sometimes called divergent validity • Example: A child's social skills as measured by the Battelle Developmental Inventory (Newborg, 2005a) should not correlate with the child's ability to count objects as measured by the Brigance Inventory of Early Development-II (Brigance & Glascoe, 2004).
Face	Refers to "what the test appears to measure, not what it actually does measure" (Sattler, 2001, p. 115) • Is important because if the test does not appear to measure what it is supposed to measure, examinees may become skeptical and not perform adequately • Example: While an assessment's items have been aligned to Office of Special Education Program child outcomes (see Chapter 9 regarding crosswalks), and the assessment appears to measure a child's performance regarding positive social relationships, without at least some sort of expert or social validation, the extent to which the assessment actually measures a child's performance on federal outcomes is not truly known.
Social	"Takes into account the perceived usefulness of the scale's items" (McCloskey, 1990, p. 55) • Extent to which assessment procedures and findings are found to be meaningful, useful, and accurate by consumers • Example: Both providers and parents are satisfied with the procedures and findings from a play-based assessment using Transdisciplinary Play-Based Assessment, Second Edition (TPBA2; Linder, 2008)
Treatment	"Refers to the degree to which an assessment or assessment process is shown to contribute to beneficial treatment or intervention outcomes" (Meisels & Atkins-Burnett, 2000, p. 252) • Leads to constructive changes and effective interventions • Sometimes called treatment or instructional utility • Example: Documented evidence that by conducting an assessment, more meaningful and relevant individualized family service plans or individualized education programs are developed and that the correct amount/type of instruction is then provided.

Generally speaking, higher correlation coefficients indicate more reliable assessment instruments. Further, the higher the stakes in terms of the decisions made from the assessment, the higher the correlations should be. For example, when making decisions about whether a child is eligible for special education services. (A high-stakes decision), reliability correlations should be .80 and higher.

There are two main forms of reliability: test–retest and interrater reliability. *Test–retest reliability* indicates how stable or consistent scores are when the tests

---

**Box 4.3.   Suggestions for Examining
the Validity of an Assessment's Scores and Procedures**

Users should look for evidence of one or more of the following: (a) content reviews by experts verifying that the items of the scale adequately represent behaviors thought to be associated with the trait, (b) results of practitioner surveys listing behaviors commonly associated with the trait and evidence that survey responses were used to develop the scale items, and (c) references to research studies that identified behaviors common to a trait. (p. 54)

The scale manual should (a) discuss the current knowledge base regarding the nature of the trait being rated (e.g., if the trait is thought to change over time or in certain situations or if the trait is rated differently for males and females) and (b) provide data to substantiate that rating scale scores accurately reflect the trait's nature. (p. 55)

A scale must show evidence of validity for each purpose for which it will be used, and with each group of raters who will be using it. Users also must confirm that validation efforts have been conducted with children similar to those with whom the scale is to be used. (p. 56)

From McCloskey, G. Topics in Early Childhood Special Education (10, 3) pp. 39–64, Copyright A9 1990 by SAGE Publications. Reprinted by permission of SAGE Publications.

---

are administered to the same group of individuals at least (indeed, generally) twice and within a short span of time (Sattler, 2001). The basic idea behind test–retest reliability is to make sure that the scores that are calculated at the end of the assessment are accurate and do not fluctuate greatly. For example, if a child scores 85 out of 100 and 2 weeks later scores 90 on the same assessment, then the assessment could be considered reliable. Conversely, a test that produced a score of 85 the first time and then 1 week later a 65 would be considered less reliable. The basic aim is that even though a score from administration to administration may change, the scores are within the stated or accepted confidence interval.

A *confidence interval* is a range of scores that indicates where a child's true score would fall, if there were no error in the administration. There is, however, always error associated with assessment administration. For example, extraneous variables that the examiner is unable to control (e.g., the child's access to quality health care, the child's exposure to toxic stress) or may not even think about (e.g., systemic racism, their implicit biases related to class or language) may affect the child's performance. Therefore, confidence intervals were created to give an idea of where the child's true score would be, and test–retest reliability provides a gauge of the child's ability in a given area. If, after several administrations of a test within a short period, the scores fall outside the confidence interval, then there is little reliable information to be gained. If a test, however, produces the same information about a child after multiple assessments conducted within the relatively same period of time, then there is a better understanding of the child's abilities.

The second aspect of reliability is *interrater reliability*. Interrater reliability, unlike test–retest reliability, usually applies to observation, as would be used in assessing a child's behavior. The purpose of interrater reliability, however, remains that of ensuring that the assessment score is an accurate representation of the child. Because a child's behavior can vary from one day to the next, interrater reliability is conducted by having two or more (usually two) individuals observe the child at the exact same time, using the same metric. Once the observation is complete, the ratings of the observers are compared. The more similar the ratings, the higher the reliability is between the observers. Higher reliability indicates that the assessment is a more reliable gauge of the child's behavior.

Bias

Various empirical processes can be used to determine whether a particular assessment is biased (meaning that systematic differences are obtained) on the basis of children's membership in a particular group (e.g., race, ability, gender, language). These groups are typically social constructs and have nothing to do with the child's biology and/or true ability. Fairness, a related issue, "is a value judgment about the appropriateness of decisions or actions based on test scores" (Thorndike & Thorndike-Christ, 2010, p. 193).

Bias and fairness affect all types of assessments; however, norm-referenced assessments (discussed in the next section in greater detail) are particularly susceptible. Assessments with a normative sample or group allow for comparisons between a child and other children of the same age, gender, race, ethnicity, ability, geographic location, economic status, and so forth and provide a basis for interpreting tests (Kritikos, 2010). The concept of normal and the composition of the normative group also impacts teacher interpretations and should be examined before an assessment instrument is selected and used. That is, normal is a myth.

> We can spend a great deal of time and energy in school systems clarifying just how many standard deviations a student is from the norm. But the concept of norm marginalizes students based on issues of differences such as perceived ability, behavior, race, and language. We often do this with the best of intentions; however, the negative impact begs us to shift our practices to understanding difference is the only norm. This means that normal behavior, normal academic achievement, normal communication styles, or normal social skills—frankly, whatever you are attempting to normalize!—are myths. Every human being in our school system, student, teacher, family, and administrator, differs greatly in every single area of development and learning. And only when we can see differences as a form of valuable human diversity can we have the mindset and heartset for this important work. (Causton et al., in review)

Further, schools are often incentivized to segregate students with disabilities based on test scores. This leads to social oppression and marginalization of students who are labeled as disabled (Broer, 2018; Karlsudd, 2021; Stern et al., 2015).

In addition to the concerns around bias and the construct of normal, teachers also need to critically examine the year the norms were established (e.g., norms from 20 years ago may not provide accurate comparisons), characteristics of the normative sample (e.g., representation, size), and whether the sample is relevant to the target population and includes children with disabilities. With regard to *representativeness* in particular is the idea that the normative sample should "match as closely as possible the major demographic characteristics of the population as a whole" (Sattler, 2001, p. 96). Representativeness can be made up of multiple factors, such as age, grade, gender, geographic location, ethnicity, and socioeconomic status (SES), and should relate to and be a relatively accurate depiction of the population for which the assessment is being used. The manual that accompanies the assessment will often have information about many, if not all, of these factors. When examining norms for an assessment instrument, a teacher must take into consideration the specific child being assessed and how closely they resemble the norm. The more a child resembles a normative group for an assessment instrument, the more valuable the results of the assessment can be (Waterman, 1994).

Although it is unlikely for an assessment instrument to have perfect representation of a population, information such as the U.S. Census, or the equivalent, can help in determining whether the assessment instrument is appropriate or beneficial. It is important, however, to examine the date (year) in which the normative information was taken—the older it is, the greater the likelihood that it is not truly representative of children today (Waterman, 1994). Another factor to examine is the idea that results for some assessments may appear skewed for a particular gender, ethnicity, or SES group. Skewed in this sense means that the information is not representative or is biased. Knowing whether the information is skewed is just as important as finding out how the normative sample compares against the general population and can help teachers determine whether they should use the instrument for a child from an affected group. Finally, teachers should look for deficiencies in the sample (e.g., geographic area, age, gender). Although a deficiency will not indicate which children should not be assessed by a particular instrument, a sample that is not representative should signal caution. Deficiencies, if indicated, are sometimes stated in a sentence or two that can be easily overlooked. When information regarding the population that is supposed to represent the child is lacking, teachers should be cautious about using the assessment instrument. It is important to note that lack of information about a particular population does not necessarily mean that the instrument is faulty or that the population was not represented; there simply may have been nothing to report. Either way, professional judgment may be necessary to determine the appropriateness of the instrument.

The size of a sample is very important. In general, the sample should be large enough to ensure accurate representation (Sattler, 2001). In addition, subgroups within the population should be represented within the sample.

Typically, when reviewing information about size, the more individuals in the norm group, the more stable the group. A general rule of thumb for actual size is at least 100 participants per group (e.g., per age grouping, per gender, per SES categorization). Often, the size of the sample will be abbreviated as N or n. Big N, as it is sometimes referred to, depicts the number of the whole population or the whole sample of the normative group (e.g., a total of 2,000 participants in the normative sample). Little n refers to the number of individuals in the sample or of a particular group (e.g., 24 boys or 600 4-year-olds within the whole sample of 2,000).

A final aspect of normative samples is the issue of *relevance*, which also refers to scoring accuracy. Without having an appropriate scale to measure a child's performance, results do not have much meaning. Often, the assessment instruments normative samples that are used are based on national and/or local norms, which are based on children living in the United States. Comparing a child living outside of the United States, a child who has recently immigrated to the United States, and/or a child whose identity is associated with a group historically marginalized and oppressed in the United States is highly problematic. National norms are found in mass-published assessments, like the Battelle Developmental Inventory–Second Edition (BDI-2). Local norms may be employed as well, particularly when ranking the child with individuals from the local population (Sattler, 2001) and monitoring progress and comparing children with their peers. This is a technique that is common when schools benchmark using Dynamic Indicators of Basic Early Literacy Skills (DIBELS) or a similar instrument.

Also related to relevance is the group or sample to which a child is being compared. For example, comparing a 3-year-old child's ability to identify 5 out of 20 numbers with a 5-year-old child's ability to identify 20 out of 20 does not provide valuable assessment information about the 3-year-old. However, comparing the 3-year-old child with other 3-year-old children with respect to their ability to identify numbers would be an appropriate group comparison.

Relevance is also affected by whether children with disabilities were included in the normative sample. According to McLean et al. (2004), children with disabilities are rarely incorporated into the normative sample. The rationale for excluding children with disabilities is that usually the comparative tests were designed to accurately represent typical development, so including children with disabilities would be unfair. The contrary viewpoint holds that children with disabilities should be included in the normative sample, and assessment instruments do exist that contain normative information about children with disabilities that would, for example, "compar[e] the development of a child with a hearing impairment . . . with that of a hearing child" (McLean et al., p. 28). (See Box 4.4 for examples.)

The technical adequacy terms defined and described here fall under a larger measurement model referred to as classical test theory (CTT), or true score theory (see Crocker & Algina, 1986). Increasingly, however, ECI assessments are being developed and their scores or procedures validated under a

---

Box 4.4. Examples of Normative Samples From Common ECI Norm-Referenced Assessments

Adaptive Behavior Assessment System–Second Edition (ABAS-II; Harrison & Oakland, 2003)

- Individuals with intellectual disability, learning difficulties, ADD/ADHD, or other impairments
- $n \geq 2,500$ in national norms for preschool ages.

Battelle Developmental Inventory–Second Edition (Newborg, 2005a)

- Sample is nationally representative in the areas of age, gender, ethnicity, geographic location, and SES (based upon the 2001 U.S. Census)
- $n = 2,500$ children ages birth through 7 years, 11 months

Bayley Scales of Infant Development–Second Edition (Bayley, 1993)

- Sample is based on age, gender, region, race/ethnicity, and parent education
- $n = 1,700$ children 1–42 months

Behavior Assessment System for Children–Second Edition (BASC-2; Reynolds & Kamphaus, 2004)

- Multiple norms are available for each scale, including norm groups of the general population, all clinical conditions, LDs, ADHD, male only, female only, and clinical 19–21 years still in high school
- Preschool norm group sizes range from 125 to 1,200.

Devereux Early Childhood Assessment (DECA; LeBuffe & Naglieri, 1999)

- DECA-I/T: $n = 2,183$
- DECA: $n = 2,000$

McCarthy Scales of Children's Abilities (McCarthy, 1972)

- Sample is based on race, geographic region, father's occupational status, in accordance with the 1970 U.S. census
- $n = 1,032$ children 2.5–8.5 years old

Pediatric Evaluation of Disability Inventory (PEDI; Haley et al., 1992)

- Sample of children with neuro-physiological concerns and/or combined physical and cognitive deficits
- $n = 402$ children 2–7.5 years old

Key: ADD, attention-deficit disorder; ADHD, attention-deficit/hyperactivity disorder; LDs, learning disabilities; SES, socioeconomic status.

modern measurement approach: the item response theory (IRT), otherwise known as latent trait models (see Hambleton & Swaminathan, 2013). For example, the developers of the Assessment, Evaluation, and Programming System for Infants and Children (Bricker et al., 2003; 2008), the Desired Results Developmental Profile access (Desired Results Access Project; California Department of Education, Special Education Division, 2008), and the Galileo Preschool (Bergan et al., 2009) have used IRT to describe and track children's performance on a developmental path versus their relative standing compared to a normative group. Many believe that IRT is more flexible than CTT, is sophisticated, and provides more information for a researcher to improve the reliability of an assessment instrument. Another possible advantage of IRT is its focus on items versus scores—in other words, the latent trait (e.g., gross motor ability) of interest versus the test. IRT analyses use the difficulty of items in an effort to differentiate between children with low and high ability. Meisels (2007) and others have recommended using IRT to develop ECI assessments, particularly for assessing the efficacy and quality of instructional efforts, which are by nature complex and multidimensional.

CLASSIFICATION OF MEASURES

As previously discussed, assessment instruments are used for a wide variety of purposes, and most were developed for a single or dedicated purpose. As the demands for more testing and accountability have increased, so too has the use of assessment instruments for purposes for which they were not designed or validated. To better understand which instruments might be right for the job, it is important to first understand the broad classifications of assessment instruments. In ECI, instruments can roughly be classified as criterion-referenced, curriculum-based assessments, curriculum-based measures, and norm-referenced. Table 4.2 includes common ECI assessment classifications, common uses, and examples of instruments that fall within a given classification. Readers may also be interested in Huitt's (1996) table that compares criterion-referenced and norm-referenced tests. Although most assessment instruments are of a particular type, some are hybrids. For example, some assessment instruments 1) may have a normative sample but do not require any standardized administration of all items or 2) may be normed and criterion referenced.

Although Table 4.2 may be useful in helping providers know which assessments fall under which category and might in turn guide selection and use, critical consumers should also understand that very few assessments have been validated for the population or purposes for which they were designed (Bagnato et al., 2010). Specifically, in a review of 11 common ECI assessments, Brown and Hubbell (2009) found that nine had no validation studies for at least one of the instruments' intended purpose. In their review, Brown and Hubbell defined intended purposes as the use advertised by the publisher. For example, the Work Sampling System (Meisels et al., 2001) is marked for use

Table 4.2. Alphabetical listing of long form assessment types, definitions, common uses, and examples

Type	Definition(s)	Common uses	Example(s)
Criterion-referenced	"CRTs determine what test takers can do and what they know, not how they compare to others" (Anastasi, 1988, p. 102). "Typically have nonstandardized item administration procedures and, as a result, items can be administered in various contexts using a variety of methods (e.g., direct observation, caregiver report)" (Andersson, 2004, p. 59). "A criterion-referenced test is one which scores are available that compare student performance to a criterion for mastery. Standards for mastery can be developed for any test. The term is sometimes applied to tests which were developed to show instructional progress rather than to compare students to each other. Thus, test questions would be selected for the test to measure important learning outcomes, regardless of whether or not they spread students out in terms of achievement" (Arter, 1988, p. 9). "Compare the individual's performance to some predetermined standard (i.e., pass/fail)" (Hart & Shaughnessy, 2013, p. 50). "Measure mastery of specific objectives defined by predetermined standards of criteria" (Losardo & Notari-Syverson, 2001, p. 16).	• Establish current skill level of individual children as compared to a criterion of mastery • Measure a child's own progress over time	• The Assessment of Basic Language and Learning Skills-Revised (ABLLS-R; Partington, 2010) • Behavioral Characteristics Progression (BCP; Holt et al., 1997) • Functional Emotional Assessment Scale (FEAS; Greenspan et al., 2001) • School Function Assessment (SFA; Coster et al., 1998)
Curriculum-based assessment (CBA)	"A form of criterion-referenced measurement wherein curricular objectives act as the criteria for the identification of instructional targets and for the assessment of status and progress" (Bagnato, 2009, p. 119). "Measurement that uses direct observation and recording of a student's performance in the local curriculum as a basis for gathering information to make instructional decisions" (Deno, 1987, p. 41). "Curriculum-based assessment incorporates three key features: Test stimuli are drawn from students' curricula; repeated testings occur across time; and the assessment information is used to formulate instructional decisions" (Fuchs & Deno, 1991, p. 488).	• Plan and revise instructional efforts • Develop IFSPs/IEPs • Monitor ongoing progress • Some CBAs provide a direct link to a "curriculum" or what should be taught (i.e., they are embedded); others can be used across various curricular objectives (i.e., they are referenced)	Direct link to a specific educational program: • Assessment, Evaluation, and Programming System for Infants and Children, Third Edition (AEPS®-3; Bricker et al., 2022) • The Carolina Curriculum for Preschoolers with Special Needs, Second Edition (Johnson-Martin et al., 2004) • The Creative Curriculum for Preschool: Developmental Continuum, Fourth Edition (Dodge et al., 2002) • HighScope Child Observation Record (High Scope Educational Research Foundation, 2002) • The SCERTS® Model (Prizant et al., 2006)

Table 4.2.   (continued)

Type	Definition(s)	Common uses	Example(s)
	"A curriculum-based assessment (CBA) is a criterion-referenced test that is teacher constructed and designed to reflect curriculum content" (Idol et al., 1996, p. 1). "Direct application of criterion-referenced assessment strategies to educational content" (Losardo et al., 2001, p. 17). "Curriculum-based assessment includes any approach that uses direct observation and recording of a student's performance in the school curriculum as a basis for obtaining information to make instructional decisions" (Mercer, 1997, p. 530).		Compatible with most educational programs: • Adaptive Behavior Assessment System–Third Edition (ABAS-III; Harrison & Oakland, 2015) • Functional Assessment and Curriculum for Teaching Everyday Routines (FACTER; Arick et al., 2004) • The New Portage Guide Birth to Six (Larson et al., 2004) • Partners in Play (PIP; Ensher et al., 2007)
Curriculum-based measurement (CBM)	CBM is one type of CBA and most often involves standardized procedures for measuring student performance in reading, math, and writing (Hosp et al., 2007). CBM is used to assess instructional interventions and generally consist of standardized, short tests (i.e., 1–5 minutes) (Shinn, 1989, 1998, 2008). "Curriculum-based measurement encompasses an assessment methodology that can be used to develop goals, benchmarks, or short-term objectives for individualized educational programs for students with disabilities. Teachers also use curriculum-based measurement as a means for monitoring student progress across the year" (Stecker, 2003, p. 1). "CBM is a reliable and valid assessment system for monitoring student progress in basic academic skill areas, such as reading, writing, spelling and mathematics" (Stecker, 2003, p. 1).	• Track basic growth trends/patterns using a standard set of procedures • Measure progress over time	• 8th Edition of Dynamic Indicators of Basic Early Literacy Skills (DIBELS; University of Oregon, 2018) • AIMSwebplus (Pearson, 2017) • Individual Growth and Development Indicators for Young Children (e.g., Carta et al., 2010)

(continued)

Table 4.2. *(continued)*

Type	Definition(s)	Common uses	Example(s)
	"CBM is an alternative assessment system that also borrows some features from standardized, norm-referenced assessment. The CBM procedures, including test administration, scoring and interpretation, are standardized; that is, tests are given and scored in the same way each time. The content of the CBM tests may be drawn from a specific curriculum or may represent generalized outcomes for a student at that grade level. In either case, CBM test content represents important, global outcomes for the year and not just an individual objective or series of objectives representing current instructional lessons" (Stecker, 2003, p. 1). "CBM data reflect generalized outcome performance, producing trend data that can be used to make within- and between-child comparisons. Additionally, CBM data form the basis for meaningful normative and bench-mark comparisons" (Vanderheyden, 2005, p. 32).		
Norm-referenced	Provides ability to compare an individual child to a reference group by indicating corresponding location within a normal distribution (Anderson, 2004; Salvia & Ysseldyke, 2004). "A norm-referenced test is one in which scores are available that compare student performance to that of other similar students. . . . The term is sometimes used to refer to standardized, published tests, but most tests can be normed" (Arter, 1988, p. 9). "Allow the individual's performance to be compared to performance of other individuals with similar characteristics (e.g., age, gender, location, etc.). Norm-referenced tests typically report percentiles or standardized scores to help in assessing the individual's performance" (Hart & Shaughnessy, 2013, p. 50). "Provide information on how a child is developing in relation to a larger group of children of the same chronological age" (Losardo et al., 2001, p. 16). "In norm-referenced measurement, we compare an examinee's performance with the performance of a specific group of subjects. A norm provides an indication of the average, or typical, performance of a specified group and the spread of scores above and below the average" (Sattler, 2001, p. 124).	• Compare a child's performance with that of a group of children of the same age, often to make decisions regarding eligibility for EI/ECSE services	• Behavior Assessment System for Children, Third Edition (Reynolds & Kamphaus, 2015) • Behavior Rating Inventory of Executive Function-Preschool Version (BRIEF-P; Gioia et al., 2003) • Bayley Scales of Infant Development (Bayley, 1993) • Devereux Early Childhood Assessment (LeBuffe & Naglieri, 1999) • Infant-Toddler Social and Emotional Assessment (Carter & Briggs-Gowan, 2006) • McCarthy Scales of Children's Abilities (McCarthy, 1972) • Stanford-Binet Intelligence Scales, Fifth Edition (Roid, 2003)

as an assessment of progress monitoring and for Office of Special Education Programs (OSEP) accountability reporting. In their review, no evidence that the system has been validated for these purposes, however, was found. Of the 11 assessments examined, only the Pediatric Evaluation of Disability Inventory (Haley et al., 1992) and the Developmental Observation Checklist System (Hresko et al., 1994) had research to support the validity of all its publisher-defined intended uses.

COMMON PRACTICES RELATED TO CONVENTIONAL ASSESSMENT

Despite concerns about their efficacy, conventional assessments (see Chapter 2) are commonly used in ECI, particularly given state rules regarding eligibility for special services. For example, providers are often required to use conventional assessments as they screen children and determine whether they qualify for early intervention/early childhood special education services. (See Chapter 8 for more information on screening and eligibility.) Further, although neither necessary nor federally required, many states have chosen to use conventional assessments for program evaluation and accountability purposes. Thus, as critical consumers, ECI providers need to have basic skills to correctly administer conventional assessment, including calculating chronological age (CA), establishing basals and ceilings, and interpreting reports.

Calculating Chronological Age

CA is the exact age of the child on the date of the test (typically represented in years, months, and days). A child's CA is calculated by subtracting the child's date of birth from the date of the test. Figure 4.1 provides three examples of how a child's CA is typically calculated.

As highlighted in Figure 4.1, an issue that arises in determining CA is the fact that the months of the year have different numbers of total days (i.e., some have 30, 31, or even 28 days). In general, most assessments consider all months to have 30 days for CA calculation. It is good practice, however, to double-check the manual to determine how CA is calculated for each particular assessment, in case there are any differences from the general rule. Also noted in Figure 4.1, there are rules for rounding children's ages. Again, the assessment manual should be consulted to determine when (i.e., on what day) one should round up to the next month, for example.

A helpful trick for calculating CA is using online calculators. An Internet search will result in a variety of CA calculators, some of which can be downloaded onto a computer or handheld device. The following is a site that professionals have used when making calculations or double-checking a calculation performed by hand: https://agesandstages.com/free-resources/asq-calculator/. Providers should be cautious because CA calculators have different orders in which test date and birth date are entered and may not disclose the algorithm being used to round. The Pearson calculation device, however, does go by the guideline of 30 days per month.

Example 1: March 2, 2005, as the child's date of birth and the assessment date of June 10, 2009:

	Year	Month	Day
Test date	2009	06	10
Date of birth	2004	03	02
Age	**5**	**3**	**8**

This child's chronological age is 5 years 3 months (this can also be written as 5–3). The following two examples will help guide these calculations:

Example 2: September 8, 2007, as the child's date of birth and the assessment date of December 14, 2009:

	Year	Month	Day
Test Date	2009	12	14
Date of Birth	2007	09	08
Age	**2**	**3**	**6**

In this example, the child's CA is 2 years 3 months, or 25 months. Because 15 or fewer days have passed into his 25th month (in this case, 6 days), the child's CA is rounded downward.

Example 3: November 24, 2004, as the child's date of birth and the assessment date of February 10, 2008:

	Year	Month	Day
Test Date	2008	02	10
Date of Birth	2004	11	24
Age	**3**	**2**	**16**

In the third example, the child's CA is 3 years 3 months (9 months). On February 10th, the test date, 16 days have passed since the 15th of the previous month. Therefore, even though he has not yet reached 39 months, because more than 15 days have passed into his 39th month, his age is rounded upward to 39 months.

For the third example, you may have noticed that the date of birth was larger than the testing date. When this occurs, there are a few steps that can be taken to make this calculation. When the birthday is larger than the day of testing, borrow 30 days (no matter how many days are actually in the month). Be sure to adjust the month column to reflect the change of a month to days. It would look something like this for the third example:

	Year	Month	Day
Test Date	2008	01	40
Date of Birth	2004	11	24
			16

The next step is to subtract the birth month from the test month. However, we run across the same issue of the birth number being larger than the test number. This time we borrow from the year column (remembering to adjust for the year) and adding 12 to the month column. This step is displayed as follows:

	Year	Month	Day
Test Date	2007	13	40
Date of Birth	2004	11	24
		2	**16**

Now the calculation can be completed by subtracting the birth year from the test year:

	Year	Month	Day
Test Date	2007	13	40
Date of Birth	2004	12	24
Age	**3**	**2**	**16**

Figure 4.1. Example of how to calculate chronological ages. (From Bricker, D., Pretti-Frontczak, K., Johnson, J. J., & Straka, E. [2002]. *Assessment, Evaluation, and Programming System for Infants and Children [AEPS®], Second Edition: Volume I. AEPS administration guide.* Paul H. Brookes Publishing Co.; reprinted by permission.)

Establishing Basal Ceiling

When administering conventional assessments, providers need to know when to start and stop testing. The technique of establishing and using basals and ceilings will help guide providers in administering conventional assessments appropriately. The basic premise is that basals and ceilings serve as indicators of where to begin and end an assessment. Before starting the assessment, however, providers should familiarize themselves with the instrument's protocol or testing sheet. (For the purposes of this chapter, the testing sheet will be referred to as the examiner's record, although it may be called by different names, depending on the assessment instrument being used.) In general, the examiner's record is used as the item sheet on which the test administrator keeps scores and tallies of the skills being assessed or the questions the child answers (either correctly or incorrectly).

The examiner's record also will likely have a cover sheet or page. On the cover page of the examiner's record, general information about the child is noted, typically including name, gender, grade, school, examiner, date of birth (DOB), and CA. Also depending upon the assessment instrument, the results of the assessment may be placed on the cover page. (Information about results is recorded only after completion of the assessment and scoring of items). In terms of conventional assessments, there are often multiple components that focus on different skills or developmental areas; these are generally referred to as subtests or subdomains. The cover sheet may provide a place to record the child's performance across each of the subdomains. Figure 4.2 contains a cover page of the examiner's record from the BDI-2 (Newborg, 2005a).

Once general information about the child has been recorded, an administrator is ready to begin the assessment (i.e., to establish a basal). The starting point is often based upon the child's CA. Using the BDI-2 as an example, one can see how the subtests have age indicators for groups of questions. For example, if a child is 2 years and 4 months (2-4) old, a teacher would begin the assessment at the 2-year-old mark, starting with Question 11, and work through the rest of the assessment.

If a child is unable to perform Question 11 (i.e., help dress him- or herself by holding out arms and legs), it would be marked as a 0. Receiving scores of 0 on several other items within the 2-year-old portion of the assessment suggests that the child did not meet basal for the self-care subtest. The basal for self-care is "a score of 2 on three consecutive lowest-numbered items administered or the first item in the subdomain if a basal cannot be established" (Newborg, 2005b, p. 3). The basal rule indicates that if a child does not get a score of 2 on the first three questions within the age range, the assessment administrator needs to reverse the order of questions being asked—instead of continuing to Question 12, the administrator will go back to Question 10. The action of moving to an earlier question (e.g., moving to Question 10 instead of 12) is called a reversal, or following the reversal rule. An administrator then continues to move in reverse order until the child has met the basal of three consecutive questions receiving a score of 2 or the first question of the subdomain is reached.

Battelle Developmental Inventory
2nd edition

Name _____
　　　Last　　　　　　　　　　First　　　　　　　　　MI
Sex　M ☐　F ☐　ID# _____
Examiner _____
School/Program _____
Teacher _____ Classroom/Grade _____

Items Administered in: ☐ English Only　☐ Spanish Only　☐ Mixed English and Spanish
Assessment Period:　☐ Beginning of year ☐ Mid-year ☐ End of year

Summary Profile

Domains and Subdomains	Age Equivalent (see Appendix A)	Subdomain Raw Score Totals (from pgs 4–28)	Subdomain Percentile Rank (See Appendix B)	Subdomain Scaled Score (See Appendix B)	Sums of Subdomain Scaled Scores
Adaptive (ADP)					
Self-Care (SC)					
Personal Responsibility (PR)					+
Total					=
Personal-Social (P-S)					
Adult Interaction (AI)					+
Peer Interaction (PI)					+
Self-Concept and Social Role (SR)					+
Total					=
Communication (COM)					
Receptive Communication (RC)					+
Expressive Communication (EC)					+
Total					=
Motor (Mot)					
Gross Motor (GM)					+
Fine Motor (FM)					+
Perceptual Motor (PM)					+
Total					=
Cognitive (COG)					
Attention and Memory (AM)					+
Reasoning and Academic Skills (RA)					+
Perception and Concepts (PC)					+
Total					=
DBI-2 Total					=

	Year	Month	Day
Date of Testing			
Date of Birth			
Chronological Age		*	**
Age in Months***			

***Number of years(*)×12 + number of months (**), Ignore all days.

Conversion Table for Sum of Scaled Scores (Appendix C)

	Sum of Scaled Scores	Developmental Quotient	Percentile Rank	% Confidence Interval
Adaptive				to
Personal-Social				to
Communication				to
Motor				to
Cognitive				to
BDI-2 Total				to

Developmental Quotient Composite Profile

	ADP	P-S	COM	MOT	COG	BDI-2 TOTAL	
160							160
145							145
130							130
115							115
100							100
85							85
70							70
55							55
40							40

Subdomain Profile – Scaled Scores

	SC	PR	AI	PI	SR	RC	EC	GM	FM	PM	AM	RA	PC	
	Self-Care	Personal Responsibility	Adult Interaction	Peer Interaction	Self-Concept and Social Role	Receptive Communication	Expressive Communication	Gross Motor	Fine Motor	Perceptual Motor	Attention and Memory	Reasoning and Academic Skills	Perception and Concepts	
	Adaptive		Personal-Social			Communication		Motor			Cognitive			
19	•	•	•	•	•	•	•	•	•	•	•	•	•	19
18	•	•	•	•	•	•	•	•	•	•	•	•	•	18
17	•	•	•	•	•	•	•	•	•	•	•	•	•	17
16	•	•	•	•	•	•	•	•	•	•	•	•	•	16
15	•	•	•	•	•	•	•	•	•	•	•	•	•	15
14	•	•	•	•	•	•	•	•	•	•	•	•	•	14
13	•	•	•	•	•	•	•	•	•	•	•	•	•	13
12	•	•	•	•	•	•	•	•	•	•	•	•	•	12
11	•	•	•	•	•	•	•	•	•	•	•	•	•	11
10	•	•	•	•	•	•	•	•	•	•	•	•	•	10
9	•	•	•	•	•	•	•	•	•	•	•	•	•	9
8	•	•	•	•	•	•	•	•	•	•	•	•	•	8
7	•	•	•	•	•	•	•	•	•	•	•	•	•	7
6	•	•	•	•	•	•	•	•	•	•	•	•	•	6
5	•	•	•	•	•	•	•	•	•	•	•	•	•	5
4	•	•	•	•	•	•	•	•	•	•	•	•	•	4
3	•	•	•	•	•	•	•	•	•	•	•	•	•	3
2	•	•	•	•	•	•	•	•	•	•	•	•	•	2
1	•	•	•	•	•	•	•	•	•	•	•	•	•	1

1984, 2005 LINC Associates, Inc. and The Riverside Publishing Company.

Figure 4.2. Cover sheet from the BDI-2. (Copyright © 2004 by The Riverside Publishing Company. Cover Sheet from the Battelle Developmental Inventory™, Second Edition [BDI-2™] reproduced with permission of the publisher. All rights reserved.)

If a child is known to have a developmental age that is not commensurate with their chronological age or a delay is suspected, it is permissible for the team to start the testing at a lower age range than the actual age of the child. There will be times when an assessment administrator will need to engage in the reversal rule (in order to establish basal), but the possibility of having to use the reversal rule is not a reason to start every child at an earlier set. For most children, beginning the subtest at an earlier starting point will just add more questions or criteria to the testing procedure than is necessary.

As an assessment administrator proceeds through the subtest, the questions or criteria become harder or more advanced, and the child's performance will likely begin to decline. It is important to note that an assessment should not be stopped when the end of an age bracket is met. However, there are instances where the age bracket is the end of a test. As such, starting and stopping instructions should be verified by consulting the assessment instrument's manual. For example, the assessment of the child in the 2-year-old range should not end with Question 16, where the age bracket ends. It is important to end only when the assessment indicates that testing should be completed. Typically, the ending point will come in the form of a ceiling rule. The ceiling rule is the reverse of the basal—it tells you when to stop. According to the ceiling for the self-care subtest, testing should continue until "a score of 0 on *three consecutive* highest-numbered items administered or the last item in the subdomain if the ceiling cannot be established" (Newborg, 2005a, p. 3). In other words, an assessment administrator will continue the subtest until the child receives a 0 score on three consecutive questions or the administrator runs out of questions to ask, due to the completion of the subtest. As can be viewed on the example examiner's record, even though the child had to have questions below the age 2 starting point to get a basal, the ceiling for the child is in the 3-year-old range.

Determining basals and ceilings can be difficult, particularly if a child has to go through several reversals to get the basal or has several close calls in reaching a ceiling (e.g., getting two consecutive questions wrong and then getting the third correct). For the administrator, it can be difficult to watch the child thinking and struggling to answer a question they do not fully comprehend several times in a row, only to have to do it all over again because one question was answered correctly. The important thing to remember is that the purpose of an assessment is to better understand what the child knows or is able to do. Basals and ceilings make the testing procedure more efficient (i.e., spending less time asking unnecessary questions, avoiding frustrating the child by asking questions that are clearly too easy or too difficult).

Adjusting for Prematurity

Adjusting for prematurity may be an important consideration when a child was born 1 or more months preterm. Use of the actual date of birth during the first 2 years of life for preterm infants may lead to inappropriate developmental expectations. Adjustment for prematurity allows more accurate determinations of the child's developmental skills (or maturity) based on the expected date of birth rather than the actual date of birth. When adjusting for prematurity, subtract the months a child is preterm from their CA. For example, a child whose CA is 18 months but was 2 months premature would have an adjusted age of 16 months.

Historically, it was believed that if age was not corrected for during the first 2 years of life, there was an increased risk of a child being misdiagnosed as having a cognitive deficit (Wilson & Cradock, 2004). The practice of adjusting for prematurity has not changed much since the 1930s. Today, it is often left to the clinician to determine, on a case-by-case basis, how and when age should be adjusted. However, many feel it is important to adjust for prematurity in children 3 and younger in the areas of cognitive, language, and motor function (Aylward, 2020). There are, however, issues related to adjusting for prematurity. First, given that adjustment for prematurity is performed on a case-by-case basis, not everyone may adjust for a given child, leading to inconsistent and incomparable scores. Second, agreement has not been reached as to when teams should stop adjusting. Some individuals believe that correction should be made up to 2 years of age, whereas others believe it should only be the first year. Last, agreement has not been reached regarding what is considered full term (e.g., full term may mean "anytime from 37 to 40 weeks"; Aylward, 1994).

Although there is no definitive set of rules for how and when to adjust for prematurity, there are suggestions that may help. Wilson and Cradock (2004) suggested that infants who were born 3–5 weeks premature might need to have their age adjusted only for the first year. Research has shown that children who were 3–5 weeks premature tend to catch up with their full-term peers. For children who were born before 28 weeks, however, adjustment may be needed for up to 2 years. Aylward (2020, abstract) stated that "not correcting for prematurity in cognitive, language, and motor functioning at 3 years and younger places preterm infants at a disadvantage when compared to peers with few exceptions, suggesting that such correction should be routine." Romeo (2018) stated that it is a common practice to correct for prematurity up to 2–3 years because the American Academy of Pediatrics recommends an age correction for preterm infants up to 3 years of age. He also found that at 12 months, the age adjustment for prematurity in preterm low-risk infants "should be applied differently in the cognitive, language, and motor domains."

Interpreting Reports

Interpreting the results from a conventional assessment can be intimidating, given the use of jargon and the need to convert scores and notes to other types of information. Understanding the reports that come from the test results can be even more difficult if an individual is unfamiliar with the assessment instrument. And although it is critical that teachers gain confidence in using and understanding results from all types of assessments, it is equally important that they have a deep and reflective practice so they are continually aware of implicit and explicit biases, and then work with other teachers and professionals to discontinue the use of assessments that promote inequities and cause harm to the children they serve. This will not always be an easy action to take; however, it is critical that teachers question assessment practices from start (the identification of an assessment) to finish (interpreting results and making high-stakes decisions). As a first step, teachers should review the assessment instrument's manual as a refresher about the types of scores that will be generated. The jargon that is used to describe conventional assessment results is based on a great deal of statistical background. Therefore, an understanding of the basic statistics referenced in reports may aid in interpreting and using the results to make sound decisions. The following provides basic information about interpreting reports, particularly when numerical scores are involved.

There are two common types of numerical scores that aid teachers in interpreting results: raw scores and standard scores. A *raw score* is simply the score the child receives on a particular test or subtest or a numerical representation of a child's performance (e.g., number of times they asked a question, the distance they are able to walk independently, the number of letters correctly identified). As discussed in greater detail in Chapter 5, however, there is no real meaning behind a raw score—it is just a number. Standard scores, on the other hand, which are generated from conventional assessments, are derived from a child's raw score.

A standard score allows for comparisons to be made among children and across different tests by having a set mean and standard deviation. A *mean* is defined as the sum of all the scores divided by the number of scores (Howell, 2002). In other words, the mean is the average. *Standard deviation (SD)* is defined as "a statistic that measures a distribution's amount of dispersion" (Wodrich, 1997, pp. 6–7). Means and *SD*s for standard scores can be placed onto a normal curve for help with visual interpretation. The *SD* can help determine how much a child's score differs from the mean (Wodrich). A *normal curve* is defined as "a representation of scores based on the population" (Kritikos, 2010, p. 37). A normal curve is often referred to as a bell curve and sometimes a normal distribution. (See Figure 4.3 for an illustration of a normal curve.) Underneath the normal curve, and in the top row of Figure 4.3, is an indication of where the mean score would be (indicated with the 0 and sometimes with the word Mean) and how the normal curve is divided into plus (+) and minus (–) *SD*s. The ±1 indicates that the child's performance is within 1 *SD* of the mean performance for the normative group, with ±2 *SD*s being well above or below average. The *SD* area of ±1 is the largest group from a sample, with 68% of the total represented. The further away from average (i.e., the mean) a score is, the smaller the percentage of children from the sample. In other words, there are fewer people who have that score.

As stated previously, to understand or compare a child's performance on a conventional assessment, their raw score is converted to a derived or standard

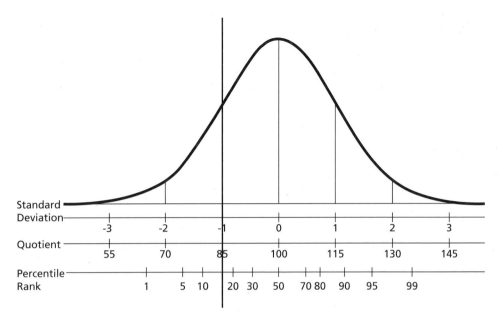

Figure 4.3. Illustration of a normal curve with means of 0 and 100 with associated standard deviations (*SD*s) and percentile rank indices.

score, often either a developmental quotient or a percentile rank. A *developmental quotient* (DQ) is a score that is calculated by dividing a child's developmental age by their CA and multiplying the results by 100 (McLean et al., 2004). A *percentile rank* simply indicates where a child's score falls in a grouping of 100 possible data points. The percentile may be easier for team members to understand because it allows for a child's score to be compared to their peers. As standard scores, both DQ and percentile rank show or compare a child's performance against the mean. As noted on Figure 4.3, a child who receives a DQ of 85 is in the 16th percentile and is −1 *SD* from the mean of the normative group. All three pieces of information (i.e., a DQ, a percentile rank, and an indication of how many *SD*s the child is from the mean) give a teacher the same information regarding a child's performance compared with the normative sample (i.e., how close or far the child is from the mean). Any score within 1 *SD* of the mean is considered acceptable; even −1.3 *SD*s is considered to represent how children who are typical would perform. It is not until the child's performance reaches −1.5 that concerns are raised or special services considered.

Although having a better understanding of what is a mean, a standard deviation, and so on helps teachers make informed decisions, comparing a child's performance to the construct of normal is highly problematic. The continued use of conventional tests as a practice is highly questionable. Teachers should work together to replace outdated and biased assessment practices and engage in the authentic practices described throughout this book, even when determining eligibility for early childhood special education (see Chapter 8).

SUMMARY

This chapter has offered suggestions and strategies for using the right assessment tool for the job at hand. Assessment instruments are often used with little consideration for their technical adequacy or appropriateness for a given purpose or population. Terms related to technical adequacy were defined and standards and examples provided. Specifically, validity, reliability, and bias were addressed. The chapter also provided a summary of how ECI assessments are classified and included definitions for the various classifications as well as examples of corresponding assessment instruments. Having information regarding an instrument's technical adequacy and classification should serve teachers in selecting and using the right tool for each job.

The chapter also provided descriptions of the mindset and the skill set needed for using conventional assessments. Specifically, strategies and suggestions for avoiding bias, calculating chronological age, when and why teams adjust for prematurity, and how to establish basals and ceilings were provided. Last, key statistical terms (e.g., mean, standard deviation, percentile rank) were defined and illustrated. Teachers need to be aware of their own biases and to have the confidence to advocate for more authentic assessment practices and/ or to move with caution when generating reports and making decisions from conventional assessments.

REFERENCES

American Educational Research Association, American Psychological Association, & National Council on Measurement in Education. (1999). *Standards for educational and psychological testing.* American Educational Research Association.

Anastasi, A. (1988). *Psychological testing* (6th ed.). Macmillan Publishing Co., Inc.

Andersson, L. L. (2004). Appropriate and inappropriate interpretation and use of test scores in early intervention. *Journal of Early Intervention, 27*(1), 55–68.

Arick, J. R., Nave, G., Hoffman, T., & Krug, D. A. (2004). *FACTER: Functional Assessment and Curriculum for Teaching Everyday Routines.* PRO-ED.

Arter, J. A. (1988). *Curriculum-referenced test development workshop series: Workshops one through three.* Office of Educational Research and Improvement.

Aylward, G. P. (1994). Critical issues in developmental and behavioral pediatrics. *Practitioner's guide to developmental and psychological testing.* Plenum Medical Book Co/Plenum Publishing Corp. https://doi.org/10.1007/978-1-4899-1205-3

Aylward, G. P. (2020). Is it correct to correct for prematurity? Theoretic analysis of the Bayley-4 normative data. *Journal of Developmental & Behavioral Pediatrics, 41*(2), 128–133. http://doi.org/10.1097/dbp. 0000000000000739

Bagnato, S. (2009). *Authentic assessment for early childhood intervention: Best practices.* Guilford Press.

Bagnato, S. J., Neisworth, J. T., & Pretti-Frontczak, K. (2010). *Linking authentic assessment and early childhood intervention: Best measures for best practices* (2nd ed.). Paul H. Brookes Publishing Co.

Bayley, N. (1993). *Bayley Scales of Infant Development* (2nd ed.). Psychological Corp.

Bergan, J. Richard, Burnham, C. G., Feld, J. K., & Bergan, J. Robert (2009). *The Galileo pre-K online system for the electronic management of learning technical manual.* Assessment Technology Incorporated.

Bracken, B. A. (1987). Limitations of preschool instruments and standards for minimal levels of technical adequacy. *Journal of Psychoeducational Assessment, 5*(4), 313–326. https://doi.org /10.1177/073428298700500402

Bracken, B. A., Keith, L. K., & Walker, K. C. (1998). Assessment of preschool behavior and social–emotional functioning: A review of thirteen third-party instruments. *Journal of Psychoeducational Assessment, 16*(2), 153–169. https://doi.org/10.1177/073428299801600204

Bricker, D., Clifford, J., Yovanoff, P., Pretti-Frontczak, K., Waddell, M., Allen, D., & Hoselton, R. (2008). Eligibility determination using a curriculum-based assessment: A further examination. *Journal of Early Intervention, 31*(1), 3–21.

Bricker, D., Dionne, C., Grisham, J., Johnson, J. J., Macy, M., Slentz, K. L., & Waddell, M. (2022). *Assessment, Evaluation, and Programming System for Infants and Children–Third Edition (AEPS®-3).* Paul H. Brookes Publishing Co.

Bricker, D., Pretti-Frontczak, K., Johnson, J. J., & Straka, E. (2002). *Assessment, Evaluation, and Programming System for Infants and Children (AEPS®), Second Edition: Volume I. AEPS administration guide.* Paul H. Brookes Publishing Co.

Bricker, D., Yovanoff, P., Capt, B., & Allen, D. (2003). Use of a curriculum-based measure to corroborate eligibility decisions. *Journal of Early Intervention, 26*(1), 20–30. https://doi.org/10.1177/105381510302600102

Brigance, A. H., & Glascoe, F. P. (2004). *Brigance Diagnostic Inventory of Early Development—Second Edition (IED-II).* Curriculum Associates.

Broer, N. A. (2018, July 6–8). *Teaching as a normative practice* [Conference Session]. Paper International Conference Liverpool.

Brown, T., & Hubbell, S. P. (2009). *Evidence-base of commonly-used assessments in early childhood special education.* Center for Excellence in Early Childhood Research and Training, Kent State University. http://ohioeicommunityofpractice.weebly.com/uploads/1/8/6/0/18607188/evidence_base_for_assessment.pdf

California Department of Education, Special Education Division. (2008). *Reliability and validity of the Desired Results Developmental Profile access (DRDP access): Results of the 2005–2006 calibration study.*

Callahan, S. M., Bergan, J. R., Feld, J. K., Larson, M. C., Burnham, C. G., & Bergan, J. R. (2013). *The Galileo Pre-K Online Educational Management System.* Assessment Technology, Incorporated. http://www.ati-online.com/pdfs/researchPreschool/GalileoTechManual.pdf

Carta, J., Greenwood, C. R., Walker, D., & Buzhardt, J. (2010). *Individual Growth and Development Indicators for Young Children.* Paul H. Brookes Publishing Co.

Carter, A. S., & Briggs-Gowan, M. J. (2006). *Manual for the Infant–Toddler Social & Emotional Assessment (ITSEA)* Psychological Corporation. https://doi.org/10.1177/073428290831715

Causton, J., MacLeod, K., & Pretti-Frontczak, K. (in review). *Ready, set, success: Leading the way to inclusive compassionate behavioral supports.* Association for Supervision and Curriculum Development.

Chieh, C., Squires, J., Chen, C.-I., Wu, R., Xie, H. (2020). The adaptation and psychometric examination of a social-emotional developmental screening tool in Taiwan. *Early Education and Development, 31*(1), 27–46. https://doi.org/10.1080/10409289.2019.1611126

Clifford, J., Chen, C. I., Xie, H., Chen, C., Murphy, K., Ascetta, K., Frantz, R., & Hansen, S. (2018). Examining the technical adequacy of the ages & stages questionnaires: Inventory. *Infants & Young Children, 31*(4), 310–325. https://doi.org/10.1097/IYC.0000000000000124

Coster, W. J., Deeney, T., Haltiwanger, J. T., & Haley, S. M. (1998). *School Function Assessment (SFA).* Psychological Corporation. https://doi.org/10.1177/073724770102600407

Crocker, L., & Algina, J. (1986). *Introduction to classical and modern test theory.* Harcourt Brace.

Deno, S. L. (1987). Curriculum-based measurement, program development, graphing performance, and increasing efficiency. *Teaching Exceptional Children, 20*, 41–47. https://doi.org/10.1177/004005998702000109

Dodge, D. T., Colker, L. J., & Heroman, C. (2002). *The creative curriculum for preschool* (4th ed.). Teaching Strategies.

Eisert, D. C., Sturner, R. A., & Mabe, P. A. (1991). Questionnaires in behavioral pediatrics: Guidelines for selection and use. *Journal of Developmental and Behavioral Pediatrics, 12*(1), 42–50. https://doi.org/10.1097/00004703-199102000-00009

Ensher, G., Bobish, T. P., Gardner, E., Reinson, C. L., Bryden, D. A., & Foertsch, D. J. (2007). *Partners in Play: Assessing infants and toddlers in natural contexts (PIP).* Thomson Delmar Learning.

Fuchs, L. S., & Deno, S. L. (1991). Paradigmatic distinctions between instructionally relevant measurement models. *Exceptional Children, 57*, 488–501. https://doi.org/10.1177/001440299105700603

Gioia, G. A., Espy, K. A., & Isquith, P. K. (2003). *Behavior Rating Inventory of Executive Function, Preschool version (BRIEF-P)*. Psychological Assessment Resources, Inc.

Greenspan, S. I., DeGangi, G., & Wieder, S. (2001). *The Functional Emotional Assessment Scale (FEAS): For infancy and early childhood*. The Interdisciplinary Council on Developmental and Learning Disorders.

Grisham, J., Waddell, M., Crawford, R., & Toland, M. (2021). Psychometric properties for the Assessment, Evaluation, and Programming System for Infants and Children (AEPS®-3). *Journal of Early Intervention, 43*(1), 24–37. https://doi.org/10.1177/1053815120967359

Haley, S. M., Coster, W. J., Ludlow, L. H., Haltiwanger, J. T., & Andrellos, P. J. (1992). *Pediatric Evaluation of Disability Inventory (PEDI)*. New England Medical Center Hospitals.

Hambleton, R. K., & Swaminathan, H. (2013). *Item response theory: Principles and applications*. Springer Science & Business Media.

Harrison, P. & Oakland, T. (2003). *Adaptive Behavior Assessment System–Second Edition (ABAS-II)*. Harcourt Assessment.

Harrison, P. L., & Oakland T. (2015). *Adaptive Behavior Assessment System–Third Edition (ABAS-III)*. Western Psychological Services.

Hart, M. A., & Shaughnessy, M. F. (2013). Assessment of the psychomotor skills and physical fitness. In R. Davidson, E. Laman, & M. F. Shaughnessy (Eds.), *Accessing the general physical education curriculum for students with sensory deficits* (pp. 45–59). Nova Science Publishers, Inc.

HighScope Educational Research Foundation. (2002). *High Scope Child Observation Record*. HighScope Press.

Holt, T., Gilles, J., Holt, A., & Davids, V. (2004). *HELP for preschoolers*. Vort Corporation.

Holt, T., Gilles, J., Holt, K., Holt, A., Mooney, J., & Teaford, P. (1997). *Behavioral characteristics progression (BCP)*. Vort Corporation.

Hosp, M. K., Hosp, J. L., & Howell, K. W. (2007). *The ABCs of CBM: A practical guide to curriculum-based measurement*. Practical Intervention in the Schools Series. Guilford Press.

Howell, D. C. (2002). *Statistical methods for psychology* (5th ed.). Duxbury.

Hresko, W., Miguel, S., Sherbenou, R., & Burton, S. (1994). *Developmental observation checklist system*. PRO-ED.

Huitt, W. (1996). Measurement and evaluation: Criterion- versus norm-referenced testing. *Educational Psychology Interactive*. Valdosta State University.

Idol, L., Nevin, A., & Paolucci-Whitcomb, P. (1996). *Models of curriculum-based assessment: A blueprint for learning* (2nd ed.). PRO-ED.

Johnson-Martin, N., Jens, K. G., Hacker, B. J., & Attermeier, S. M. (2004). *The Carolina curriculum for preschoolers with special needs* (2nd ed.). Paul H. Brookes Publishing Co.

Karlsudd, P. (2021). When differences are made into likenesses: The normative documentation and assessment culture of the preschool. *International Journal of Inclusive Education*. https://doi.org/10.1080/13603116.2021.1879951

Kritikos, E. P. (2010). *Special education assessment: Issues and strategies affecting today's classroom*. Merrill Pearson Education.

Larson, N., Herwig, J., Wollenburg, K., Olsen, E., Bowe, W., Chvojicek, R., & Copa, A. (2004). *The New Portage Guide Birth to Six*. Cooperative Educational Service Agency 5, Portage Project.

LeBuffe, P. A., & Naglieri, J. A. (1999). *The Devereux Early Childhood Assessment*. Kaplan Press.

Losardo, A., Notari-Syverson, A., & Bricker, D. D. (2001). *Alternative approach to assessing young children*. Paul H. Brookes Publishing Co.

Macy, M., Bagnato, S. J., Lehman, C., & Salaway, J. (2007). *Research foundations of conventional tests and testing to ensure accurate and representative early intervention eligibility*. TRACE: Center for Excellence in Early Childhood Assessment, Early Childhood Partnerships, Children's Hospital/University of Pittsburgh; U.S. Department of Education, Office of Special Education Programs, and Orelena Hawks Puckett Institute.

McCarthy, D. (1972). *McCarthy Scales of Children's Abilities*. Psychological Corp.

McCloskey, G. (1990). Selecting and using early childhood rating scales. *Topics in Early Childhood Special Education, 10*(3), 39–64.

McLean, M. E., Wolery, M., & Bailey, D. B. (2004). *Assessing infants and preschoolers with special needs* (3rd ed.). Pearson, Merrill, Prentice Hall.

Meisels, S. J. (2007). Accountability in early childhood: No easy answers. In R. C. Pianta, M. J. Cox, & K. Snow (Eds.), *School readiness and the transition to kindergarten in the era of accountability* (pp. 31–47). Paul H. Brookes Publishing Co.

Meisels, S. J., & Atkins-Burnett, S. (2000). The elements of early childhood assessment. In J. P. Shonkoff, & S. J. Meisels (Eds.), *Handbook of early childhood intervention* (2nd ed., pp. 231–257). Cambridge University Press.

Meisels, S. J., Jablon, J. R., Dichtelmiller, M. K., Marsden, D. B., & Dorfman, A. B. (2001). *The work sampling system* (4th ed.). Pearson Learning Group.

Mercer, C. (1997). *Students with learning disabilities* (5th ed.). Merrill, Prentice Hall.

Newborg, J. (2005a). *Battelle Developmental Inventory–2nd Edition*. Riverside Publishing. http://doi.org/10.1177/0734282907300382

Newborg, J. (2005b). *Battelle Developmental Inventory–2nd Edition, Normative Update examiner's manual*. Riverside Publishing.

Partington, J. W. (2010). *The Assessment of Basic Language and Learning Skills-Revised (ABLLS-R): An assessment, curriculum guide and skills tracking system for children with autism or other developmental disabilities*. Behavior Analysts, Inc.

Pearson (2017). *Aimswebplus technical manual*. NCS Pearson, Inc.

Prizant, B. M., Wetherby, A. M., Rubin, E., Laurent, A. C., & Rydell, P. J. (2006). *The SCERTS® Model: A comprehensive educational approach for children with autism spectrum disorder*. Paul H. Brookes Publishing Co.

Rabinowitz, S., Sato, E., Worth, P., Gallagher, C., Lagunoff, R., & Crane, E. (2007). *Evaluation of the technical evidence of assessments for special student populations*. WestEd, Assessment and Accountability Comprehensive Center. https://csaa.wested.org/wp-content/uploads/2019/11/AACC_Evaluation.pdf

Reynolds, C. R., & Kamphaus, R. W. (2004). *Behavior Assessment System for Children* (2nd ed.). Pearson Assessments.

Reynolds, C. R., & Kamphaus, R. W. (2015). *Behavior Assessment System for Children,* (3rd ed.). NCS Pearson, Inc.

Roid, G. H. (2003). *Stanford-Binet intelligence scales* (5th ed.). Riverside Publishing.

Romeo, D. M. (2018). Correcting for prematurity with the Bayley Scales of Infant Development. *Developmental Medicine & Child Neurology, 60*(8), 736–737. https://doi.org/10.1111/dmcn.13741

Salvia, J., & Ysseldyke, J. E. (2004). *Assessment in special and remedial education*. Houghton Mifflin.

Sattler, J. M. (2001). *Assessment of children: Cognitive applications* (4th ed.). Jerome M. Sattler Publisher.

Shinn, M. R. (1989). *The Guilford school practitioner series. Curriculum-based measurement: Assessing special children*. Guilford Press.

Shinn, M. R. (1998). *The Guilford school practitioner series. Advanced applications of curriculum-based measurement*. Guilford Press.

Shinn, M. R. (2008). Best practices in using curriculum-based measurement in a problem-solving model. In A. Thomas & J. Grimes (Eds.), *Best practices in school psychology* (5th ed., Vol. 2, pp. 243–262). National Association of School Psychologists.

Stecker, P. M. (2003). *Monitoring student progress in individualized educational programs using curriculum-based measurement*. National Center on Student Progress Monitoring. https://files.eric.ed.gov/fulltext/ED502450.pdf

Stern, M., Clonan, S., Jaffee, L., & Lee, A. (2015). The normative limits of choice: Charter schools, disability studies, and questions of inclusion. *Educational Policy, 29*(3), 448–477. https://doi.org/10.1177/0895904813510779

Thorndike, R. M., & Thorndike-Christ, T. (2010). Qualities desired in any measurement procedure: Validity. In *Measurement and evaluation in psychology and education* (8th ed., pp. 154–198). Pearson.

University of Oregon. (2018). *8th Edition of Dynamic Indicators of Basic Early Literacy Skills (DIBELS)*. Author. https://dibels.uoregon.edu

Vanderheyden, A. M. (2005). Intervention-driven assessment practices in early childhood/early intervention: Measuring what is possible rather than what is present. *Journal of Early Intervention, 28*(1), 28–33. https://doi.org/10.1177/105381510502800104

Waterman, B. B. (1994). Assessing children for the presence of a disability, section 2: Methods of gathering information. *NICHCY News Digest, 4*(1).

Wilson, S. L., & Cradock, M. M. (2004). Review: Accounting for prematurity in developmental assessment and the use of age-adjusted scores. *Journal of Pediatric Psychology, 29*(8), 641–649. https://doi.org/10.1093/jpepsy/jsh067

Wodrich, D. L. (1997). *Children's psychological testing: A guide for nonpsychologists* (3rd ed.). Paul H. Brookes Publishing Co.

CHAPTER 5

Critical Decision-Making Practices

Lynn D. Sullivan, Kristie Pretti-Frontczak, and Jennifer Grisham

After learning about authentic assessment and gaining a better understanding of the critical role that the context in which a child and their family are situated plays on educational decisions, Charlotte now recognizes she must build her capacity to interpret data in ways that do not continue to produce inequities and/or rely heavily on biased test scores. Charlotte is ready to employ a framework that will help her to not only better understand the children she serves, but also notice and be able to discuss with her team areas of structural inequality and oppression. Her goal is to make sound decisions that will help children thrive and will celebrate the diversity of families served by her school. While searching for a system that incorporates authentic assessment practices, Charlotte discovered a process referred to as early education-based decision making. She knows it will take time to fully implement this process in ways that will help her achieve her goals . . . but she is ready to take action.

OVERVIEW OF THE DECISION-MAKING PROCESS

Teachers make decisions on a regular basis. In fact, early research on teacher decision making and efficacy estimated that teachers made as many as 1,300 decisions daily (Jackson, 1990; Sandall & Schwartz, 2002). At the heart of making sound decisions is the ability to gather and use information for the benefit of children served. Two key decisions most commonly made by teachers center on planning meaningful learning experiences for children and then monitoring the impact of their decision. There are many other decisions teachers make, and several of these key decisions are described in detail in Section II of this book. In this chapter, a five-step process is suggested to guide teachers in making decisions: gathering information, documenting, summarizing, analyzing, and interpreting (Pretti-Frontczak et al., 2011, 2015; Pretti-Frontczak & Winchell, 2014a, 2014b). See Figure 5.1 for an illustration of the five-step process.

As depicted in Figure 5.1, the first step is to gather information about children and families, as well as about the contextual and social factors that influence them. The second step is to document (i.e., record) what has been gathered across time, people, and procedures. The third step is to summarize the information in order to begin to make sense of what was gathered and documented. The fourth step is to critically analyze the summaries, looking for patterns and trends to inform decision making. The fifth step is to interpret and make meaning out of the information. These interpretations lead to making important decisions such as who needs to learn what, whether certain outcomes are a higher priority than others, the type and level of instruction that are needed, how and when to revise instructional efforts, and, perhaps most importantly, where inequities within the curriculum and policies exist.

The goal in this chapter is to help teachers engage in more effective decision-making practices and essentially to support making decisions that are trustworthy, accurate, equitable, and useful for the children and families they serve. The following sections provide a detailed definition of each step of the decision-making process. The following sections also provide recommended practices for implementing each step. The chapter concludes with Appendix A,

Figure 5.1.   An illustration of the five-step decision-making process.

which contains lists with recommended practices for each step in the decision-making process. These recommendations offer teachers practical and effective ways to make meaningful decisions with families about individual children and groups of children.

STEP ONE: GATHERING

The first step of the decision-making process is to gather enough of the right type of information to make sound decisions. Teachers gather when they are collecting, capturing, and/or obtaining information. Most often they are doing this to truly learn about a child's strengths and needs, a family's hopes and vision for the future, and a family's resources, priorities, and concerns. There are many different ways teachers gather information, including observing, interviewing, reviewing records, and administering tests/measures. The following section is devoted to key practices for observing children during daily activities. Refer to Chapter 3 for practical tips for interviewing families and other important caregivers. Chapter 8 provides several tips for reviewing records and administering tests/measures. Last, Section III of this book illustrates how to gather information for a variety of more specific reasons.

Observation can be defined as a "rigorous act of examining a specific behavior of interest in the context of daily routines" (Johnson et al., 1998, p. 218). Observing involves watching an interaction, activity, or event in which a child is engaged to gain information about the child" (Grisham-Brown & Pretti-Frontczak, 2011, p. 21). However, observations can also take place by watching videos of children's past birthdays, listening to audio recordings captured of children's language during play, and even looking at photos in an album or photos on a smartphone. Observations should be conducted during children's daily interactions with others and should be conducted across materials, settings, and time. In general, there are four key guiding principles related to observing children:

1. Determine what to observe.

2. Determine who conducts the observation.

3. Determine when and where to conduct the observation.

4. Determine how often to conduct observations.

Guiding Principle: What to Observe

Observing young children is a major component of authentic assessment practices. Observation, however, is more than looking at a specific event or activity in which a child is engaged. Rather, observation involves watching an interaction, activity, or event in which a child is engaged to gain information about the child. Because, in fact, children are constantly showing us that they know what they like and when they may need more support. The number of things that could be observed, however, is endless and can unintentionally lead to watching without purpose or engaging in forced observations to see whether a child can demonstrate a preset number of arbitrary skills in a prescribed sequence. To avoid these pitfalls, teachers need to clearly define what they are watching for. For example, is the teacher observing how a child interacts with other children, how they use objects and toys, or how long they can remain with a group? If a child is playing at the water table and splashing, pouring, sharing, and so forth, which behavior should be observed, noted, and considered important? In other words, what should the teacher pay attention to? The skills and behaviors of interest should also be observable. Observable skills and behaviors are those that can be seen and/or heard and that multiple people can agree have occurred (i.e., the behaviors are actions that have a beginning and end). Table 5.1 contains examples of observable and unobservable child behaviors.

Guiding Principle: Who Observes

To ensure that information is valid and reliable, multiple team members should observe children. Team members can include teachers, teaching assistants, related service providers, family members, and community child care providers. Responsibility for observing should be shared across team members for at least three reasons. First, shared responsibility permits the observations across

Table 5.1.   Examples of observable and unobservable child behaviors

Observable child behaviors	Unobservable child behaviors
Spontaneously or on request, child names at least 20 letters of the alphabet.	Child knows letters of the alphabet.
Child prints any three upper- or lowercase letters without a model. Errors are permissible; however, individual letters should be recognizable.	Child tries to write first name.
Child follows directions, answers questions, or identifies objects, people, or events using at least eight different terms that describe color.	Child demonstrates understanding of color.
Child responds with verbal or motor action to group direction provided by an adult.	Child participates during group activities.
Child manipulates at least three different objects/toys/materials with both hands, each hand performing a different action.	Child improves fine motor skills.
Child greets peers by vocalizing, verbalizing, hugging, patting, touching, or smiling.	Child gets along with peers.

From Bricker, D. (Series Ed.). (2002). *Assessment, Evaluation, and Programming System for Infants and Children (AEPS®), Second Edition: Volume 2: AEPS test for birth to three.* Paul H. Brookes Publishing Co.; adapted by permission.

perspectives and settings, limiting the influences of cultural norms or bias. Second, shared responsibility allows for more opportunities to observe a child to get an accurate picture of their skills and abilities. Third, shared responsibility, particularly with caregivers, ensures trustworthy conclusions made about a child's development and learning. Figure 5.2 provides a number of specific strategies for involving caregivers in observing and gathering information.

Guiding Principle: When and Where to Observe

As discussed in Chapter 2, observations of a young child should be conducted in familiar settings with familiar objects. These types of authentic situations ensure that children are observed when they are likely or need to use the skills and/or processes of interest. In other words, times when the child is likely or needs to perform the targeted behavior(s). For example, if the behavior "uses phrases to request objects" is the target of observation, then the child should be observed during ongoing and daily activities when they need to make verbal requests (e.g., when they request a toy, request an object, request food). Teachers cannot always collect data during ongoing activities given other responsibilities (e.g., facilitating the activity, positioning children, preparing materials), but with advance planning and with the selection of the most efficient data collection method, it is possible to incorporate observations into the daily routine. Observations can also be spontaneous and unpredictable. Teachers should resist the temptation to observe by taking the child to a quiet, individual setting to see if they can do something or know something. If teachers are using computerized assessment or child progress monitoring software, observations should be conducted during ongoing activities, notes recorded, and then data entered or synchronized into the computer at a later time rather than simultaneously testing the child and entering data into the computer.

Ask caregivers to provide written or verbal information regarding
• the child's background
• family's priorities and concerns
• child's likes and dislikes
• family daily routine
Ask caregivers to confirm or question information previously gathered.
Ask caregivers to
• observe the child in other settings
• gather information regarding the child's skills in other settings and activities
Ask caregivers to facilitate observations of children during conventional and authentic assessment activities.
Ask caregivers to complete formal and informal checklists regarding the child's skills and behaviors.
Ask caregivers to identify strategies and procedures for best observing and documenting their child's performance.
Ask caregivers to help interpret information and to participate in all steps of the process.

Figure 5.2. Strategies for involving caregivers in observing and gathering information. (From Grisham-Brown, J., Hemmeter, M. L., & Pretti-Frontczak, K. [2005]. *Blended practices for teaching young children in inclusive settings.* Paul H. Brookes Publishing Co., Inc.; adapted by permission.)

Guiding Principle: How Often to Observe

In general, teachers need to monitor children's performance often enough to provide an accurate picture of performance across environments (e.g., home, school) and to ensure that all children have access to and are making progress in the general curriculum and on individualized educational program (IEP) goals and objectives. This said, teachers should consider what they want to know about a child's performance. For example, do they want to know how often the child performs the behavior, know how well the child performs the behavior, or determine the amount of assistance the child needs to perform the behavior? Answers to questions such as these will guide how often observations are needed. Teachers need to also consider existing resources (e.g., training, time, staff availability) when determining how often to observe.

This section provided a detailed definition of the first step in the decision-making process—gathering. Four guiding principles were also described to help teachers gather information about children during daily routines and activities. Appendix A includes a checklist with additional recommended practices for gathering. Next, the second step of the process, documenting, is explored.

STEP TWO: DOCUMENTING

The second step of the decision-making process is to document information needed to make important decisions. Teachers are documenting when they are recording, chronicling, or otherwise detailing the information gathered in step one. This step can be defined as the process of recording relevant information by writing, tallying, scoring, and/or creating permanent products (e.g., videos, audio, photos). Given the demands on teachers, it is important that they learn strategies to effectively document information. There are at least three effective ways to document information: 1) written descriptions, 2) visuals and artifacts, and 3) counts and tallies. The three ways to document, along with examples, are described next.

Written Descriptions

Written descriptions can be typed and/or handwritten. For example, written narratives can be placed on sticky notes, mailing labels, index cards, text messages, or even a note-recording app found on smartphones. The most common examples of written descriptions include running records, anecdotal notes, and jottings. Basically, each of these includes the information that was gathered with differing amounts of detail.

Documenting with running records (also called descriptive narratives, specimen descriptions, or transcripts) provides a rich description of children's and/or a family's behaviors and related events observed within a particular time frame. Wortham (2008) states a running record "is a more detailed narrative of a child's behavior that includes the sequence of events" (p. 119). Good examples of running records include transcripts of interviews with family members, and language samples of children's social communication efforts. Running records often describe the complete sequence of events, the back-and-forth interactions between people, and/or actions by a child/family within the environment (i.e., a play-by-play of what was observed).

Anecdotal notes are a second type of written documentation. Anecdotal notes are brief accounts of behaviors, events, or activities that record a child's skill level and are written after the behavior or event takes place (Ratcliff, 2001). The notes should be detailed, precise, and nonsubjective, omitting observer thoughts and feelings (McNair et al., 1998). Anecdotal notes provide an objective written account of what occurred (e.g., who was observed and what they were observed doing). Anecdotal notes typically provide highlights of what was observed versus the play-by-play account of running records. By collecting meaningful anecdotal notes over days, weeks, and months, the educational team soon has a variety of written accounts of a child's developmental skills (Diffily & Fleege, 1993) and should be able to make valid decisions about a child's development (McNair et al., 1998).

Jottings are a third way to document the information that has been gathered; this is the least time-consuming method. Jottings provide a single statement regarding a specific incident or occurrence while leaving out words that are needed to make a complete sentence or to contextualize the information. Combining jottings from across several days or activities tends to convey more meaning and can be used in combination with other data to guide intervention efforts and decisions.

Visuals and Artifacts

Visuals and artifacts, also known as permanent products or records, are a second means of documenting the information that was gathered. The most common examples of visuals and artifacts include children's writing samples such as scribbling, pictures or shapes that are drawn, photographs of children's work, and audio/video recordings. Visuals and artifacts are most useful when what is documented represents products that are created naturally from the child and/or involvement in a wide variety of activities typical in a classroom day.

Two common examples of documenting using visuals and artifacts is when teachers create documentation panels or portfolios. "Documentation panels including photographs, teacher's notes, transcriptions, and artifacts, artfully and prominently displayed, serve as a visual archive of children's learning" (Kline, 2008, p. 1). For steps to making pedagogical documentation panels, visit http://www.everyarteverychild.org/assessment/documentationpanels.html. Portfolios are an authentic documentation method that teachers can use to monitor a child's development. Meadows and Karr-Kidwell (2001) state that a portfolio "is a record of a child's progress of learning including how a child thinks, questions, analyzes, and interacts" (p. 44). In both, the samples can include artwork, anecdotal notes, running records, checklists, and pictures (Diffily & Fleege, 1993).

Counts and Tallies

The third way to document information involves the use of counts and tallies, where numbers (or symbols) are used to represent what was gathered. Checklists, event and time sampling, rating scales, and rubrics are examples of documenting using counts or tallies. See Table 5.2 for examples of skills and associated count or and tally procedures.

Table 5.2. Examples of skills and suggested count or tally documentation procedures

Skills	Procedure
Objects the child manipulates with both hands	Checklist of objects
Sounds the child can differentiate between that are the same and are different	Checklist of target sounds
Behaviors a child can perform consistently and without assistance	Checklist of expected behaviors
Number of times (how often) a child needs reminders to take one item and pass the rest to a friend	Event sampling within a time frame (frequency)
How long it takes a child to start cleaning up following a directive/request	Event sampling within a time frame (latency)
Number of times a child initiates needing to use the bathroom	Event sampling within a time frame (frequency)
Type of participation during group activities	Time sampling with descriptors
Type of play engaged in at different points in the daily routine	Time sampling with descriptors
Amount of assistance needed to move around the classroom	Rating scale
How a child's writing skills are developing	Rubric

Checklists can be a valuable tool for a teacher who is assessing the developmental progress of every child in his or her classroom or of a number of children in the classroom who are working toward the same goal. Using a checklist, "teachers can quickly and easily observe groups of children, and check the behavior or skill each child is demonstrating at a particular moment" (Ratcliff, 2001, p. 67). Checklists are used as a means of indicating which behaviors were demonstrated or which behaviors the child possesses and those he or she does not (Cavallaro & Haney, 1999). Table 5.3 contains common questions and answers around the use of checklists.

If a teacher wants to document the frequency of a behavior (how often it occurs), the duration (how long it lasts), the latency (how long it takes for it to begin), and/or the endurance (how many times it is repeated), then event sampling may be the documentation strategy that is chosen (Grisham-Brown et al., 2005). Event sampling can be used to document a variety of behaviors from aggressiveness to "social skills, affective expressions, cognitive attributes, creativity, and enhancement to self" (Mindes, 2007, pp. 83–84). Similarly, time sampling, "involves recording the occurrence of a behavior at a given time or time interval" (McLean et al., 2004, p. 558). In time sampling, teachers count or tally how many times a targeted behavior occurs within a given period, providing the frequency of a behavior within that period. However, for the meaning of the data to remain clear, it is important that the recorded behavior be clearly defined

Table 5.3. Tips for using checklists

Common Questions	Answers to Common Questions
Why use a checklist?	Quick, reliable, objective
When can a checklist be used?	During a variety of activities and across the daily routines
Who can collect information in a checklist?	Teachers, teaching assistants, family members, related services providers, and other assigned adults with training
What types of information can be collected?	Specific skills and behaviors
	Descriptions of actions/steps taken, attempted, completed in a routine
	Things a child likes/prefers
	Types of support needed
Where can a checklist be used?	Any location where described skills and behaviors are likely to occur
How can items on a checklist be arranged?	Logical presentation for easy scoring
	Easy to more difficult
	Simple to complex
	Increasing quantities (items, distance, time)
	Sequence of steps in a routine
	In dichotomies (yes/no, with/without, a.m./p.m.)
How is checklist information used?	Plan lessons and activities
	Adjust instruction for individuals and groups of children
	Monitor performance over time
	Quickly gather information from family members and other team members

Source: Head Start Early Childhood Learning and Knowledge Center (2020).

by the teacher. Time sampling includes having a set time scheduled to observe a behavior. Therefore, teachers may be more likely to record data if a time is preassigned to a particular teacher. Time sampling also allows planned observation during times and events in which the targeted behavior is most likely to occur.

Another way for teachers to document a child's skills and behaviors is by using rating scales and rubrics, which "allow teachers to record observations, inferences, or judgments quickly based on predetermined definitions of behavior" (Grisham-Brown et al., 2005, p. 133). Teachers have to determine prior to the observation what behavior or skill will be observed and what criteria will be used for rating it. Rating the behavior can range from circling a number showing how many times the child performed the targeted behavior to denoting "always, sometimes, or never" if the behavior occurred. A rubric, like a rating scale, also provides a quick way for teachers to numerically document behaviors. In developing rubrics, teachers "create standards and rules for judging performance" (Mindes, 2007, pp. 150–151). These standards can be based on developmentally appropriate skill levels or state and/or agency requirements. Once teachers decide what behaviors will be assessed, they can circle the criterion that best matches the behavior they observed from the child.

Regardless of the way in which information is documented, to be effective and efficient, documentation practices should:

1. Occur immediately or as soon after the observation as possible

2. Match the resources of the team/program and should not be arbitrarily set as a one size fits all type of policy

3. Include the date, time, basic information about the child (e.g., name, age, target skill), and the person(s) who is making or made the documentation

4. Include objective statements without judgment or labeling; what is documented must be objective, factual (versus impressions, perceptions, or feelings), and provide description of actions (what was done/created/accomplished), conversations, and/or interactions

This section provided a detailed definition of the second step in the decision-making process—gathering. An overview of effective ways to document information using written descriptions (e.g., running records, anecdotal records, jottings), visuals and artifacts (e.g., permanent products), and counts and tallies (e.g., checklists, event and time sampling, rating scales, rubrics) were explored. Last, key practices to ensure documentation is effective and efficient were briefly described. Appendix A includes a checklist with additional recommended practices for documenting information. Next, the third step of the decision-making process, summarizing, is explored.

STEP THREE: SUMMARIZING

The third step of the decision-making process is to summarize information needed to make important decisions. Teachers are summarizing when they compile, recap, or describe in a nutshell information needed to make important decisions. This step can be defined as the process of compiling relevant information by creating written reports, adding and totaling numbers, and by generating illustrations (e.g., graphs). Summarizing allows the whole child to emerge from the abundance of details and information. Summaries also provide the necessary context in which to draw conclusions about observations from across time, place, and people. There are three broad ways teachers can summarize the information collected: 1) numerical summaries, 2) visual summaries, and 3) narrative summaries. Each way is described next; however, teachers often find that using a combination of different types of strategies helps them make more accurate and less biased decisions.

Numerical Summaries

The first way teachers can summarize information is numerically. Generally speaking, numerical summaries allow teachers to take large amounts of information and condense it into something more manageable. Examples of numerical summaries include developmental quotients, percentile ranks, percentages, frequency, length of time, totals, and means (averages) such as mean length of utterance (MLU). Using numbers, although efficient, can lead to misunderstandings and, in general, should be paired with narrative and/or visual summaries. Certain types of numerical summaries can be confusing to professional team members and families alike. Refer to Chapter 4 for concerns around two main types of numerical summaries that are particularly confusing (i.e., raw scores and age equivalencies).

This said, raw numbers can be used to summarize information when shared as frequency counts, length of time, totals, and means (averages). For example, teachers can use raw numbers to summarize the total number of 4-year-olds who are able to perform a set of skills without reminders, or the number of children in the toddler morning class versus the afternoon class who are able to engage in parallel play. Additionally, teachers can summarize how many minutes a child stays engaged at a center, or how many times a child needs reminders. Teachers can summarize how long a child's tantrum lasts, or the number of books a group of children has read. Last, teams can calculate the mean (average)—for example, the number of steps a child can take, the mean length of their sentences, or the mean number of concepts they know. Further, teachers can convert raw scores into a percentage, which is another useful way to create numerical summaries. Percentages are particularly useful when used over time to determine if the child is making progress toward meaningful and desired outcomes. Examples of useful types of percentages include the following:

- Percentage of assessment items for which a child needed assistance across three time periods

- Percentage of items when their behavior interfered with their ability to perform across 3 weeks

- Percentage of assessment items a child can demonstrate across settings

- Percentage of assessment items a child can do without support

Visual Summaries

It is often said that a picture is worth 1,000 words, thus making visual summaries useful and powerful. Visual summaries include graphs, charts, diagrams, pictures, videos, bulletin boards, documentation panels, portfolios, slideshows, movies, and even maps. Graphs, for example, allow teachers to summarize things such as the number of acquired skills, the number of emerging skills, and the number of skills that are not yet mastered. "Organizing child performance data into graphic displays can promote the systematic use of data in educational decision-making, which enhances outcomes for all students" (Gischlar et al., 2009, p. 16). Graphs can easily be generated using a computer program or by hand. (See Gischlar et al. for specific directions for creating and interpreting graphs.)

Teachers can also use permanent products to document mastered skills or skills that still need to be targeted. For example, the teacher may notice that the child wrote their name at the top of a piece of artwork in the wrong direction; therefore, writing letters from left to right may be a target area for the child, and the artwork may serve as a physical documentation of this need. Skill levels may also be recorded in photographs. The teacher may photograph the child in the writing center holding the writing implement incorrectly; therefore, holding a writing implement appropriately may be a skill to target. See Figure 5.3 for an

Figure 5.3. Two examples of documentation panels.

example of a documentation panel with pictures of children's play, their art-work, their narratives, and the teacher's self-reflections.

Last, visual summaries help 1) identify trends or patterns in children's performance, 2) quickly determine the effects of instruction, 3) communicate with others regarding children's progress over time, 4) help identify even small increments of change, and 5) help teachers look across children and see where harmful social constructs such as racism, classisms, and ableism influence results.

Narrative Summaries

A third technique for summarizing information is using written narratives. Written narratives can be combined into a single report or single set of statements about individuals or groups of children. For example, teachers are using narrative summaries when they generate evaluation reports, develop IEPs (especially statements regarding current competencies), and/or when communicating with families (e.g., report cards, communication notebooks, blogs). Narrative summaries are a common way to represent a child's performance across time, settings, materials, and people, including family members and community-based providers. When creating narrative summaries, teachers need to avoid opinions and labels grounded in their feelings or judgments (e.g., a child is kind, happy, cute, sweet, overly active, tired). Narrative summaries should also be written so that different readers can understand and won't be overly confused by jargon or technical terms. When teachers include real-life examples from all who gathered and documented the information across the child's daily routine, it helps to provide a context for the information. Relatedly, narrative summaries that include information about the form and the function of a child's behavior can be less biased and depict the complexity of what was observed. In other words, they provide a narrative of the form (description of the actual skill that was performed) as well as the function (one or more known or inferred purpose behind the action). Describing form and function is preferred because it provides a more descriptive, more accurate, and less biased summary of a child's performance. Focusing solely on the form places an overreliance on a belief in objectivity, whereas both form and function allow teacher interpretations through critical reflection to be shared. For example, a child with a hearing impairment may be unable to turn and look at a noise-producing object (i.e., form) but be perfectly capable of attending to and responding to environmental stimuli (i.e., function).

Regardless of the way in which information is summarized, there are four guiding principles to help teachers summarize information to guide subsequent decisions:

1. Summaries should be generated before moving to analysis and interpretation.

2. Summaries should provide a context for drawing conclusions and should judiciously include information that provides a comprehensive picture.

3. Summaries should incorporate multiple perspectives and examples while avoiding labels or judgments.

4. Summaries should depict the child in the most positive ways and support subsequent decisions to help children (and families) achieve optimal functional, developmental, and academic outcomes.

This section provided a detailed definition of the third step in the decision-making process—summarizing. Four guiding principles were also described to help teachers summarize information about children during daily routines and activities. The Appendix to this chapter includes a checklist with additional recommended practices for summarizing. Next, the fourth step of the decision-making process, analyzing, is explored.

STEP FOUR: ANALYZING

The fourth step of the decision-making process is to analyze information needed to make important decisions. Teachers are analyzing when they are exploring or scrutinizing information to make important decisions. This step can be defined as a process of examining relevant information by looking for patterns and trends from what has been gathered, documented, and summarized. And although beyond the scope of this chapter, analysis also includes a teacher's ability to notice areas of equity and inequity, when more data are needed, and eventually make systemic changes that lead to a more just educational system (Dodman et al., 2021). Next, two common ways teachers analyze information for planning and monitoring instructional efforts, examining patterns and identifying trends through visual inspection, are briefly discussed.

Patterns

When teachers look for patterns in children's behaviors, they are looking for recurring events, or those that repeat in a predictable manner (i.e., event or behavior will occur at the same time, under the same conditions, and in the similar way). Patterns are found in all three types of summaries: narrative, visual, and numerical. Patterns are indicated using phrases such as every time, consistently, across materials, settings, or people. There are at least six different types of patterns that teachers look for when analyzing. Go to https://kristiepf.com/patterns-handout to download a printable handout where each pattern is defined and examples are provided. Table 5.4 contains a brief summary of synonyms, explanations, and implications regarding each pattern.

1. Patterns of strength

2. Patterns of unexpected performance

3. Patterns of quality

4. Patterns of assistance

5. Patterns of interfering behavior

6. Patterns of time toward task

Table 5.4.   Description of patterns and associated implications

Pattern	Synonyms	Explanation	Implications for decision making
Strength	Can do, on target	Demonstrates what a child knows and/or can do, independently, consistently, and/or across settings	More intensive interventions are not warranted Provides a foundation for skill building
Unexpected performance	Splinter skill, isolated skill	Instances in which a child is missing a skill that should have emerged earlier in development or demonstrates some easier or prerequisite skills and some harder and more complex skills that should be developing concurrently (at the same rate and degree of difficulty)	Places skills in a context of consistent performance Acknowledges efforts on highly valued isolated skills Performance may be associated with disability, cultural influences, dual language learning, etc.
Quality	Too fast, slow, tight, loose, loud, soft	Instances in which the child demonstrates a concept or skill in a unique way and can be understood as performance that may hinder understanding by others, impedes the accuracy of the performance of the skill, and/or gests in the way of completing the task in a normal amount of time	Concern if quality interferes with ability to participate in daily routines or activities May appear as unquantified impressions or judgment statements in gathering and documenting steps
Assistance	Multiple reminders, adult holds object	Instances in which objects from the environment and/or people have to complete part or all of the task/response for the child	Concern if reliance on assistance interferes with ability to participate in daily routines or activities Level of assistance should decline over time
Interfering behavior	Biting, kicking, throwing, tearing, head banging, outbursts, ignoring, complacency, disengagement, lack of initiation, lack of responsiveness	Instances in which stressors cause a child to struggle with coregulation and/or self-regulation and often result in the demonstration of nondesired responses (e.g., fight, flight, freeze, faint)	Concern if interfering with ability to participate in daily routines or activities Level of assistance should decline over time Focus on supports and strategies for more constructive responses
Time toward task	Latency, time lag, impulsive	Instances in which the amount of time that passes from the directive or request to perform specific tasks, skills, or behaviors to the time the child demonstrates/initiates the required/desired tasks, skills, or behaviors is too long or too short	Concern if interfering with ability to participate in daily routines or activities Focus on supports and strategies for more constructive responses

Table 5.5. Visual analysis key terms

Term	Definition
Baseline phase	The phase in a graph or period of data collection that represents the period before instruction or support is provided or changed
Intervention phase	The phase in a graph or period of data collection that represents the period when instruction or support is provided or changed
Trends	The direction or way in which something is headed. A key way to examine trends is through visual analysis.
Stability	The extent that the line in a phase on a graph is stable, meaning that the line is relatively horizontal and lacking big peaks and valleys. This indicates that the behavior or skill occurred at a consistent level across the phase.
Variability	Any factor that can change or vary. In regard to assessment, we think about variables as being any factor that may be attributed to or may affect a child's performance. In applied behavior analysis (ABA), these can include independent and dependent variables
Immediacy	A significant or noticeable rise in level between two phases in a graph
Phase	A term that is used to describe an aspect of a graph or period of data collection that depicts a specific period of time during which data were collected, usually baseline or intervention
Mean	The average performance observed during a phase on a graph. It can be calculated by taking the data on the y axis and dividing by the number of data points in the phase.
Level	The position of the data on a graph during a given phase. We can look at the general level across the phase (e.g., whether it is low or high) or the level of the data on the last day of one phase compared to the first day (or first few days) of the next phase to determine if an immediacy of change is present.

Used with permission from Lyons, A., & Pretti-Frontczak, K. (2019). *Early childhood assessment terms primer* (2nd ed.). B2K Solutions℠, Ltd.

Trends

Trends are defined as the direction or general way in which something is headed. A primary way teachers use trends is through visual analysis or visual inspection, which allows for comparing individuals or groups of children's performance to one another or over time in response to instructional efforts. Table 5.5 contains words that are commonly used when we engage in visual analysis, particularly as it applies to line graphs. For an assessment primer with even more definitions like these (Lyons & Pretti-Frontczak, 2019), visit https://kristiepf.com/assessment-primer.

This section provided a detailed definition of the fourth step in the decision-making process—analyzing. How to identify patterns and trends was also briefly discussed. The Appendix to this chapter includes a checklist with additional recommended practices for analyzing. Next, the fifth and final step of the decision-making process, interpreting, is explored.

STEP FIVE: INTERPRETING

The fifth step of the decision-making process is to interpret information needed to make important decisions. Teachers are interpreting when they are making meaning, setting/revising a course, deciphering, and coming to conclusions about information that has been gathered, documented, summarized, and analyzed. This step can be defined as a process of exploring or scrutinizing relevant information to make meaningful decisions.

Perhaps most broadly, teachers interpret information by making decisions regarding children's strengths, emerging skills, and areas of need, as well as families' strengths, needs, priorities, and concerns. More specifically, depending upon their role, teachers make critical decisions in determining the following:

- If additional testing and/or information is needed when concerns around development and learning have been raised

- If a child is eligible for services, and if eligible, if there is a need for early intervention and/or early childhood special education services

- What are the meaningful and equitable child and family outcomes that are important to focus on

- The supports and services the child and family would benefit from

- Whether there are desired changes in a child's performance over time

- Whether the family's priorities are being addressed

- The degree to which curricular and policy adoptions are not perpetuating harmful social constructs and systemic oppression

- Whether program evaluation and accountability efforts are equitable, just, and socially valid

As teachers engage in interpreting, there are several guiding questions they can ask to ensure critical, thoughtful, and collaborative conclusions are made and that conclusions are based upon sound, unbiased, and trustworthy information. Box 5.1 includes these guiding questions, which can be used in self-reflection and/or team discussions.

SUMMARY

Chapter 5 explained how Charlotte prepared to implement the five-step decision-making process to achieve ethical and equitable results for her school system. The five steps start with gathering information on the child, their families, and environment through observations, interviews, records, and as needed test administration. Step two is documenting through written descriptions, visuals and artifacts, and counts and tallies. Step three is summarizing information needed to assess the whole child by using numerical, visual, and narrative summaries. Step four is analyzing and exploring patterns and trends based on gathered, documented, and summarized information. Then step five is interpreting information through developing an understanding of the child's overall strengths and skills and their families' needs to make critical decisions in determining eligibility for support and services.

Box 5.1.   Guiding Questions for Critical Self-Reflection and/or Team Discussions Regarding Interpretation of Information

- Is there clarity about the underlying concern (e.g., reason for referral, presenting issue), and is there implicit bias driving the concern?

- Is there clarity around the desired outcomes, are these outcomes meaningful for the child/family/stakeholder group, and have harmful societal influences been recognized?

- Is enough known about the context in which the information was obtained and/or people, situations, and beliefs that may be influencing the information at hand?

- Is there sufficient information to draw meaningful conclusions?

- What is our hope for the future? If we were to imagine a time without this concern, what would it look like, and how would we feel?

- What solutions are we seeking (realistic and hopeful)? Are there different solutions we see given our points of reference?

- Are there patterns of disparity and inequity that need a larger conversation?

The next section of the book focuses on the different reasons teachers engage in authentic assessment, including program planning, performance monitoring, identification for special education, and conducting program evaluations. The decision-making process described here in Chapter 5 is illustrated across these chapters.

REFERENCES

Cavallaro, C. C., & Haney, M. (1999). *Preschool inclusion.* Paul H. Brookes Publishing Co.

Diffily, D., & Fleege. P. O. (1993). *Sociodramatic play: Assessment through portfolio* (ED354079). ERIC. https://files.eric.ed.gov/fulltext/ED354079.pdf

Dodman, S. L., Swalwell, K., DeMulder, E. K., View, J. L., & Stribling, S. M. (2021). Critical data-driven decision making: A conceptual model of data use for equity. *Teaching and Teacher Education, 99*, 103272. https://doi.org/10.1016/j.tate.2020.103272

Gischlar, K. L., Hojnoski, R. L., & Missall, K. N. (2009). Improving child outcomes with data-based decision making: Interpreting and using data. *Young Exceptional Children, 13*(1), 2–18. http://doi.org/10.1177/1096250609346249

Grisham-Brown, J., Hemmeter, M. L., & Pretti-Frontczak, K. (2005). *Blended practices for teaching young children in inclusive settings.* Paul H. Brookes Publishing Co.

Grisham-Brown, J., & Pretti-Frontczak, K. (2011). *Assessing young children in inclusive settings: The blended practices approach.* Paul H. Brookes Publishing Co.

Head Start Early Childhood Learning and Knowledge Center. (2020). *Using checklists.* https://eclkc.ohs.acf.hhs.gov/video/using-checklists

Jackson, P. W. (1990). *Life in classrooms* (Rev. ed.). Teachers College Press.

Johnson, L. J., LaMontagne, M. J., Elgas, P. M., & Bauer, A. M. (1998). *Early childhood education: Blending theory, blending practices.* Paul H. Brookes Publishing Co.

Kline, L. S. (2008) Documentation panel: The "making learning visible" project. *Journal of Early Childhood Teacher Education, 29*(1), 70–80. http://doi.org/10.1080/10901020701878685

Lyons, A., & Pretti-Frontczak, K. (2019). *Early childhood assessment terms primer* (2nd ed.). B2K Solutions℠, Ltd. https://kristiepf.com/assessment-primer

McLean, M., Wolery, M., & Bailey, D. B. (2004). *Assessing infants and preschoolers with special needs* (3rd ed.). Pearson.

McNair, S., Thomson, M., & Williams, R. (1998). *Authentic assessment of young children's developing concepts in mathematics and science* (ED445922). ERIC. https://files.eric.ed.gov/fulltext/ED445922.pdf

Meadows, S., & Karr-Kidwell, P. J. (2001). *The role of standardized tests as a means of assessment of young children: A review of related literature and recommendations of alternative assessments for administrators and teachers* (ED456134). ERIC. https://files.eric.ed.gov/fulltext/ED456134.pdf

Mindes, G. (2007). *Assessing young children* (3rd ed.). Pearson.

Pretti-Frontczak, K., Bagnato, S., & Macy, M. (2011). Data driven decision-making to plan programs and promote performance in early childhood intervention: Applying best professional practice standards. In C. Groark (Series Ed.) & S. P. Maude (Vol. Ed.), *Early childhood intervention: Shaping the future for children with special needs and their families* (Vol. 2, pp. 55–80). ABC-CLIO, Praeger.

Pretti-Frontczak, K., Lyons, A. N., & Travers, K. (2015). *Five steps to functional assessment: Evaluation and assessment base training and coaching content* [PowerPoint]. B2K Solutions℠, Ltd.

Pretti-Frontczak, K., & Winchell, B. (2014a). *Analyzing patterns: Data-driven decision-making.* B2K Solutions℠, Ltd. https://kristiepf.com/patterns-handout

Pretti-Frontczak, K., & Winchell, B. (2014b). *Manual for assessing patterns in early childhood development.* B2K Solutions℠, Ltd.

Ratcliff, N. J. (2001). Using authentic assessment to document the emerging literacy skills of young children. *Childhood Education, 78,* 66–69.

Sandall, S., & Schwartz, I. (2002). *Building blocks for teaching preschoolers with special needs.* Paul H. Brookes Publishing Co.

Wortham, S. C. (2008). *Assessment in early childhood education* (5th ed.). Pearson.

Lists of Recommended Practices for the Decision-Making Process

This appendix contains five lists with recommended practices for each step in the decision-making process described in Chapter 5. These recommendations offer teachers practical and effective ways to make meaningful decisions with families about individual children and groups of children.

Checklist for Gathering Information

1. Collect information using multiple methods, including daily observation, typical interactions, and formal and informal interviews.

2. Use clear definitions for the skills, knowledge, and behaviors being assessed.

3. See the whole child across all areas of development and learning, including their strengths, interests, preferences, and areas of needed support.

4. Gather in familiar settings, with familiar people, interacting with familiar objects, in familiar ways.

5. Gather across time (at least three different sessions) and across settings/locations.

6. Decide who is gathering what to limit duplication and redundancy.

7. Gather only essential information that is needed to make meaningful decisions.

8. Gather while interacting with the child to avoid pulling them out of familiar contexts and situations.

9. Know when the best times are for the child to show what they know and can do.

10. Engage in critical self-reflection to limit the impact of implicit bias and systemic inequities.

Checklist for Documenting Information

1. Use multiple methods including written descriptions, visuals, and counts and tallies.

2. Document only the relevant information, which is necessary to make sound decisions.

3. Include situational information to provide a context.

4. Document within a reasonable time frame.

5. Document the perspectives of all team members, including family members.

6. Write about and talk about children using descriptive and positive language.

7. Collaborate using efficient and effective methods, including the use of digital technologies (e.g., Google Drive, Dropbox, YouTube, Evernote, e-mail, shared cloud/server space, smartphone/tablet).

8. Maintain confidentiality and confirm who can have access to what information.

9. Ensure safe storage and transfer of information.

10. Adhere to program, agency, and/or district privacy policies related to sharing pictures and other child and family information in public places, including social media.

Checklist for Summarizing Information

1. Use multiple methods to summarize and, when possible, combine methods (e.g., visuals paired with narratives).

2. Provide examples of what the child knows and can do.

3. Use objective language and define terms as needed.

4. Explain scores, numbers, and other information using easy-to-understand terms.

5. Provide a rich description of the child's current knowledge and skills.

6. Generate reports that describe children and families based upon their chosen identities, highlight their strengths, and limit the use of labels.

7. Summarize the child's strengths, gifts, talents, and contributions.

8. Confirm that summaries make sense to others and represent their perspectives.

9. Think beyond the box by expecting summarized information to not always fit neatly into provided data fields, forms, and templates.

10. Summarize in ways that support sound instructional decision making.

Checklist for Analyzing Information

1. Identify recurring and/or predictable patterns and trends.

2. Ensure enough information to identify trustworthy patterns and trends.

3. Examine patterns of strength as a starting point.

4. Look for similarities in the child's performance based upon time of day, people who were present, demands of the situation, and so forth.

5. Look for differences in the child's performance based upon time of day, people who were present, demands of the situation, and so forth.

6. Consider if anything expected or unexpected was found in the patterns.

7. Compare the child's performance to trustworthy sources regarding development and learning.

8. Compare the child's performance to unbiased indicators, standards, and/or benchmarks.

9. Determine if the child's performance is changing over time or staying the same.

10. Confirm that all team members understand the identified patterns and trends.

Checklist for Interpreting and Making Decisions

1. Confirm that the right tool(s) were used for the right purpose(s) in earlier steps before making decisions.

2. Reflect upon biases and judgments, which can cloud decision making.

3. Consider mediating factors (e.g., attendance, health status, exposure to other therapies, changes in medications, systemic factors related to inequity) before making decisions.

4. Determine if more or different information is needed before making decisions.

5. Address family priorities in the decision-making process.

6. Work with others to ensure multiple perspectives are present in making decisions.

7. Identify ways the same data can be used to make multiple decisions and/or for multiple purposes.

8. Confirm known evidence for context, methods, and sources used throughout the decision-making process.

9. Make meaningful instructional decisions (e.g., determine who needs to learn what, how best to create learning opportunities, and which instructional efforts need to be revised).

10. Confirm that all team members, including family members, agree with decisions.

Reasons for Conducting Assessment (Assessment Purposes)

CHAPTER 6

Assessment for
Program Planning Purposes

Kristie Pretti-Frontczak, Jennifer Grisham, Lynn D. Sullivan, and Sarah Hawkins-Lear

Jason teaches in a rural public preschool program in Appalachia. Jason teaches 4 days a week to two groups of children: one group that attends in the morning and another that attends in the afternoon. The children in the program attend for one of three reasons. Some 4-year-old children are placed in the classroom because they are considered to be at risk, which is defined by Jason's state as being socioeconomically disadvantaged. A second group of children attends the program because they have diagnosed disabilities and are 3 or 4 years of age. In addition, the school district for which Jason works contracts with Head Start, so some children in the classroom are eligible for that program.

The school district has chosen a curriculum-based assessment (CBA) called Help Children Grow and Learn to be used for planning instruction. Jason must administer the assessment to all the children in both his morning and afternoon preschool classrooms (18 and 16 children, respectively) within the first 45 days of the school year, beginning in August. Jason finds the idea of giving this test to so many children in a short amount of time overwhelming. In addition to being concerned about collecting all of the data, Jason is concerned about the instrument itself. Jason was taught that a high-quality CBA should allow for the use of authentic assessment practices. However, the Help Children Grow and Learn CBA requires the use of direct testing as the primary way of collecting data on the children in the classroom. In addition, Jason is having difficulty determining how the CBA will help plan instruction. The items on the Help Children Grow and Learn don't seem very functional. For example, there are items related to tasks such as stringing beads and putting puzzles together. Another concern is that some of the children in the program are 3 or 4 years old but function developmentally at a much younger age. The Help Children Grow and Learn CBA was designed for children who are 3 to 5 years of age. Jason fears that the assessment will not yield any useful programming information for children who have developmental delays. With Jason's concerns about the usefulness and sensitivity of the assessment in mind, Jason decides to approach the preschool director before school starts and seek guidance about selecting another assessment, as well as help with efficiently collecting and meaningfully using all of the data.

The situation described in the vignette highlights the difficulties that early childhood intervention teachers face when they conduct assessments that promote development and learning for program planning purposes. Program planning assessment can be defined simply as the process of determining, based upon authentic information, what, where, and how to teach the whole class, small groups, and individual children. In order for quality program planning to occur, programs need to utilize tools and practices that link assessment with instruction. In other words, the items on the assessment instrument are the skills, behaviors, and experiences teachers and families want their children to learn as part of the daily curriculum. As described in Chapter 4, assessment tools are developed for particular purposes. Unfortunately, programs frequently utilize assessment instruments for program planning that were intended for another purpose (e.g., screening, diagnosis, accountability). When assessment instruments that were not intended for program planning are used, teachers feel frustrated because there is no obvious link between what the assessment tells them about the children in their program and what they need to teach.

The purpose of this chapter is to describe recommended practices for program planning for individual children and groups based upon authentic assessment information that has been gathered, documented, summarized, and analyzed. The chapter includes three main sections. The first section provides a definition and discussion of assessment practices for program planning. This is followed by a section with information on selecting and administering a CBA. Last is a section with information on using CBAs to plan instruction for individual children and groups following the decision-making process described in Chapter 5. For a more detailed explanation and illustration of designing and delivering blended and tiered instruction, see Grisham-Brown and Hemmeter (2017).

DEFINITION AND PURPOSES OF ASSESSMENT FOR PROGRAM PLANNING

In Chapter 1, a curriculum framework was defined as a way of conceptualizing the practices in which early childhood intervention teachers engage to plan for, implement, and evaluate instruction. A curriculum framework includes four elements: assessment, scope and sequence, activities and instruction, and performance monitoring. The assessment element of the curriculum framework is for the purpose of program planning. Program planning is intended to guide instruction. Information gained from the assessment process for programming purposes serves as the baseline that allows educators to make appropriate instructional decisions. Quality program planning is comprehensive in nature (meaning that information is assessed on all areas of development and content), and practices are authentic (meaning that information is gathered from multiple worthwhile, significant, and meaningful sources). See Chapter 2 for more on authentic assessment practices.

Quality program planning assessment yields information on children's developmental status (strengths and needs), their preferences, and the priorities and concerns of their families. In order to design effective instruction for all young children, educators need information about each of these factors. Table 6.1 summarizes the purposes for conducting program planning assessment and the specific types of information gained for each purpose.

In blended classrooms, the purposes for conducting assessment for program planning apply to both individual children and the group. Information on each child's developmental status can be used in combination with information gathered from the child's family to determine individualized outcomes for each child in the class. Information on each child's preferences, in combination with knowledge about routines that they enjoy, can be useful in individualizing instruction. For example, if a teacher finds out that a child likes to take baths and play in water, the teacher may consider using water play as an activity for

Table 6.1. Purposes of program planning assessment and information gained

Assessment purposes	Information gained
Understand child's developmental status	• Children's performance across all areas of development (e.g., motor, adaptive, cognitive, communication, social) • Children's performance across all subject areas (e.g., language arts, science, social studies, math, technology, health) • Interrelatedness of children's performance across development, subjects, and identities • Children's strengths, emerging skills, and unique support needs
Interests and preferences	• What motivates children • Children's preferred activities, toys/materials, people, and actions • What sustains children's interest, participation, and engagement
Priorities and concerns	• Family and other familiar caregivers' priorities regarding a child's participation in daily routines and events • Family and other familiar caregivers' perspectives and concerns

teaching a high-priority skill such as sharing materials with peers. Furthermore, a child's preferences can assist teachers in selecting matched instructional strategies. If a child prefers instruction from certain teachers, support in a particular format (e.g., physical, verbal), or small-group versus large-group activities, teachers must consider these preferences when designing individualized instruction for the child.

Teachers also need to consider what program planning assessment data tell them collectively about the children in their classroom. As teachers examine both conventional and authentic assessment data, they should look for trends that provide guidance in designing curricular goals for the group of children with whom they are working during a given year. The assessment data will help them determine appropriate materials and activities to use with the children, based on the children's preferences. For example, a teacher may have a group of young 3-year-olds who have difficulty with basic social skills (e.g., sharing materials) and adaptive skills (e.g., opening their milk carton, washing their hands). The assessment data help the teacher design curricular activities that focus on social and adaptive outcomes for the children. The assessment might also assist the teacher in determining the interests of the children in order to teach relevant content. For example, if the teacher notices, while gathering assessment data, that the children really enjoy playing grocery store, they might design activities focused on food, where it comes from, and how it is sold. Also, in any given school year, there may be priorities that children's families share. Perhaps a teacher has a group of children who will be entering kindergarten the following year. Those children's families might desire the curriculum to focus on early literacy skills that children need as they approach kindergarten.

CONDUCTING PROGRAM PLANNING ASSESSMENTS

A primary strategy for assessing all young children for program planning is to administer a CBA. As discussed in Chapters 4 and 12, a primary purpose of CBAs is to serve as a direct link between assessment and instructional efforts (i.e., to ensure that what is assessed is taught, and vice versa). CBAs may also guide teachers in looking at children's overall development and interests and preferences during daily activities, as well as provide direct and indirect opportunities for families to discuss priorities and concerns. The National Early Childhood Technical Assistance Center (NECTAC) investigated the pros and cons of using CBAs. Some of the pros included yielding valid results due to the use of authentic assessment measures, being useful for ongoing intervention planning, providing accountability and progress monitoring, and being individualized in nature where accommodations are built into the environment. An unfortunate con of using CBAs for program planning is that often the whole system must change in order to promote full implementation (NECTAC, 2005). On the basis of their purpose and associated pros, CBAs are viable options in helping teachers gain needed information to plan and subsequently revise instruction. (See Chapter 7 on using a CBA to monitor children's performance over time and revise instruction.) The next section provides strategies and supports for selecting a CBA, reviews how to use a CBA rating rubric, and explains how to administer CBAs.

Selecting a Curriculum-Based Assessment for Program Planning

Many different CBAs are available. For example, some CBAs have age expectations or cutoff scores, whereas others do not include such information. The absence of cutoff scores can make it difficult to establish developmental level if the assessor does not have a strong knowledge of child development. Some CBAs also require the assessor to have extensive training in order for the results to be reliable (NECTAC, 2005). Table 6.2 provides an overview of commonly used early childhood intervention CBAs. The table's description of the assessment instrument includes skill areas covered, age ranges, uses, technology components, and advantages and disadvantages. Not all CBAs, however, help teachers plan intervention or instruction. Unfortunately, as mentioned in Chapter 4, many CBAs lack technical adequacy, are not sensitive to small changes in performance, do not provide strategies to involve families, lead to biased decisions, and/or fail to support family involvement (Bagnato et al., 2010; Brown & Hubbell, 2010).

Curriculum-Based Assessment Rating Rubric

Pretti-Frontczak et al. (2005) created a rating rubric to guide teachers in selecting, implementing, and using high-quality CBAs for program planning purposes. The rubric allows teachers to rate the critical elements of various CBAs, including technical adequacy (i.e., reliability, validity), degree of family involvement, and appropriateness for children with diverse abilities. Appendix B contains a slightly revised version of this rubric that teachers can use as they examine various CBAs to ensure that they are high quality and will meet their needs given the specific population of children they serve. The revisions were based on a review of current research, current trends in early childhood assessment,

Table 6.2. Overview of commonly used early childhood intervention curriculum-based assessments

Name of assessment	Description	Advantages	Disadvantages
Assessment, Evaluation, and Programming System for Infants and Children, Third Edition (AEPS®-3); Bricker et al. (2022)	• Assesses fine motor, gross motor, adaptive, cognitive, math, literacy, social-communication, and social areas of development • Continuous assessment for children birth to age 6 • Links assessment data to a tiered curriculum organized around activities and routines • Actively involves families by gathering input • Technology features include a web-based management system called AEPSinteractive™(AEPSi™) (https://aepsinteractive.com/).	• Can be used with children who are typically developing, those who are at risk, and those with developmental delays • Targets functional skills; child can use alternate behavior forms to demonstrate mastery of the skills • Allows for modifications for children with disabilities • Data are collected using authentic assessment methods. • Has strong research bases to validate its use for specific and varied purposes • Includes a school readiness component with subtest entitled Ready-Set	• Given the comprehensive nature of the system, can be overwhelming, particularly for those without a strong background in child development • Large number of components • Requires a time investment
The Carolina Curriculum for Preschoolers with Special Needs, Second Edition; Johnson-Martin et al. (2004b) The Carolina Curriculum for Infants and Toddlers with Special Needs, Third Edition; Johnson-Martin et al. (2004a)	• Assessment is used for gaining information on a child's mastery level in five developmental domains, including personal-social, cognition, communication, fine motor, and gross motor. • Assessment is divided into two age levels: 0–24 months and 24–60 months. • System directly links assessment items to curricular activities for children with special needs. • Provides special attention for children with atypical developmental pathways and serious impairments • Technology features include assessment logs and developmental progress charts available on CD-ROM or online in PDF format.	• Produces information that is useful when developing goals/objectives • Provides information on skills child has mastered, those that are emerging, and those the child has not yet developed • Allows for adaptations for children with specific disabilities • The latest revision of the Carolina made assessment items and related interventions continuous from birth to age 5 to meet the needs of preschool children developmentally functioning below 36 months in one or more domains.	• No specific component for family involvement • Designed only for use with children who have disabilities • Age scores are not validated. • Lacks research to demonstrate the reliability, validity, and utility of scores and inferences made

Table 6.2. *(continued)*

Name of assessment	Description	Advantages	Disadvantages
COR Advantage; HighScope Educational Research Foundation (2013)	• Assesses 34 items in six categories, including approaches to learning, social and emotional development, physical development and health, language, literacy and communication, mathematics, creative arts, science and technology, and social studies • Assessment can be used with children from birth to age 6 years. • Linked to HighScope Infant-Toddler and Preschool Curriculum • Technology features include an online data management system (mycoreadvantage.com).	• Looks broadly at all key areas of development using a strength-based approach • Process of gathering data takes place over a number of weeks or months and requires no change in the child's daily routine. • Allows child to express self using alternative forms of expression • Families can connect to online system and receive messages through the system.	• Users need a strong foundation in child development and the ability to document children's performance using narrative methods. • Lacks research to validate the COR for reporting Office of Special Education Programs (OSEP) outcomes • Users might find that the COR is not sensitive enough to detect small increments of change in development.
Hawaii Early Learning Profile 0–3; Parks-Warshaw (2006) Hawaii Early Learning Profile 3–6; Teaford (2010)	• Covers cognitive, language, gross motor, fine motor, social, and self-help skills • Composed of two separate age levels: birth–3 years and 3–6 years • Includes materials for how to address each assessment item at home • Technology features include a free score calculator for generating accountability reports.	• Can be used with different populations (children with disabilities, typically developing children, or children who are at risk) • Can assist in determining child's present levels of performance • Links assessment with curriculum that is designed to be implemented in child's home or classroom • Data can be collected using authentic assessment methods.	• Many items, so therefore large time investment • Limited research on 0–3 years and none on 3–6 years

(continued)

Table 6.2.   *(continued)*

Name of assessment	Description	Advantages	Disadvantages
The Ounce Scale; Meisels et al. (2003)	• Observational method used to assess a young child's growth and development in six developmental areas: personal connections, feelings about self, relationships with other children, understanding and communicating, exploration and problem solving, and movements and coordination • Designed for children from birth to 42 months • Consists of three elements: the observational record, the family album, and the developmental profile • Technology features include web-based data entry and electronic scoring.	• Family-oriented tool that promotes collaboration among parents and professionals • Gives "well-rounded" perspective on the child's development • Can be used to meet IDEA Part C early intervention eligibility criteria	• Scoring procedure may lead itself to subjectivity. • Additional research is needed to validate use for eligibility and accountability, particularly with children with disabilities.
Teaching Strategies GOLD Objectives for Development and Learning: Birth Through Kindergarten; Heroman et al. (2010)	• 38 objectives across social-emotional, physical, language, cognitive, literacy, mathematics, science and technology, social studies, the arts, and English language acquisition • Designed for children from birth to third grade • Linked to Creative Curriculum • Technology features include a data management system.	• Can be used by a wide range of early childhood professionals, particularly those without a strong foundation in development and/or developmentally appropriate practices • Uses authentic assessment methods • Strategies for actively involving families in assessment process • Includes technical report about the psychometrics of the test	• Insufficient items to show progress for children with disabilities • Items lack specificity, calling into question whether they can be scored reliably. • No adaptations or modifications for children with disabilities. • Some teachers find the amount of data collection necessary to score items unwieldy.

Table 6.2. (continued)

Name of assessment	Description	Advantages	Disadvantages
Transdisciplinary Play-Based Assessment, Second Edition (TPBA2); Linder (2008)	• Used to gain a comprehensive look regarding a child's cognitive, social-emotional, communication and language, and sensorimotor development through observation of play and observation/interaction with a teacher or peer • Technology features include a CD-ROM with forms and OSEP reporting tool.	• Parents can serve as play facilitators, so the process is less intimidating for children. • Emphasis on transdisciplinary teaming • Easy to use and does not require the use of a standard set of toys or materials • Includes specific assessment items for children who use American Sign Language	• Time consuming—total of 386 items, which take 1–2 hours to administer • Lacks sufficient research to support all intended and promoted purposes (e.g., identifying intervention targets, eligibility determination, and OSEP reporting)
Work Sampling System (WSS); Meisels et al. (2013)	• Covers the following domains: personal and social, language and literacy, mathematical thinking, scientific thinking, social studies, the arts, and physical development, health, and safety • Can be used with children in pre-kindergarten through third grade • Technology features include a data management system, online scoring, summary report completion, design lesson plans, and class profiles.	• Several studies have validated its use as an effective curriculum-embedded assessment. • Incorporates different types of information to assist the teacher in deciphering the child's strengths and planning appropriate instruction • Promotes collaboration among parents and professionals in sensible and friendly ways	• Scoring procedure may lend itself to subjectivity. • Lacks evidence of validity and reliability for OSEP child outcome reporting • May not be sensitive enough to show change in children with disabilities

and recommendations of professional organizations (i.e., Division for Early Childhood, National Association for the Education of Young Children). The rubric is currently composed of 11 alphabetized elements: 1) collaboration, 2) comprehensive coverage, 3) equitable design, 4) family involvement, 5) multifactors, 6) professional development, 7) reliability, 8) sensitivity, 9) technology, 10) usefulness for intervention, and 11) validity. (See Appendix B for complete definitions of each element.)

The rubric is to be completed by a team of stakeholders that may include teachers, administrators, related service providers, and parents. Some aspects of the rubric (e.g., reliability, validity) may need to be completed by a member of the team who understands how to interpret psychometric properties. To use the rubric, the team selects a CBA to review, compares the assessment instrument with the stated criteria on the rubric, and decides which rating best describes the CBA. The 11 elements are rated using a Likert scale in which 0 = *unsatisfactory*, 1 = *basic*, 2 = *satisfactory*, and 3 = *excellent*. The team circles the rating directly on the rubric. A total score can also be calculated for each CBA that the team reviews. When the team is comparing CBAs in order to select one, it can focus on the assessments that received higher overall ratings. The team may want to consider which elements are most important and must achieve at least a satisfactory rating. For example, a team may feel that, in order to be useful, a CBA must receive a satisfactory rating for the criteria of validity, family involvement, and sensitivity to children with diverse abilities.

There are times, however, when using a CBA is not possible. For example, teachers may be required to use a boxed curriculum that doesn't have an assessment component, may be required to administer a curriculum-based measure (CBM) focused only on literacy (see Chapter 12 for the distinction between CBAs and CBMs), may only have information gathered during the eligibility process, or, for a variety of other reasons, may need program planning information without the use of a CBA. Box 6.1 provides general recommendations for program planning without the use of a CBA. The following section returns to how to use a CBA, to administer a CBA with fidelity, and to do so in ways that will aid the program planning process.

Other guiding questions are in Box 6.3 as part of interpreting in the decision-making process.

Even when a team uses a quality CBA, they may want to consider if there is anything else needed to make informed decisions for program planning (e.g., Do we need more family input? Do we know about the stressors for this child? Do we know enough about their strengths?). For example, a team may want to use existing checklists designed to provide much needed information for program planning, such as the Positive Student Profile (available at https://prekteachandplay.com/PSP), the All About Me Map (available at https://prekteachandplay.com/rftsmap), and the Stress Detective Checklist (available at https://prekteachandplay.com/stress-detective-checklist/).

Box 6.1.   General Recommendations for Program Planning Without the Use of a Curriculum-Based Assessment

Start with a review of information that has already been collected or that is required outside of the use of a CBA. Information sources can be formal and informal and stem from the transition process from early intervention to preschool or preschool to kindergarten. Information can be obtained from the eligibility process for early childhood intervention and even from multi-tiered systems of support problem-solving teams. Last, program planning information can stem from completing the district's required kindergarten readiness measure or a CBM (see Chapter 12).

Next, discuss limitations and/or concerns with any of the information that is accessible. For example, as highlighted in Chapters 2, 8, and 12, although there are many sources of data, not all are useful for program planning. Teams are encouraged to harvest existing information as they can, link assessment purposes, and, at the same time, recognize the potential limitations of what they have access to (e.g., only have literacy data, child's performance is stated in comparison to a normative sample, information was obtained using standardized procedures).

Once existing data have been identified and the limitations addressed, the team may want to generate a simple list of what they still need in order to make sound decisions regarding the child or group of children. In essence, the team is looking for gaps in terms of what they know about a child's development and learning, preferences and interests, and family and other caregiver priorities and concerns.

Here are a number of questions the team can ask:

- What information do we have?

- What are the limitations of what we have?

- Do we have information across all developmental areas and from a range of settings and caregivers?

- What do we still want to know for program planning?

- What are possible authentic data sources and/or steps we can take?

- Who will get the additional sources of information and by when?

Administering Curriculum-Based Assessments

Although using CBAs is an effective way to conduct assessment for program planning purposes, they involve two administration issues that must be addressed. First, administration of CBAs should follow the recommended authentic assessment practices of familiar people, interacting with the child in familiar settings, while doing familiar things, found in Chapter 2. Given that there are clear parameters for administering CBAs, consideration should be given to the fidelity with which teachers conduct the assessment and, at the same time, to how families' cultures and values are honored and incorporated. Second, experience has shown that teachers sometimes need support in gathering data on all CBA items. As a result, assessment activities are suggested as a method for gathering data on individuals or groups of children. We will discuss determining fidelity of administration and using assessment activities next.

Assessment Fidelity

The term fidelity often refers to instructional efforts and is commonly defined "as the determination of how well an intervention is implemented in comparison with the original program design during an efficacy and/or effectiveness study" (O'Donnell, 2008, p. 33). Issues surrounding fidelity, however, be they related to adherence, implicit bias, duration, quality, or program differentiation, are important when it comes to assessment practices (Grisham-Brown et al., 2008). In other words, evidence is needed that an assessment such as a CBA is administered, summarized, interpreted, and used in not only the way it was designed and validated, but also to ensure unbiased practices and equitable practices.

With regard to use, there may be any number of reasons that CBAs are not completed with fidelity. Teachers may find the actual implementation of a CBA to be overwhelming, particularly in classrooms where large amounts of data have to be collected on many children. Sometimes teachers lack the training or support to administer the CBA. In such a situation, the teacher may become frustrated and implement the assessment with low fidelity. Finally, if teachers do not understand the usefulness of the CBA, they may reluctantly use it but not as it was intended.

The likelihood that teachers complete CBAs with fidelity will increase if they are given 1) adequate support, 2) sufficient training, and 3) information regarding the usefulness of the CBA for identifying children's goals, curriculum planning, and progress monitoring. Grisham-Brown and colleagues (2008) used a fidelity measure to determine the assessment fidelity of Head Start teachers who used the AEPS. Figure 6.1 contains a sample of the measure, which rated the fidelity with which teachers 1) set up and prepared assessment activities (i.e., the extent to which observations occurred in natural activities), 2) selected materials that were part of natural activities, 3) used procedures that elicited assessment items in a natural way, 4) made decisions that allowed children to demonstrate behavior in numerous ways, 5) embedded opportunities for child responses related to the activities in which they were engaged, and 6) allowed for child choice about activities. A complete copy of the authentic assessment fidelity measure is available at https://prekteachandplay.com/shop/authentic-assessment-procedural-fidelity-measure. Again, decisions made from CBAs are only as credible and trustworthy as the data that guide them. Therefore, teachers must make a concerted effort to avoid factors that lead to a lack of

Feature	Indicators of Authentic Assessment Procedures	Indicators of Nonauthentic Assessment Procedures	Score
Set up and Preparation	❑ Assessment activity is set up within typical class-room environment/routine (e.g., at the snack table, on the playground, at the reading corner). ❑ Teacher/team is famil-iar with the activity as evidenced by the flow (e.g., children are engaged; there are not long pauses in the activity; teacher/team refers to the activity protocol mostly for data recording purposes). ❑ Activity follows a plan or seems organized, and items targeted seem appropriate to the activity.	❑ Assessment activity is set up outside the typical classroom environment/routine (e.g., in hallway or empty room, special "texting" area in the classroom). ❑ Teacher/team is unfamil-iar with the activity as evidenced by the flow (e.g., children are disen-gaged; there are long pauses in the activity; teacher constantly refers to the description of the activity/lesson). ❑ Activity does not seem to follow any set plan or organization around assessment items.	0 1 2 3

Figure 6.1. Sample portion from an authentic assessment activity fidelity measure. (From Grisham-Brown, J., & Pretti-Frontczak, K. [2018]. *Authentic assessment procedural fidelity measure*. B2K Solutions^SM, Ltd.; reprinted by permission.)

assessment fidelity. (See Box 6.2 for common pitfalls and remedies for increas-ing assessment fidelity.)

Assessment Activities

One way to make collecting information for a CBA more efficient is to collect data during pre-established assessment activities (Grisham-Brown et al., 2005, 2006). Assessment activities are semistructured events that allow teams to use observation as the primary method of gathering information. The intent is to structure observations by embedding assessment instrument items into com-monly occurring home and classroom activities. Teachers can create assess-ment activities for individuals or groups of children. First, teachers identify activities that are motivating and interesting to young children and that offer opportunities for the teacher to observe skills related to several areas of development/content (i.e., many items from the CBA). Next, teachers intention-ally embed skills that they would like to assess into the identified activities. Skills selected should be ones that can logically be observed during the selected activities. For example, teachers would likely observe certain adaptive skills (e.g., pouring liquids, eating with utensils), social skills (e.g., initiating inter-actions, sharing materials), and social-communication skills (e.g., requesting assistance, answering questions) during snack time. After they have identified skills that may be embedded into selected activities, teachers choose materi-als that might be needed for the child to demonstrate the identified skills. For

---

Box 6.2.   Common Pitfalls and Remedies for Increasing Assessment Fidelity

Pitfall 1: Most ECI assessments, even those with standardized procedures, do not include administration checklists that can be used for integrity/fidelity checks. Such integrity and/or fidelity checks also often prioritize objective procedures, which may not account for cultural, linguistic, and/or individual differences and diversity of children and families served.

Remedies:

- Use the authentic assessment fidelity measure by Grisham-Brown and colleagues (2008).

- Use the checklist designed by Hoover (2009) to determine the degree to which the assessment itself, the assessment practices, and assessment accommodations (if applicable) were followed.

- Develop a fidelity measure that relates to procedures of the assessment being used by your program.

- Review procedures (often stated in the manual) ahead of time and avoid deviating from the directions, particularly for standardized tests.

- Critique fidelity checklists to ensure guidelines for valuing diversity and ensuring children, families, educators, and/or programs are not penalized for changes in practice to better align with family priorities and community values.

Pitfall 2: Teams administer assessments without sufficient training or ongoing support.

Remedies:

- Build opportunities for frequent checks by experts for scoring accuracy and correct administration and use.

- Utilize a coaching system in which teachers check one another and provide support for those who are new to using the assessment.

- Engage in ongoing professional development to ensure accuracy in scoring and use and avoid drift over time.

- Keep up to date with changes in the assessment being used, including securing revised editions and/or new features as they become available.

---

example, if teachers want to observe whether children pour liquids at snack time, they will need to have pitchers of preferred drinks and cups for pouring. Figure 6.2 shows an example of an assessment protocol for observing developmental skills during a story time routine.

Teachers can plan assessment activities across the classroom routine to elicit information from groups of children. The assessment activities should

Examiner:

AEPS Level: II

Group Name: **Sample Level II**

Status:

Test Date: 02/17/2010 (mm/dd/yyyy)

Short Description:
story time provides opportunity to assess skills such as establishing joint attention, functional use of reading materials, locating objects, and sounding out words.

SYMBOL KEYS

Child's Name:	Damien Roberts	Bob Wire
Date of Birth:	07/09/03	09/22/05
Area: Congnitive	IFSP IEP S N	IFSP IEP S N
C. Sequencing		
3. Retells event in sequence		
3.1 Completes sequence of familiar story or event		
F. Play		
1. Engages in cooperative, imaginary play [N]		
1. Enacts roles or identities		
1.2 Plans and acts out recognizable events		
1.3 Uses imaginary props		
H. Phonological Awareness and Emergent Reading		
1. Demonstrates phonological awareness skills [N]		
1.1 Uses rhyming skills		
1.2 Segments sentences and words		
1.3 Blends single sounds and syllables		
1.4 Identifies same and different sounds at the beginning and end of words		
2.Uses letter-sound association to sound out and write words [N]		
2.1 Writes words using letter sounds		
2.2 Sounds out words		
2.3 Produces correct sounds for letters		

Save Test In Progress   Finalize Area

Figure 6.2. An example of an assessment activity administered during storytime. (From AEPSinteractive™ Storybook Samples, http://www.aepsinteractive.com; reprinted by permission.)

be part of the classroom schedule. Teachers may elect to make two or three activities per week available as a way to elicit specific items from their CBA. Children should not be forced to participate in the activities, but when they decide to participate in an assessment activity, an adult can collect data on CBA items that are embedded in that particular activity. For example, if a group of children are playing with playdough, the observer could gather information regarding children's fine motor skills (e.g., removing lid from playdough), social-communication skills (e.g., asking for assistance), and concept knowledge (e.g., naming colors of playdough, identifying numbers on cookie cutters). The teacher also may want to assign specific team members to these centers to collect data (Grisham-Brown et al., 2006). They may place a teaching assistant in the writing center, a teacher in the art center, and an occupational therapist in the manipulative center.

Sometimes teachers may need to conduct an assessment activity during which various team members observe a child during a common activity. For example, if a team is trying to determine whether a child who is learning multiple languages has a language delay or whether a child who is having difficulty participating during a small-group activity needs a different type of instruction, a team approach may lead to greater insight. The teacher may use a transdisciplinary approach to collect data (Grisham-Brown, 2000) and may also use an assessment activity to guide the teams' observations and subsequent conclusions. The teacher would facilitate an assessment activity and invite all of the needed service providers (e.g., speech and language pathologist [SLP], occupational therapist, physical therapist [PT]) to observe the child. During the assessment activity, such as playing with playdough, the SLP could collect data on social-communication skills, the occupational therapist could collect data on fine motor skills, and the PT could collect data on gross motor skills, while the teacher collects data on concept knowledge.

Although the SLP may focus on social-communication skills and the PT may focus on gross motor skills, the transdisciplinary model encourages cross-role observations. For example, if the SLP notices that the child is using an abnormal movement pattern during the playdough activity, they would note it. Or if the PT notices that the child is making articulation errors in communications to peers while playing with playdough, they would note that. Using this model, team members provide input not only from their own domain, but from other domains as well. With a transdisciplinary assessment approach, the teacher and therapists work and collaborate as a team, which is the best practice for collecting assessment data for programming purposes. Once the team has conducted the assessment through cross-role observations and has reached decisions about what skills to target, members can engage in role release for teaching the target skills. For example, the SLP may demonstrate specific skills to the teacher, such as how to produce the initial /l/ sound, and then the teacher can embed that skill within activities and routines across the child's day (Hawkins & Schuster, 2007). Similarly, the PT may demonstrate or model a specific positioning technique for a student, and the teacher then can embed that technique within classroom activities and routines. Parents also should be involved in role release. If the therapist can model the parents' specific skills, then those skills will be addressed not only during the school day but in the home as well (Jung & Grisham-Brown, 2006).

USING INFORMATION FROM
CURRICULUM-BASED ASSESSMENTS TO PROGRAM PLAN

As we noted earlier in this chapter, when teachers complete a CBA for program planning purposes, they should do so with the intent of using the information to determine what to teach, when to teach, how to teach, and which supports children may benefit from. The temptation here is to complete a CBA, enter the data into a computer or put it in the child's folder, and then plan instruction that is based on a holiday, favorite book, season, or idea discussed during an in-service or topics suggested by a commercial curriculum rather than making decisions based upon findings from the CBA. Essentially, teachers must recognize that program planning involves much more than the completion of a CBA. After systematically gathering and documenting (the first two steps in the decision-making process described in Chapter 5), teachers now finish the decision-making process by summarizing the information, analyzing patterns and trends, and interpreting to make critical decisions about instruction. Specifically, teachers need to make decisions regarding the needs and priorities of individual children as well as groups of children as it relates to services, supports, and experiences offered. The sections that follow provide suggestions and strategies for engaging in a decision-making process for planning instruction when using a CBA. (See Chapter 5 for an overview of the decision-making process).

Making Decisions for Program Planning

Regardless of how information is gathered, documented, summarized, or analyzed, if it isn't used to plan and guide instruction, then the process is a waste of the teacher's time and provides no advantage for children. Thus, assessment information, like that obtained from a CBA, should be used to identify who needs to learn what, to determine how to sort children's strengths and needs, and to identify the level of support individuals and groups of children need.

Identifying Who Needs to Learn What

Once a CBA has been completed, teachers can use the information to determine which children need to learn which skills or outcomes. The following section, and Grisham-Brown and Hemmeter (2017), provide more details on how to make program planning determinations regarding "who needs to learn what." Generally speaking, however, deciding who needs to learn what is determined by using assessment summaries and the patterns and trends identified during analysis of the CBA or other authentic assessment information. More specifically, and as described in Grisham-Brown and Hemmeter (2017), teachers in a blended classroom use assessment results to help sort children's strengths and needs across three types of outcomes and then plan instruction accordingly.

The first type of outcome is often referred to as a common outcome. Common outcomes are general expectations that states, agencies, funding sources, and programs have for all children within a given age group. The second type of outcome is often termed targeted. Targeted outcomes are skills that require more support in order to help children who are struggling or whose learning and development have stalled. The third type of outcome is termed individualized. Individualized outcomes are based upon a child's unique needs and are sometimes documented on various individualized plans, including IEPs for children with identified disabilities (Johnson et al., 2015). However, individualized outcomes are not limited to or an indicator of children receiving special education

---

Box 6.3. Questions to Ask Regarding Related and Mediating Factors

- Was the CBA completed by familiar people in familiar settings?

- Were sufficient amounts of information collected to create rich summaries?

- Were summaries objective and free from bias?

- Did summaries provide a complete picture of the child or groups of children within the context of their family and community?

- During the analysis of patterns and trends, were factors such as attendance, change in medications, exposure to other therapies, fidelity of implementation, stressors, and health status considered?

- Was the influence of family and culture and the child's personal and contextual identities considered?

- Were the interrelatedness and interdependence of development considered?

---

services. Individualized outcomes include when children need instructional support regarding prerequisite skills or foundational skills, or need teachers to remove barriers to learning (i.e., things that are preventing children's access, participation, and ability to make progress in daily activities and experiences). Individualized outcomes can also include mediating factors discovered while administering a CBA. Box 6.3 includes examples of mediating factors that may require consideration as teachers plan instruction.

Sorting Children by Outcomes

Teachers then sort children by using the assessment information and comparing results to the three types of outcomes. This can be done quite literally by drawing something like a triangle with three layers, by drawing three buckets or squares, by creating an embedding schedule, and/or by using a tiered intentional instructional sequence. (See Grisham-Brown & Hemmeter, 2017, for more on embedding schedules and the intentional instructional sequence for sorting assessment data by outcome.) The more experienced the teacher, the more automatic the sorting process; however, teachers who are new to the field, those serving large numbers of children, and/or those trying to address the complexities of including a child with significant support needs may want to draw/type a tiered image or shape (e.g., a triangle with three layers) to aid with identifying and sorting children's strengths and needs. Regardless of approach, a key part of the instructional team's planning time should be used to sort. That is, a core part of planning time should be spent determining, for a child or group of children, whether they are on track, whether their development has stalled, or whether they are struggling, and/or whether there is an individualized

Individualized outcome examples:
1. Remove and reduce stressors such as noisy or cluttered learning environment.
2. Address a prerequisite to phonological awareness such as one-to-one correspondence.
3. Address a foundation for learning phonological awareness such as imitation of sounds.

Targeted outcome example:
Address a component of phonological awareness, such as rhyming, with which a child or a group of children may struggle.

Common outcome example:
Phonological awareness is commonly defined as an awareness of speech sounds such as rhyming and alliteration as well as more advanced skills such as onset-rime awareness and full phonemic awareness.

Figure 6.3. Illustration of a tiered image for each of the three outcomes in a blended approach using phonological awareness as the common outcome.

outcome that needs to be addressed for a particular child or group of children. Again, teachers can simply take a sheet of paper or open a digital document, create three tiers/layers/rows, and then, starting at the bottom, identify and clearly define a common outcome (e.g., state standard, big idea, milestone), the targeted outcome(s) associated with the common outcome, and, last, any individualized outcomes. See Figure 6.3 for an illustration of a tiered image with each of the three outcomes in a blended approach using phonological awareness (PA) as the common outcome. As a teacher plans to teach PA to the group of children, they also use assessment information to determine which children may need additional support regarding a component of PA (e.g., rhyming), and even which children need support to also address individualized outcomes that at first glance seem quite unrelated to PA (e.g., removing auditory stimuli, teaching one-to-one-correspondence, teaching imitation). These individualized outcomes, however, require intentional instruction to allow some children to fully access, participate, and make progress during daily activities and experiences, while still being exposed to the broader outcome for all (i.e., PA).

Then, using the information from the CBA, the teacher sorts children by each main common outcome that is part of their curriculum. They do so by placing children's names or initials on the tier or next to the outcome that matches

**Begins to
ignore
distractions**
Child with an
instructional focus
on a foundational
skill: LM

**Remains with
or near the group**
Children struggling with participation (i.e.,
remaining with the group): RR, MC, JP

**Participates by watching, interacting,
following directions, exchanging materials,
and remaining with the group**

Children on track to learn and grow regarding participation:
MJ, SP, AL, ML, SC, XR, IL, JG, LS, AL, KP, IJ, IG, JC, KM, KA, TR, LC

Figure 6.4. Classroom of children sorted by the common outcome of participants during group activities, the targeted outcome of remains with or near the group, and the individualized outcome of begins to ignore distractions.

their readiness. The sorting process can also be done through a conversation with others and by holding the information in one's mind/memory. Because sorting is ideally completed by major outcomes or big ideas and for a group of children, however, it can result in a lot of information. Capturing who is ready to learn which outcome by typing, drawing, and/or writing can be helpful. See Figure 6.4 for an example of how the data for a classroom of children were sorted by the common outcome of participation, the targeted outcome of remains with the group, and the individualized outcome of begins to ignore distractions. The key thing to note in Figure 6.4 is that given the complexity of development, and that all children have strengths and needs that will vary based upon the outcome, content, or situation and the support provided, a child is not referred to as a Tier 3 child, nor do a group of children require Tier 2 instruction. Rather, the type of instruction they receive is predicted on an outcome-by-outcome basis. Further, once children have been sorted, teachers have a map of where to begin instruction and which outcomes to embed during daily activities and experiences. They can also determine performance monitoring procedures to help revise instruction. See Chapter 7's Case Example 2 of using assessment information to plan and revise instruction for a child named Mikey. See Grisham-Brown and Hemmeter (2017) for more on how to match instruction to an individual child's and groups of children's strengths and needs.

Multi-Tiered Systems of Support

What was previously described regarding program planning decision making mirrors much of the practices and terminology associated with what is often referred to as multi-tiered systems of support (MTSS). For example, in 2021, the Division for Early Childhood (DEC) published a position statement for conceptualizing MTSS for young children. At its core, like a blended approach, MTSS begins with collecting assessment data for the purposes of making decisions about what and how to teach children. In an MTSS model, the term universal screening is used to determine if children are performing at benchmark levels. Although there are some instruments that have been designated as MTSS universal screeners (e.g., Individual Growth and Development Indicators; Carta et al., 2002), which are often norm-referenced, it is acceptable to use a CBA for universal screening and to make decisions about tiered supports needed for individuals or groups of children. Specifically, benchmarks from a CBA can be established by setting local norms, meaning that the child scores lower on certain aspects of the test than their classmates (DEC, 2021). Unlike a norm-referenced universal screener that yields standardized scores and benchmarks based on those scores, using a CBA allows teams to make decisions about the need for increased support based on using an assessment that can be administered using authentic practices described in Chapter 2. Within an MTSS model, the establishment of benchmarks guides decisions about the tier or level of support that a child needs in order to learn important skills. As we described previously, an important decision that can be made in an early childhood MTSS model is to consider the type of outcome a child needs to learn. In general, the model for using program planning assessment data to determine what to teach and design instruction described in this chapter is very much in keeping with the tenets of MTSS.

SUMMARY

The purpose of Chapter 6 was to describe recommended practices for program planning for individuals and groups of children. In essence, we highlighted how authentic assessment information is used to aid in the design and delivery of tiered or differentiated instruction. First, the chapter defined and discussed assessment for program planning purposes. Next, we provided information on how to conduct program planning assessments, including how to select a CBA using a rating rubric, as well as how to administer the CBA with fidelity and engage in authentic assessment activities. The chapter concluded with a description of how to identify, sort, and align instruction to meet the individual needs of the child or groups of children using a tiered model (DEC, 2021). In the next chapter, we will describe how to revise instruction continuously to support individual and/or group needs.

REFERENCES

Bagnato, S. J., Neisworth, J. T., & Pretti-Frontczak, K. (2010). *LINKing authentic assessment and early childhood intervention: Best measures for best practices* (2nd ed.). Paul H. Brookes Publishing Co.

Bricker, D., Dionne, C., Grisham, J., Johnson, J. J., Macy, M., Slentz, K., & Waddell, M. (2022). *Assessment, Evaluation, and Programming System for infants and children, Third Edition (AEPS®-3)*. Paul H. Brookes Publishing Co.

Brown, T., & Hubbell, S. P. (2010, January). *Evidence-base of commonly-used assessments in early childhood special education*. Center for Excellence in Early Childhood Research and Training, Kent State University.

Carta, J. J., Greenwood, C. R., Walker, D., Kaminski, R., Good, R., McConnell, S., & McEvoy, M. (2002). Individual growth and development indicators (IGDIs): Assessment that guides intervention for young children. *Young Exceptional Children Monograph Series, 4*, 15–28.

Division for Early Childhood (DEC). (2021). *Multitiered system of support framework for early childhood: Description and implications*. Author.

Grisham-Brown, J., & Pretti-Frontczak, K. (2018). *Authentic assessment procedural fidelity measure*. B2K Solutions, Ltd.

Grisham-Brown, J., Hallam, R., & Brookeshire, R. (2006). Using authentic assessment to evidence children's progress toward early learning standards. *Early Childhood Education Journal, 34*(1), 45–51.

Grisham-Brown, J., Hallam, R. A., & Pretti-Frontczak, K. (2008). Preparing Head Start personnel to use a curriculum-based assessment: An innovative practice in the "age of accountability." *Journal of Early Intervention, 30*(4), 271–281.

Grisham-Brown, J. L. (2000). Transdisciplinary activity-based assessment for young children with multiple disabilities: A program planning approach. *Young Exceptional Children, 3*, 3–10.

Grisham-Brown, J. L., & Hemmeter, M. L. (2017). *Blended practices for teaching young children in inclusive settings* (2nd ed.). Paul H. Brookes Publishing Co.

Grisham-Brown, J., Hemmeter, M. L., & Pretti-Frontczak, K. (2005). *Blended practices for teaching young children in inclusive settings*. Paul H. Brookes Publishing Co.

Hawkins, S., & Schuster, J. (2007). Using a mand-model procedure to teach preschool children initial speech sounds. *Journal of Developmental and Physical Disabilities, 19*(1), 65–80.

Heroman, C., Burts, D. C., Berke, K. L., & Bickart, T. S. (2010). *Teaching Strategies GOLD objectives for development and learning: Birth through kindergarten*. Teaching Strategies, LLC.

HighScope Educational Research Foundation (2013). *COR Advantage*. HighScope Press.

Hoover, J. J. (2009). *RTI assessment essentials for struggling learners*. Sage.

Johnson, J. J., Rahn, N. L., & Bricker, D. (2015). *An activity-based approach to early intervention*. Paul H. Brookes Publishing Co.

Johnson-Martin, N. M., Attermeier, S. M., & Hacker, B. J. (2004a). *The Carolina Curriculum for Infants and Toddlers with Special Needs (CCITSN), Third Edition*. Paul H. Brookes Publishing Co.

Johnson-Martin, N. M., Hacker, B. J., & Attermeier, S. M. (2004b). *The Carolina Curriculum for Infants and Toddlers with Special Needs (CCITSN), Second Edition*. Paul H. Brookes Publishing Co.

Jung, L. A., & Grisham-Brown, J. L. (2006). Moving from assessment information to IFSPs: Guidelines for a family-centered process. *Young Exceptional Children, 9*(2), 2–11.

Linder, T. (2008). *Transdisciplinary play-based assessment* (2nd ed.) (TPBA2). Paul H. Brookes Publishing Co.

Meisels, S. J., & Atkins-Burnett, S. (2000). The elements of early childhood assessment. In J. P. Shonkoff & S. J. Meisels (Eds.), *Handbook of early childhood intervention* (pp. 231–257). Cambridge University Press. https://doi.org/10.1017/CBO9780511529320.013

Meisels, S. J., Dombro, A. L., Marsden, D., Weston, D., & Jewkes, A. (2003). *The ounce scale: Standards for the developmental profiles, birth-42 months*. Pearson Early Learning.

Meisels, S., Marsden, D. B., Jablon, J. R., & Dichtelmiller, M. (2013). *The Work Sampling System* (5th ed.). Pearson.

National Early Childhood Technical Assistance Center (NECTAC). (2005). *Norm-referenced versus curriculum-based assessment tools.* http://www.nectac.org/topics/quality/childfam.asp

O'Donnell, C. L. (2008). Defining, conceptualizing, and measuring fidelity of implementation and its relationship to outcomes in K-12 curriculum intervention research. *Review of Educational Research, 78*(1), 33–84.

Parks-Warshaw, S. (2006). *Hawaii Early Learning Profile 0-3.* VORT Corporation.

Paul H. Brookes Publishing Co. (2022). *AEPSinteractive™ (AEPSi™) storybook samples.* https://aepsinteractive.com/

Pretti-Frontczak, K., Vilardo, L., & Kenneley, D. (2005). *Curriculum-based rating rubric.* Kent State University.

Teaford, P. (2010). *Hawaii Early Learning Profile 3-6* (2nd ed.). VORT Corporation.

Revised Curriculum-Based Assessment Rating Rubric and Glossary

Element	Unsatisfactory (0)	Basic (1)	Satisfactory (2)	Excellent (3)
Collaboration	Assessment is completed and summarized by one team member.	Several team members work independently to complete the assessment (i.e., separate protocols or sections are completed by different professionals). Family members are not involved. Assessment reports are often created by individual team members.	Several team members (often from different disciplines) work together to complete the assessment. Family members are involved in the assessment process; however, their role is prescribed, dictated, or limited. Assessment reports may be created by individual team members.	Assessment process encourages different recommended models of teamwork (e.g., transdisciplinary) and role sharing among parents and professionals. All team members work together to complete the assessment. Families have choices and can play a variety of roles. Assessment reports are summarized as a whole by the team.
Comprehensive coverage	Assessment items cover a single developmental area (e.g., communication) OR a single content area (e.g., literacy) AND many critical concepts and skills are missing.	Assessment covers either several developmental areas OR several content areas but not both, AND some of the areas may be missing critical concepts and skills.	Assessment covers many traditional developmental areas and some content areas, which may be missing critical concepts and skills. The assessment is fairly comprehensive but mostly covers traditional developmental areas with some inclusion of content areas.	Assessment covers the major areas of development (i.e., motor, adaptive, cognitive, communication, social) AND major content areas (e.g., early math, reading). Assessment may combine content and developmental areas (e.g., literacy may be covered under the cognitive domain); however, most critical concepts and skills are included.

Assessing Young Children in Inclusive Settings: The Blended Practices Approach, Second Edition, by Kristie Pretti-Frontczak and Jennifer Grisham, with Lynn D. Sullivan. Copyright © 2023 by Paul H. Brookes Publishing Co., Inc. All rights reserved.

Element	Unsatisfactory (0)	Basic (1)	Satisfactory (2)	Excellent (3)
Equitable design	Children are expected to demonstrate competence according to biased and narrowly defined criteria. Modifications are not allowed, thus a child is penalized due to sensory, physical, behavioral, social-emotional, linguistic, and/or cultural differences or functional limitations. Emphasis is on topographical content or form rather than the context and function of the child's performance.	Children are expected to demonstrate competence according to a predefined criterion. Extensive modifications would be needed to ensure that all children are able to show their competencies due to sensory, physical, behavioral, social-emotional, linguistic, and/or cultural differences or functional limitations. Emphasis is on topographical content or form rather than the context and function of the child's performance.	Children can demonstrate competence using a variety of expressions (verbal and nonverbal); however, some modifications may be needed to ensure that all children are able to show their competencies due to sensory, physical, behavioral, social-emotional, linguistic, and/or cultural differences or functional limitations. Emphasis is on the context and function of the child's performance rather than topographical content or form.	All children can demonstrate competence using a variety of expressions (verbal and nonverbal). The diversity among children is celebrated and no child is penalized due to culture, language, individual differences, or other intersecting identities, thus making assessment modifications or adaptations relatively unnecessary. In other words, children are allowed multiple and alternate ways to show their competencies despite sensory, physical, behavioral, social-emotional, linguistic, and/or cultural differences. Emphasis is on the context and function of the child's performance rather than topographical content or form.
Family involvement	No opportunities for family involvement.	Minimal opportunities for involvement, mostly passive roles (e.g., answering questions, observing but not participating).	Several opportunities for passive and active involvement (e.g., families are encouraged to answer questions and to observe and participate by gathering information or scoring protocols).	Assessment practices enable the integral engagement of parents, family members, and friends via friendly jargon-free materials and procedures, and practices that respect cultural values, among which the family and partners can voice a preference. Specific supports, strategies, and/or content to help improve communication and partnerships with families are provided. Families are viewed as equal team members and have a variety of options or ways of participating in assessment and instructional efforts.

Element	Unsatisfactory (0)	Basic (1)	Satisfactory (2)	Excellent (3)
Multifactors	Uses a single method of gathering information at a single point in time, in an unfamiliar single setting, by a single and unfamiliar team member.	Uses a single method of gathering information in multiple settings, but with unfamiliar people.	Uses multiple methods of gathering information during a single setting or time period, with familiar people.	Gathers information through multiple methods across time points in familiar settings/situations with familiar people.
Professional development	Nothing in the assessment materials (manual, website, etc.) addresses the need for training and/or approaches to training.	Very little in the materials (manual, website, etc.) addresses the need for training and/or approaches to training.	Either some of the materials (manual, website, etc.) address the need for training to ensure accuracy and fidelity of assessment **OR** suggestions and/or procedures for training (e.g., additional downloads, tutorials, list of trainers, menu of training options, training videos, self-study materials, FAQ blogs) are provided.	Considerable attention is given in the materials (manual, website, etc.) to the need for training to ensure accuracy and fidelity of use without bias **AND** suggestions and/or procedures for training (e.g., additional downloads, tutorials, list of trainers, menu of training options, training videos, self-study materials, FAQ blogs) are systematically provided.
Reliability	Multiple assessors do not agree on the scoring **AND** child scores differently when reassessed within a short amount of time.	Multiple assessors do not agree on the scoring **OR** child scores differently when reassessed within a short amount of time.	Multiple assessors agree on the scoring **OR** child scores similarly on items when reassessed within a short amount of time.	Multiple assessors agree on the scoring **AND** child scores similarly on items when reassessed within a short amount of time.
Sensitivity	Assessment does not contain a sufficient number of items to record low or high levels of functioning, items are not organized in sequences that guide instruction, **AND** ratings are dichotomous (e.g., yes/no, ready/not ready, mastered/not mastered, +/–).	Assessment contains a sufficient number of items to record low **OR** high levels of functioning, items are not consistently organized in sequences that guide instruction, **AND** ratings are dichotomous (e.g., yes/no, ready/not ready, mastered/not mastered, +/–).	Assessment contains a sufficient number of items to record low **AND** high levels of functioning, most items are organized in sequences that guide instruction, **AND** uses quantitative ratings (e.g., multipoint ratings) **OR** qualitative methods (rich anecdotal notes and permanent records).	Assessment contains a sufficient number of items to record low and high functional levels **AND** to detect the smallest increments of changes. Items are consistently organized in sequences that guide instruction. Child's performance is measured using a range of quantitative and qualitative methods (e.g., multipoint ratings or classifications are used as well as procedures to document the extent and conditions under which children demonstrate competence).

Element	Unsatisfactory (0)	Basic (1)	Satisfactory (2)	Excellent (3)
Technology	Assessment does not incorporate any electronic and/or web-based features.	Assessment incorporates only static technology options (e.g., CD-ROM of forms).	Assessment incorporates a single interactive/dynamic technology-based support **OR** a combination of static options.	Assessment incorporates multiple interactive (e.g., blog, discussion board, online data management system, handheld devices, etc.) **AND** static technology-based supports (e.g., downloads, FAQs, tutorials) exist, including materials that promote the link between assessment and instruction.
Usefulness for intervention	Assessment information serves no purpose related to intervention (i.e., for planning or revising).	Assessment information has limited use and is not linked to daily plans, individual intervention plans, or performance monitoring efforts.	Assessment information can be used for multiple purposes (e.g., developing present levels of performance, identifying children's needs, planning instruction, monitoring progress) and is somewhat linked to daily plans, individual intervention plans, and performance monitoring efforts.	Assessment information can be used for multiple or interrelated purposes **AND** is linked to daily plans or individual intervention plans **AND** administration of the assessment leads to improved outcomes and measures important skills that accurately portray the child's abilities.
Validity	Little to no evidence exists to validate the tool for the purposes for which it was developed, designed, or intended **AND** there is little to no evidence that the assessment links well to instruction.	Little to no evidence exists to validate the tool for the purposes for which it was developed, designed, or intended but there is some evidence that the assessment links well to instruction.	At least some evidence exists to validate the tool for the purposes for which it was developed, designed, or intended **OR** there is evidence that the assessment links well to instruction.	Considerable evidence exists to validate the tool for the purposes for which it was developed, designed, or intended **AND** there is evidence that the assessment links well to instruction.

Collaboration—The assessment instrument can be used by a group of people (e.g., educators, service providers, professionals, assistants, family members, therapists) who engage in a process of planning, conducting, summarizing, interpreting, and using the assessment for a variety of purposes.

Comprehensive coverage—The assessment instrument encompasses all areas/competencies of children's early development and learning. In other words, the assessment instrument covers all content areas (e.g., literacy, mathematics, science) and developmental areas (e.g., motor, communication, social-emotional) and shows the interrelationships of early development.

Equitable design—All children are able to demonstrate their underlying and often unrealized functional capabilities. The assessment allows alternate and often multisensory means for children to show their competencies despite sensory, physical, behavioral, social-emotional, linguistic, and cultural differences or functional limitations. The CBA emphasizes context and functional rather than topographical content (form) and adheres to universal design concepts (i.e., it is designed for all children, including those with disabilities, without relying heavily on adaptations or special design; it promotes full integration; and it acknowledges differences as a part of everyday life). For example, an assessment would determine whether a child can *"get or move* across the room" versus *"walk* across the room." The team is aware of, explores, and takes action to minimize when a child and/or family's intersectionality of identities leads to implicit and/or explicit oppression and marginalization.

Family involvement—Families are viewed as equal team members and given a variety of options or ways of participating in assessment and instructional efforts. Families (and other important caregivers) are included throughout the assessment process (e.g., asked to share information, be present during the assessment process, help administer assessment items, help with summarizing and interpreting).

Multifactors—Assessment information is gathered and recorded about children's competencies across diverse places (e.g., classroom, home, community), routines (e.g., group circle, playground, lunch), and situations (e.g., morning, evening). Information is pooled from several familiar caregivers (e.g., parents, family, friends, professionals) who have attachments to the child and interact with the child during daily events, life activities, and across different settings. Information is gathered through multiple methods (i.e., interview, direct probes, permanent products, observations).

Professional development—An assessment contains supports, strategies, and/or content related to its initial and ongoing use to ensure that it is conducted accurately, without bias, and with fidelity. For example, the publisher or authors provide access to ongoing professional development activities through live expert trainings, webinars, online tutorials, or instructional videos.

Reliability—CBA results are stable and consistent. The more reliable scores and procedures are, the more confidence users can have in their accuracy. Reliability correlation coefficients range from –1 (i.e., an inverse relationship) to +1.00 (i.e., a perfect relationship). Generally speaking, the higher the correlation coefficient, the better the assessment. Furthermore, the higher the stakes in terms of the decisions made from the assessment, the higher the correlations should be.

Sensitivity—An assessment can differentiate between small variances in skills—there are a sufficient number of items to record low and high functional levels. Sensitivity can be measured by using quantitative methods that analyze the density of items in a skill hierarchy and using graduated scoring of children's performance on those items, as well as by using qualitative methods that document the extent and conditions under which children demonstrate competence.

Technology—The CBA has electronic and/or web-based features that are designed to support any aspect of the assessment process (e.g., online tutorials, interactive website or even a place to download additional materials, scoring assist, handheld data-entry devices, online data management system, and/or interface with state databases).

Usefulness for intervention—This measure refers to "the degree to which an assessment or assessment process is shown to contribute to beneficial treatment or intervention outcomes" (Meisels & Atkins-Burnett, 2000, p. 252). For example, teachers might be interested in the usefulness of the assessment process, often called its treatment validity, to accomplish specific early childhood intervention purposes, especially planning and evaluating interventions.

Validity—Evidence that an assessment instrument correctly and accurately measures what it was intended to measure (i.e., the overall degree of justification for test interpretation and use).

CHAPTER 7

Assessment for Progress Monitoring Purposes

Jennifer Grisham, Kristie Pretti-Frontczak,
Ashley Lyons-Picard, Sarah Hawkins-Lear, and Lynn D. Sullivan

Yashika is a teacher in a blended preschool classroom that serves children with and without disabilities. The classroom consists of children ages 3 through 6. Four of the children have individualized educational programs (IEPs) with specific goals and outcomes; six of the children are developing typically, and two children do not currently have an IEP, but data are being collected on their progress due to concerns related to their development. Using the strategies described in Chapter 6, Yashika assessed all of the children with the use of a curriculum-based assessment (CBA) and engaged in the decision-making process to determine the children's needs and to match instruction to those needs. Yashika now realizes that a systematic approach to plan instruction is vital. However, Yashika isn't sure how to complete the task. The prospect of tracking so many children and different abilities makes Yashika feel a little overwhelmed. Yashika wonders: How will the instruction change the children's behavior? How will it be possible to monitor multiple children's progress toward different outcomes? What kinds of information assist in making good decisions about the impact of instruction and intervention? When should the instruction change, and how long should the current instruction and intervention continue?

Teachers make decisions on a regular basis; as discussed in Chapter 5, early research on teacher decision making and efficacy estimated that teachers made as many as 1,300 decisions daily (Jackson, 1968; Sandall & Schwartz, 2002). Subsequent research has confirmed that both novice and experienced teachers make continuous decisions before, during, and after they provide instruction to their students (Ysseldyke et al., 1987). The decisions that teachers make are often quick and are done under ever-changing situations. Thus, teachers frequently rely on their past experience in order to make decisions.

The complexities of blended classrooms, however, have changed the types of decisions that teachers need to make. For example, when teachers serve children who are multilanguage learners, who may have a delay or disability, or who may exhibit challenging behaviors, the teachers need to rely on the systematic use of data, rather than their past experiences or intuition, to inform their decisions. Furthermore, the decisions that are made regarding instruction have implications for children's growth, development, and learning and thus should be based on valid, reliable, and sufficient evidence (Ysseldyke & Tardrew, 2007). To address the challenges of ongoing data collection and use, teachers need both informal and formal methods of gathering and using data to support instructional decisions, particularly until they become more experienced, and the decisions become more common and automatic.

The processes and procedures for conducting assessment to plan instruction were addressed in Chapter 6. The purpose of Chapter 7 is to assist teachers in conducting assessment for the purpose of revising instruction (referred to as progress monitoring) in an effort to continuously support children. Chapter 7 is divided into four sections. First, we define assessment for the purpose of revising instruction. Second, we describe two broad recommended practices for progress monitoring. Third, we share a tiered model of progress monitoring as a means of addressing the challenges of systematically collecting data for children in blended classrooms. Last, we discuss suggestions and strategies for sharing progress monitoring reports.

PROGRESS MONITORING

Progress monitoring is an assessment purpose in which teachers revisit initial instructional decisions in terms of their accuracy and efficacy (i.e., they determine whether instructional efforts are promoting growth and development, leading to family satisfaction, and resulting in quality programming). The notion of monitoring is key to understanding this assessment purpose. In general, monitoring refers to the systematic collection of information that provides ongoing feedback regarding children's progress over time. Monitoring allows teachers to track children's progress on common, targeted, and individualized outcomes. Monitoring also allows for the systematic collection of comparative data to determine the significance or effect of instruction for individual children and groups of children (Raver, 2003). Ongoing data collection is necessary for determining instruction's effectiveness and any need for revision (Division for Early Childhood [DEC], 2014).

The term progress monitoring is used for three main reasons. First, progress views children's growth and development in terms of the acquisition of skills and the use of functional abilities. In this context, the term progress may lead to thoughts about vertical gains in the development and acquisition of skills to a mastery criterion (i.e., as a child learns one skill, teams automatically move to the acquisition of the next and the next, without considering the child's developmental readiness or function) (Kearney, 2008). In other words, progress monitoring stresses the need to describe and examine changes in children's behaviors more broadly, in terms of acquisition and mastery as well as other critical and often both quantitative and qualitative attributes.

Second, many people associate the term progress with IEP data collection efforts. We prefer to use more blended or universal language, and progress seems more applicable to all children. Progress emphasizes the continuous process of collecting and analyzing data on multiple and often interrelated domains of development. In addition, progress indicators can compare the impact of instruction on goals and objectives and compare actual results against expected results (achievement of outputs and progress toward outcomes).

Third, other terms, such as formative assessment and summative assessment (see Box 7.1), could be used for progress monitoring, but they may be unfamiliar to many teachers, may be used more often to refer to older students, and might not clearly convey or emphasize the type of practices that are necessary for use with young children, particularly those with diverse abilities (Fuchs & Fuchs, 1986, 1999).

Progress monitoring is applicable to all types of early childhood programs and philosophies. The implementation of assessment for progress monitoring purposes, however, may vary in terms of who collects data; how they do

---

Box 7.1.   What Is the Difference?
Definitions of Formative Versus Summative Assessment

Formative	Summative
Part of instructional practice	Given periodically to determine at a particular point in time what children know
Allows timely adjustments to instruction	
Helps teachers determine next steps during the learning process	Is an accountability measure that is generally used as part of the grading process
Provides information at the classroom level to assist in making instructional revisions	Allows teachers to gauge child learning relative to content standards at a particular point in time
	Provides a snapshot of the child's progress at a specific interval of time
Engages children in the assessment of their own learning through descriptive feedback	Illustrates cumulative representation of children's current competency through comprehensive monitoring

---

so; and what information is gathered, documented, and summarized for use (McAfee & Leong, 2002; McConnell, 2000; McLean et al., 2004). In other words, the recommended practices and tiered model of progress monitoring described here in Chapter 7 hold true regardless of the type of program or educational philosophy; however, the look or feel of progress monitoring may vary.

It is beyond the scope of the chapter to describe in detail how teachers working in different programs conceptualize and define progress monitoring. However, Table 7.1 highlights key characteristics of progress monitoring with regard to widely accepted early childhood programs and philosophies (e.g., HighScope, Montessori). In general, although programs following particular philosophies may conceptualize and define progress monitoring differently, it is recommended that all teachers serving young children engage in a set of monitoring practices that are holistic and data-driven (Branscombe et al., 2003; Copple & Bredekamp, 2009; Gestwicki, 1999; Grisham-Brown et al., 2005, 2008; Pretti-Frontczak & Bricker, 2004; Sandall et al., 2005).

RECOMMENDED PROGRESS MONITORING PRACTICES

As in the case of any assessment process, there are recommended practices to guide teachers. In regard to progress monitoring, two recommendations are prevalent across the literature. First, progress monitoring should be conceptualized holistically and should use both qualitative and quantitative methods, consider mediating factors, and consider the interdependence or the relationship among development, culture, and experiences (Brinton & Fujiki, 2003; Hojnoski et al., 2009a, 2009b, 2009c; Klingner et al., 2007; Ross et al., 1998). Second, progress monitoring should be data-driven and serve as a recursive process that involves gathering information, documenting, summarizing, conducting analysis, and interpreting data to inform and revise instruction (Division for Early Childhood of the Council for Exceptional Children, National Association for the Education of Young Children, and National Head Start Association, 2013; National

Table 7.1. Illustration of how various program types conceptualize and define progress monitoring

Program type	Who tends to gather information and how?	What information is documented, and what methods are used to document?	How is information summarized for use in monitoring performance?
Activity-Based Intervention (ABI) (Macy, 2007; Pretti-Frontczak & Bricker, 2004)	WHO: Transdisciplinary teams that include family members HOW: Through observation of children during routine, planned, and child-directed activities; through interviews and conversations with familiar caregivers	WHAT: Children's strengths, interests, emerging skills, as well as their interests and preferences METHODS: Written descriptions, permanent products, and counts/tallies	HOW: Narratively, numerically, and/or visually, most often by compiling information on a curriculum-based assessment (CBA)
Discrete Trial Training Programs (Eikeseth et al., 2002; Lovaas, 1987)	WHO: Therapist/consultant HOW: Through direct testing and prompting during intervention sessions	WHAT: Children's performance on individualized and discrete skills METHODS: Counts and tallies; time sampling procedures	Visually, most often through graphs
HighScope (HighScope Educational Research Foundation, 2002, 2003, 2013)	WHO: Teachers and teaching assistants HOW: Through observation during the plan, do, review sequence of daily activities	WHAT: Children's actions and abilities METHODS: Written descriptions (i.e., anecdotal notes, interviews) and counts and tallies	Narratively and numerically, most often through discussions of work time
Montessori (Montessori, 1976)	WHO: Directress/guide/teacher HOW: Observe children engaged during individual work that follows their own natural interests	WHAT: Children's inner directives from nature METHODS: Written descriptions (i.e., interviews, portfolios, audio/visual recordings of children's work, individual conferences, anecdotal notes, counts and tallies)	Narratively, numerically, and/or visually, most often through word task analysis journals and panel boards
Project-based (Katz & Chard, 2000)	WHO: Teacher and teaching assistants HOW: Observe children in classroom activities following children's interests	WHAT: Children's interest and involvement in their own learning METHODS: Anecdotal/observational notes and records, graphic organizers (e.g., curriculum web), interviews, permanent products, counts and tallies (i.e., interviews)	Narratively, numerically, and/or visually, most often through a display of objects
Reggio Emilia (Fraser & Gestwicki, 2000)	WHO: Teacher and parents HOW: Observation of children during daily activities, guided by specific questions and hypotheses	WHAT: Children's principles of respect, responsibility, and community METHODS: Family interviews, panel boards, photos, text, sculptures, drawings, and paintings	Narratively and visually, most often through various media and symbols and display of objects
Teaching Strategies GOLD (Heroman et al., 2010)	WHO: Teachers and teaching assistants HOW: Through observation during classroom activities	WHAT: Children's actions and abilities METHODS: Written descriptions and numerical ratings	Narratively and visually, most often through portfolios

Association for the Education of Young Children & National Association of Early Childhood Specialists in State Departments of Education, 2003; Rous & Hyson, 2007). Each of the recommended practices is described next.

Holistic Approach to Progress Monitoring

Recommended practices indicate that children's progress should be monitored holistically, meaning that teachers should understand the importance of viewing the whole child and the interdependence of all variables (e.g., all the factors that may affect progress; Copple & Bredekamp, 2009; Hojnoski & Missall, 2007; National Association for the Education of Young Children & National Association of Early Childhood Specialists in State Departments of Education, 2003; Rous & Hyson, 2007; Sandall et al., 2005). The first way to examine a child's progress holistically is to measure a child's progress qualitatively and quantitatively. The use of qualitative and quantitative measurement strategies provides a more complete picture of the child and the relative effectiveness of the instruction. Integration of both types of data informs and influences the development of an effective intervention. Qualitative data are rich descriptions of characteristics, cases, and settings (Blankenship, 1985). Quantitative data ascertain the magnitude, amount, or size of attributes, behaviors, or opinions. See Box 7.2 for an analogy of qualitative and quantitative measurement approaches to describe a farm.

In an effort to gather qualitative and quantitative information regarding children's progress, teachers should aim to examine more than the frequency of a child's progress, which tends to be quantitative in nature (e.g., the number of times that the behavior occurs), or the accuracy of a child's progress, which tends to be qualitative in nature (e.g., descriptions of how well a child performs an action). Teachers should consider qualitative attributes of frequency and quantitative attributes of accuracy, as well as the dimensions of latency (the time between a trigger and the occurrence of the behavior being monitored), duration (how long the desired and undesired behavior lasts), and endurance (how long the desired and undesired behavior is repeated). Children's progress and abilities are quite complex; thus, it is necessary to look at multiple dimensions of progress, using qualitative and quantitative measurement to understand those dimensions and make sound decisions. Teachers often use qualitative methods to assess all the children in their classroom. The qualitative method is based on observations, anecdotal notes, and family interviews, and it explores children's interests and preferences. Data collected through qualitative methods are often viewed as "richness of information" (Creswell & Plano Clark, 2007).

Consider the example of a teacher who has decided that a child in their class needs instruction toward the common outcome of participation. The teacher will need to measure how many times the child participates; whether the child's participation was appropriate, maintained, and pleasurable; and whether it resulted in positive interactions among children (Ingersoll &

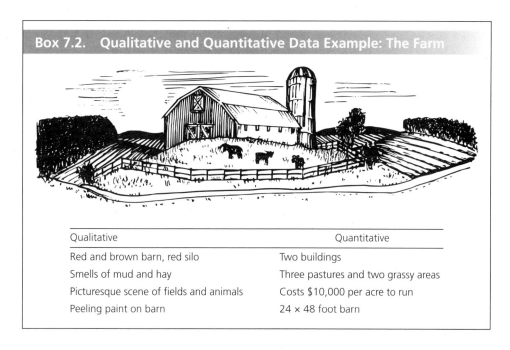

Box 7.2.   Qualitative and Quantitative Data Example: The Farm

Qualitative	Quantitative
Red and brown barn, red silo	Two buildings
Smells of mud and hay	Three pastures and two grassy areas
Picturesque scene of fields and animals	Costs $10,000 per acre to run
Peeling paint on barn	24 × 48 foot barn

Schreibman, 2006). By collecting both qualitative and quantitative information, the teacher is able to gain a complete picture of the child's progress. Both methods have utility within the early childhood setting. Table 7.2 provides several examples of the quantitative and qualitative information that is needed to understand changes in children's progress across dimensions.

When teachers monitor children's progress holistically, they also understand the importance of viewing the interdependence of all variables that may affect progress, sometimes called mediating factors (Ross et al., 1998). Mediating factors are the social and psychological conditions that moderate the effects of instructional efforts. In other words, mediating factors are integral elements that may influence or contribute to the child's overall progress. Mediating factors can include attendance, home or community situations, medications, past exposure to instruction, and even the novelty of the situation. The mediating factors directly affect the child's rate of progress. For example, if the child is absent numerous days and does not receive instruction, then monitoring the child's progress of the skills that were taught when the child missed instruction is somewhat futile. Likewise, if a child's medication has recently changed, the data collected on the child's current level of progress may not accurately depict the child's overall capability.

Another aspect of understanding progress monitoring holistically is to recognize the interdependence among development, culture, and experience (i.e., the variables form a mutual and reciprocal relationship; Creswell & Plano Clark, 2007; Darling-Hammond & Snyder, 2000). The interaction of skills from developmental domains or areas means that multiple skills may need to be addressed before a child demonstrates improvement in a single skill.

Table 7.2. Examples of quantitative and qualitative information needed to understand changes in child's performance

Dimensions of behavior	Associated quantitative statements	Associated qualitative statements
Frequency (Number of times/how often)	• Number of times a child initiates • Number of times a child manipulates • Number of times a child participates • Number of times a child is successful	• Each morning • Each afternoon • During most structured activities • On each occasion • Daily • Weekly
Accuracy (How well/how intended)	• Number/percent correct • Number of steps completed correctly • Number/percent of trials completed correctly	• Independently • Recognizably • Correctly • Quickly • Intelligibly • Functionally • Purposively • Precisely
Latency (Length of time to respond)	• Time between direction and child response • Time between cue and child response • Time between direction and child response • Time between request and child response	• Within the allotted time • Within the given time • Within a reasonable time
Duration (How long behavior lasts)	• How long a child cries • How long a child participates • How long a child plays near peers • How long a child stays on task	• Across the majority of the school day • As long as expected • As long as expected of others • Throughout supper • During the field trip • While shopping at Target
Endurance (How many times behavior is repeated)	• Takes 10 steps • Communicates for two or more exchanges • Counts 10 objects • Remains seated for 3 minutes	• With persistence or perseverance • By overcoming challenges and increased difficulty • During most of the activity or event • With concentration or attentiveness • With sensitivity to physical stimuli

For example, Travis is missing both the skill of bringing hands to midline and the skill of joint attention (Godfrey et al., 2003; Ingersoll & Schreibman, 2006). Joint attention is defined as looking at an appropriate object, person, or event during small-group activities (Bricker, 2002). Travis will need to make progress on both skills in order to attain either.

In addition to being affected by skill interrelatedness, children's development and growth are affected by culture. In the example of Travis, progress monitoring on the two skills—bringing hands to midline and joint attention—reveals that Travis is making significant progress on joint attention but minimal progress on the skill of bringing hands to midline. The teacher reviews the qualitative data from the family and discovers that the family feeds and dresses Travis, as is customary in their culture, so he has fewer opportunities to practice each skill than do other children his age, possibly contributing to a difference in Travis's progress.

Last, developmentally appropriate experiences promote children's active exploration of their world, manipulation of real objects, learning through hands-on activities, direct experiences, and exposure to contextual clues, all of which provide children with multiple opportunities to engage skills across developmental domains. Not all children may have had these experiences or any experience on a specific skill or outcome. Progress monitoring should occur across the child's experiences and consider the child's repertoire of learning in order to provide the teacher with accurate data. The recommended practice for being holistic is illustrated in a project approach for a group of children in Case Example 7.1.

Case Example 7.1. Holistic Progress
Monitoring Within a Project-Based Approach

S. Wolf is a teacher in a blended preschool classroom that incorporates the project approach to plan, employ, and evaluate instruction. At the beginning of the year, S. Wolf assessed all the children in their classroom through quantitative methods regarding performance on specific skills. To do this, they completed the Get It Got It Go! and the Early Language and Literacy Classroom Observation. They qualitatively assessed all the children in the classroom through observations, anecdotal notes, family interviews, and an exploration of children's interests and preferences. S. Wolf determined the needs of each child in the classroom relative to specific skills and outcomes.

They then set up a bird feeder in an isolated spot on the playground. The children observed the bird feeder and the birds that visited it. Capitalizing on the children's interest in the birds and the bird feeder, S. Wolf prepared a project involving birds and bird feeders. They determined that the project integrated multiple content area outcomes, such as reading and math. They narrowed their focus within the content areas to address the outcomes of comprehension and counting. In the classroom, S. Wolf serves as a researcher and as a resource to children, providing guidance, information, and materials while stimulating independent thinking.

In order to assess the children's performance, S. Wolf sent home a questionnaire to the family to help inform the current children's knowledge and to continually inform regarding mediating factors that might moderate the effects of instructional efforts. Concurrently, S. Wolf assessed the children to determine which topics were locally relevant and valued by them, by developing a web with the children. S. Wolf also considered the culture of the community and the children (e.g., do the children live in homes with windows through which they can see birds, do they have bird feeders at home, do they live mainly on farms and view birds from a different perspective as a source of food?). S. Wolf's next step was to implement multiple activities throughout the classroom focused around the topics from the web and the chosen outcomes.

During the project, S. Wolf continued to use the recommended practices to track how and why the children were performing or not performing toward the outcomes of comprehension and counting (e.g., if a child is not performing toward an outcome, is it because the child has been absent, because medication has changed, or because the instruction has no relevance to the child?) by discussing, expanding, and/or narrowing the web with the children. S. Wolf also continually analyzed and interpreted artifacts, experiences, discussions, and interviews with the children and the family to revise their instruction.

S. Wolf continued to consider the children's interest and involvement to revise instruction. The children continued to choose from a variety of activities provided. S. Wolf capitalized on children's proficiencies as they considered their families' influence and the families' climate for learning. For example, they considered whether the family was providing additional instruction and whether there were any families that could share their knowledge of birds. When S. Wolf selected outcomes for the project, they knew to be aware that the children were the experts and that the mediating factors continued to influence the direction, activities, and outcomes of the bird project. The web they had created with the class demonstrated the way in which outcomes in different domains connect to one another. S. Wolf continued to monitor the progress of the children and revised instruction as necessary by observing the children, taking anecdotal notes, conducting family interviews, and taking into account children's preferences and interests, as well as summarizing, analyzing, and interpreting the children's pictures, narratives, bulletin boards, panel boards, and webs.

Progress Monitoring Decision Making

The second recommended practice is that progress monitoring should be data-driven. Chapter 5 provides more explicit information on the five-step process of gathering information, documenting, summarizing, analyzing, and interpreting. These steps are particularly critical with regard to progress monitoring. Unless teachers engage in decision making to carry out progress monitoring tasks, how will they make decisions regarding when and how to revise instruction? How will their instructional efforts be informed? How will a teacher know whether a child is responding to instructional efforts and when and how to change their approach? Chapter 5 described the five-step process to determine initial instruction that would meet individual and groups of children's needs. For progress monitoring, the process remains the same; however, the purpose is to revisit initial decisions and systematically modify teaching practices to ensure that all children are progressing toward identified outcomes. See Case Example 7.2 for an illustration of the decision-making model in action for monitoring a child's progress.

Case Example 7.2. Progress Monitoring
Decision Making in Action: The Case Study of Mikey

Mikey is a 4-year, 3-month-old boy enrolled in a blended preschool program. Results from a CBA, family interviews, and team conversations suggested that there was concern regarding Mikey's ability to hold or steady an object with one hand while manipulating an object with the other hand. For example, he had trouble holding a bowl and feeding himself with a spoon and opening containers such as his milk carton, and he tended to avoid activities such as putting puzzles together and making jewelry. The ability to hold or steady an object with one hand while manipulating an object with the other hand is a prerequisite for Mikey to later create and represent ideas and concepts, play with toys cooperatively, and engage in more advanced fine motor activities such as writing, cutting, and zipping up a coat. Thus, Mikey's need was labeled an individualized need requiring intentional, intensive, individualized instruction within and across daily activities and experiences. This case example describes how Mikey's teacher went through the five-step decision-making process to 1) determine a starting place for instruction, 2) track Mikey's subsequent response to instruction, and 3) revise instruction as needed.

Step 1: Gathering Information

The teacher and classroom assistant observed Mikey during a variety of daily activities to see when he was able to perform the desired action or behavior (holding or steadying an object with one hand while manipulating an object with another). For example, the teacher and assistant watched to see whether Mikey could pour juice into a cup, hold a book and turn the pages, zip a coat's zipper, cut a piece of paper in half, hold a pot and stir, or hold a nail and hammer.

Step 2: Documentation

The teacher and classroom assistant created a simple data collection system of counts and tallies to document how often and where Mikey held or steadied an object with one hand while manipulating an object with the other hand. To minimize the time they spent writing, they created a checklist of possible ways that Mikey could demonstrate the behavior. They walked around the room and made a comprehensive list of the different ways that Mikey could hold or steady an object with one hand while manipulating an object with the other hand by considering the opportunities at each classroom center and during the daily routine. (See Figure 7.1 for a copy of their data collection sheet.) The form also allowed them to indicate other examples when he demonstrated the desired behavior and to indicate the setting or activity where the desired behavior was observed. The teacher and classroom assistant merely marked whether they saw Mikey do any of the behaviors that were listed.

Step 3: Summarization

At the end of each day, the teacher and classroom assistant summarized Mikey's progress numerically by totaling the number of times he held an object with one hand and manipulated an object with the other hand. The total number for each day was then summarized visually by plotting the total number on a graph. Figure 7.2 illustrates Mikey's progress during baseline (i.e., his progress before more intensive and intentional instruction was provided). The period of time when data are collected and specific or desired instruction is not provided is referred to as baseline, and otherwise thought of as where a child started.

Examples of target behavior (holding or steadying an object with one hand while manipulating an object with the other)	Tally each time target behavior is observed	Setting/Activity
Hold backpack and unzip		
Hold paper and scribble		
Hold puzzle steady and place pieces		
Hold a book and turn the page		
Hold container (e.g., playdough) and remove lid		
Hold a cup and pour liquid		
Hold a bowl/container and use spoon		
Hold a container and stir		
Hold paper and tear		
Hold paper and peel a sticker		
Hold paper and crease		
Hold a lace and string beads onto it		
Hold workbench and use hammer		
Hold a block while stacking another one on top		
Hold pop-up toy and press button		
Hold bowl and scoop snack		
Hold bucket and scoop sand		
Other: _____		

Narrative Comments:

Mikey responds more often and with more success with increased prompts and continuous positive reinforcement.

Figure 7.1.   Documentation sheet for Mikey's desired behaviors.

Step 4: Analysis

Mikey's teacher reviewed the daily visual summaries at the end of the week, looking for patterns and trends related to Mikey's progress. At the end of a week of taking baseline data, the teacher was able to determine that Mikey demonstrated the ability to hold an object with one hand and manipulate an object with the other hand only three times during five consecutive days of data collection. The teacher concluded that Mikey's predictable response (i.e., patterned response) was either to avoid touching or manipulating

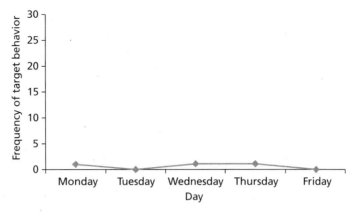

Figure 7.2. Mikey's baseline performance.

objects and toys or to try once and give up. The teacher also concluded that the trend (i.e., the way the direction of his performance was going) was relatively flat (i.e., it was not going up or down). The data showed little variability in the number of times that Mikey exhibited holding or steadying an object with one hand while manipulating an object with another over the 5 days. To better direct instruction, the teacher went back to the data collection sheets to review which activities Mikey was participating in when performing the behavior and noted that all three times were during sand play.

Step 5: Interpretation

Using the analysis of the data, Mikey's teacher was able to make decisions concerning how to better address Mikey's needs. The teacher chose to embed frequent learning opportunities across daily routines and activities, particularly during sand play. The embedded learning opportunities matched Mikey's interests and preferences and increased the chance for participation in the activities and demonstrated the individualized outcomes, referred to throughout the case example as the desired behavior.

First Week: Instruction

As the individualized, intensive, and intentional instruction was provided, the teacher and classroom assistant continued to gather information about Mikey and document progress using the checklist in Figure 7.1 At the end of each week, they numerically summarized Mikey's performance by totaling the number of times Mikey held or steadied an object with one hand while manipulating an object with the other. Then they summarized the total number for each day visually by plotting that number on a graph as they had done during baseline. Figure 7.3 provides a visual summary of the data that were collected during the first week of instruction.

As the teachers had done for the data collected during the baseline week, they analyzed the data summaries and looked for patterns and trends related to Mikey's progress. The teacher asked the following questions as a guide during the analysis: Is Mikey exhibiting the same desired behavior or lack of the same desired behavior across multiple settings? Is the intervention affecting the desired behavior? When, why, and how is the intervention changing Mikey's progress? The teacher expected, given the

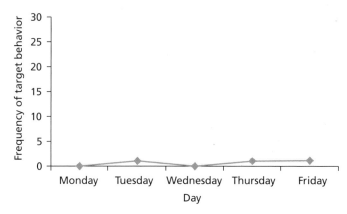

Figure 7.3. First week of systemic instruction.

*more intensive instructional efforts, that there would be a change in Mikey's progress;
however, there were no changes during the first week of instruction (i.e., there wasn't
a change in the pattern, trend, or variability of the desired behavior compared with
baseline). In other words, Mikey continued to rarely demonstrate the desired behavior
and to exhibit it in only one setting, the sandbox. From the data, the teacher interpreted
that additional learning opportunities were needed and that they needed to consistently
prompt and give feedback to Mikey during a variety of other situations. Therefore,
the teacher revised the intervention plan to include specific ways to prompt Mikey to
engage in the desired behavior. For example, the intervention plan included phrases
that teachers could say or things that teachers could do during activities to prompt
Mikey (e.g., help him hold an object while acting on another, model how they held one
object and acted on another, direct Mikey to demonstrate the desired behavior). The
teacher also determined ways for classroom staff to consistently respond to Mikey
depending on whether or not the desired behavior was demonstrated. Staff responses
would include providing Mikey with positive feedback (e.g., smiles, high fives, clap-
ping) when the desired behavior was demonstrated and increased adult support when
it was not.*

Week 2: Instruction Revised

*Because progress monitoring is a continuous process, the teacher and classroom assis-
tant continued to provide intentional and individualized instruction. At the end of
each week, they summarized Mikey's progress. Figure 7.4 provides a visual summary
of the data that were collected during the second week of intervention, following the
implementation of the revised instruction plan.*

*Again, Mikey's teacher considered the guiding questions and looked for pat-
terns and trends. Furthermore, the teacher considered whether there was a change
in the level of his progress during the second week, which might indicate that Mikey
was engaging in the behavior more often and how quickly that change occurred.
By the second week, Mikey began to predictably demonstrate the behavior multiple
times a day and during more than one activity (i.e., now during housekeeping and
sand play). Week 2 data also showed an upward trend in terms of the frequency with*

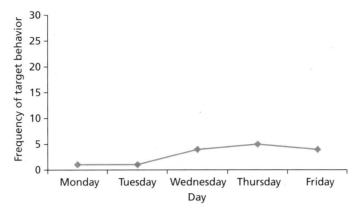

Figure 7.4. Second week of systemic instruction.

which he demonstrated the desired behavior. The visual summary also showed that the level increased rather quickly and consistently compared with the level in the first week.

On the basis of the teacher's analysis of the data, it was interpreted that they should continue with the revised intervention plan because Mikey appeared to be responding to the instruction. The teacher made sure to focus on encouraging Mikey to engage in many activities that would require and increase his generalization and use of the desired behavior.

The five-step process continued for 2 more weeks of instruction. Figure 7.5 shows a visual summary of the data collected during the third and fourth weeks. Because the teacher wanted Mikey to generalize the desired behavior (i.e., use it consistently across activities), they reviewed the checklists to see whether any new patterns emerged in terms of where the desired behavior was being used. The teacher discovered that Mikey was consistently demonstrating the desired behavior across many settings and in a variety of activities. These settings and activities included snack time (pouring and using a spoon), art center (scribbling, tearing, opening the glue stick), and construction

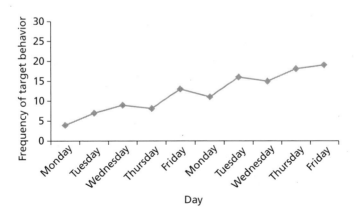

Figure 7.5. Third and fourth weeks of intentional, intense, individualized instruction.

(building with blocks and using a workbench). In reviewing the data, Mikey's teacher was also able to see a continued upward trend, meaning that Mikey engaged in the desired behavior with increasing frequency. When the teacher compared the summary from week two with those of weeks three and four, Mikey's teacher saw that the level continued to increase and that there was little variability in performance from day to day.

Maintenance

On the basis of the analysis of 4 weeks of data, Mikey's teacher decided that the intervention plan continued to be effective. Because Mikey was demonstrating the desired behavior across multiple settings and activities, the teacher decided to reduce the intensity of the instruction. The teacher also decided to continue to provide many opportunities for Mikey to practice the desired behavior throughout the day; however, the staff did reduce the number of specific prompts and consequences provided. Mikey's teacher also decided to collect data by means of weekly probes of the behavior. Thus, 1 day per week the teacher gathered information about Mikey across activities and documented his use of the desired behavior in the absence of specific prompts and consequences (i.e., they repeated the five-step process for 4 more weeks). Figure 7.6 shows a visual summary of the data collected over 4 weeks of maintenance.

On the basis of these data, Mikey's teacher saw continued demonstration of the desired behavior, and a review of the checklists revealed that Mikey continued to demonstrate the desired behavior across multiple settings and activities. In all, the maintenance data continued to show an upward trend, meaning that Mikey was continuing to increase use of the desired behavior. On the basis of the analysis, Mikey's teacher decided that they had sufficient data to conclude that Mikey had accomplished the desired behavior. Thus, it was time for the teacher to reevaluate Mikey's overall performance across common outcomes on the CBA and determine what skill or concept would be the next considering developmental readiness and the need to engage and participate during daily activities.

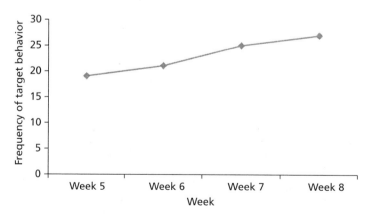

Figure 7.6. Maintenance data. Mikey's overall performance across common outcomes determined what skill or concept he needed to learn next considering his developmental readiness and need to engage and participate during daily activities.

TIERED MODEL OF PROGRESS MONITORING

A tiered model of progress monitoring provides a framework for making revisions to instruction and matches instructional efforts to children's needs. In other words, just as tiered levels of instruction were matched to identified needs, tiered progress monitoring efforts match the frequency, intensity, and intent of efforts to the level of need and instruction. For example, if the needs of a child on a particular skill are determined to be targeted outcomes, then progress monitoring efforts should align and be at the frequency and intensity depicted in the middle tier of Figure 7.7, which illustrates a tiered model of progress monitoring.

Within Tier 1 of the model, all children's progress toward common outcomes are monitored. As defined earlier, common outcomes are the standards and milestones that all children are expected to achieve, regardless of ability, at a given age. Teachers monitor children's progress toward standards and developmentally appropriate milestones at least once a year, preferably (given the variability of development during the early years) three or four times a year. Tier 1 progress monitoring can include a re-administration of an authentic and comprehensive assessment for all children (i.e., re-administration of a CBA). Systematic monitoring of children's Tier 1 progress informs teachers whether children's needs have continued to develop as expected and whether they require a change in the frequency and intensity of instruction and/or the skills identified for additional instruction.

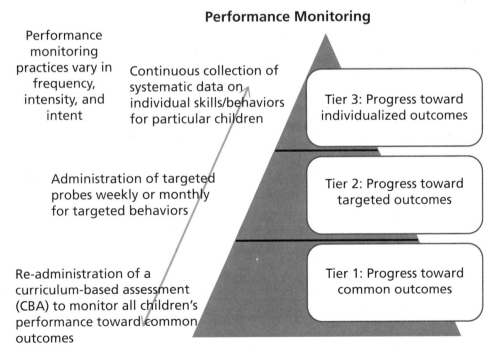

Performance Monitoring

Performance monitoring practices vary in frequency, intensity, and intent

Continuous collection of systematic data on individual skills/behaviors for particular children

Administration of targeted probes weekly or monthly for targeted behaviors

Re-administration of a curriculum-based assessment (CBA) to monitor all children's performance toward common outcomes

Tier 3: Progress toward individualized outcomes

Tier 2: Progress toward targeted outcomes

Tier 1: Progress toward common outcomes

Figure 7.7.   Depiction of progress monitoring as a tiered model.

For example, Yashika readministers a CBA to all children halfway through the year and summarizes and analyzes the information she collects. Then she uses the information from the second administration of the CBA to determine whether any of the children who were previously determined to have a Tier 1 need now require a different level of instruction, given any of the mediating factors that were discussed earlier. For example, after interpreting Danny's information, Yashika noticed that Danny fell below the cutoff score for the gross motor area of development provided in the CBA administered. Back in October, Danny's gross motor skills were on track; however, after Danny had surgery to repair a tendon in his foot, he was unable to receive the universal instruction (i.e., missed several weeks of preschool). Now Danny's needs in gross motor development may require more focused instruction for a temporary length of time while his foot is recovering.

Tier 2 progress monitoring consists of more frequent efforts and is not conducted on all skills for all children. In other words, teachers gather information on select groups of children who may have similar needs related to a component of a common outcome, may be challenged to express themselves verbally or nonverbally as expected for their age, or may have a skill that has stalled and needs a boost of instruction to become more sophisticated and/or reach the expected level. Teachers may collect weekly or monthly data (i.e., administer select probes) to better track how children are responding to focused instructional efforts. In Danny's situation, for example, Yashika may determine a plan for focused instruction to improve Danny's range of motion for his foot and ankle based on recommendations from his physical therapist. She may design activities where Danny has the opportunity to kick a ball back and forth with a peer daily and then perform weekly assessments of Danny's progress, measuring the frequency and duration that he can kick the ball back and forth with a peer. Each week after gathering and documenting the information, Yashika summarizes, analyzes, and interprets the data. On the basis of the five-step decision-making process, she may come to realize that Danny has increased the frequency (the number of times he kicks the ball back and forth) as well as the duration (how long he is able to continue kicking the ball back and forth). By the end of the third week, Yashika may conclude that Danny no longer needs focused instruction, and she and the physical therapist return Danny to universal instruction and monitoring around gross motor development.

Tier 3 progress monitoring consists of continuous collection of systematic data on individualized outcomes for particular children. (Refer to Figure 7.5.) In other words, at Tier 3 teachers gather data for individual children who are missing foundational or prerequisite skills that are deemed necessary for the children to make progress toward a common goal or outcome. At Tier 3, teachers may collect minute-by-minute, hour-by-hour, or daily counts and tallies, written narratives, and/or permanent products that are related to individualized skills. On the basis of the five-step decision-making process, Yashika may keep a tally sheet that records each time the correct or incorrect response occurred, then monitor Danny's progress on the skill every hour to inform instruction. At the end of the day, she may summarize, analyze, and interpret the data to determine whether Danny is performing the individualized skill as expected (i.e., whether he is showing an immediacy of change and a positive trend line and/or pattern) or whether the instruction needs to be modified and, if so, how (i.e., through examination of antecedent, behavior, and consequence). Tier 3 progress monitoring is designed and employed to supplement, enhance, and support systematic instruction. Tier 3 progress monitoring on the same skill is intentionally revisited and modified on the basis of the present level of functioning. Closely monitoring progress allows teachers to revise instruction routinely to ensure that the child is reaching their maximum potential.

SHARING PROGRESS MONITORING INFORMATION

A logical step after decisions are made regarding children's progress may be to report the changes (good, bad, or otherwise) to other team members, including families. However, family members and other team members should be involved throughout the progress monitoring process, thus making an additional step of reporting to others unnecessary. There are times however, when teachers are expected to share progress monitoring information, such as during parent–teacher conferences, transition meetings, and IEP meetings. The next section provides suggestions and strategies for sharing progress monitoring information.

Communicating With Families

As was noted in Chapter 3, teachers can employ a number of specific strategies to involve family members as partners in their children's education and to enhance communication with families (Woods & McCormick, 2002). Table 7.3 provides communication strategies that may be useful to teachers when they discuss progress monitoring information with families. The overarching suggestion is to ensure that communication is bidirectional, meaning that teachers should avoid a one-way reporting of information to families and should strive to have a conversation during which both parties share information, concerns, and ideas. Despite their best efforts to communicate effectively, teachers often express their concern about how to talk to families regarding a child who isn't making desired progress, how to deliver news about a child's lack of progress in development, and how to discuss challenging behaviors that are seen in the classroom. When families are involved throughout the processes of program planning, instruction, and progress monitoring, the conversations about difficult topics become less like meetings in which teachers are telling families something and more like a partnership in which each partner jointly recognizes when there may be reason for concern. Thus, sharing progress monitoring information should not be a point-in-time event, but rather a continuous effort (Wolrey, 2004).

Teachers also express concern and frustration when they feel that their attempts to share information with families have been made to no avail.

Table 7.3. Useful communication strategies for discussing a child's performance with families

Strategies	Teacher actions
Active listening	• Allow for wait time (i.e., allow for time in between comments, questions, suggestions) • Be willing to listen to the family's concerns/questions/suggestions and preferences • Demonstrate active listening through nonverbal communication (e.g., nodding head, eye contact) • Engage in reflective listening skills (i.e., repeat what was heard) to affirm understanding • Use verbal and nonverbal communication (i.e., lean forward and show interest, mirror the other person's body language)
Acknowledgment	• Share relevant and pertinent data from the family • Recognize family's priorities and opinions through verbal and nonverbal means • Allow for differences in opinions • Mention child's strengths
Collaborate	• Seek alternative solutions aimed to meet the needs of families • Engage in a two-way process of information sharing and understanding (i.e., cultural reciprocity) • Adapt professional recommendations to the value system of the family • Aim for consensus versus total agreement
Participation	• Actively participate in conversations, minimize distractions • Respond in a timely manner • Promote a positive atmosphere (welcome, reduce silence) • Allow families to access data (qualitative and quantitative data)
Respect	• Allow for differences in opinions • Seek alternative solutions that meet the needs of families • Realize the family is the first teacher • Allow families to complete thoughts and sentences before responding • Minimize use of jargon
Sharing	• Maximize opportunities to use or enjoy something jointly with others • Communicate strengths of child and family • Keep information confidential • Share information in a variety of ways (i.e., in person, e-mails, notes, text, websites)

For example, a teacher may write notes home using a communication notebook, but family members never write back, leading the teacher to assume that the notebook has never been opened. Before becoming frustrated, teachers need to consider several factors. First, has the teacher discussed with families the intent of the communication notebook? In other words, do families know what to expect from the teacher and what the teacher expects in return? Second, has the teacher considered literacy and language as possible barriers to a family member's access and participation in communicating through a written format? Third, has the teacher talked to the family about their preferences in terms of mode and frequency of sharing information? In other words, some families may enjoy communicating back and forth on a daily or weekly basis; others may appreciate a less interactive mode such as a monthly newsletter, an updated website, or more personal, but less frequent, phone calls; whereas still others may want frequent, informal modes of communication such as texting, tweeting, and e-mailing.

Keeping the proper perspective on the interaction can make it easier for teachers to share difficult or sensitive information. For example, if a teacher has evidence that a child's development is delayed and that the child needs further testing or perhaps special services, the teacher may fear that the family will not agree or may become upset at hearing the news. Keep in mind that it is not the teacher's job to convince a family how it should feel or what it should think, or to keep family members from hearing objective concerns. It is the teacher's job, as a developmental specialist, to share all information as objectively and mean-ingfully as possible and then engage in a discussion with the family about what the information may mean, what the next steps might be, and how the family feels about the information. Sometimes families will need time to process the information or need to hear it again or in a different way, and they need to know that they can ask questions and express their own concerns. Thus, the key to any difficult situation is to ensure that there is a relationship of trust and open communication already in place.

How and When to Share Progress Monitoring Information

When teachers share progress monitoring information with families, as dis-cussed in Chapter 5 with regard to summarizing, it is best for them to use a mixture of methods to convey children's strengths, emerging skills, and areas of continued need. For example, matching a picture with a few written notes or a graph with percentages may have more meaning than a picture, a note, a graph, or a percentage standing alone. Mixing and matching methods also ensure that the information is being conveyed through multiple means of rep-resentation. In other words, teachers should document progress data by vary-ing portrayals of the child's current level of progress. Documenting data in a mixed manner helps teachers to prepare and articulate their findings to others.

Furthermore, as is the case with needs and instruction, progress moni-toring reporting efforts should be tiered (i.e., the frequency and intensity of sharing should be tiered). For example, Tier 1 progress toward common out-comes may be shared with all children's families two, three, or four times a year. Tier 2 progress monitoring information on targeted skills may be shared only with the families of select groups of children each month. Last, Tier 3 progress monitoring information may be shared with individual families on a weekly basis. Again, like other aspects of a tiered model, the frequency and intensity (meaning the amount of effort that is put forth) vary, given the tier of progress monitoring. Teachers should avoid a one-size-fits-all approach such as doing a comprehensive, detailed report on each individual child regarding all skills and abilities (Schwartz & Olswang, 1996). When common outcomes are being addressed through universal instruction, broad samples of a child's progress are sufficient.

Regardless of the format or frequency of sharing information, most teach-ers will be faced at one point or another with the task of creating a report card

---

Box 7.3.   Suggestions for Developing Report Cards Within Blended Programs

1. Create report cards that contain information regarding children's progress on Tier 1 outcomes. For example, children's progress as measured by and summarized using a comprehensive curriculum-based assessment.

2. Organize Tier 1 outcomes into manageable parts of developmental domains and content areas (i.e., create classifications or strands that represent behaviors from a broad domain/content area, but not all the specific skills). For example, Tier 1 outcome reports should include what is expected of all children regarding participation, counting, classifying, one-to-one correspondence, and engaging in cooperative activities.

3. Include qualitative and quantitative data regarding children's progress toward common outcomes. For example, information on how the child has increased the number of activities they participate in and the types of activities (e.g., small group, large group, those with movement and music, those requiring manipulation of small objects) in which the child consistently participates within the classroom.

4. Include information as needed for subgroups or individual children regarding progress toward Tier 2 and Tier 3 target behavior. For example, include narrative, numerical, and/or visual summaries of a child's progress toward targeted or individualized behaviors such as the degree to which they are understood by others; the extent to which they have gained prerequisite or foundational skills that will increase their access, participation, and progress toward common outcomes; and/or how they have responded to instruction regarding a missing component of a common outcome.

---

and sharing a child's progress with families. Unfortunately, report cards are a feature of push-down policies that may work in a K-12 environment but that are not very helpful in blended early childhood classrooms (Cavallaro & Haney, 1999; Schwartz & Olswang 1996). Given that young children who are served in blended classrooms have diverse abilities and that all children will have tiered needs, the idea of reporting progress data for all children across levels can be an overwhelming task. Box 7.3 includes suggestions for developing report cards within blended programs.

SUMMARY

The purpose of Chapter 7 was to describe recommended practices for progress monitoring for individuals and groups of children. First, the chapter defined and discussed assessment for the purpose of revising instruction (i.e., for progress monitoring). Second, information was provided on two broad rec-ommended practices for progress monitoring—a holistic approach and a data-driven process—and the recommendations were illustrated. Next, a tiered model of progress monitoring was shared as a means of addressing the challenges of systematically collecting data for children who are served in blended classrooms. Multiple case examples exemplified how to engage in the tiered model. Last, suggestions and strategies for sharing progress monitoring reports were discussed.

REFERENCES

Blankenship, C. S. (1985). Using curriculum-based assessment data to make instructional decisions. *Exceptional Children, 52,* 233–238.

Branscombe, N. A., Castle, K., Dorsey, A. G., Surbeck, E., & Taylor, J. B. (2003). *Early childhood curriculum: A constructivist perspective.* Houghton Mifflin.

Bricker, D. (2002). *Assessment, Evaluation, and Programming System for Infants and Children (AEPS®), Second Edition.* Paul H. Brookes Publishing Co.

Brinton, B., & Fujiki, M. (2003). Blending qualitative and quantitative methods in language research and intervention. *American Journal of Speech–Language Pathology, 12,* 165–171.

Cavallaro, C. C., & Haney, M. (1999). *Preschool inclusion.* Paul H. Brookes Publishing Co.

Creswell, J. W., & Plano Clark, V. L. (2007). *Designing and conducting mixed methods research.* Sage Publications.

Copple, C., & Bredekamp, S. (Eds.). (2009). *Developmentally appropriate practice in early childhood programs serving children from birth through age 8* (3rd ed.). National Association for the Education of Young Children.

Darling-Hammond, L., & Snyder, J. (2000). Authentic assessment of teaching in context. *Teaching and Teacher Education, 16*(5), 523–545.

Division for Early Childhood (DEC). (2014). *DEC recommended practices in early intervention/ early childhood special education 2014.* http://www.dec-sped.org/recommendedpractices

Division for Early Childhood of the Council for Exceptional Children, National Association for the Education of Young Children, and National Head Start Association. (2013). *Frameworks for response to intervention in early childhood: Description and implications.* DEC.

Eikeseth, S., Smith, T., Jahr, E., & Eldevik, S. (2002). Intensive behavioral treatment at school for 4- to 7-year old children with autism: A 1-year comparison controlled study. *Behavior Modification, 26*(1), 49–68.

Fraser, S., & Gestwicki, C. (2000). *Authentic childhood in the classroom.* Nelson.

Fuchs, L. S., & Fuchs, D. (1986). Effects of systematic formative evaluation: A meta-analysis. *Exceptional Children, 53,* 199–208.

Fuchs, L. S., & Fuchs, D. (1999). Monitoring student progress toward the development of reading competence: A review of three forms of classroom-based assessment. *School Psychology Review, 28*(4), 659–671.

Gestwicki, C. (1999). *Developmentally appropriate practice: Curriculum development in early education* (2nd ed.). Delmar.

Godfrey, S. A., Grisham-Brown, J., Schuster, J. W., & Hemmeter, M. L. (2003). The effects of three techniques on student participation with preschool children with attending problems. *Education and Treatment of Children, 26*(3), 255–272.

Grisham-Brown, J., Hallam, R., & Pretti-Frontczak, K. (2008). Preparing Head Start personnel to use a curriculum-based assessment: An innovative practice in the "age of accountability." *Journal of Early Intervention, 30*(4), 271–281.

Grisham-Brown, J., Hemmeter, M. L., & Pretti-Frontczak, K. (2005). *Blended practices for teaching young children in inclusive settings.* Paul H. Brookes Publishing Co.

Heroman, C., Burts, D. C., Berke, K., Bickart, T. (2010). *Teaching Strategies GOLD objectives for development and learning: Birth through kindergarten.* Teaching Strategies.

HighScope Educational Research Foundation. (2002). Development and validation. In *User Guide: HighScope Child Observation Record for Infants and Toddlers* (pp. 31–36). HighScope Press.

HighScope Educational Research Foundation. (2003). Preschool COR development and validation. In *User Guide: HighScope Preschool Child Observation Record* (pp. 29–31). HighScope Press.

HighScope Educational Research Foundation. (2013). *COR Advantage.* http://kaymbu.com/assessment

Hojnoski, R. L., Gischlar, K. L., & Missall, K. N. (2009a). Improving child outcomes with data-based decision making: Collecting data. *Young Exceptional Children, 12,* 32–44.

Hojnoski, R. L., Gischlar, K. L., & Missall, K. N. (2009b). Improving child outcomes with data-based decision making: Graphing data. *Young Exceptional Children, 12,* 15–30.

Hojnoski, R. L., Gischlar, K. L., & Missall, K. N. (2009c). Improving child outcomes with data-based decision making: Interpreting and using data. *Young Exceptional Children, 13,* 2–18.

Hojnoski, R. L., & Missall, K. N. (2007). Monitoring preschoolers' language and early literacy growth and development. *Young Exceptional Children, 10,* 17–27.

Ingersoll, B., & Schreibman, L. (2006). Teaching reciprocal imitation skills to young children with autism using a naturalistic behavioral approach: Effects on language, pretend play, and joint attention. *Journal of Autism and Developmental Disorders, 36*(4), 487–505.

Jackson, P. (1968). *Life in classrooms.* Holt, Rinehart, & Winston.

Katz, L., & Chard, S. C. (2000). *Engaging children's minds: The project approach* (2nd ed.). Ablex Publishing.

Kearney, A. J. (2008). *Understanding applied behavior analysis: An introduction to ABA for parents, teachers, and other professionals.* Jessica Kingsley Publishers.

Klingner, J. K., Sorrells, A. M., & Barrera, M. (2007). Three-tiered models with culturally and linguistically diverse students. In D. Haager, S. Vaughn, & J. Klingner (Eds.), *Validated practices for three tiers of reading intervention.* Paul H. Brookes Publishing Co.

Lovaas, O. I. (1987). Behavioral treatment and normal educational and intellectual functioning in young autistic children. *Journal of Consulting and Clinical Psychology, 55,* 3–9.

Macy, M. (2007). Theory and theory-driven practices of activity-based intervention. *Journal of Early & Intensive Behavior Intervention, 4*(3), 561–585.

McAfee, O., & Leong, D. (2002). *Assessing and guiding young children's development and learning.* Allyn & Bacon.

McConnell, S. (2000). Assessment in early intervention and early childhood education: Building on the past to project the future. *Topics in Early Childhood Education, 20*(1), 43–48.

McLean, M., Wolery, M., & Bailey, D. B. (2004). *Assessing infants and preschoolers with special needs* (3rd ed.). Prentice Hall.

Montessori, M. M. Jr. (1976). *Education for human development: Understanding Montessori.* Schocken Books.

National Association for the Education of Young Children & National Association of Early Childhood Specialists in State Departments of Education. (2003). *Early childhood curriculum, assessment, and program evaluation building an effective, accountable system in programs for children birth through age 8.* http://www.naeyc.org/files/naeyc/file/positions/CAPEexpand.pdf

Pretti-Frontczak, K., & Bricker, D. (2004). *An activity-based approach to early intervention* (3rd ed.). Paul H. Brookes Publishing Co.

Raver, S. (2003). Keeping track: Using routine-based instruction and monitoring. *Young Exceptional Children, 6*(3), 12–20.

Ross, D., Roberts, P., & Scott, K. (1998). *Mediating factors in child development outcomes: Children in lone-parent families.* Applied Research Branch, Human Resources Development Canada.

Rous, B., & Hyson, M. (Eds.). (2007). *Promoting positive outcomes for children with disabilities: Recommendations for curriculum, assessment and program evaluation.* Division for Early Childhood of the Council for Exceptional Children. https://www.decdocs.org/position-statement-promoting-positi

Sandall, S., Hemmeter, M. L., Smith, B., & McLean, M. (2005). *DEC recommended practices: A comprehensive guide for practical application.* Sopris West.

Sandall, S., & Schwartz, I. (2002). *Building blocks for teaching preschoolers with special needs.* Paul H. Brookes Publishing Co.

Schwartz, I. S., & Olswang, L. B. (1996). Evaluating child behavior change in natural settings: Exploring alternative strategies for data collection. *Topics in Early Childhood Special Education, 16*(1), 82–101.

Wolrey, M. (2004). Monitoring child progress. In M. McLean, M. Wolrey, & D. B. Bailey (Eds.), *Assessing infants and preschoolers with special needs* (3rd ed., pp. 545–584). Prentice Hall.

Woods, J. J., & McCormick, K. M. (2002). Toward an integration of child and family-centered practices in the assessment of preschool children: Welcoming the family. *Young Exceptional Children, 5*(3), 2–11.

Ysseldyke, J., & Tardrew, S. (2007). Use of a progress monitoring system to enable teachers to differentiate mathematics instruction. *Journal of Applied School Psychology, 24*(1), 1–28.

Ysseldyke, J. E., Thurlow, M. L, & Christenson, S. L. (1987). *Teacher effectiveness and teacher decision-making: Implications for effective instruction of handicapped students* [Monograph No. 5]. Instructional Alternatives Project, University of Minnesota.

CHAPTER 8

Recommended Practices in Identifying Children for Special Services

Kristie Pretti-Frontczak and Jennifer Grisham

*Marcus is the lead teacher in a preschool classroom at the Hope for Tomorrow
Learning Center. There are 19 children in the all-day program. Three of the children
in the program have diagnosed disabilities. He receives assistance from the local school
district to support the children with disabilities. Marcus has grown concerned about
Edwin, a 4-year-old in the class. Edwin lives with his maternal grandmother, who has
asked Marcus to keep an eye on Edwin because she is concerned about her grandson's
development. When Edwin was enrolled, Marcus noticed that he talked very little
to other children or to the teachers. When he talked, Edwin's speech was sometimes
difficult to understand, resulting in the other children struggling to interact with him.
Lately, Edwin is becoming very frustrated when he cannot get others to understand
him. As a result, he has started throwing materials and screaming when he wants
something.*

*Marcus suspects that Edwin may have speech delays and is concerned that if
not addressed quickly, he will begin to develop serious behavior problems. He plans to
meet with Edwin's grandmother and work alongside her to follow up on both of their
concerns. Although Marcus has children with diagnosed disabilities in his classroom,
he has never been involved at the beginning of the special education process and does
not know what he needs to do to get the ball rolling so that Edwin can get evaluated
and receive services if he needs them.*

The scenario described in the vignette is one that commonly occurs in early
childhood programs. After children have attended a preschool program for
a certain length of time, classroom staff begin to develop concerns regarding
some children who do not have diagnosed disabilities and begin to suspect
that there are potential developmental problems. Such situations require that
teachers understand how to work within the system to provide the support and
services children need and/or may qualify for.

Identifying children for services is a multistep process designed to limit
over identification or underidentification for special education services, particularly for children from marginalized and oppressed groups. This is because
of the possible negative impact on a child once they are identified as having a
disability. For example:

> In schools with reported use of restraint or seclusion at least 10 times, students with
> disabilities were 200% more likely to be subject to restraint or seclusion relative
> to their peers; students attending elementary schools were more likely to receive
> restraint or seclusion than students attending secondary schools. Similarly, Black
> students were almost 200% more likely and Hispanic students were 45% more likely
> to experience a restraint or seclusion than their White counterparts. (Katsiyannis
> et al., 2020, abstract).

Given numbers like these, it is essential that the steps be taken to accurately
1) locate children who may have developmental delays, 2) screen children who
may have developmental delays to determine whether there is reason for concern, and 3) validate the existence of a developmental delay before making
decisions and assigning labels that have significant consequences for children.

Teachers like Marcus must understand recommended Child Find, screening, and eligibility evaluation processes and their role in ensuring that children get special services if they need them.

The Individuals with Disabilities Improvement Education Act of 2004 (IDEA 2004; PL 108-446) is the legislation that provides federal funding for special education services for children with disabilities from birth to age 21. In addition, IDEA provides federal regulations about how services can be delivered, who can receive services, and who can deliver services. IDEA includes three major components that will be discussed throughout this chapter. The first is Part B, which describes regulations that affect children ages 3 to 21. Part B is sometimes referred to as the school-age component of IDEA. Within Part B is Section 619, which describes specific regulations for preschool special education/early childhood special education programs. Finally, Part C describes regulations that apply only to programs that serve infants and toddlers. Part C is also called the early intervention component.

The purpose of the chapter is to describe the steps associated with identifying children for special services under IDEA, and it is divided into three sections. The first section describes the purpose and requirements of Child Find, as well as common Child Find activities and associated recommended practices. The second section provides an overview of traditional and contemporary screening approaches, types of screening instruments, ways of conducting screenings, and recommended practices for implementing screenings. The third, and last, section explains the legal requirements for conducting eligibility assessments and determining eligibility, along with a model for conducting eligibility assessments while adhering to recommended assessment practices. Figure 8.1 shows the entire process for ensuring that children are identified for special services. All key elements (i.e., Child Find, screening, and eligibility determination) are described in this chapter.

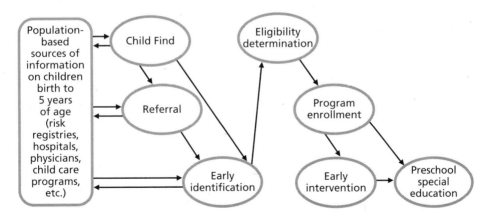

Figure 8.1.   Illustration of the process for ensuring that entitled children are identified for special services. (From Tracking, Referral, and Assessment Center for Excellence website, http://tracecenter.info/model.php. Copyright © 2006–2009 Orelena Hawks Puckett Institute. Reprinted by permission.)

CHILD FIND

The first step toward getting young children special services is to find children who may need such services. The following section explains the purpose and requirements for conducting Child Find activities. In addition, common activities for implementing Child Find efforts and associated recommended practices are summarized.

Purpose and Requirements

Child Find is considered a set of activities for locating children potentially eligible for early intervention or preschool special education services by making families aware of the availability of screening (Meisels & Atkins-Barnett, 2005). Child Find activities "include outreach, initial screening, tracking, and referral" (Pavri & Fowler, 2001, p. 1).

IDEA requires that lead agencies of states provide services to children under Part C to ensure that all eligible infants and toddlers are identified, located, and evaluated for services. This includes infants and toddlers with disabilities living on Indian reservations as well as those who are in foster care, homeless, or wards of the state. Similarly, in Part B of IDEA, state education agencies are directed to ensure the same thing of all children with disabilities who may qualify under Part B.

The intent of Child Find is to ensure that young children receive special services as early as possible. The agency or agencies responsible for delivering Part C (i.e., early intervention) and Section 619 (preschool special education) services are responsible for coordinating and conducting Child Find activities. Important features of Child Find are 1) the activities and coordinating partners and 2) the referral process.

Further, IDEA requires agencies responsible for delivering special education services to young children to coordinate Child Find efforts with other statewide agencies that provide services to young children, including, but not limited to, maternal and child health programs under Title V, child protection programs, and the office of coordination of Education for Homeless Children and Youth under the McKinney-Vento Homeless Assistance Act. In addition, local agencies work with community-based programs that serve young children, such as child care or Head Start, to make families aware of the availability of special services and solicit referrals. In addition to traditional early childhood intervention programs, local agencies coordinate Child Find efforts with local pediatrician offices, hospitals, and health departments who frequently see young children. Other community services that should be aware of the availability of special services for young children are social service agencies, recreation services (e.g., YMCA), and houses of faith.

Common Activities and Recommended Practices

Key components of Child Find activities are public awareness and referrals made by anyone who knows a child whom they suspect has a developmental delay. Agencies use a variety of methods for letting the community know of the availability of services for children who have special needs, including flyers, electronic notices, public service announcements, websites, printed materials, and even billboard messages (Dunst & Clow, 2007). Referrals are likely to be made by physicians, family members, child care providers, and hospital staff. As it relates to teachers, the period between post toddlerhood and prekindergarten is one of the most critical in terms of making referrals, a responsibility that often falls to teachers working in blended programs.

Unfortunately, in a review of the literature, Dunst and Clow (2007) found that even though states used 630 different public awareness and Child Find activities, most were in the form of nontargeted print materials, such as brochures. In all, they concluded that public awareness activities used by Part C programs "were not consistent with research evidence on practices found effective for child find purposes" (p. 5). Other researchers state that there is a lack of follow-through by families for eligibility evaluation and that public awareness initiatives are inefficient or nonexistent (Macy et al., 2014).

In other words, the largest percentage of these activities used by states involved practices that generally were found ineffective for either changing people's help-seeking behavior or influencing referrals from primary sources. Recommendations to the field, including more active and direct contact with primary referral sources (e.g., pediatricians) and targeted activities (such as working directly with visiting nurses), are more effective in changing referral patterns and rates. To meet the requirement to reach populations that have traditionally not been involved in early intervention services, agencies need to do even more. For example, agencies need to make materials available in a variety of languages, provide alternative ways to contact persons and agencies, make Child Find materials accessible, and ensure that the delivery of culturally and linguistically appropriate activities does not conflict with the assumptions, values, or beliefs of those intended to be reached (Pavri & Fowler, 2001), as well as identify and implement new strategies to improve inter agency collaboration (Ko et al., 2020).

As with public awareness, there are key attributes to ensuring a referral system is effective. When a child is believed to have a developmental delay, the person making the referral contacts someone in their community who oversees Child Find efforts. As mentioned previously, the local education agency (LEA) is responsible for such efforts. Most early intervention systems, however, have a process by which referrals can be made when a child has a suspected delay. (See Box 8.1 for how to design an effective referral process.)

Box 8.1.   How to Design an Effective Referral Process

Examination of available research evidence, with a focus on the characteristics of the practices that are associated with referrals, indicates that four sets of factors are most important if outreach to primary referral sources is to be successful:

1.   Building rapport and establishing credibility with primary referral sources

2.   Highlighting and repeating a focused message about the benefits of making a referral to both the primary referral source and the child being referred

3.   "Using concise, graphic written materials that describe the services, the primary referral source, and the child being referred will receive from program"

4.   Making follow-up visits to reinforce primary referral source referrals, answer questions, and provide additional information as needed

From Dunst, C. J. (2006). Improving outreach to primary referral sources. *Trace Practice Guide, 1*(2), 1–2; adapted by permission.

SCREENING

After a child is referred to as potentially being in need of special services, the next step in the identification process is developmental and behavioral screening. Meisels and Atkins-Burnett (2005) define this type of screening as a process of identifying "children who may have developmental or learning problems or disabilities" (p. 7). The following section describes traditional and contemporary screening approaches, types of screeners, formats for conducting screening, and recommended screening practices.

Traditional and Contemporary Screening Approaches

Traditionally, screening in early intervention and early childhood special education has been viewed as a process that answers the assessment question, Does the child need further assessment? Figure 8.2 demonstrates a common screening process. The figure shows that screening results puts children into two categories: at risk (meaning that the results of the screener indicate that the child should be further evaluated) or not at risk (meaning that the results of the screener indicate that the child should not be further evaluated). Children who are not at risk are enrolled in the regular classroom with no further assessment. Children who are found to be at risk are then further evaluated to determine whether they are in need of special services. This type of screening is different from universal screening, often conducted in K-12 as part of tiered

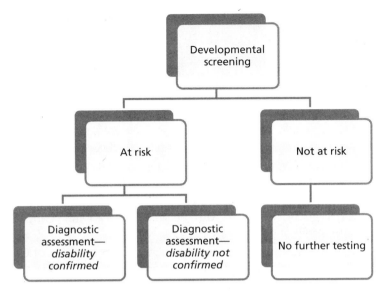

Figure 8.2. Common developmental screening process. (*Source:* Meisels & Atkins-Burnett, 2005.)

intervention practices. See Box 8.2 for a comparison between universal screening used within tiered frameworks and developmental screening used in the Child Find process.

However, referral and screening in preschool can at times mirror practices in K–12 special education. The reason for this is twofold. First, special services for preschoolers are increasingly delivered within public school buildings (Early Childhood Technical Assistance Center, 2019; U.S. Department of Health and Human Services and the U.S. Department of Education, 2015), and second, there are increased efforts to bridge preschool with K-12 practices and policies (National Institute for Early Education Research [NIEER], 2020; Reynolds et al., 2010). Thus, across P-12, and following guidelines set forth in IDEA 2004, districts work to prevent overidentification of children for special services by ensuring that intervention is provided for children in need before formal referrals to special education are made. These efforts are broadly referred to as response to intervention (RTI) and/or multi-tiered systems of support (MTSS). According to the Division for Early Childhood, and others, such efforts should not be used as a gateway for determining eligibility for special services or to delay or deny services early (DEC, 2009; U.S. Department of Education, 2016, 2017). Rather, such tiered models are viewed as quality instructional frameworks (Pretti-Frontczak et al., 2014). Thus, although each state, and sometimes each agency within a state, may approach the referral process differently, the procedures are similar to those found in Figure 8.2. In the more contemporary scenario (see Figure 8.3), children are screened and placed into one of three categories: delay suspected, at risk due to socioeconomic reasons, or typically developing. For children who are typically developing, nothing else is done.

> **Box 8.2.   Comparison Between Universal Screening Used Within an MTSS Framework and Developmental Screening Used in the Child Find Process**
>
> "Universal screening is distinct from developmental screening in that universal screening is a process by which teams determine whether or not a child would likely benefit from additional services and/or supports, whereas developmental screening is a process by which teams determine whether the child's development is typical and whether further testing is warranted.
>
> The systematic nature of universal screening identifies children in need of additional instruction before they fall significantly behind. Universal screening supports the delivery of instruction with the goal of ameliorating early learning difficulties before special education services are needed.
>
> Developmental screening, on the other hand, serves as a part of Child Find obligations and helps teams make decisions regarding a child's need for further developmental evaluation or monitoring for special education services." (Division for Early Childhood, 2021, p. 6)
>
> Universal screening answers the question, "Is this child performing at benchmark levels?"
>
> Developmental screening answers the question, "Does the child need further assessment or testing?"

Children who are at risk due to economic factors are enrolled in a preschool on the basis of being economically disadvantaged. Children who have a suspected delay are first provided access to a developmentally appropriate curriculum in a preschool classroom (Tier 1 intervention). Data are collected on children's suspected areas of delay while in that class to determine whether exposure to high-quality early childhood intervention positively affects the area of suspected delay. If exposure alone does not improve the child's functioning in the area of the suspected delay, interventions that are more intentional (i.e., Tier 2) are provided and data are collected to determine the impact of the interventions on the suspected delay. If progress is made (see Chapter 7 for a discussion of performance-monitoring efforts), the referral process stops and no further testing occurs. If no progress is made after intentional interventions are provided, a formal referral for evaluation for special education services is made. Again, the intent of providing interventions to children before they are formally tested for special education is to determine whether less-intrusive services will improve the child's functioning in the area of the suspected delay so that the child will not be diagnosed and labeled unnecessarily.

Screening Types and Formats

Within the Child Find process, there are a variety of types and formats of screenings, beyond universal, which was described previously. All serve the purpose

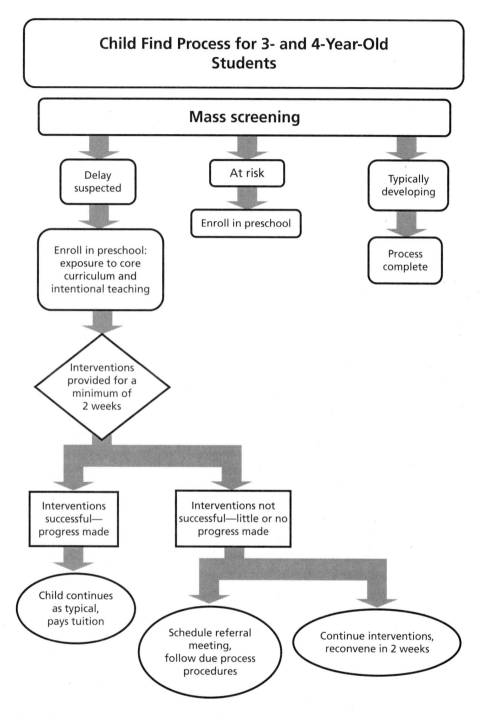

Figure 8.3. Contemporary Screening Process. (Created by Christy Brock, Preschool Coordinator, Franklin County Public Schools, Frankfort, KY [2010]. Reprinted by permission.)

of determining a child's need for further evaluation. Universal newborn, sensory, and developmental screeners are common types. Also, screenings can be conducted in a variety of formats. Both types and formats are discussed in the next section.

SCREENING TYPES

Universal newborn screening is one of the first types of screenings that young children might experience. Universal newborn screening implies that all newborns are screened. Universal or comprehensive newborn screening is designed to ensure that health or mental conditions are detected early so that children can receive needed intervention and associated problems can be prevented (Save Babies Through Screening Foundation, 2008). Some universal newborn screenings are associated with health conditions. For example, the heel prick test, or PKU (phenylketonuria) test, is conducted within the first 24–48 hours of a baby's life to determine whether the child has a metabolic condition that can be treated if detected early. Although there are no federal requirements that states screen newborns for any conditions, the National Institutes of Health recommend screenings for three conditions: sickle-cell diseases, PKU, and congenital hypothyroidism (U.S. General Accounting Office, 2003).

Second, sensory screening should be conducted on young children. Early identification of vision and hearing difficulties and appropriate follow-up are essential to children's overall well-being and development. According to Meisels and Atkins-Burnett (2005), indicators of vision and hearing problems include "rubbing eyes, bringing reading materials close to face, turning head to hear something, or not following directions" (p. 11). Visual impairments are associated with delays in other areas of development, particularly gross motor development (Celeste, 2002) and literacy development, especially in the area of letter identification (Gonpel et al., 2004). Hearing impairments are associated with delays in communication development, behavior, psychosocial well-being, and educational development (U.S. Preventive Services Task Force, 2008).

Recommended strategies for screening young children's vision include 1) observing children's visual behaviors (e.g., Are the child's eyes working together? Does the child tilt their head to see?), 2) examining children's distance vision by having the child read letters or pictures at a distance of 10 feet, and 3) photoscreening for nonverbal children, where a photograph of the child's eyes is examined for signs of vision problems (Prevent Blindness America, 2015). In some states, hearing screening is part of universal newborn screening. In other states, hearing screening is regularly conducted as part of preschool screening events. Box 8.3 describes hearing screening tests commonly used with young children.

Finally, the most common type of screeners conducted on preschoolers is developmental screeners. Developmental screeners can be administered in a relatively short period of time (e.g., 15–30 minutes). Most developmental screeners are used to find delays in all developmental areas (i.e., adaptive, language, cognitive, motor, and social), although some screen for potential delays

---

Box 8.3.   Commonly Used Hearing Screening Tests

Visual reinforcement audiometry (VRA) is the method of choice for children between 6 months and 2 years of age. With VRA, the child is trained to look toward (localize) a sound source. When the child gives a correct response (e.g., looking toward a source of sound when it is presented), the child is rewarded through visual reinforcement such as a toy that moves or a flashing light.

Conditioned play audiometry (CPA) can be used as the child matures and is widely used for children 2–3 years of age. In CPA, the child is trained to perform an activity each time a sound is heard. The activity may be putting a block in a box, placing pegs in a hole, putting a ring on a cone, and so forth. The child is taught to wait, listen, and respond.

Tympanometry introduces air pressure into the ear canal, making the eardrum move back and forth. A special machine then measures the mobility of the eardrum. Tympanograms, or graphs, are produced that show stiffness, floppiness, or normal eardrum movement.

Acoustic reflex measures the response of a tiny ear muscle that contracts when a loud sound occurs. The loudness level at which the acoustic reflex occurs and/or the absence of the acoustic reflex give important diagnostic information.

Static acoustic measures estimate the physical volume of air in the ear canal. This test is useful in identifying a perforated eardrum or whether ear ventilation tubes are still open.

See https://www.asha.org/public/hearing/pure-tone-testing for more information.

---

in only one developmental area (e.g., social). For example, given the importance of children's social-emotional well-being and the increasing number of children who are at risk for social-emotional disorders, teachers can administer screening instruments such as the Ages and Stages Questionnaires®: Social-Emotional (Squires et al., 2002) or Temperament and Atypical Behavior Scale (Bagnato et al., 1999) to determine whether social-emotional concerns are warranted and whether a child should be referred for additional evaluation in the social-emotional area. Rather than evaluating the child's performance in motor skills or cognition, which are not concerns in this example, the teacher can target the screening to the specific area of concern, in this case social-emotional.

In general, developmental screeners yield comparative information between children taking the test and those who were part of the normative sample on whom the test was developed. Information from developmental screeners is typically expressed in some type of standard score. As discussed in Chapter 4, a standard score allows for comparisons to be made among children and across different tests by having a set mean and standard deviation. Scores representing children's performance on a screening instrument help teachers determine whether further evaluation is warranted (i.e., further evaluation is warranted when the child performs significantly lower than the mean of the normative sample). Information on commonly used developmental screeners includes the publisher, cost, developmental areas covered, age range, type of score produced, length of administration, administration methods, and qualifications of administrators.

SCREENING FORMATS

Screening instruments are completed using a variety of formats depending on the screening purpose. A primary format is to complete screening instruments during mass community setting roundups. For example, an agency may set up stations at a local library, at a YMCA, or even during kindergarten registration where other children (e.g., kindergarteners' younger siblings) are screened in the areas of motor, language, and cognition. Screening instruments can also be administered in a format that is part of a larger surveillance or monitoring system. Sometimes referred to as tracking, surveillance efforts are broad in scope, are flexible, and include observations of children in routine settings across time. (For instance, pediatricians observe and discuss a child's health and development during a well-child checkup, or a child care provider completes a monitoring questionnaire every 3 months for children who are at risk due to socioeconomic reasons.) Last, professional or family members of the team can complete screening instruments. For example, the Ages and Stages Questionnaires (ASQ-3®; Squires & Bricker, 2009) is a developmental screening questionnaire completed by a parent then scored by a professional. Although some have questioned the use of parent-completed screening instruments, considerable evidence can be cited recognizing that such instruments have sound psychometric properties (McLean & Crais, 2004; Puckett & Black, 2008).

Recommended Screening Practices

Meisels and Atkins-Burnett (2005), along with Puckett and Black (2008), provide several recommendations for screening practices. As with other assessment purposes, screening instruments and practices should be sensitive to the child's cultural background, administered in the child's primary language, and based upon multiple sources of information (inclusive of families). In addition, the screener should be administered by trained personnel, particularly when standardized screening instruments are used. Further, screening instruments should have adequate normative samples (see Chapter 4 for a discussion on adequacy of normative samples), be inexpensive, and be easily administered.

As discussed in Chapter 4, the screening instrument's scores and procedures should have documented technical adequacy. In other words, a screener should be valid (measure what it is intended to measure) and reliable (produce the same results if used on the same population multiple times, by different administrators, or with different forms of the test). In addition to the traditional standards regarding technical adequacy, sensitivity, specificity, positive predictive value, and negative predictive value are four indices relative to the quality of a screening instrument. *Sensitivity* (or true positive rate) refers to the ability of a screening instrument to correctly identify children in need of further evaluation

(Squires, 2000). *Specificity* (or true negative rate) refers to the ability of a screening instrument to accurately exclude children who do not need further evaluation (Squires, 2000). A *positive predictive value* refers to the proportion of children who do not pass a screening and were later identified as needing special services (i.e., screening results correctly determined the proportion of children needing further evaluation due to needing special services). A *negative predictive value* refers to the proportion of children who pass a screening and were not later identified as needing special services (i.e., proportion of children who were correctly identified as not needing further evaluation due to not needing special services).

In addition to the four indices, teachers will hear the terms *true positives* (meaning that the children identified as needing additional evaluation were correctly identified as needing special services), *true negatives/correct rejection* (meaning that the children identified as needing additional evaluation were later determined not to need special services), *false positives/false alarms* (meaning that the children referred for evaluation based on the results of a screening were later found not to be in need of special services), and *false negatives/with miss* (meaning that the children who passed the screening and are not referred for evaluation are later identified as needing special services). Figure 8.4 is an illustration of the relationship among indices related to the technical adequacy of screening instruments.

	The child *did* need to be tested further because they *needed* special services	The child did *not* need to be tested further because they did *not* need special services	
Screener indicated child should be tested further (i.e., the child failed the screener)	A True positive	B False positive	Leads to index of positive predictive value (precision) $\dfrac{a}{a+b}$
Screener indicated child should *not* be tested further (i.e., the child passed the screener)	C False negative	D True negative	Leads to index of negative predictive value $\dfrac{d}{d+c}$
	Leads to index of sensitivity $\dfrac{a}{a+c}$	Leads to index of specificity $\dfrac{d}{d+b}$	

Figure 8.4. Illustration of the relationship among indices related to the technical adequacy of screening instruments.

Although the terms can be confusing, it is critical that teachers are able to interpret the effectiveness of various screening instruments. For example, if sensitivity were reported at 100%, it would mean that the screening instrument identifies all actual positives resulting in low type II errors, or false negatives. If specificity were reported at 100%, it would mean that the screening instrument identifies all actual negatives resulting in low type I errors, or false positives. False negatives can lead to underidentification of children, which can have serious consequences for the children who might have benefited from special services but did not receive the services due to errors (e.g., a lack of technical adequacy). False positives can lead to over identification of children, which can cause undue anxiety for families and unnecessary expenses for agencies. False positives, however, are often preferred over false negatives. Some suggest that the positive predictive value is the most critical index for screeners (Glover & Albers, 2007), but the index is dependent upon the prevalence of children needing further evaluation. For example, a screening instrument can have low precision (i.e., a low positive predictive value) and high specificity if there are far more true negatives than true positives. Thus, others have suggested that screening instruments should be evaluated in terms of sensitivity, specificity, and positive predictive values, all of which should be above 70–75% (sometimes noted as a decimal such as .70 or .75). In general, the higher the stakes, the higher the index percentages that teachers should look for (Meisels & Atkins-Burnett, 2005).

As a guide to help teachers be critical consumers of screening instruments, Jackson et al. (2008) created a rating rubric to guide in selecting, implementing, and using high-quality developmental screening instruments. The rubric allows teachers to rate various developmental screening instruments across 17 critical elements, including cost, multiple means of expression, representative norm sample, training, and usefulness of follow-up information. In addition to employing the rubric, teachers can use reviews of screening instruments to guide their decision making. (See Box 8.4 for a brief summary of screening instrument compendia and reviews.)

Recommended practice repeatedly indicates that any assessment instrument should be used for the purposes for which it was intended and validated. Increasingly, however, practitioners and researchers have expressed interest in stretching the uses of screening tools for assessment and evaluation purposes beyond the typical scope of screening (Bricker et al., 2010). For example, professionals are asking whether they can use a screening instrument to develop goals, evaluate progress, measure developmental changes and thereby establish eligibility for special services, and meet federal accountability mandates. As stated by Bricker et al.:

> Screening measures such as the ASQ were not designed to develop intervention goals and content or to [monitor] child progress over time and currently no empirical base exists to suggest how well or how poorly a screening measure may contribute to these assessment/evaluation purposes. (2010, p. 19)

Box 8.4.   Screening Instrument Reviews

American Academy of Pediatrics. (2020). Promoting optimal development: Identifying infants and young children with developmental disorders through developmental surveillance and screening. https://publications.aap.org /pediatrics/article/145/1/e20193449/36971/Promoting-Optimal-Development -Identifying-Infants

Bellman, M., Byrne, O., & Sege, R. (2013). Developmental assessment of children. *BMJ, 346*, e8687. https://www.researchgate.net/profile/Robert_Sege /publication/234141651_Developmental_assessment_of_children/links /568d346108aead3f42ed8d7f/Developmental-assessment-of-children.pdf

Canadian Task Force on Preventive Health Care. (2016). Recommendations on screening for developmental delay. *CMAJ, 188*(8), 579–587. https://www .ncbi.nlm.nih.gov/pmc/articles/PMC4868607/pdf/1880579.pdf

Fischer, V. J., Morris, J., & Martines, J. (2014). Developmental screening tools: Feasibility of use at primary healthcare level in low- and middle-income settings. *Journal of Health, Population, and Nutrition, 32*(2), 314. https://www .ncbi.nlm.nih.gov/pmc/articles/PMC4216967/pdf/jhpn0032-0314.pdf

Mackrides, P. S., & Ryherd, S. J. (2011). Screening for developmental delay. *American Family Physician, 84*(5), 544–549. https://www.aafp.org/afp/2011 /0901/p544.html

Moodie, S., Daneri, P., Goldhagen, S., Halle, T., Green, K., & LaMonte, L. (2014). *Early childhood developmental screening: A compendium of measures for children ages birth to five*. OPRE Report 2014-11. U.S. Department of Health and Human Services. https://files.eric.ed.gov/fulltext/ED561406.pdf

U.S. Department of Health and Human Services. (2013). *Birth to 5: Watch me thrive! A compendium of screening measures for young children*. Author. https://eclkc.ohs.acf.hhs.gov/sites/default/files/pdf/screening-compendium -march2014.pdf

Thus, teachers need to recognize that screening instruments should not be used to diagnose children, write individualized goals, plan instruction, monitor children's performance over time as a response to instruction, or evaluate a program; nor should they be used for state or federal accountability purposes (Meisels & Atkins-Burnett, 2005). Screening instruments "can only alert teachers and families to areas of concern for further evaluation and consultation" (Printz et al., 2003, p. 4).

DETERMINING ELIGIBILITY FOR SERVICES

Public funding (under IDEA) is available to support the educational needs of children with disabilities through federal grants to states that choose to participate. In order to qualify for the grant, a state must abide by the relevant federal laws and regulations. The grant covers only a portion of the cost of educating children with disabilities. State education agencies (SEAs) and LEAs are responsible for covering the remaining portion of the costs. It is important to understand the basic funding structure that supports the educational needs of children with disabilities because it directly affects who receives services, what services children receive, and how services are delivered. The next section describes federal regulations and state variations related to determining eligibility for services.

Federal Regulations

In addition to stating regulations related to funding, IDEA lists several general requirements for completing eligibility determination. Eligibility determination is the process by which a child meets the federal and state definitions of a child with a disability. (See Box 8.5 for the IDEA definition of a child with a disability.) Once a child is determined to be eligible, the child is entitled to receive special education services under IDEA funding. IDEA describes essential characteristics of assessments used for eligibility and regulations about assessment administration, which apply to children from birth through age 21. IDEA regulations can be grouped into five minimum standards for eligibility measures and procedures as follows.

Box 8.5. IDEA Definition of a Child With a Disability

PUBLIC LAW 108-446—DEC.3, 2004 118 STAT. 2653

   STATUTE/REGULATIONS—PART B—SUBPART A-SECTION 300.8 CHILD WITH A DISABILITY

   (3) CHILD WITH A DISABILITY—

   (A) IN-GENERAL—

   (i) Child with a disability means a child evaluated in accordance with §§300.304 through 300.311 as having an intellectual disability, a hearing impairment (including deafness), a speech or language impairment, a visual impairment (including blindness), a serious emotional disturbance (referred to in this part as "emotional disturbance"), an orthopedic impairment, autism, traumatic brain injury, an other health impairment, a specific learning disability, deaf-blindness, or multiple disabilities, and who, by reason thereof, needs special education and related services.

   (a) If a child has one of the disabilities identified in paragraph (a)(1) of this section, but only needs a related service and not special education, the child is not a child with a disability under this part.

   (b) If the related service required by the child is considered special education rather than a related service under State standards, the child would be determined to be a child with a disability under paragraph (a)(1) of this section.

Box 8.5. *(continued)*

(B) CHILDREN AGED 3 THROUGH 9 EXPERIENCING DEVELOPMENTAL DELAYS—

Child with a disability for children aged 3 through 9 (or any subset of that age range, including ages 3 through 5), may, subject to the conditions described in §300.111(b), include a child—

(i) Who is experiencing developmental delays, as defined by the State and as measured by appropriate diagnostic instruments and procedures, in one or more of the following areas: Physical development, cognitive development, communication development, social-emotional development, or adaptive development; and

(ii) Who, by reason thereof, needs special education and related services.

(C) 13 FEDERAL CATEGORIES/DISABILITY TERMS—

(1) Autism

(2) Deaf-blindness

(3) Deafness

(4) Emotional disturbance

(5) Hearing impairment

(6) Intellectual disability

(7) Multiple disabilities

(8) Orthopedic impairment

(9) Other health impairment

(10) Specific learning disability

(11) Speech or language impairment

(12) Traumatic brain injury

(13) Visual impairment.

Source: The Individuals with Disabilities Education Improvement Act of 2004 (PL 108-446).

First, when assessing a child for eligibility, no one procedure can be used as the sole criterion for determining eligibility; a variety of tools and strategies should be employed (Evaluation Procedures, 2005). For example, though a child clearly presents with a speech impairment, it is unacceptable to find the child eligible solely on the basis of a speech therapist's report. Even if the child has an expressive language score on a norm-referenced assessment that is two standard deviations below the mean, additional data must be used to determine the child's eligibility. Anecdotal information about how the child communicates their wants and needs during an observation in child care and parent reports of the child's functional language skills at home and in other familiar environments should be used to support the speech therapist's conventional assessment results for eligibility determination.

Second, the eligibility determination process, including all measures, should be free of racial and cultural bias (Evaluation Procedures, 2005). It is nearly impossible to find an early childhood assessment instrument that is free from cultural bias because many typical early childhood skills are linked to cultural preferences. For example, dressing oneself independently is a skill linked to cultural beliefs about developing independence. In a culture that places a high value on children developing independence from their parents or caregivers at an early age, it may be typical for a 3-year-old to dress themselves independently. In another culture that values community and family over independent expression, it may be typical for a 5-year-old to be dressed by their mother on a daily basis. When selecting and administering developmental assessment instruments, teachers can address issues of item-embedded racial or cultural bias by being aware of such biases, not relying solely on the results of one measure for eligibility, and gaining an understanding of each child's racial and cultural background through observations and parent interviews.

Third, any test given as part of the eligibility process to children with sensory impairments must be selected and administered such that the results adequately represent the children's abilities and aptitude (Evaluation Procedures, 2005). For example, it would be clearly inappropriate to use a picture naming test to identify the vocabulary of a child who has a vision impairment. When a child has a significant sensory impairment, such as blindness (in the previous example), it may seem obvious that certain tests would be inappropriate. When a child demonstrates some functional vision, however, the necessity for using an alternative test instrument for the child to demonstrate their true abilities and aptitude may not be as clear.

Fourth, the measure (or measures) used for eligibility must cover all areas related to the suspected disability and be sufficiently comprehensive to determine the needed educational supports, including related services (Evaluation Procedures, 2005). The suspected disability is the eligibility category that the LEA determines is most appropriate for the child on the basis of the referral and/or results of a screening. The category of suspected disability drives the types of data collected about a child during the eligibility process.

Fifth, any standardized assessment used in the eligibility process must be administered according to the published instructions by an individual with knowledge and training related to its administration (Evaluation Procedures, 2005). This guideline emphasizes the necessity for LEAs to administer tests as the publishers intended. In order for the test results to be reliable and valid, all accompanying instructions must be followed, including any publisher-specified training or credentials required of the test administrators.

Federal Categories

IDEA describes 14 categories under which children ages 3–21 can be found eligible. Although brief definitions of each category are provided in IDEA, SEAs are responsible for determining the specific criteria that children in their state must meet in order to qualify under each specific category. Two federal eligibility categories contain more in-depth descriptions in the federal law: specific learning disability and developmental delay. Specific learning disability is the only eligibility category for which detailed federal eligibility criteria are given. The specific learning disability category, however, is rarely, if ever, used to identify preschool-age children. On the other hand, developmental delay is widely used in the preschool-age group and so deserves special attention.

Developmental Delay

Developmental delay is the only optional federal category and the only category with federally imposed age restrictions. IDEA (2004), at the discretion of the SEA and LEA, permits states to use the term to identify children ages 3 through 9, or any subset of that age range, including children experiencing developmental delays in one or more of the following areas: physical, communication, cognitive, social-emotional, and/or adaptive development for special services eligibility. The developmental delay category, however, was introduced in federal special education law in the 1986 Education for All Handicapped Children Act with the advent of special services for infants and toddlers with disabilities. The 1991 authorization of IDEA permitted states to use developmental delay as an eligibility category for children ages 3–5 years, as well as for infants and toddlers. The current age range (birth to 9 years) has been in effect since IDEA 1997.

The phrase developmental delay, when used as a category of eligibility, characterizes a condition that represents a significant delay in development and is likely to interfere with a child's future educational performance unless it is addressed with special services (McLean et al., 1991). Beginning at age 3, children must meet criteria under a category defined by the features of their disabilities in order to be eligible for special education services. Any child who is transitioning from Part C services to Part B services will have some type of noncategorical label, such as infant or toddler with a disability or child at risk of developmental delay. Although some states use other terms in place of developmental delay for preschool eligibility, such as preschool child with a disability, noncategorical, or preschool special needs, all states have some general category for preschool eligibility with a range of definitional variations (Danaher, 2005).

The Division for Early Childhood (2009) recommends using the developmental delay category for children from birth through age 8 and supports its use through age 9. Further, the use of categories other than developmental delay for children ages birth to 8 is generally not recommended by the DEC because such classifications may be inaccurate and considered a unique developmental period by the DEC, Council of Exceptional Children, and National Association for the Education of Young Children. The use of developmental delay can allow children to be found eligible for services even if they do not meet the criteria for eligibility under any of the school-age categories. Therefore, the use of the developmental delay category helps to catch children early who may otherwise not be identified until their disabilities present a significant detrimental impact on their performance in school. Children with some types of disabilities, such as specific learning disabilities, mild cognitive disabilities, or social-emotional disabilities that are difficult to diagnose at early ages, may benefit most from the use of the developmental delay eligibility category in early childhood. For example, to meet the federal qualifications under the category of specific learning disability, a child must either demonstrate a significant discrepancy between their academic performance and intellectual ability or demonstrate an inability to make adequate progress in the general curriculum with research-based instruction and interventions. Further, it must be demonstrated that the reason the child met either condition listed was not from lack of appropriate instruction. A preschool-age child who has no school experience prior to referral for special education cannot meet the criteria for a child with a specific learning disability because there is no evidence of prior appropriate instruction.

In a longitudinal study of over 2,000 children who received preschool special education services under the developmental delay category in Florida, Delgado et al. (2006) found that about one-fourth of the children exited special education by third grade. Of the remaining three-fourths, more than half were served under the specific learning disability or educable mentally handicapped (a term for mild cognitive disability) categories in third grade. The results of the study illustrate the importance of using a noncategorical option, such as developmental delay, to identify children with mild disabilities or disabilities with complicated or unknown etiologies so that young children can receive necessary intervention at an early age.

Although there are many positive aspects of using the developmental delay category, one drawback is that it is commonly documented through the use of percent delay. Box 8.6 provides more detailed information on the topic of percent delay in relation to the early childhood eligibility process. In addition, there are a few situations in which use of eligibility categories other than developmental delay in early childhood is essential for children to access appropriate services, including specialized interventions, specific therapies, adaptive equipment, material and environmental modifications, and augmentative and alternative communication systems. Special programs, and sometimes funding, are available for children who have been identified under specific eligibility categories such as autism, deaf or hard of hearing, and visually impaired. However, by using the term developmental delay, some family members, administrators, and service providers may cover a child's disability and cause issues in determining future service eligibility. Therefore, DEC recommends that young children with low incidence, multiple, or significant disabilities be identified under their specific eligibility categories rather than using the developmental delay category. IDEA also requires the child's services to be individualized and determined by the individualized educational program (IEP)/individualized family service plan (IFSP) team.

Box 8.6.   Issues Related to Percent Delay

Percent delay is defined as the difference between a child's chronological age and developmental age expressed as a percent of the chronological age. Percent delay is often used to determine a child's eligibility for services, particularly in early intervention (birth to 3/Part C). Examples of state criteria using percent delay include the following:

- 25% delay in one or more areas

- 50% delay or equivalent standard deviation *(SD)*

- 33.33% delay in one or more areas prior to 24 months and 50% in one area or a continued 33.33% in two or more areas after 24 months

- 25% delay or 1.5 *SD*s in one or more developmental areas

- 25% (or 1.3 *SD*s below the mean) in one or more areas of development

    To calculate the percent delay, teams are to determine "the discrepancy between the child's chronological age and the developmental score the child receives on tests administered during the evaluation" (Andersson, 2004, p. 63). When using percent delay as a criterion, there is a positive emphasis on natural environments, parent reports, and informed clinical opinions throughout the assessment process. There are, however, a number of concerns with using percent delay as a criterion for eligibility or measure of a child's performance. See Andersson for a more thorough discussion of the issues, which are outlined as follows:

- First, unlike the scaled or standard scores described earlier in the chapter, percent delay is calculated differently from assessment to assessment, team to team, and state to state. Further, percent delay calculations are not equitable to particular *SD*s, thus confusing the issue when state criteria use them interchangeably or suggest an equivalency exists.

- Second, percent delay is based upon the notion of age equivalencies. Age equivalencies are problematic for at least two reasons: 1) For many tests, the age associated with a given item is not determined empirically; rather, the item is assigned an age based on how ages are assigned in other tests or generally agreed upon developmental milestones. 2) Age equivalencies do not inform teams about a child's strengths, emerging skills, or needs, which a team is responsible for assessing.

- Third, having chronological ages assigned to items may lead interventionists and caregivers to select intervention targets based on the age level of an item rather than selecting items that address children's individual developmental needs.

(continued)

Box 8.6. *(continued)*

- Fourth, a 25% delay in one particular area of development (e.g., motor skills) may have greater or lesser implications than a 25% delay in another area of development (e.g., language skills) at a given period in development.

- Fifth, many tests commonly used for determining eligibility, particularly for Part C, indicate that providers cannot generate percent delay from the tool being used, yet providers do so on a daily basis. For example, the HELP utility from VORT Corporation indicates on its website that it "is not standardized or normed. As such, it is not intended to be used to calculate a child's single-age equivalent (score or % delay)" (https://www.vort.com /pages.php?pageid=1#q320).

- Sixth, many of the assessments used for eligibility do not have systematic procedures for generating percent delay and leave it up to the provider or team. However, some states and/or authors/publishers have provided guidance in the calculation of percent delay. (See the examples that follow.) Generally speaking, however, comparing age equivalencies to chronological age generates percent delay.

Examples:

- Sample of guidance from an early childhood intervention provider: Our team calculates 25% by taking the child's chronological age (CA), multiplying it by .25, and subtracting the months from the CA. So a 24-month-old child with a 25% delay would have an age equivalency of 18 months or less, and a 14-month-old with a 25% delay would be performing only at an age equivalency of 10–11 months.

- In Virginia, teams are given the formula of CA – DA/CA = percent delay. For example, if the child's CA was 38 and developmental age (DA) was 24, the team would subtract 24 from 38, divide the difference by 38, and round up to 37%.

- The West Virginia Department of Health and Human Resources provides a birth to 3 percentage conversion chart to assist providers in determining percent delay for eligibility under the developmental delay category (see https://www.wvdhhr.org/Birth23/files/WVBTT_PercConvChartInst3409.pdf).

State Variations

Several regulations in IDEA allow flexibility for states, which ultimately affects children's eligibility for services and the services children receive. One state variation that can affect the services children receive is whether states choose to serve 3- to 5-year-olds under Part B or Part C. According to IDEA, children who turn 2 years old during the school year and who qualify for special services can be served under either Part B or Part C. This regulation primarily affects children who will transition from Part C to Part B services because children who receive services under Part C must be evaluated for Part B eligibility when they age out of Part C eligibility. Children who are being evaluated for services for the first time close to their third birthdays, however, could also be affected by this regulation. For example, in Ohio, children cannot be served under Part B until their third birthday. In New York, parents can choose to keep their 3-year-olds in Part C services until September 1 or January 2, whichever comes sooner after the child's third birthday. In Maryland, children with disabilities can be served under Part C until they are age-eligible for kindergarten.

Eligibility criteria can vary from state to state and from category to category. In order to understand the variations among state eligibility criteria, it is important to understand how states define such criteria. There are three general types of data that states use to define eligibility criteria: diagnosis by a licensed professional, test scores, and informed clinical opinion.

Diagnosis by a licensed professional occurs when a child has been evaluated by a physician, psychologist, audiologist, or other therapist and meets diagnostic criteria for a specific condition or disease. Diagnoses are most commonly included in the eligibility process for sensory impairments and other biologically based impairments with clear etiology, such as Down syndrome or spina bifida. Diagnoses are helpful for initial identification of children who are eligible for services and provide general guidance as to the services that a child may require. However, diagnoses rarely provide information sufficient for determining the precise educational needs of a child and, therefore, cannot be used as a sole eligibility factor. For instance, in the Down syndrome example, the diagnosis suggests that the child is likely to have a language delay, a mild to moderate cognitive delay, motor delay, and health complications due to heart defects. However, the diagnosis of Down syndrome does not provide information about the extent of the delays, nor does it give any information about the child's functional abilities. A child with Down syndrome may or may not qualify for occupational or physical therapy due to motor delays, depending on their functional motor abilities.

Test scores are the most prevalent sources of data used to determine eligibility. Different types of tests result in different types of scores. (See Chapter 4 for more information about different types of tests and their uses in early childhood.) Conventional assessments are the primary type of test used in the eligibility process. As described in Chapter 4, conventional assessments generate standard scores, percentile ranks, and age equivalencies. Standard scores can be used to determine the distance in number of SDs that a child's score falls from the mean. The number of SDs below the mean for an area of development is a pervasive requirement for eligibility across categories and states. The following examples illustrate state SD requirements for preschool eligibility under the developmental delay or similar category:

- The most common quantitative criterion for preschool eligibility (representing 36 states) is 2 SDs below the mean in one developmental domain or 1.5 SDs below the mean in two domains (Danaher, 2007).

- States range from qualifying children who score as little as 1 *SD* below the mean in one domain to requiring a score as much as 3 *SDs* below the mean in one domain (Danaher, 2007).

Some states use age-equivalent scores (refer to Chapter 4 for inherent limitations of age equivalencies) expressed as percent delay to determine eligibility. Box 8.6 defined percent delay in detail, described how to calculate percent delay, and listed issues related to using percent delay. Although test scores tend to provide more detailed information about children's strengths and weaknesses than diagnoses, like diagnoses, test scores offer limited information about children's functional skills. Therefore, test scores should not be used as the sole criterion for determining eligibility.

The final type of data used to determine eligibility is qualitative. Qualitative data include descriptive or anecdotal information gathered through interviews and observations and provide the most detailed information about children's functional abilities, compared with other types of data. Qualitative data are often measured or reported using informed clinical opinion, or clinical judgment. Bagnato (2007) identifies five practices that are necessary for accurate decision making based on clinical judgment. First, the assessment team should create operational definitions of attributes of the constructs or functional domains that will be examined. For example, if clinical judgment will be used to identify a child as eligible for services due to a language impairment, the team must define the functional language skills that they consider typical, at risk, and delayed. The second essential practice is to use structured rating formats to record informed opinions. Using the previous example, the team would create a checklist and/or rating scale to record the child's functional language skills. Next, the team should gather data from multiple sources. The fourth essential practice is to establish a consensus decision-making process for the team to use. Clearly defining a decision-making process facilitates the resolution of disagreements among team members and results in more accurate eligibility decisions. The fifth, and final, essential practice is to provide training to facilitate reliable ratings.

Often, states require specific types of data to determine eligibility. For example, to qualify under the autism category, several states require a diagnosis from a licensed physician, whereas some states permit diagnosis by school psychologists and other states do not require a diagnosis at all. A few states list specific team members who must be included (e.g., a speech language clinician, school social worker, psychiatrist) in order to determine eligibility under the autism category. Some states require an observation of the child, whereas others define specific tests that must be used, as well as specific test scores that must be met for eligibility (Muller & Markowitz, 2004). For further information about state-specific special education laws and policies, refer to Box 8.7.

Box 8.7.   State-Specific Special Education Law and Policy Resources

IDEA regulations are minimum federal requirements. States always have the option of creating state laws and policies that exceed the minimum requirements described in the federal law. Therefore, it is important to know about related state laws and policies in addition to understanding the federal laws. Here are some resources for finding state-specific information on special education laws and policies:

The Early Childhood Technical Assistance Center, State Part C Regulations and Policies: https://ectacenter.org/partc/statepolicies.asp

The Early Childhood Technical Assistance Center, State Part B Section 619 Regulations and Policies: https://ectacenter.org/sec619/stateregs.asp

The Early Childhood Technical Assistance Center, Section 619 Coordinators by State: https://ectacenter.org/contact/619coord.asp

The Early Childhood Technical Assistance Center, Part C Coordinators by State: https://ectacenter.org/contact/ptccoord.asp

State Performance Plans (SPP) Letters and Annual Performance Report (APR) Letters: https://sites.ed.gov/idea/spp-apr-letters

National Center on Educational Outcomes, Policy Topics by State: https://nceo.info/state_policies

Division for Early Childhood (DEC) State Subdivision Pages and Resources: https://www.dec-sped.org/subdivisions

---

RECOMMENDED PRACTICES FOR ELIGIBILITY DETERMINATION

Understanding federal and state laws, regulations, and common practices is an important step toward understanding the eligibility determination process. The next step is to incorporate recommended practices in early childhood intervention assessment with federal and state requirements to create the ideal eligibility determination process. The recommendations that follow represent ideal practices that programs should strive to implement as much as possible, recognizing that time demands, financial resources, scheduling conflicts, and personal preferences may dictate deviations from these practices.

Transdisciplinary Teaming During Eligibility

When conducting eligibility assessment, teams of professionals are often involved in the process. Teams can be structured in one of four ways: unidisciplinary, multidisciplinary, interdisciplinary, and transdisciplinary. Each of these structures is explained in Box 8.8. The transdisciplinary team structure, as described in Chapter 1 in terms of its value for assessment of children with

---

Box 8.8.   Team Structure Variations

Unidisciplinary

- Each team member completes their discipline-specific evaluation of the child individually, including the related report.

- Team members do not communicate with each other about any aspect of the assessment process or intervention.

- Parents are not included in the team.

Multidisciplinary

- Each team member completes their discipline-specific evaluation of the child individually, including the related report.

- Team members share their results and recommendations with each other.

- Each team member implements their intervention independently.

- Parents are not included in the team.

Interdisciplinary

- Each team member completes their discipline-specific evaluation of the child either individually or simultaneously with other team members.

- Team members combine their results to create one report and make recommendations together as a team with the child's parents.

- Team members may collaborate minimally to implement interventions.

Transdisciplinary

- Team members collaborate on every aspect of the assessment and intervention processes, including report writing.

- Parents are essential members of the team throughout the assessment process and intervention.

- Each team member contributes to assessment and intervention across all disciplines.

---

diverse abilities, is the recommended structure for preschool special education eligibility assessment (Sandall et al., 2005). Grisham-Brown (2000) describes a process of conducting a transdisciplinary assessment with young children who may have disabilities. The first step of the transdisciplinary assessment process is for the individual coordinating the assessment (e.g., school psychologist) to gather information from the child's family and other familiar caregivers. The information collected should focus on not only what the child can do, but also any priorities and concerns families have about the child's development. In addition, the assessment coordinator needs to collect information about the child's preferences (e.g., activities, materials). (See Chapter 3 for information on methods of gathering information from families.) If applicable, the assessment coordinator should request any prior school records, including IFSPs or IEPs, health information, and reports from previous related-service providers. While meeting with the family, the assessment coordinator explains the assessment process to the family.

Once information is gathered from the child's family and previous records, the assessment coordinator determines who should comprise the assessment team. The team reviews the assessment information, gathered by the assessment coordinator, and plans the assessment. Based on information from the family, the assessment team identifies activities in which they will conduct the assessment. They also select appropriate assessment instruments to use while conducting the evaluation. If the team works in a state where the use of a conventional assessment instrument is required as part of the state's eligibility criteria, the team should rely on a curriculum-based assessment instrument to assist in gathering functional assessment data.

During the assessment, one team member is selected to facilitate the assessment. This individual can be anyone on the team, including a member of the child's family. The facilitator engages the child in activities that have been planned by the team as opportunities to observe developmental skills in the areas in which the child was referred. For example, if the child was referred for potential speech/language and fine motor delays, the team might plan a snack activity in which its members can observe the child's use of speech/language skills to request, describe, and comment on the snack. The team might also provide open containers, a sandwich spread, and liquids for the child to pour. (Chapter 6 includes further information on how to create assessment activities.) The assessment facilitator creates opportunities for the observing team members to see the child demonstrate behaviors that might indicate delay. For example, the facilitator might not give the child a spoon to eat their yogurt, in order to determine whether the child will request a spoon. Similarly, the facilitator might leave the top on the cream cheese container to see if the child can independently use both hands together to remove the top. Observations are documented by team members and noted on test-scoring protocols. The goal of a transdisciplinary eligibility assessment is to conduct as much of the assessment through observation as possible. In situations where the use of conventional assessment instruments is required, the team should abide by the following guidelines: 1) Most conventional assessments allow for some flexibility in scoring some of the items. (If an item can be scored through observations, then the team member should score while observing.) 2) If the administration guidelines of the assessment disallow the collection of data through observation or the team member does not observe the child demonstrate the behavior, the team member should wait until after the observation period and then complete any direct testing that is required.

Team Meeting Grid	
Skills	**Activities**
Communication • Express wants and needs (hungry, tired, belly hurts, drink, sick)	• Across all activities (home, school, community) • Teach through role play with dolls or puppets during dramatic play or story time • Activities that she enjoys (movement, water)
Supports	**Adaptations**
• Parents • Interpreter • Therapists • Vision services • Functional vision assessment • Other school personnel • Peers	• Use a combination of BIGmack and SpeakEasy communication devices. • Some messages ("My belly hurts") need to be with her at all times. • Expand switches (3 or 4) on the SpeakEasy so that the number of choices can be expanded. • Try placing one switch on her tray and one on her foot plate. • If switches remain on her tray, change their angle to vertical, instead of horizontal, as they are now. • Provide stable position in her wheelchair so that she can use her upper extremities better to touch the switches on the communication device.

Figure 8.5. Example of a grid used to capture information about priorities. (From Grisham-Brown, J. [2000]. Transdisciplinary activity assessment for young children with multiple disabilities: A program planning approach. *Young Exceptional Children, 3*[3], 3–10; reprinted by permission.)

After the assessment is complete, the team (including the family) meets to debrief the assessment. Each member shares the data they collected about the child with the team. The team then sorts the data to determine the child's strengths, weaknesses, and primary educational needs (i.e., priorities). The team structures the discussion around the child's primary educational needs that emerged during the assessment. For each of those priorities (e.g., making requests), the team brainstorms 1) sample activities in which the child might learn the skill, 2) adaptations and modifications that the child needs in order to learn the skill, and 3) supports the child needs in order to learn the skill (i.e., people). Figure 8.5 shows an example of a grid that can be used to capture information about each priority. After determining the child's priority educational needs, the final step in the transdisciplinary assessment process is to summarize the team's findings in a written report.

Report Writing

The purpose of an assessment report is to merge all the information from pertinent sources into one document to generate a complete picture of the child. Kritikos (2010) indicated that there are five main areas to report writing: background/history, assessment tools used, informal information, results, and interpretations and recommendations. Because the middle three sections (assessment tools used, informal information, and results) often overlap with or have relevant data, they will be discussed primarily as a whole, rather than as individual parts.

The background or history section provides basic information about the child's age, grade, dates of assessments, and so forth. The background should include any pertinent information about the pregnancy, birth, and early development. Medical information (e.g., allergies, hospitalizations, surgeries, disorders or impairments), academic information, and information about the child's social history would also be located in the history.

The next section involves the assessment instruments and procedures used. There are many different assessments and assessment types (speech and language, cognitive, achievement, etc.) that can be included in a single report. The assessment section should list all of the tools that were used to gather information. For instance, if cognitive, achievement, and sensory assessments were given to a child, all three of the assessments would be listed in assessments-used sections. The full name, with the edition or version, should be given, along with any abbreviations.

A description of the assessment purpose can serve as an introductory paragraph into the results of the assessment. The overall score of the test should be given along with the results of each of the subtests administered. In terms of standardized tests, a standard score and percentile are reported. Using two different ways of reporting the score (standard score and percentile) helps to explain the test more effectively than just reporting the standard score.

Along with the reporting of scores, information about what the scores mean should also be given here. It is appropriate to describe what a particular score implies for the child. Information to guide score interpretations can often be found within the manual that accompanies the assessment tool. A report is most informative when it provides implications, based upon the child's score, rather than just restating the standard score and percentile (Wodrich, 1997).

Qualitative information can include all of the observations made during the assessment procedures. Observations about the child's willingness to participate, attitude, and so forth are all important variables that should be noted. In addition, information about the assessment itself and the environment should be noted. Aspects such as testing location, number of breaks needed or given, interruptions (e.g., a fire drill), and other factors that could affect the results should be mentioned. Most importantly, team members should provide information on the child's demonstrated functional behaviors during each of the assessment activities.

The final section, interpretation and recommendation, focuses on the identified priorities. Each team member contributes recommendations related to their area of expertise for how to teach each priority. In the example in Figure 8.5, the priority is expressing wants and needs. In the report, the speech therapist would provide suggestions on the type of assistive technology for the child to use. The occupational therapist might contribute ideas about how to position the communication device for optimal fine motor use. The physical therapist would suggest how to position the child so that her fine motor functioning is maximized. The teacher would supply suggestions of motivating activities for teaching the prioritized skill. By including suggestions from each team member related to the identified priorities, the report exemplifies true transdisciplinary service delivery in which shared goals are identified and role release is intimated (Cloniger, 2004).

Regardless of form or framework used for report writing, teachers are encouraged to follow several key guiding principles. First, teachers should write about and talk about children in the most positive ways. Second, whenever possible, teachers should lose the labels and describe the child in life-giving and affirming ways. Third, teachers should respect family preferences in terms of the language and/or format in which information is shared. Fourth, as described in Chapter 3, teachers should co-construct the report with families, avoid the use of jargon, and ensure the report guides future decision making that is as unbiased as possible and leads to supports and services a child will benefit from. To learn more about best practices in authentic assessment in early childhood, visit https://prekteachandplay.com/ece-authentic-assessment/. This website offers numerous resources, including but not limited to a do's and don'ts chart about recommended practices for writing reports, a play-based assessment guide for early childhood education teams, a reproducible form for teams to combine data and create a positive student profile, an affirmative vocabulary handout with guidelines and suggested reframes to support positive language use in report writing, as well as many other mindset, heartset, skillset, and on-demand resources.

SUMMARY

This chapter has described the process used to identify children who are eligible for federally funded special services, including Child Find, screening, and assessment for eligibility determination. In addition, the chapter has identified areas of weakness within current practices related to each component of the process and identified recommended practices for improvement.

Overall, the process of identifying children for special services should be viewed as a process with dual purposes: to identify whether a child qualifies for federally funded special services and to identify educational needs and appropriate services. Therefore, even when conventional testing or other nonrecommended practices (such as diagnosis by a single professional) are required for eligibility, it is important to consider what additional assessment activities are necessary to fully understand the child's educational needs.

The eligibility determination process should utilize authentic assessment measures, particularly with young children. LEAs are often burdened by state and federally mandated time lines, poor interagency cooperation during transitions, scheduling issues with families, and scheduling issues with team members. Conventional testing, as described in Chapter 2 and Chapter 4, certainly speeds up the eligibility determination process and may be necessary at times. However, LEAs should strive to use a system that is truly authentic, uses multiple methods, and relies on a transdisciplinary team. Further, assessment should focus on a child's educational needs and functioning rather than deficits and test scores.

REFERENCES

American Academy of Pediatrics. (2020). *Promoting optimal development: Identifying infants and young children with developmental disorders through developmental surveillance and screening.* https://publications.aap.org/pediatrics/article/145/1/e20193449/36971/Promoting-Optimal-Development-Identifying-Infants

Andersson, L. L. (2004). Appropriate and inappropriate interpretation and use of test scores in early intervention. *Journal of Early Intervention, 27,* 55–68.

Bagnato, S. J. (2007). *Authentic assessment for early childhood intervention: Best practices.* Guilford Press.

Bagnato, S. J., Neisworth, J. T., Salvia, J. J., & Hunt, F. M. (1999). *Temperament and atypical behavior scale.* Paul H. Brookes Publishing Co.

Bellman, M., Byrne, O., & Sege, R. (2013). Developmental assessment of children. *BMJ, 346,* e8687. https://www.researchgate.net/profile/Robert_Sege/publication/234141651_Developmental_assessment_of_children/links/568d346108aead3f42ed8d7f/Developmental-assessment-of-children.pdf

Bricker, D., Squires, J., & Clifford, J. (2010). Developmental screening measures: Stretching the use of the ASQ for other assessment purposes. *Infants & Young Children, 23*(1), 14–22.

Canadian Task Force on Preventive Health Care. (2016). Recommendations on screening for developmental delay. *CMAJ, 188*(8), 579–587. https://www.ncbi.nlm.nih.gov/pmc/articles/PMC4868607/pdf/1880579.pdf

Celeste, M. (2002). A survey of motor development for infants and young children with visual impairments. *Journal of Visual Impairments and Blindness, 96*(3), 169–175.

Cloninger, C. J. (2004). Designing collaborative educational services. In F. P. Orelove, D. Sobsey, & R. K. Silberman, *Educating children with multiple disabilities: A collaborative approach* (4th ed., pp. 1–30). Paul H. Brookes Publishing Co.

Danaher, J. (2005). Eligibility policies and practices for young children under Part B of IDEA. *NECTAC Notes, 15,* 1–18. National Early Childhood Technical Assistance Center.

Danaher, J. (2007). Eligibility policies and practices for young children under Part B of IDEA. *NECTAC Notes, 24.* National Early Childhood Technical Assistance Center.

Delgado, C. E. F., Vagi, S. J., & Scott, K. G. (2006). Tracking preschool children with developmental delay: Third grade outcomes. *American Journal on Mental Retardation, 111,* 299–306.

Division for Early Childhood (DEC). (2009, April). *Developmental delay as an eligibility category.* https://www.decdocs.org/concept-paper-developmental-delay

Division for Early Childhood (DEC). (2021). *Multi-tiered system of support framework in early childhood: Description and implications.* Author.

Dunst, C. J., & Clow, P. W. (2007). Public awareness and Child Find activities in Part C early intervention programs. *Cornerstones, 3*(1), 1–7. http://www.puckett.org/Trace/cornerstones/cornerstones_vol3_no1.pdf

Early Childhood Technical Assistance Center. (2019). *IDEA Part B, Section 619 National Survey Summary Report.* http://ectacenter.org/sec619/sec619data.asp

Education of the Handicapped Act Amendments of 1986, PL 99-457, 20 U.S.C. §§ 1400 *et seq.*

Evaluation Procedures, 34 CFR 300.532 (2005).

Fischer, V. J., Morris, J., & Martines, J. (2014). Developmental screening tools: Feasibility of use at primary healthcare level in low- and middle-income settings. *Journal of Health, Population, and Nutrition, 32*(2), 314. https://www.ncbi.nlm.nih.gov/pmc/articles/PMC4216967/pdf/jhpn0032-0314.pdf

Glover, T., & Albers, C. (2007). Considerations for evaluating universal screening assessments. *Journal of School Psychology, 45*(2), 117–135.

Gonpel, M., van Bon, W. H. J., & Schreuder, R. (2004). Word reading and processing of the identity and order of letters by children with low vision and sighted children. *Journal of Visual Impairments and Blindness, 98*(12), 757–772.

Grisham-Brown, J. L. (2000). Transdisciplinary activity-based assessment for young children with multiple disabilities: A program planning approach. *Young Exceptional Children, 3*(3), 3–10.

Individuals with Disabilities Education Act Amendments of 1991, PL 102-119, 20 U.S.C. §§ 1400 *et seq.*

Individuals with Disabilities Education Act Amendments (IDEA) of 1997, PL 105-17, 20 U.S.C. §§ 1400 *et seq.*

Individuals with Disabilities Education Improvement Act (IDEA) of 2004, PL 108-446, 20 U.S.C. §§ 1400 *et seq.*

Jackson, S., Korey-Hirko, S., Goss, S., & LaVogue, C. (2008). *Developmental screening rating rubric.* Ohio State Support Team Region 8 and Kent State University.

Katsiyannis, A., Gage, N., Rapa, L. J., & MacSuga-Gage, A. S. (2020). Exploring the disproportionate use of restraint and seclusion among students with disabilities, boys, and students of color. *Advances in Neurodevelopmental Disorders, 4,* 271–278. http://www.doi.org/10.1007/s41252-020-00160-z

Ko, D., Mawene, D., Roberts, K., & Hong, J. (2020). A systematic review of boundary-crossing partnerships in designing equity-oriented special education services for culturally and linguistically diverse students with disabilities. *Remedial and Special Education,* 1–14. https://doi.org/10.1177/0741932520983474

Kritikos, E. P. (2010). *Special education assessment: Issues and strategies affecting today's classroom.* Merrill.

Mackrides, P. S., & Ryherd, S. J. (2011). Screening for developmental delay. *American Family Physician, 84*(5), 544–549. https://www.aafp.org/afp/2011/0901/p544.html

Macy, M., Marks, K., & Towle, A. (2014). Missed, misused, or mismanaged? Improving early detection systems to optimize child outcomes. *Topics in Early Childhood Special Education, 34*(2), 1–12.

McLean, M., & Crais, E. (2004). Procedural considerations in assessing infants and preschoolers with disabilities. In M. McLean, M. Wolery, & D. B. Bailey (Eds.), *Assessing infants and preschoolers with special needs* (pp. 45–70). Pearson Merrill Prentice Hall.

McLean, M., Smith, B., McCormick, K., Schakel, J., & McEvoy, M. (1991). *Developmental delay: Establishing parameters for a preschool category of exceptionality.* Position Statement of the Division for Early Childhood, Council for Exceptional Children.

Meisels, S. J., & Atkins-Burnett, S. (2005). *Developmental screening in early childhood: A guide* (5th ed.). National Association for the Education of Young Children.

Moodie, S., Daneri, P., Goldhagen, S., Halle, T., Green, K., & LaMonte, L. (2014). *Early childhood developmental screening: A compendium of measures for children ages birth to five. OPRE Report 2014-11.* U.S. Department of Health and Human Services. https://files.eric.ed.gov/fulltext/ED561406.pdf

Muller, E., & Markowitz, J. (2004). *Disability categories: State terminology, definitions & eligibility criteria.* National Association of State Directors of Special Education, Project FORUM.

National Institute for Early Education Research (NIEER). (2021). *The state of preschool in 2020.* NIEER.

Pavri, S., & Fowler, S. A. (2001). *Child Find, screening, and tracking: Serving culturally and linguistically diverse children and families* (Technical report). CLAS Early Childhood Research Institute.

Orelena Hawks Puckett Institute. (2006–2009). Tracking, Referral, and Assessment Center for Excellence website. http://tracecenter.info/model.php.

Pretti-Frontczak, K., Carta, J., Dropkin, E., Fox, L., Grisham-Brown, J., Pope Edwards, C., & Sandall, S. (2014). Frameworks for Response to Intervention in early childhood: Description and implications. *Communications Disorders Quarterly, 35*(2), 108–119.

Prevent Blindness America. (2015). *Children's vision screening.* https://preventblindness.org/wp-content/uploads/2011/06/Prevent-Blindness-Statements-on-School-aged-Vision-Screening-Approved-8-2015.pdf

Printz, P. H., Borg, A., & Demaree, M. A. (2003). *A look at social, emotional, and behavioral screening tools for Head Start and Early Head Start.* Center for Children and Families, Education Development Center.

Puckett, M. B., & Black, J. K. (2008). *Meaningful assessments of the young child: Celebrating development and learning* (3rd ed.). Pearson Education, Inc.

Reynolds, A. J., Magnuson, K. A., & Ou, S. R. (2010). Preschool-to-third-grade programs and practices: A review of research. *Children and Youth Services Review, 32*(8), 1121–1131. http://www.doi.org/10.1016/j.childyouth.2009.10.017

Sandall, S., Hemmeter, M. L., Smith, B. J., & McLean, M. (2005). *DEC recommended practice: A comprehensive guide for practical application in early intervention/early childhood special education.* Division for Early Childhood.

Save Babies Through Screening Foundation. (2008). *Answers to frequently asked questions.* http://www.savebabies.org/ips_faqs.html

Squires, J. (2000). Identifying social/emotional and behavioral problems in infants and toddlers. *Infant/Toddler Intervention, 10*(2), 107–119.

Squires, J., & Bricker, D. (2009). *Ages and Stages Questionnaires®, Third Edition (ASQ®-3): A parent-completed child-monitoring system.* Paul H. Brookes Publishing Co.

Squires, J., Bricker, D., & Twombly, E. (2002). *Ages and Stages Questionnaires®: Social Emotional (ASQ®:SE).* Paul H. Brookes Publishing Co.

U.S. Department of Education. (2016). *Dear colleague letter on response to intervention* (RTI) *and preschool services.* https://sites.ed.gov/idea/files/idea/policy/speced/guid/idea/memosdcltrs/oseprtipreschoolmemo4-29-16.pdf

U.S. Department of Education. (2017). *Dear colleague letter on preschool least restrictive environment.* https://sites.ed.gov/idea/files/policy_speced_guid_idea_memosdcltrs_preschool-lre-dcl-1-10-17.pdf

U.S. Department of Health and Human Services. (2013). *Birth to 5: Watch me thrive! A compendium of screening measures for young children.* https://eclkc.ohs.acf.hhs.gov/sites/default/files/pdf/screening-compendium-march2014.pdf

U.S. Department of Health and Human Services and the U.S. Department of Education. (2015). *Policy statement on inclusion of children with disabilities in early childhood programs.* https://www2.ed.gov/policy/speced/guid/earlylearning/joint-statement-full-text.pdf

U.S. General Accounting Office. (2003, March). *Newborn screening: Characteristics of state programs* (Report no. GAO-03-449). https://www.gao.gov/assets/a237602.html

U.S. Preventive Services Task Force. (2008). Universal screening for hearing loss in newborns: U.S. Preventive Services Task Force Recommendations Statement. *Pediatrics, 122,* 143–148.

Wodrich, D. L. (1997). *Children's psychological testing.* Paul H. Brookes Publishing Co.

CHAPTER 9

Program Evaluation

Jennifer Grisham and Kristie Pretti-Frontczak

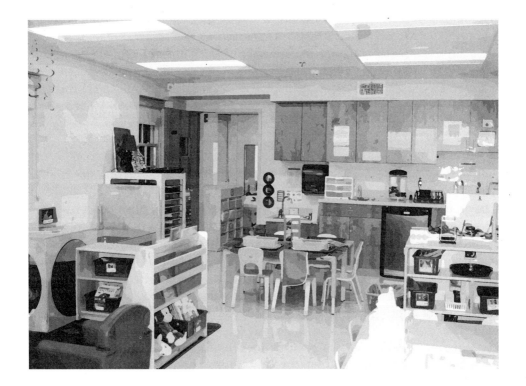

*The Building Blocks Preschool Program is a nonprofit licensed child care program
that contracts with the local public school to provide services to young children with
disabilities. The program is accredited by the National Association for the Education of
Young Children (NAEYC) and has been rated as four stars (out of five) on the state's
quality rating system. The program serves 70 children who are 2 to 5 years of age
in mixed-age classrooms. Fifteen percent of the children have diagnosed disabilities,
and 50% of the children receive child care subsidies for low-income families. Twenty
percent of the children are English language learners. In addition to its contract with
the local public school and the child care subsidy, Building Blocks receives funding
from the local United Way agency.*

*Teresa, Director of Building Blocks, is pleased with the progress the program
has made since its inception 15 years ago. She believes that the mix of funding
has afforded the program the opportunity to provide high-quality early care and
education to young children who are vulnerable to school failure. She is frustrated,
however, about the amount of paperwork she must complete to maintain her contract
with the school district, preserve NAEYC accreditation and stars rating, and seek
continued funding from United Way. Each entity requests multiple forms of data
to support the effectiveness of the services provided by Building Blocks. Therefore,
Teresa is seeking ways to provide the data that all these entities need in the most
efficient way possible.*

The scenario described in the vignette is not uncommon in blended preschool
programs. In an effort to provide high-quality inclusive services to young
children, programs often collaborate with multiple entities and agencies. Local,
state, and national agencies are increasingly requiring programs to provide
effectiveness data. Programs like Building Blocks need a comprehensive program evaluation plan that will provide the data they need to make internal
decisions about program enhancement and to satisfy funders and accreditation
agencies.

Program evaluation has been defined as the process of "systematically
collecting, synthesizing, and interpreting information about programs for the
purpose of assisting with decision making" (Snyder & Sheehan, 1996, p. 359), as
well as the " application of systematic methods to address questions about program operations and results" (Newcomer et al., 2010). The National Academy
of Sciences (2008) details three primary purposes for collecting program
evaluation data. First, data is sometimes collected to determine the impact
of a program. This purpose is limited primarily to investigations in which
researchers want to compare two (or more) programs and determine which
program had the greatest impact. Second, program evaluations may be conducted for social benchmarking purposes. For example, if researchers want to
find out whether today's 4-year-olds have better literacy skills than 4-year-olds
did 10 years ago, before the increased emphasis on literacy, they may compare
data on children's literacy abilities now with data on a group of similar children
from 10 years ago. Third, program evaluation data are collected for purposes of
determining a program's effectiveness.

Chapter 9 focuses on program evaluation for the latter purpose. The chapter describes the types of program evaluations that early childhood intervention programs might undertake at the classroom, programwide, state, and national levels. Also described are methods for collecting program evaluation data, including child assessment, program observations, stakeholder input, and record review. Finally, recommended practices used in conducting effective program evaluations will be discussed.

TYPES OF AND REASONS FOR CONDUCTING PROGRAM EVALUATION

As is evident from the vignette, blended programs often have multiple layers of program evaluation they must conduct. The Division for Early Childhood (DEC, 2007) represents the types of program evaluation as concentric circles indicating how information from each type can feed into the larger evaluation effort. Figure 9.1 is an adaptation from DEC showing the types or levels of evaluation that blended early childhood intervention programs might encounter and the reasons for collecting evaluation data at each level. In the sections that follow, we expand on each of these levels and their corresponding purposes.

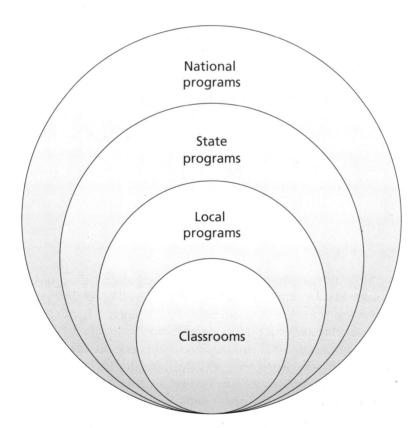

Figure 9.1. Relationship between levels of program evaluation. (Reprinted from Division for Early Childhood. [2007]. *Promoting positive outcomes for children with disabilities: Recommendation for curriculum, assessment, and program evaluation.* Missoula, MT; Author.)

Individual Classroom-Level Evaluations

For teachers, the most important form of program evaluation occurs at the classroom level. Teachers need information on the degree to which children are making progress, whether children are interested in curricular activities, whether instruction is being implemented properly, and whether the parents of their students are satisfied with the services provided. Data gathered from classroom program evaluations can be useful in making changes to the classroom curriculum. For example, if teachers determine that children are no longer engaging in activities and materials available to them, the activities and materials may need to be changed. If children have mastered the content associated with a particular topic of study, new goals need to be identified. If parents indicate that their children are really excited about coming to school and particularly enjoy an activity that has been introduced, then the activity might be maintained.

In addition to making changes to the curriculum, another important reason for collecting classroom-level program evaluation data is to determine the degree of fidelity with which instruction is being delivered. Fidelity of implementation refers to whether teachers/providers can implement curricula or interventions in the way in which they were designed (Hamre et al., 2010; Ledford & Wolery, 2013). Some curricular approaches espouse specific instructional tenets that should be demonstrated. For example, Hamre et al. (2010) found that children made significant language and literacy gains in classrooms where teachers frequently implemented MyTeachingPartner language and literacy activities with fidelity, as opposed to children in classrooms whose teachers did not. Similarly, when specialized instruction must be provided for individual children, the fidelity of implementation should be measured. This is often referred to as *procedural fidelity*, which is the degree to which a person can implement an intervention accurately after training (Ledford & Wolery, 2013). Figure 9.2 shows an example of a procedural fidelity checklist used to determine whether a teacher is implementing a procedure for teaching language to young children correctly.

Local Program-Level Evaluations

Local programs include those operated by nonprofit or for-profit agencies and school districts. Examples include community-based child care, publicly funded preschools operated by local education agencies, home-visiting programs, and Head Start. When conducting program evaluations, local programs are concerned about how well children are doing, the quality of teaching or parenting, the utility of assessment, and staff morale (Bagnato & Neisworth, 1991). Local programs conduct evaluations for a variety of reasons. First, they are interested in determining the professional development needs of their staff. Child assessment data that demonstrate consistent deficits in certain curricular areas (e.g., math) might indicate the need for staff development in that area of instruction. Observational data that demonstrate poor interactions between

Child's Name: Instructor: Date: Session #:

Are the materials ready? _____
Is the stopwatch ready? _____

          Key: + = Correct   − = Incorrect/No Response

Child's Name	Trial	Attentional cue provided?	3-second delay?	Response before CP	Response after CP	Controlling prompt provided, if needed?	Descriptive verbal praise given, if needed?	Continue activity?
	1.			+ − NR	+ − NR			
	2.							
	3.							
	4.							
	5.							
	6.							
Percent Agreement/Correct								

Figure 9.2. Procedural fidelity checklist using small-group format of 3-second delay intervention.

staff and children would be indicative of a need for training in creating positive classroom environments for young children.

Local programs, particularly nonprofit programs, often receive funding from a variety of sources, including foundation grants. Under those circumstances, program evaluation data are used to demonstrate that grant funds had an impact on the quality of the program or the children and families who receive services from the program. For example, if a local inclusive child care program receives funding from the United Way to purchase tablets for each of its four preschool classrooms in order to support interactions between children with and without disabilities, it might need a variety of data to report to the funder. The program might show how interactions between children with and without disabilities increased as a result of having tablets with interactive games. Similarly, the program might show gains in children's literacy scores on assessment measures as a result of having exposure to the technology. Finally, the program might show enhanced scores on environmental rating scales as a result of children having access to age-appropriate technology for an appropriate length of time. Generally speaking, local program funders are interested in changes in scores that come about as a result of the funding they provided.

Evaluation data are needed in order for programs to obtain accreditation from some professional bodies. Most accrediting bodies provide specific guidelines about the type of data they need in order to document evidence of quality. The most common accreditation sought by early childhood intervention programs is from the NAEYC. The intent of the voluntary accreditation process is to improve program quality for young children, because program quality has been linked to children's outcomes (Groginsky, 1999). NAEYC accreditation establishes national standards of quality (e.g., relationships, assessment of child progress, community relationships), as well as a process for improving program quality where needed. NAEYC accreditation is being used in combination with state-supported quality-rating systems. A program accredited by NAEYC is thought to be of the highest quality; therefore, accreditation is generally a requirement of a high ranking in state quality-rating systems (e.g., North Carolina, Kentucky). NAEYC accreditation involves self-evaluating classroom environments, gathering information from staff about their perceptions of the program, and determining the satisfaction of families participating in the program. Once programs have collected and submitted these data, NAEYC sends an assessor to the program for an on-site visit to determine the extent to which the program meets the 10 standards necessary for a program to receive accreditation.

Finally, local programs may collect program evaluation data for the purpose of determining the degree to which they are meeting their program goals. Often these data are reported to the program's stakeholders, such as a board of directors or parent advisory board. For example, if one of the program's goals is to improve the literacy outcomes of all children who attend the program, then child assessment pre- and posttest data would be needed to determine whether there has been growth in the area of literacy development.

State-Level Evaluations

Because of the relationship between program quality and children's readiness outcomes, some states and agencies that oversee early childhood intervention programs (e.g., child care, Head Start, education) are working together to improve the quality of early education in order to ensure that young children are ready to enter school (Burchinal et al., 2011). Generally speaking, program quality in the United States is measured using one or more measures, including "environment rating scales, the Classroom Assessment Scoring System (CLASS), national accreditation, and a quality rating improvement system" (National Academies of Science, Engineering, and Medicine, 2019, p. 12).

During the Obama administration, the Race to the Top Early Learning Challenge (RTT-ELC) provided states with grants to encourage states to improve child care quality. The emphasis of those grants, as well as other state initiatives was the development of Quality Rating and Improvement Systems (QRIS). "All states either have a quality rating and improvement system, a pilot for one, or are in the planning process for one. There is no one system in use across the United States; every state has a unique system reflecting its own priorities and context" (National Academies of Science, Engineering, and Medicine, 2019, p. 14). Thus, how quality is defined and measured is highly variable and, in many cases, highly questionable in terms of leading to positive outcomes for children. For example, Meek and colleagues (2020) state, "equitable experiences and equitable outcomes for children, have been almost universally excluded from this important definition [of quality] and as a result, from Quality Rating and Improvement Systems. . . ." (p. 10). As such, serious and legitimate concerns have been raised by advocates about whether QRIS is exacerbating inequities. Meek and colleagues go on to state, "Too often, these rating systems ignore equity content in their indicators, are inaccessible to the providers who serve the most marginalized children, and penalize programs who are experiencing systemic barriers. It is critical that these systems be redesigned, in partnership with parents and providers, to center equity" (p. 10). The California Child Care Resource & Referral Network along with Parent Voices staff have also called for a master plan, which includes acknowledging and repairing the harm done by a racist quality improvement system (California Child Care Resource & Referral Network & Parent Voices, 2020).

There are two primary purposes for conducting state-level program evaluations. First, because of the amount of public resources that are used to implement these initiatives, state legislators are interested in understanding their impact on their constituencies. Some states have started cost–benefit analyses of early care initiatives (Groginsky et al., 1999). Second, evaluations of state initiatives can help set public policy. An evaluation of Kentucky's Early Care and Education System, for example, found that kindergarten-age children who attended three- and four-star-rated centers had higher academic and language outcomes than a matched sample of children. These data were partially used to establish mandatory participation in the state's quality rating system. However, as noted above, Congress, agencies, states, and tribes, as well as local programs, need to engage in program evaluation activities by centering equity, ensure QRIS and other systems lead to overall improvements in child care and early learning programs, and ultimately dismantle systems of oppression, particularly for children traditionally marginalized (e.g., children who are poor; immigrants; Black, Indigenous, people of color; dual language learners).

Federal Program Evaluations

During the Clinton administration, all federally funded programs became subject to the Government Performance and Results Act (GPRA). As a result of that act and educational initiatives including the No Child Left Behind (NCLB) Act and later the Every Student Succeeds Act (ESSA), educational programs began reporting data to the federal government on students' performance on statewide tests. More recently, early childhood intervention programs have been held responsible for reporting data to the federal government about their success. Evaluations of federal programs are considered accountability assessments (DEC, 2007). Table 9.1 gives an overview of three federal early childhood programs that have created accountability assessment systems. The table describes each program, the evaluation system, and how local programs are affected by the evaluation.

From the federal government's point of view, the primary purpose for conducting accountability assessments is to determine whether the benefits

Table 9.1. Federal early childhood programs, associated accountability system, and local requirements

Program	Accountability system	Requirements for local programs
Head Start—Program to provide services to low-income children to improve school readiness skills https://eclkc.ohs.acf.hhs.gov/school-readiness/article/head-start-early-learning-outcomes-framework	Performance standards related to school readiness as defined by the Head Start Outcomes Framework	Local programs require assessment of child outcomes as they relate to school readiness
Office of Special Education Programs—Services provided through the U.S. Department of Education to children ages birth to 3 (Part C) and 3–5 (Section 619) with disabilities https://www2.ed.gov/about/offices/list/osers/osep/programs.html	Child outcome data on three outcomes Family outcome data	Local programs must provide child outcome data near entry and exit from early intervention (Part C) and 619 programs (Part C) and 619 programs (preschool)
Child Care and Development Block Grant (CCDBG) program—Federal funding to provide high-quality child care services to low-income children. https://childcareta.acf.hhs.gov/ccdf-fundamentals/establish-standards-and-monitoring-processes-ensure-health-and-safety-child-care-settings	States identify a lead agency to conduct oversight. The lead agency performs annual inspections, ensures staff are trained in areas of health and safety, and submits plans to federal government on use of funds, professional development for staff, and select measures of quality to report to U.S. Department of Health and Human Services.	Local programs have to follow state licensing and/or Quality Rating and Improvement System (QRIS) requirements

outweigh the costs of the program. More specifically, federal program evaluations are conducted because "policymakers are asking two questions that are corollaries of their earlier readiness query: Are children learning? and, Are public funds being used wisely" (Meisels, 2006, p. 5). Many warn that high stakes accountability systems may be detrimental to the education of young children. A qualitative study that examined the effects of high stakes accountability found that teachers of young children believe that those systems lead to developmentally inappropriate expectations of young children (Counsell & Wright, 2018). Further, researchers found that accountability systems create a culture of fear (e.g., fear of speaking out against inappropriate practices; fear of impact on children's emotional welfare).

As a result of the potential pitfalls of implementing poorly designed early childhood accountability systems, there is general agreement that child outcomes assessment should not be the only measure of the quality of a program. Specifically, federal accountability programs should measure 1) children's progress on key indicators of development, 2) teaching practices, and 3) programmatic quality (Helios Education Foundation, 2017).

According to Shultz et al. (2009), who led an accountability task force, five recommendations should be considered. First, there should be a unified system across sources of funding. Rather than having separate accountability systems for child care, publicly funded prekindergarten, and Head Start, one system should be in place. Second, standards, curriculum, and assessment should be aligned from prekindergarten to Grade 3. Vertical curriculum alignment ensures that children are prepared for the next educational level. Third, like all assessments, accountability assessment should be valid and reliable. Given the potential high-stakes nature of accountability assessment, it is very important that data be accurate and provide the intended information. Fourth, as with K-12 accountability systems, all children should be included in accountability efforts, including those children with diagnosed disabilities. In fact, there is evidence that including children with disabilities in high-stakes assessment can have positive benefits for them (Cole, 2006) because doing so ensures that assessment results for children with disabilities are valued as much as those of their nondisabled peers. Similarly to recommendations for K-12 systems, appropriate accommodations should be made. Finally, accountability systems should provide for the necessary resources to ensure that programs can adequately implement the system. Resources are needed for data management, professional development, and oversight of accountability systems.

METHODS FOR COLLECTING PROGRAM EVALUATION DATA

In deciding which assessment method to use to collect program evaluation data, a number of issues must be taken into account. Colker and Koralek (2018) and Meek and colleagues (2020) provide guidance about the various aspects of a program that should be measured. These include the following:

- Degree with which the program is developmentally appropriate, including learning through play and opportunities for choice

- How well the program meets the individual needs of each child in the program

- Whether the program reflects and values diverse cultures and home languages

- The health and safety of the program

- The degree with which adults interact with children in a positive, respectful manner

- How well programs engage families in reciprocal relationships

- The extent to which staff understand child development and engage in professional development

- The degree to which equity is centered and any observational measure used includes contextualized data (e.g., institutional and systemic racism, inequities in health care, inequities in pay and preparation of the workforce, intrapersonal biases)

The audience also will affect the methods used. Programs providing program evaluation data to groups such as funders that are unfamiliar with early childhood intervention assessment and practices would want to use methods that are understandable to those groups. In addition, those implementing program evaluations must consider available resources for collecting data. Some measures and methods require that someone outside of the program collect the data. Programs with limited funds may not have the fiscal resources to hire data collectors. Similarly, measurement systems may be cost prohibitive for some programs: Some measurement methods have expensive data management systems. Also, adequate staff training in program evaluation measures can be costly to programs. Finally, it is important to consider the need for methods that produce both quantitative and qualitative information. Quantitative data produce information such as how often something happens, how much someone likes something, and whether children make progress. Qualitative data provide information on the impact of the program on the lives of the children and families that receive its services. In the sections that follow, we describe methods of collecting child outcome data and program observation data, gathering information from stakeholders, and conducting record reviews.

Child Outcome Data

Given that child outcome data are used for program-level decision making, it is extremely important to ensure that data have been collected with fidelity and reliability. (See Chapter 6 for a discussion of the latter.) Ensuring that child assessment data are accurate is extremely important in conducting program evaluations because inaccurate data might lead to inappropriate decisions about services for children. For example, if child outcome data indicate that all children in a program are making substantial gains when in fact they are not, program funders might believe that certain services are unnecessary and cut funding as a result.

Programs need to adhere to recommended assessment practices when assessing young children for program evaluation purposes. In addition to those practices described in detail in Chapter 1, other practices should be followed during program evaluation, particularly when the evaluation is part of an accountability system. First, child outcome data need to be aggregated, meaning that all individual scores are combined and reported (National Child Care Information Center, 2005, p. 1). Individual children's scores should be unrecognizable to program evaluators. In addition, when considering the impact of a program on child outcomes, program evaluators must take into account the length of time children have been in the program and the quality of services they have received. Children who have received high-quality early intervention services for 1 year will likely have better outcomes than those who have received low-quality early childhood intervention services for 3 months. Adequacy of services and quality of care must be considered when child outcome data are used for program evaluation purposes.

One of the most important considerations programs must make when collecting child outcome data for program evaluation purposes has to do with the type of instrument that will be used. In a document entitled *Early childhood assessment policies and practices in the age of accountability*, the Helios Education Foundation (2017) provides excellent guidance for selecting instruments/ tools for assessing child outcomes as part of a program evaluation. First, the assessment should be comprehensive in nature. An underlying belief about child development is that it is interrelated. Therefore, it is essential to gather assessment information about all areas of a child's development. Second, assessment tools should be valid and reliable, meaning that they measure what they are intended to measure (i.e., validity) and the data are consistent over time (i.e., reliability). The authors also recommend that child assessment tools allow for assessing children at different time points throughout their time in the program so that growth can be measured. Finally, assessment tools used for program evaluation should be appropriate for children who are neurodiverse and who are from a variety of cultural and linguistic backgrounds, including those with identified disabilities. The assessment tool should be unbiased, be equitable in design, and allow for accommodations and/or modifications as needed.

Although using CBAs that are comprehensive, technically adequate, and unbiased is paramount for meaningful program evaluations, alignment with federal/state/agency standards and/or outcomes is also useful when engaging in program evaluations. Alignment is the process of matching two or more educational components. Alignment considers the degree to which the assessment documents children's performance toward targeted outcomes. Alignment, also referred to as crosswalking, is the process of linking curriculum, assessment, classroom instruction, and learning to a set of standards that describes what children should know and be able to do. For example, a teacher or workgroup might align an assessment instrument's items with state standards. Ensuring such alignment is important given that teachers are often expected to produce data and/or reports regarding children's performance toward agency (e.g., Head Start), state, and federal outcomes. Recommended practices state that alignment matrixes and/or crosswalks include evidence that a valid alignment between unbiased standards/outcomes and assessment items has been conducted and information or evidence regarding most of the following is available:

- Description of the steps taken to align components

- Consistency of content in the outcomes and assessment

- Comparable span of knowledge encompassed by both

- Even distribution of assessment items across outcomes

- Consistency between the cognitive demands of the outcome and the assessment items

- Expert validation or other steps taken to validate alignment

A variety of child assessment instruments/tools might be used for program evaluation. Five different types of tools are described here. Occasionally programs will select norm-referenced assessments which have been discouraged by many. In fact, in *Principles and Recommendations for Early Childhood Assessment*, the authors indicate that standardized, norm-referenced assessments should not be used with children younger than age 8 (Shepard et al., 1998). If they are used, collecting data on only a sample of children is recommended. Graham et al. (2006) describe a process called *matrix sampling* in which different groups of children are administered parts of a norm-referenced assessment so that none have to complete the entire test. Preferable to norm-referenced assessments, programs should consider using data collected from the curriculum-based assessment (CBA) for program planning purposes. Bagnato and Neisworth indicate that CBAs are the "most relevant, direct, and sensitive measure of the program's influence on the child's performance" (1991, p. 171). By demonstrating children's achievement of objectives on CBAs, programs can show a direct correlation between child outcomes and program quality. Second, judgment-based assessments, such as the Developmental System to Plan Early Intervention Services (Bagnato & Neisworth, 1991), are an alternative to norm-referenced assessments. Scores on judgment-based assessments are based on the perceptions of those who know the children on whom the data are being collected. Third, Sherow (2000) indicates that adopting goal attainment scaling is preferable to using standardized measures for program evaluation purposes because it measures the impact of services provided and the actual goals that learners acquired. According to Bagnato and Neisworth, "goal attainment scaling techniques involve identification of individual child goals and the specification of five levels of possible attainment for each along a continuum of worst to best" (1991, p. 171). Finally, general outcomes measures can be used to examine children's progress toward specific program goals (e.g., indicators of early literacy). General outcome measures are standardized measures that can be quickly administered to large groups of children over time to show the effectiveness of a curriculum or specific intervention (Hojnoski & Missall, 2007).

Program Observations

A common way program evaluation data are collected is from program observations. Program observation measures generally fall into two categories. The first set of measures assesses the global, or macro, aspects of the program. The most common global measures of program quality are the Early Childhood Environmental Rating Scale–Third Edition (Harms et al., 2014) and the Infant Toddler Environmental Rating Scale–Third Edition (Harms et al., 2017); both scales measure space and furnishings, personal care routines, language reasoning, activities, interaction, program structure, and parents and staff. The second set of measures assesses specific, or micro, aspects of program quality. For example, the Classroom Assessment Scoring System (Pianta et al., 2008) assesses emotional support (e.g., teacher sensitivity), classroom organization (e.g., behavior management), and instructional support (e.g., quality of feedback). Another example of this second type of measure is the Assessing Classroom Sociocultural Equity Scale (ACSES; Curenton et al., 2018), which examines equitable sociocultural interactions (e.g., culturally responsive pedagogy, teacher bias/differential treatment, and inequitable experiences) among teachers and students with racially minoritized learners in early childhood classrooms (pre-K to 3). Tables 9.2 and 9.3 summarize program observation instruments commonly used for evaluation purposes. Table 9.2 describes instruments used to measure global quality, and Table 9.3 lists instruments used to measure specific program components, including parent–child interactions, teacher–child interactions, content-specific evaluations, behavior, and administration.

Table 9.2. Global instruments designed to measure program quality and description

Instrument	Description
Assessing Classroom Sociocultural Equity Scale (ACSES) (Curenton et al., 2018)	Measures the equitable sociocultural interactions in pre-K–third-grade classrooms based on culturally relevant, culturally responsive, and antibias education. The framework supports these aspects within the classroom: • Freedom of expression • Connection and incorporation of children's home life • Social identities • Social justice • Equitable and positive discipline • Instruction and curriculum challenging the status quo • Children's ethnic and sociopolitical heritage
Early Childhood Environment Rating Scale, Third Edition (ECERS-3) (Harms et al., 2014)	Evaluates the overall quality of the preschool environment primarily on the basis of interactions between teacher and children and activities that occur in the classroom. Seven subscales: • Space and furnishings • Personal care routines • Language–reasoning • Activities • Interaction • Program structure • Parents and staff
Family Child Care Environment Rating Scale, Third Edition (FCCERS-3) (Harms et al., 2019)	Evaluates the overall quality of a family child care environment primarily on the basis between the teacher and children and activities that occur in the environment. Six subscales: • Space and furnishings • Personal care routines • Language and books • Activities • Interaction • Program structure

(continued)

Table 9.2. *(continued)*

Instrument	Description
Infant Toddler Environmental Rating Scale, Third Edition (ITERS-3) (Harms et al., 2017)	Evaluates the overall quality of the infant or toddler environment primarily on the basis of interactions between teacher and children and activities that occur in the classroom. Seven subscales: • Space and furnishings • Personal care routines • Language–reasoning • Activities • Interaction • Program structure • Parents and staff
Preschool Program Quality Assessment–Revised (HighScope, 2019)	Evaluates the overall quality of preschool classrooms on three dimensions: • Learning environment • Teaching and learning routines and adult–child interactions • Curriculum, planning, assessment, and parent engagement
DEC Recommended Practices Program Assessment: Improving practices for young children with special needs and their families (Hemmeter et al., 2001)	Evaluates the quality of services provided to young children with disabilities and their families in any early childhood environment such as Head Start, child care, or public preschool on the basis of the Division for Early Childhood Recommended Practices. Divided into five strands: • Interdisciplinary models • Family-based practices • Assessment • Child-focused practices • Technology applications
Global Guidelines Assessment-Third Edition (GGA) (Association for Childhood Education International, 2011)	Evaluates the overall quality of early childhood care and education programs. Segmented into five subscales: • Environment and physical space • Curriculum content and pedagogy • Early childhood educators and caregivers • Partnerships with families and communities • Young children with special needs
Inclusive Classroom Profile (ICP) (Soukakou, 2016)	Assesses the quality of classroom practices in inclusive settings and evaluates program quality as part of Quality Rating and Improvement Systems (QRIS) and informs models of professional development to support providers to meet the individualized needs of children with disabilities in inclusive settings. Separated into 12 quality indicators: • Adaptations of space and materials/equipment • Adult involvement in peer interactions • Adults' guidance of children's play • Conflict resolution • Membership • Relationships between adults and children • Support for communication • Adaptation of group activities • Transitions between activities • Feedback • Family–professional partnerships • Monitoring children's learning

Table 9.3.   Instruments designed to measure specific program components and description

Parent–child interactions	
Instrument	Description
Home Observation for Measurement of the Environment (HOME)– Third Edition (Caldwell & Bradley, 2003)	Examines infants and toddlers (birth to 3) by measuring the following: • Parent responsivity • Acceptance of child • Organization of the environment • Learning materials • Parental involvement • Variety of experience Uses the following early childhood (3–6) measures: • Learning materials • Language stimulation • Physical environment • Parental responsivity • Learning stimulation • Modeling of social maturity • Variety in experience • Acceptance of child
Parenting Interactions with Children: The checklist of observations linked to outcomes (Roggman et al., 2013)	Examines the following early childhood (10–47 months) measures: • Affection • Responsiveness • Encouragement • Teaching
The Parent-Child Early Relational Assessment (PCERA) (Clark, 1985)	Examines young children (birth–5) on the quality of affect and behavior in parent–child interactions under eight subscales: • Parental positive affective involvement and verbalization • Parental negative affect and behavior • Parental intrusiveness, insensitivity, and inconsistency • Infant positive affect and social communicative skills • Infant quality of play, interest, and attentional skills • Infant dysregulation and irritability • Dyadic mutual enjoyment and reciprocity • Dyadic disorganization and tension
The Parent-Infant Interaction Observation Scale for Health Visitors (PIIOS) (Svanberg & Barlow, 2013)	Screening tool for primary care practitioners to assess parent–child interaction and to identify parents of infants (2–7 months) in need of further support on 13 subscales: • Infant positioning • Eye contact • Vocalizations • Affect engagement and synchrony • Warmth and affection • Holding and handling • Verbal commenting (mind-mindedness) • Attunement to distress • Bodily intrusiveness • Expressed expectations • Empathic understanding • Responsive turn taking • Baby's self-soothing strategies

(continued)

Table 9.3.   *(continued)*

Parent–child interactions	
Instrument	Description
CARE-Index (Crittenden, 2005)	Evaluates the quality of parent–child interactions of parents or caregivers with infants (birth–15 months) and toddlers (15–30 months). Results are divided into seven scales for both adult and child: Adult • Sensitivity • Control • Unresponsiveness Child (infant) • Cooperativeness • Compulsiveness • Difficultness • Passivity Child (toddler) • Cooperativeness • Compulsiveness • Threateningly coercive • Disarmingly coercive
Indicator of Parent Child Interaction–II (IPCI-II) (Baggett et al., 2010)	Evaluates the quality of parent–child interactions in young children (2–42 months). Segmented into six items each for both the parent and the child, and divided into two sections: Parent facilitators • Convey acceptance and warmth • Use descriptive language • Follow child's lead • Maintain or extend child's focus Parent interrupters • Use criticism or harsh voice • Use restrictions/intrusions • Child engagement • Positive feedback • Sustained engagement • Follow through Child distress • Irritable, fusses, cries • External distress (tantrum) • Frozen, watchful, withdrawn
Parent-Infant Relational Assessment Tool (PIRAT) (Boughton, 2014)	Rates parent–child interactions for infants (birth to 2 years) and measures optimal parental behavior. Divided into 12 subscales for the infant and 11 parent subscales Infant • Infant's seeking of contact • Responsiveness to contact • Responsiveness to stranger • Ability to communicate needs • Ability to be comforted • Quality of contact • Clinging • Frightened/wary • Lack of pleasure

Table 9.3. *(continued)*

Parent–child interactions	
Instrument	Description
	• Sexualized
	• Dissociative
	• Avoidant
	Parent
	• Initiation of physical contact
	• Initiation of emotional contact
	• Playfulness in relation to infant
	• Pleasure in parenting
	• Hostility and blame
	• Quality of contact
	• Frightening
	• Sexualized
	• Dissociative
	• Avoidant
	• Consistency/predictability
Keys to Interactive Parenting Scale (KIPS) (Comfort et al., 2011)	Evaluates the quality of parent–child interactions and parent behavior during free play in young children (2 months–5 years). Divided into three domains: • Building relationships • Promoting (child's) learning • Supporting (child's) confidence

Teacher–child instruction	
Measure	Description
Caregiver Interaction Scale (Arnett, 1989)	Examines caregiver interactions with young children in home and center-based settings, measuring the following: • Sensitivity • Harshness • Detachment • Permissiveness
Child Caregiver Interaction Scale (CCIS)–Revised Edition (Carl, 2010)	Examines caregiver's interactions with young children. Three domains: • Emotional domain • Cognitive/physical domain • Social domain
Classroom Assessment Scoring System (CLASS) (Pianta et al., 2008)	Examines teacher's interactions with child across all academic areas, as well as classroom management. Three subscales: • Emotional support • Classroom organization • Instructional support
The Early Childhood Classroom Observation Measure (ECCOM; Stipek & Byler, 2004)	Examines teacher sensitivity and management style in preschool classrooms. Measure includes three subscales: • Management • Social climate • Learning climate Also includes a classroom resources checklist that is used to determine the materials in the classroom for various activities (e.g., literacy, dramatic play, art)

(continued)

Table 9.3.   *(continued)*

Teacher–child instruction	
Measure	Description
Emerging Academic Snapshot (Richie et al., 2001)	Focuses on the extent to which individual preschool children are exposed to instruction and engagement in academic activities. Subcategories include the following: • Children's activity setting • Engagement with adults • Engagement with activities • Peer interaction
Observation Record of the Caregiving Environment (NICHD Early Child Care Research Network, 1996)	Focuses on the sensitivity and responsiveness of caregivers in their interactions with infants, toddlers, and preschoolers. Different subscales are scored depending on the age of the child. The following are among the variables examined: • Positive caregiving • Language development • Fostering child's exploration • Stimulation of cognitive development • Positive talk and physical contact
Student-Teacher Relationship Scale (STRS) (Pianta, 2007)	Measures a teacher's overall view of their relationship with a particular student, with high scores suggesting higher relationship quality. Three subscales: • Conflict • Closeness • Dependency
Content-specific instruction	
Measure	Description
Early Childhood Environment Rating Scale–Extension (ECERS-E), Fourth Edition (Sylva et al., 2010)	Developed as an extension of the ECERS-R to examine the quality of instruction in preschool classrooms. The measure emphasizes instruction in four content areas: • Literacy • Mathematics • Science/environment • Diversity
Early Language and Literacy Classroom Observation—PreK (Smith et al., 2008)	Designed to measure the quality of the language and literacy environment and teacher practices in preschool classrooms. Measure examines five elements: • Classroom structure • Curriculum • Language environment • Books and book reading opportunities • Print and early writing supports
Observation Measure of Language and Literacy Instruction (OMLIT; Goodson et al., 2006)	The OMLIT is an observational tool that measures the degree with which the early childhood environment is supporting language and literacy instruction for young children. There are five instruments: • Classroom literacy opportunities checklist • Snapshot of classroom activities • Read aloud profile • Classroom literacy instruction profile • Quality of instruction in language and literacy

Table 9.3. *(continued)*

Content-specific instruction	
Measure	**Description**
Preschool Classroom Mathematics Inventory (National Institute for Early Education Research, 2007)	The Preschool Classroom Mathematics Inventory examines the quality of mathematics instruction and learning opportunities in preschool classrooms. Items are grouped into three categories: • Number • Mathematical concepts • Parent involvement
Supports for English Language Learners Classroom Assessment (National Institute for Early Education Research, 2005)	The Supports for English Language Learners Classrooms Assessment assesses the following: • Degree with which teacher incorporates culture of children in classroom • Degree with which teacher encourages parent participation • Degree with which teacher encourages children's use of native language and offers literacy materials in their native language • Degree with which the teacher supports English language development
Science Teaching and Environment Rating Scale (STERS) (Chalufour et al., 2006)	The Science Teaching and Environment Rating Learning Scale assesses the quality of classroom science instruction by measuring the following: • Instructor creates a physical environment for inquiry and learning • Instructor facilitates direct experiences to promote conceptual learning • Instructor promotes use of scientific inquiry • Instructor creates a collaborative climate that promotes exploration and understanding • Instructor provides opportunities for extended conversations • Instructor builds children's vocabulary • Instructor plans in-depth investigations • Instructor assesses children's learning
The Basic School Skills Inventory (BSSI)–Third Edition (Hammill et al., 1998)	Evaluates young children (ages 4–6) who are at risk of falling behind, may have learning disorders, or have certain areas that need improvement. Four areas: • Reading • Math • Writing • Classroom behavior

Behavior	
Measure	**Description**
Teaching Pyramid Observation Tool for Preschool Classrooms (Hemmeter et al., 2008)	Assesses the degree with which preschool teachers are implementing the teaching pyramid for supporting young children's social-emotional development. The tool measures four components: • Responsive interactions • Classroom preventive practices • Social-emotional teaching strategies • Individualized interventions
Preschool Learning Behaviors Scale (PLBS) (McDermott et al., 2002)	Evaluates early learning behaviors within early childhood educational programs under three domains: • Competence motivation • Attention/persistence • Learning strategy

(continued)

Table 9.3.   *(continued)*

Behavior	
Measure	Description
The Penn Interactive Peer Play Scale (PIPPS) (Fantuzzo et al., 1995)	Assesses the interactive play behaviors of preschool children. Three dimensions: • Play interaction • Play disruption • Play disconnection
The Social Competence and Behavior Evaluation scale (SCBE-30)–Preschool Edition (LaFreniere & Dumas, 1996)	Measures the social competence, emotion regulation and expression, and adjustment difficulties of young children (3–6). Three subscores: • Anger – Aggression • Social competence • Anxiety – Withdrawal
Behavior Assessment System for Children, Third Edition (BASC-3), Preschool Level (Reynolds & Kamphaus, 2015)	Evaluates and monitors changes in young children's (ages 2–5) behavior or emotional status. Several composite subscores are reported, as well as individual scores. Four main scores: • Externalizing problems • Internalizing problems • Adaptive skills • School problems
Preschool Self-Regulation Assessment (PSRA) (Goyette et al., 2006)	Assesses the self-regulation of young children. Three domains: • Emotional • Attentional • Behavioral
Early Childhood Behavior Questionnaire (Putnam et al., 2006)	Assesses three factors of children's temperament: • Negative affectivity • Surgency • Effortful control
Child Behavioral Checklist (CBCL/1½-5) (Achenbach & Rescorla, 2001)	Measures child behavior using seven subscales: • Emotionally reactive • Anxious/depressed • Somatic complaints • Sleep problems • Attention problems • Aggressive behavior

Administration	
Measure	Description
Program Administration Scale, Second Edition (PAS) (Talan & Bloom, 2011)	Evaluates the overall quality of administrative practices in early care and education programs using 10 subscales: • Human resource development • Personnel costs and allocation • Center operations • Child assessment • Fiscal management • Program planning and evaluation • Family partnerships • Marketing and public relations • Technology • Staff qualifications

Table 9.3. *(continued)*

Administration	
Measure	Description
Business Administration Scale for Family Child Care–Second Edition (BAS) (Talan & Bloom, 2009)	Assesses the overall quality of administrative practices family child care and education programs utilizing 10 subscales: • Qualifications and professional development • Income and benefits • Work environments • Fiscal management • Recordkeeping • Risk management • Provider-parent communication • Community resources • Marketing and public relations • Provider as employer

Stakeholder Input

Program evaluation data also can be collected through stakeholder input. Stakeholders are those who benefit from the program's services and include family members who pay for the services, staff who deliver the services, and community constituents who advise and sometimes fund the program's services. In some situations, children who receive services from the program might provide input into the quality of the program.

There are three primary ways that information from stakeholders can be gathered. First, someone can conduct individual interviews with stakeholders. For program evaluation purposes, interview questions are generally open ended and about the stakeholders' satisfaction or dissatisfaction with the program. The questions are often directed at focus groups, which generally involve 7–10 people who provide the evaluator information that will be useful in determining the effectiveness of the program. Focus groups are frequently utilized for local, state, or federal program evaluations. Table 9.4 provides sample questions for an evaluation of a state-level program evaluation.

Finally, information from large numbers of stakeholders can be gathered with a survey. Survey questions often require respondents to answer on the basis of some type of rubric or Likert scale. For example, when a program is going through the NAEYC accreditation process, both staff and families are asked to complete a comprehensive survey requesting their input into the degree with which the program is meeting certain standards. The teaching staff survey asks questions about child relationships, curriculum, teaching, assessment, health, teachers, family, community relationships, leadership, and management, among other aspects of the program. One item related to leadership and management is "Program staff are involved in a comprehensive program evaluation that measures progress toward program goals and

Table 9.4. Sample focus group questions

Components of statewide early care and education initiative	Focus group questions
Quality Rating System	1. What supports are available that encourage participation in the STARS for KIDS NOW Quality Rating System?
	2. What makes participation in the STARS for KIDS NOW Quality Rating System challenging?
	3. What might the state do to encourage or support your continued participation in the STARS for KIDS NOW Quality Rating System?
Scholarship program for early care and education providers	1. What supports are available to encourage participation in the scholarship program?
	2. What makes participation in the scholarship system challenging?
	3. What might the state do to encourage or support your (or your staff members') participation in the scholarship program?
Community Early Childhood Councils	1. What incentives or supports are available that encourage you to participate in your local Community Early Childhood Council?
	2. What makes participation in the local Community Early Childhood Council challenging?
	3. What might the state do to encourage or support your participation in the Community Early Childhood Council?
Healthy Start	1. What incentives or supports are available that encourage you to participate in your Healthy Start program?
	2. What makes participation in the Healthy Start program challenging?
	3. What might the state do to encourage or support your participation in the Healthy Start program?

objectives." Staff indicate a yes, no, or don't know response. Similarly, families complete a 24-question survey for NAEYC program accreditation. A sample item from that survey is "Teachers often share information about things happening in the program and want to know things my child is doing at home."

Information from stakeholders can provide both quantitative and qualitative information. Quantitative data may give program administrators information about the number or percentage of parents in a program who are satisfied with the services they received. Qualitative data can provide administrators with information about the impact that program services have had on their child or family. The following statement from a parent suggests the impact that the program has had on the child and family: "My child has gained so much since start[ing] Building Blocks. The staff are great about meeting her individual needs and listening to our concerns." One of the greatest benefits of surveying stakeholders is that it provides information not just about what the program is, but also about what difference the program makes. A high-quality program evaluation includes both quantitative and qualitative information. In a recent evaluation of an early reading program for English language learners, Llosa and Slayton (2009) indicate that the only way to understand all of the variables that affect program implementation is to utilize a multimethodological approach to program evaluation.

Record Review

Finally, a review of program documents is a common component of many program evaluations. A review of a program's policies and procedures will provide information about the program's philosophy, goals, and intensity and duration of services. The handbook for parents has information about family involvement options that the program offers. Information about employee professional development can be found in the program's employee records. Other administrative records will provide evidence of staff evaluations and associated professional development plans. All of these documents can give program evaluators the information they need to understand the structural variables that affect program quality.

In an evaluation of an early childhood gifted education program, Hertzog & Fowler (1999) used semistructured interviews, focus groups, and surveys conducted during classroom observations to collect data from stakeholders (i.e., teachers and parents). However, prior to conducting the evaluation, they collected and reviewed program documents including previous evaluation reports, program pamphlets, and the program's policy and procedures manual. These documents provided the evaluation team members with information about the program's philosophy, curriculum design, and staffing patterns.

RECOMMENDED PRACTICES

Certain practices should be adhered to in conducting a program evaluation. More specifically, guidance is given on how to plan the evaluation, how to conduct it, and how to use the data collected. All three topics will be covered in the next section.

Planning for Program Evaluation

There are many things to consider in planning a program evaluation. A thorough evaluation should begin prior to the start of a new program and should be designed so that it will help to improve the program (Bagnato & Neisworth, 1991). The evaluation should focus on the program's goals, and its purpose should be clear to key stakeholders, who should be actively involved in the evaluation process (DEC, 2007). The National Forum on Early Childhood Program Evaluation (2007) indicates that improving the program should be the goal of all program evaluations. Often, there is a tendency to utilize comparative research design (i.e., comparing one program against another) as the model for evaluating federal programs. This approach is problematic because there may be variables that affect program quality but that are beyond the control of the program (e.g., the quality of the service delivered, whether the children or families in the program actually received the service).

Conducting a Program Evaluation

As previously stated, a high-quality program evaluation focuses on both outcomes (the product) and procedures (the process), using a variety of measures (Bagnato & Neisworth, 1991); therefore, collecting both qualitative and quantitative data is important. Regardless of what measures are used, all should be valid and reliable (DEC, 2007). A high-quality program evaluation should consider not only child outcomes (Bagnato & Neisworth, 1991), but also variables that mediate outcomes (e.g., length of time in the program) as well as the degree of fidelity with which interventions were provided (DEC, 2007).

Using Program Evaluation Data

The DEC (2007) indicates that a high-quality program evaluation should facilitate making decisions about the program. A common way to determine how to use program-evaluation data to improve programs is to develop a logic model, "a clear and logical explanation of how the goals of the program link to the services provided and produce the expected results" (National Child Care Information Center, 2005, p. 2). The DEC describes the components of a logic model. The inputs are the program's resources, which may include the people who work in the program or fiscal resources. The activities are what the program does with its inputs to carry out its goals. For example, the staff of the program implement developmentally appropriate curricula, and resources may be used to design outdoor learning environments. "Outputs are the direct products of program activities and typically are measured in terms of the amount of services or supports provided to participants" (DEC, p. 23). For example, the output of staff implementing a developmentally appropriate curriculum might be the number of children in a 1-year period who received access to a developmentally appropriate curriculum. Finally, the outcomes are the results generated during or after the program's implementation. The DEC describes two types of outcomes. Proximal outcomes are generated from consumers of the services and are intermediate. Parents' level of satisfaction with a program's curriculum is an example of a proximal outcome. Distal, or end, outcomes are related to the expected impact of the activity. For example, a distal outcome of a developmentally appropriate curriculum might be that preschoolers possess the necessary skills to transition easily to kindergarten. Kingsbury (2002) suggests that when systems are being evaluated, external influences should be included in the logic model. External influences are those variables that might be supporting or exacerbating the implementation of the activities. For example, if the goal of a statewide preschool program is to implement developmentally appropriate curricula in blended preschool programs, an influence that might affect that goal is the absence of state funding to appropriately train teachers to implement the curricula. Policy issues are often affected by external influences.

SUMMARY

This chapter has described program evaluation systems at the classroom, programwide, state, and national levels. Among the methods examined for collecting program evaluation data were child assessment, program observations, the use of stakeholder input, and a record review. Readers were cautioned to be selective in determining the type of assessment tool to use, and in interpreting child assessment data, for program evaluation purposes. Finally, recommended practices for conducting effective program evaluations were discussed, with an emphasis on using program evaluation data to improve programs for young children and their families.

Program evaluation is a form of assessment that teachers sometimes believe does not affect them. However, teachers are an integral part of program evaluation assessment at all levels. Teachers collect data for many levels of program evaluation, and they provide data to program administrators for some program evaluation levels. Most importantly, teachers are consumers of program evaluation data. Information gained from program evaluations can assist early childhood intervention teachers in improving services to children and their families. For that reason, an understanding of program evaluation is essential for teachers who work with young children.

REFERENCES

Achenbach, T. M., & Rescorla, L. A. (2001). *Manual for the ASEBA school-age forms & profiles.* University of Vermont, Research Center for Children, Youth & Families.

Arnett, J. (1989). Caregivers in day-care centers: Does training matter? *Journal of Applied Developmental Psychology, 10,* 541. https://doi.org/10.1016/0193-3973(89)90026-9

Association for Childhood Education International. (2011). *ACEI global guidelines assessment* (3rd ed.). Association for Childhood Education International.

Baggett, K. M., Carta, J. J., & Horn, E. A. (2010). Indicator of parent child interaction. In J. Carta, C. Greenwood, D. Walker, & J. Buzhardt (Eds.), *Individual growth and developmental indicators: Tools for monitoring progress and measuring growth in very young children.* Paul H. Brookes Publishing Co.

Bagnato, S. J., & Neisworth, J. T. (1991). *Assessment for early intervention: Best practices for professionals.* Guilford Press.

Broughton, C. (2014). Measuring parent-infant interaction: The Parent-Infant Relational Assessment Tool (PIRAT). *Journal of Child Psychotherapy, 40*(3), 254–270. http://doi.org/10.1080/0075417X.2014.965420

Burchinal, M., Kainz, K., & Cai, Y. (2011). How well do our measures of quality predict child outcomes? A meta-analysis and coordinated analysis of data from large-scale studies of early childhood settings. In M. Zaslow, I. Martinez-Beck, K. Tout, & T. Halle (Eds.), *Quality measurement in early childhood settings* (pp. 11–31). Paul H. Brookes Publishing Co.

Caldwell, R. H., & Bradley, B. M. (2003). *Home Observation for Measurement of the Environment: Administration manual* (3rd ed.). Family & Human Dynamics Research Institute, Arizona State University.

California Child Care Resource Network & Referral & Parent Voices. (2020). *Quality improvement in California.* Child Care Law Center. https://rrnetwork.org/assets/general-files/Master-Plan-QRIS.pdf

Carl, B. (2010). *Child Caregiver Interaction Scale (CCIS) manual–revised edition.* https://annenberginstitute.org/instruments/child-caregiver-interaction-scale

Clark, R. (1985). *The Parent-Child Early Relational Assessment: Instrument and manual.* University of Wisconsin Medical School, Department of Psychiatry.

Chalufour, I., Worth, K., & Clark-Chiarelli, N. (2006). *Science Teaching and Environment Rating Scale (STERS)*. Education Development Center.

Cole, C. (2006). Closing the achievement gap series: Part III. What is the impact of NCLB on the inclusion of students with disabilities? *Center for Evaluation and Education Policy, 4*(11), 1–12.

Colker, L. J., & Koralek, D. (2018). *High quality early childhood programs: The what, why, and how.* Redleaf Press.

Comfort, M., Gordon, P. R., & Naples., D. (2011). KIPS: An evidence-based tool for assessing parenting strengths and needs in diverse families. *Infants & Young Children: An Interdisciplinary Journal of Early Childhood Intervention, 24*(1), 56–74.

Counsell, S. L., & Wright, B. L. (2018). High stakes accountability systems: Creating cultures of fear. *Global Education Review, 5*(2), 189–202.

Crittenden, P. M. (2005). Der care-index als hilfsmittel für früherkennung, intervention und forschung. *Frühförderung interdisziplinär, 3,* S.99–106.

Curenton, S. M., Iruka, I. U., Humphries, M., Jenson, B., Durden, T., Rochester, S. E., Sims, J., Whittaker, J., & Kinzie, M. (2019). Validity for the Assessing Classroom Sociocultural Equity Scale (ACSES) in early childhood classrooms. *Early Education and Development, 31*(1), 1–20. http://doi.org/10.1080/10409289.2019.1611331

Curenton, S. M., Jensen, B., Iruka, I., Durden, T., Humphries, M., & Rochester, S. E. (2018). *Manual for Assessing Classroom Sociocultural Equity Scale (ACSES)–Version 2.5.* Boston University.

Division for Early Childhood (DEC). (2007). *Promoting positive outcomes for children with disabilities: Recommendation for curriculum, assessment, and program evaluation.* Author.

Fantuzzo, J., Sutton-Smith, B., Coolahan, K. C., Manz, P. H., Canning, S., & Debnam, D. (1995). The Penn Interactive Peer Play Scale. *Early Childhood Research Quarterly, 10*(1), 105–120.

Goodson, B. D., Layzer, C., Smith, W. C., & Rimdzius, T. (2006). *Observation Measures of Language and Literacy Instruction* (OMLIT). Abt Associates.

Goyette, P., Carroll, K., Smith-Donald, R., Metzger, M., Young, T., & Raver, C. C. (2006). *Field administration of an emotional and behavioral assessment of Head Start children: Preliminary findings from the Preschool Self-Regulation Assessment.* Poster presented at Head Start's Eighth National Research Conference.

Graham, J. W., Taylor, B. J., Olchowski, A. E., & Cumsville, P. E. (2006). Planning missing data designs in psychological research. *Psychological Methods, 11*(4), 323–343.

Groginsky, S., Robison, S., & Smith, S. (1999). *Making child care better: State initiatives.* National Conference of State Legislators.

Hammill, D. D., Leigh, J. E., Pearson, N. A., & Maddox, T. (1998). *Basic School Skills Inventory: A readiness measure for teachers.* PRO-ED.

Hamre, B. K., Justice, L. M., Pianta, R. C., Kilday, C., Beverly, S., Downer, J. T., & Leach, A. (2010). Implementation fidelity of MyTeachingPartner literacy and language activities: Association with preschoolers' language and literacy growth. *Early Childhood Research Quarterly, 25*(3), 329–347. https://doi.org/10.1016/j.ecresq.2009.07.002

Harms, T., Clifford, R. M., & Cryer, D. (2014). *Early Childhood Environment Rating Scale–Third Edition* (ECERS-3). Teachers College Press.

Harms, T., Clifford, R. M., & Cryer, D. (2017). *Infant/Toddler Environment Rating Scale–Third Edition.* Teachers College Press.

Harms, T., Cryer, D., Clifford, R. M., & Yazejian, N. (2019). *Family Child Care Environment Rating Scale–Third Edition* (FCCER-3). Teachers College Press.

Helios Education Foundation. (2017). *Early childhood assessment policies and practices in the age of accountability: Core considerations for system development.* Helios.

Hemmeter, M. L., Fox, L., & Snyder, P. (2008). *The Teaching Pyramid Observation Tool.* Vanderbilt University.

Hemmeter, M. L., Joseph, G. E., Smith, B. J., & Sandall, S. (2001). *DEC Recommended Practices Program Assessment: Improving practices for young children with special needs and their families.* Sopris West.

Hertzog, N. B., & Fowler, S. A. (1999). *Roeper Review, 21*(3), 222–227.

HighScope. (2019). *Preschool Program Quality Assessment–Revised Edition.* HighScope Press.

Hojnoski, R. L., & Missall, K. N. (2007). Monitoring preschoolers' language and literacy growth and development. *Young Exceptional Children, 10*(17), 17–27.

Kingsbury, N. (2002). *Program evaluation: Strategies for assessing how information dissemination contributes to agency goals* (GAO-02-923). U.S. GAO.

LaFreniere, P. J., & Dumas, J. E. (1996). Social Competence and Behavior Evaluation scale in children ages 3 to 6 years: The short form (SCBE-30). *Psychological Assessment, 8*(4), 369.

Ledford, J. R., & Wolery, M. (2013). Procedural fidelity: An analysis of measurement and reporting practices. *Vanderbilt University, 35*(2), 173–193. http://doi.org/10.1177/1053815113515908

Llosa, L., & Slayton, J. (2009). Using program evaluation to improve the education of young English language learners in US schools. *Language Teaching Research, 13*(1), 35–54.

McDermott, P. A., Leigh, N. M., & Perry, M. A. (2002). Development and validation of the Preschool Learning Behaviors Scale. *Psychology in the Schools, 39*, 353–365.

Meek, S., Iruka, I. U., Allen, R., Yazzie, D., Fernandez, V., Catherine, E., McIntosh, K., Gordon, L., Gilliam, W., Hemmeter, M. L., Blevins, D., & Powell, T. (2020). *Fourteen priorities to dismantle systemic racism in early care and education.* The Children's Equity Project.

Meisels, S. J. (2006). *Accountability in early childhood: No easy answers* (Report No. 6). Herr Research Center for Children and Social Policy at Erikson Institute. https://www.erikson.edu/research/accountability-in-early-childhood-no-easy-answers/

National Academies of Science, Engineering, and Medicine. (2019). *5 indicators of disparities in access to educational opportunities. Monitoring educational equity.* National Academies Press. http://doi.org/10.17226/25389

National Academy of Sciences. (2008). *Early childhood assessment: Why, what, and how.* National Academies Press. http://doi.org/10.17226/12446

National Child Care Information Center. (2005). *Assessment and evaluation: Becoming an educated consumer. Part II: Program evaluation.* Author.

National Forum on Early Childhood Program Evaluation. (2007). *Early childhood program evaluation: A decision-making guide.* Center on the Developing Child at Harvard University.

National Institute for Early Education Research. (2005). *Support for English Language Learners Classroom Assessment.* Author.

National Institute for Early Education Research. (2007). *Preschool Classroom Mathematics Inventory.* Author.

Newcomer, K. E., Hatry, H. P., & Wholey, J. S. (2010). Planning and designing useful evaluations. *Handbook of Practical Program Evaluation, 19*(5).

NICHD Early Child Care Research Network. (1996). Observational Record of the Caregiving Environment. *Early Childhood Research Quarterly, 11*(3), 169–306.

Pianta, R.C. (2007). *STRS: Student-Teacher Relationship Scale: Professional manual.* Psychological Assessment Resources.

Pianta, R. C., La Paro, K. M., & Hamre, B. K. (2008). *Classroom assessments: Scoring system.* Paul H. Brookes Publishing Co.

Putnam, S. P., Garstein, M. A., & Rothbart., M. K. (2006). Measurement of fine-grained aspect of toddler temperament: Early Childhood Behavior Questionnaire. *Infant Behavior and Development, 29*(3), 386–401.

Reynolds, C. R., & Kamphaus, R. W. (2015). *Behavior Assessment System for Children* (3rd ed.). American Guidance Service.

Richie, S., Howes, C., Kraft-Sayre, M., & Weiser, B. (2001). *Emerging Academic Snapshot.* University of California at Los Angeles.

Roggman, L. A., Cook, G. A., Innocenti, M. S., Jump, V. K., Christiansen, K., & Anderson, S. (2013). *Parenting interactions with children: The checklist of observations linked to outcomes.* Paul H. Brookes Publishing Co.

Shepard, L. A., Kagan, S. L., & Wurtz, E. (1998). *Principles and recommendations for early childhood assessments.* The National Education Goals Panel.

Sherow, S. M. (2000). Adult and family literacy adaptations of goal statement scaling, *Adult Basic Education, 10*(1), 1–4.

Shultz, T., Kagan, S. L., & Shore, R. (2009). *Taking stock: Assessing and improving early childhood learning and program quality.* National Early Childhood Accountability Task Force.

Smith, M. W., Brady, J. P., & Anastasopoulos, L. (2008). *Early Language and Literacy Classroom Observation—Pre-K.* Paul H. Brookes Publishing Co.

Snyder, S., & Sheehan R. (1996). Program evaluation in early childhood special education. In S. L. Odom & M. E. McLean (Eds.), *Early intervention for infants and young children with disabilities and their families: Recommended practices* (pp. 359–378). PRO-ED.

Soukakou, E. P. (2016). *Inclusive Classroom Profile (ICP) manual.* Paul H. Brookes Publishing Co.

Stipek, D., & Byler, P. (2004). The Early Childhood Classroom Observation Measure. *Early Childhood Research Quarterly, 19*, 375–397.

Svanberg, P. O., & Barlow, J. (2013). The effectiveness of training in the Parent-Infant Interaction Observation Scale for Health Visitors. *Journal of Health Visiting, 1*(3), 162–166.

Sylva, K., Siraj-Blatchford, I., & Taggart, B. (2010). *ECERS-E: The four curricular subscales extension to the Early Childhood Environment Rating Scale (ECERS-R).* Teachers College Press.

Talan, T. N., & Bloom, P. J. (2009). *Business Administration Scale for Family Child Care, BAS* (2nd ed.). Teachers College Press.

Talan, T. N., & Bloom, P. J. (2011). *Program Administration Scale: Measuring early childhood leadership and administration* (2nd ed.). Teachers College Press.

Special Topics in the Assessment of Young Children

Recommended Practices for Assessing Children Who Are Dual Language Learners or Multilanguage Learners

Lin Zhu, Jennifer Grisham, Kristie Pretti-Frontczak, and Ashley Lyons-Picard

Jaden is a teacher in an inclusive preschool classroom serving children both with and without disabilities in a culturally and linguistically diverse neighborhood. At the start of the school year, Jaden has 12 children registered to attend her classroom. Within the group of 12 children registered to start preschool in Jaden's class, seven different cultural backgrounds are represented, with four of the children primarily speaking languages other than English. Jaden understands that it is her responsibility to assess each child in an individually appropriate and nonbiased way. Jaden is very worried about how she is going to design a high-quality learning experience for all of the children when she is unsure of even where to begin facilitating an appropriate, nonbiased assessment process for a group of children with such diverse backgrounds.

As the number of children with disabilities who are served in community settings has increased, so has the overall diversity of the population of young children being served. The number of young children who are dual language learners (DLLs) or multilanguage learners has grown rapidly in the United States since 2000, with DLL children making up one-quarter or more of all young children in 19 states and the District of Columbia (Park et al., 2018). Schools in the United States have faced rapid changes in student demographics with a concomitant increase in the number of dual language learners. Many children use one language at home and are expected to use another language to communicate in their larger environment (Peña, 2016).

As a result of these demographic changes, early childhood educators need support to assess and meet the needs of children from diverse cultural and linguistic backgrounds. Children who are DLLs show diversity in many aspects, including race and ethnicity, countries of origin, and languages spoken. All of these aspects of diversity affect the assessment process. The purpose of this chapter is to discuss the application of recommended assessment practices discussed in Chapters 2–4 as they apply to children who are DLLs or multilanguage learners. The text that follows is divided into three main sections. The first section provides an overview of the challenges and general considerations for assessing children who are DLLs or multilanguage learners. In the second section, specific recommendations and suggestions are made for the assessment process. Finally, the last section concludes the chapter with a discussion of the measures available for assessing young children who are DLLs or multilanguage learners. Practices for serving children with diverse cultural experiences, and children who are dual or multilanguage learners, will be emphasized throughout the chapter.

GENERAL CONSIDERATIONS FOR ASSESSING CHILDREN WHO ARE DUAL LANGUAGE OR MULTILANGUAGE LEARNERS

The next section provides general considerations for assessing children who are DLLs or multilanguage learners. The section discusses some of the challenges teachers face when conducting assessments for these children and presents an overview of the general issues surrounding the measures teachers have available to them.

Challenges of Assessing Children Who Are Dual or Multilanguage Learners

When children from particular racial or ethnic groups are identified as having a disability at a greater or lesser rate than all other students, then that group is said to be disproportionately represented in special education (Williams, 2007). When a particular group is represented at a greater rate than the population in general, that group is said to be overrepresented (e.g., when a group represents 10% of the population but constitutes 20% of children being served in special education). Children who are dual or multilanguage learners have historically been, and continue to be, under- and overrepresented in special education placements (Umansky et al., 2017). Many professionals would agree that at least a portion of the overrepresentation of culturally and linguistically diverse children is directly related to errors in the assessment process (Counts et al., 2018). In her speech *Assessing young dual language learners: Challenges and opportunities*, L. M. Espinosa stated, "[when] children are assessed in a language they do not fully use or comprehend or with invalid measures, their language skills will be underestimated." She went on to say, "invalid measures of language will result in over-referral of typical language learners or under-referral of at risk children" (personal communication, May 2010).

Children are all too often found eligible for special education services when cultural or linguistic characteristics are confused with a skill deficit or a need for special education service. For instance, children from linguistically diverse backgrounds are often overidentified with language impairment (LI) because the teacher may not have appropriate expectations for their language and communication development. School districts sometimes label DLLs or multilanguage learners with learning disabilities when they struggle to understand the English language (Artiles et al., 2005). Moreover, once DLLs are classified for special education, they are more likely than their English-speaking peers to be taught outside mainstream classrooms and unlikely to receive extensive language services (Ackerman & Tazi, 2015).

In reality, the confusion and frequent misinterpretation of results are due not to professional misunderstanding, but to an overreliance on culturally and linguistically biased assessments (Espinosa, 2005, 2015). In fact, assessment tools are often culturally or linguistically biased (Banerjee & Guiberson, 2012). The field of education has identified a combination of a shortage of assessors trained in second-language acquisition and the absence of tests that are scientifically validated for children who do not speak proficient English (Russakoff, 2011). For example, in some school districts, DLLs or multilanguage learners are required to take the same high-stakes tests as their English-speaking peers. Although 75% of DLLs are Spanish speakers, these tests are not addressing their unique language and cultural needs, either (Russakoff, 2011).

Children from various cultural backgrounds have different approaches to learning (Gutiérrez & Rogoff, 2009). Many assessment items require children to engage in tasks or activities using predetermined sequences or actions (e.g., self-help skills) that they are not expected to engage in or that they engage in differently at home. Children also have unique experiences with, and exposure to, materials that are dependent on their cultural surroundings. For example, a child may be familiar with real objects rather than pretend or play items, or a child's family may encourage certain toys for boys or for girls. Given that many assessments use picture or object naming as a test of cognition or communication skills, the child's exposure to the testing materials, or lack thereof, contributes to testing bias (Qi et al., 2003). It may not be that the child's communication skills or cognition are lacking; instead, it may be that the child's performance is simply a product of things experienced within their unique family and culture.

The ways in which children approach adults also varies greatly among cultures, presenting yet another barrier to the assessment process. In some cultures, children are told not to talk until they are spoken to or perhaps not to call attention to themselves (California Department of Education, 2016). The following example illustrates such a difference in approaches: A typical social skill assessment might examine the ways in which children approach their peers and familiar adults in the preschool setting. Children are expected to look at the teacher when the teacher is talking and to respond verbally. It is also assumed that the children will use verbal means of approaching their peers. Philips (1983) conducted a study of classroom participation comparing Anglo-American and Native American students. The Native American children looked at the teacher less often, were less likely to respond to the teacher verbally, and showed attentiveness to peers through physical contact. A Native American child in the scenario might be labeled as displaying inappropriate behavior and assigned a low score on a social skill assessment when, in fact, the child is only acting the way they were taught to interact with others at home.

Home–school collaboration is highly valued in the assessment process (Lewis & Ginsburg-Block, 2014). The National Association for the Education of Young Children (2005) recommends that programs should closely involve families of young DLLs or multilanguage learners in the assessment process using a variety of methods. However, cultural barriers exist in DLLs' or multilanguage learners' family involvement, especially for immigrant families. Often, first-generation immigrant families are less familiar with the U.S. educational system, and do not have enough knowledge about the assessments to initiate or be involved in the processes (De Feyter & Winsler, 2009). In some cases, immigrant parents do not see themselves as responsible for their children's education because they were not involved with the educational system in their home country (Pelletier & Corter, 2005). For additional support for individuals searching for appropriate assessment tools for children who are DLLs or multi-language learners, see Box 10.1.

Children who are DLLs or multilanguage learners are especially vulnerable to culturally and linguistically biased testing (Farnsworth, 2018; Peña & Halle, 2011). DLLs or multilanguage learners come from a variety of cultural experiences; moreover, they are expected to access assessment items presented in a language other than their own. Similar to children with language or communication impairments, children who are dual or multilanguage learners will

---

Box 10.1.   Support for Individuals Searching for Assessment Tools Appropriate for Children Who Are Dual Language or Multilanguage Learners

The American Speech-Language-Hearing Association (ASHA) has a valuable website with a variety of resources for individuals seeking assessments designed for children who are dual language or multilanguage learners. For example, they include descriptive information about a bilingual vocabulary assessment measure, a language proficiency questionnaire, a verbal ability test, and a classroom communication profile.

- ASHA website: http://www.asha.org

The Dual Language Learners Program Assessment (DLLPA) assists Head Start, child care, and pre-K programs to assess their management systems and services to ensure the full and effective participation of children who are DLLs and their families.

- DLLPA website: https://eclkc.ohs.acf.hhs.gov/culture-language/dual
  -language-learners-program-assessment-dllpa-users-guide/dual
  -language-learners-program-assessment-dllpa-users-guide

The Center for Early Care and Education Research–Dual Language Learners (CECER-DLL) is a national center that is building capacity for research with DLLs ages birth through 5 years. CECER-DLL aims to improve the state of knowledge and measurement in early childhood.

- CECER-DLL website: https://cecerdll.fpg.unc.edu/

The Center for Law and Social Policy (CLASP) is a national, nonpartisan, nonprofit organization advancing policy solutions for people with low income. This includes a blog that advocates for federal and state policy reforms to promote health, economic security, and overall success for immigrant children, youth, and families.

- CLASP website: https://www.clasp.

have varying degrees of capability to understand test instructions and communicate the correct response. In the early childhood setting, children who are dual or multilanguage learners will be at different stages of the additional language learning process (Barone & Xu, 2008). During the first stage of the additional language learning process, often referred to as the silent stage, a child is observing the environment and using little or no verbal communication (Clarke & F.K.A. Multicultural Resource Centre, 1992; Drury, 2007). During this stage, it is all too easy for a team to misinterpret the child's nonverbal behavior as a language delay or disorder (Farnsworth, 2018).

In recognition of the obstacles surrounding the assessment of children who are DLLs or multilanguage learners, the Individuals with Disabilities Education Improvement Act (IDEA) of 2004 (PL108-446) requires that assessments be provided in a child's native language, unless it is clearly not feasible to do so. For example, if a child speaks Spanish, teachers are expected to administer a Spanish version of the same assessment that is given to all children. The intentionality of IDEA is good; however, most assessments fail to adapt to DLLs' and multilanguage learners' cultural and linguistic diversity and further fail to distinguish between DLLs' language development and need for special education services (Montenegro & Jankowski, 2017; Spinelli, 2008; Umansky et al., 2017). Furthermore, standardized tests, such as those utilized for statewide mandated assessments, cannot be readily provided in a language other than English, as translation could compromise the validity of the test (Menken, 2000, 2008; Menken et al., 2014) or translation may be mismatched for some assessments (Russakoff, 2011). In recent years, researchers began to address the need for valid, reliable instruments for assessment of speech and language ability. For example, the Bilingual English–Spanish Assessment (BESA™; Peña et al., 2018) is a comprehensive assessment of 4- to 6-year-old English–Spanish bilingual children's speech and language abilities in both languages.

SPECIFIC RECOMMENDATIONS

This section provides specific recommendations for assessing children who are DLLs or multilanguage learners. The section provides specific recommendations regarding what and how information is gathered across assessment purposes. For more details on gathering information, refer to Chapter 5, step one.

What to Assess

When assessing children who are DLLs or multilanguage learners, teachers should gather information about the child's culture and language patterns in the home (DEC, 2014; Espinosa, 2015). It would be wise to collect information about the child's learning style and experience with materials, the family's preferences and child-rearing practices, as well as what behaviors and ways of approaching adults are culturally appropriate before conducting screening and assessment (California Department of Education, 2016). Furthermore, teachers should determine who in the child's family speaks or understands which languages and for what purposes (e.g., reads the newspaper, watches TV, listens to the radio, talks to friends or socializes). Simply determining the language spoken in the home is not enough. Parent surveys or family interviewing (Bedore et al., 2012) can be used for gathering information regarding the language a child is exposed to and how and when they use various languages, and for gaining a better understanding of the family context and preferences. These methods can also be used to ask parents about home educational practices and beliefs to better understand their home culture (Farver et al., 2013).

Gathering information about language patterns in the home can provide insight about the acculturation of the child and family. The term acculturation refers to the process in which members of one cultural group adopt the beliefs, behaviors, language, or cultural traits of another cultural group (Schumann, 1978). Understanding the level of acculturation is important, given that young children who are DLLs or multilanguage learners are acquiring not just a new language, but a new culture as well. When children experience culture shock, their academic and social behaviors can appear to mirror those of a student with special needs (Grassi & Barker, 2010). Consider the preschool child who is not expected to feed himself at home. At preschool, food is placed in front of the child with the expectation that he will feed himself. The child might scream, cry, or simply shut down out of fear or frustration, not understanding the situation, or not being able to perform the task. During the assessment process, teachers might interpret the child's behavior as a number of things that are untrue about the child's abilities (e.g., a fine motor delay, challenging behavior, sensory processing issue). See Box 10.2 for further examples of behaviors exhibited by DLLs or multilanguage learners experiencing culture shock, keeping in mind that the goal is not for children and families to become acculturated to the White Dominant Culture in which they are being served. Rather, it is to understand the uniqueness of each family in making assessment decisions.

Box 10.2. Behaviors Exhibited by Dual Language or Multilanguage Learners Experiencing Culture Shock

Constantly asking to go to the bathroom or school nurse
Crying or exhibiting signs of depression
Throwing chairs or books across the room
Being unable to stay focused on tasks
Falling asleep during class
Exhibiting outbursts of anger, violence, frustration, or sadness
Getting into fights at recess
Leaving the classroom or asking to go home
Being out sick from school for many days

From Grassi, E., & Baker, H. B. (2010). *Culturally and linguistically diverse exceptional students: Strategies for teaching and assessment.* Copyright A9 2003 by SAGE Publications. Reprinted by permission of SAGE Publications.

Finally, when assessing the language skills of children who are dual or multilanguage learners, it is critical to gather information about the child's language acquisition for each language the child speaks and avoid comparisons with children who are native English speakers (Goodz, 1994; Guzman-Orth et al., 2017). For example, teachers should determine whether the child who is a DLL or multilanguage learner has an age-appropriate level of vocabulary and syntax in his or her native language in order to evaluate the child's English language acquisition. If there is no communication disorder in the child's native language, then the likelihood is that there is no communication disorder in English. If possible, another strategy is to compare children who are DLLs or multilanguage learners with same-age peers who are also dual or multilanguage learners. If the child is acquiring English at the same rate as other nonnative English speakers of the same age, then chances are there is no significant communication disorder. In other words, the likelihood of both children exhibiting a communication disorder at the same rate is small. That being said, when making comparisons between children, teachers should consider the length of time each child has been exposed to the new language because children spend a predictable amount of time in each stage of the language acquisition process (Haynes, 2006; Paradis et al., 2021).

How to Assess

The remainder of the section provides recommendations for how transdisciplinary teams should approach the assessment process for children who are from diverse cultural backgrounds, or who are DLLs or multilanguage learners. Assessments for DLLs or multilanguage learners in early education settings should include multiple methods, measurements, and repeated assessment and use interchangeable cuing systems and alternative materials. Teachers need to consider the influences and biases involved with the assessment process, be knowledgeable about the uniqueness of language development on children who are learning more than one language, and allow children to provide alternative responses (Losardo & Syverson, 2011). See Table 10.1 for recommended assessments to use with DLLs and multilanguage learners.

Influences and Biases

When gathering information for a child who is from a diverse cultural background or who is a dual or multilanguage learner, teachers should match the child with an examiner who is knowledgeable about the child's culture and who speaks the same language, and gather information from families (Ackerman & Tazi, 2015; Bedore et al., 2011; McLean, 2000). Teachers and DLL families often do not share similar cultural or linguistic backgrounds. Therefore, it is essential that the teacher understand how child development is viewed and expected in the family's culture and avoid assumptions that differences in development are due to developmental delays, instead of common cultural practices. For example, some East Asian cultures value an extended family structure, and

Table 10.1. Recommended assessments to use with dual language learners and multilanguage learners

Assessment	Brief assessment description	Target audience	Age span	Contact information
Ages & Stages Questionnaires®, Third Edition (ASQ®-3) (Squires & Bricker, 2009)	Available in Arabic, Chinese, English, French, Spanish, and Vietnamese Time: 10–15 minutes for parents to complete and 2–3 minutes for professionals to score Capture parents' in-depth knowledge Highlights a child's strengths as well as concerns Teaches parents about child development and their own child's skills Highlights results that fall in a monitoring zone to make it easier to keep track of children at risk Can be completed at home, in a waiting room, during a home visit, or as part of an in-person or phone interview	Parents/caregivers of children ages 1 month to 66 months	Ages 1 month to 66 months	https://agesandstages.com /products-pricing/asq3/
Bilingual English–Spanish Assessment (BESA™) (Peña et al., 2018)	Three Spanish subtests are a part of the BESA: phonology subtest, morphosyntax subtest, and semantics subtest A language assessment for use with children ages 4 through 6 years who have varying degrees of bilingualism Standardized and norm-referenced The subtests take about 15 minutes each and address the key domains of morphosyntax, semantics, and phonology	Spanish–English language learners	Ages 4 through 6 years	https://www.northernspeech.com /spanish-bilingual-therapy/besa -protocols-spanish/
Bilingual Language Proficiency Questionnaire–English and Spanish (Mattes & Santiago, 1985)	The Spanish/English edition of this parent interview questionnaire can be used to obtain information about bilingual children's development and functional use of a variety of speech and language skills in English and Spanish Articulation, language, voice, fluency, and the pragmatic aspects of communication are examined The individual items are listed in English and Spanish on the questionnaire	Parents of English–Spanish language learners ages 3 and up	Ages 3 and up	https://acadcom.com/acawebsite /prodView.asp?idproduct=442

(continued)

Table 10.1. *(continued)*

Assessment	Brief assessment description	Target audience	Age span	Contact information
Clinical Evaluation of Language Fundamentals–Fifth Edition (CELF-5) (Wiig et al., 2013)	CELF-5 provides clinicians with a streamlined, flexible battery to assess semantics, morphology, syntax, and pragmatics for students ages 5–21 CELF-5 features structured and authentic tests of language ability (including observational and interactive measures) for a complete picture of students' language skills	All children	Ages 5–21 years	Elisabeth H. Wiig, PhD Eleanor Semel, EdD Wayne A. Secord, PhD https://www.pearsonassessments.com/store/usassessments/en/Store/Professional-Assessments/Speech-%26-Language/Clinical-Evaluation-of-Language-Fundamentals-%7C-Fifth-Edition/p/100000705.html
Comprehensive Test of Phonological Processing–Second Edition (CTOPP-2) (Wagner et al., 2013)	This test measures phonological awareness, phonological memory, and naming Applicable across two age levels, 4–6 and 7–24 Manual scoring Completion time: 40 minutes	Korean–English bilingual children	Ages 4 years to 24 years, 11 months	https://www.pearsonassessments.com/store/usassessments/en/Store/Professional-Assessments/Speech-%26-Language/Comprehensive-Test-of-Phonological-Processing-%7C-Second-Edition/p/100000737.html?tab=product-details
Expressive One-Word Picture Vocabulary Test-4 (EOWPVT/ EOWPVT-4 SBE, English and Spanish) (Martin, 2015)	The test measures total acquired vocabulary; it is not a test of language proficiency Bilingual vocabulary Individual administration Norm-referenced (1,200+ U.S. Spanish-bilingual individuals) Administration and scoring time: 20–25 minutes	Spanish–English language learners	Ages 2 through 70+	https://www.academictherapy.com/detailATP.tpl?action=search&eqskudatarq=8623-9
Individual Growth & Development Indicators–Español (IGDIs-E) (Wackerle-Hollman et al., 2018)	This test is a universal screener within a multi-tiered systems of support (MTSS) or response to intervention (RTI) model of service delivery This test is not a translation of the English Individual Growth and Development Indicators (IGDIs 2.0) Measures oral language, phonological awareness, and alphabet knowledge A universal screening measure	Spanish-speaking preschoolers	4- to 5-year-olds	https://conservancy.umn.edu/bitstream/handle/11299/201548/IGDIs-E-technical-manual-2018.pdf?sequence=1&isAllowed=y

Table 10.1. *(continued)*

Assessment	Brief assessment description	Target audience	Age span	Contact information
MacArthur-Bates Communicative Development Inventories (CDIs) (Fenson et al., 2006)	The MacArthur-Bates CDIs, and the corresponding Spanish-Language Inventories, provide a systematic way for professionals to use parents as informants regarding their child's language They enable professionals to tap into parents' knowledge about their young children's communicative development for use in screening and developing a prognosis for children with language delays. It also ensures they are meeting mandates for including parent input in child evaluation procedures	Completed by parents/caregivers of children 8–37 months	Ages 8 to 37 months (can be used for older children who have developmental delays)	https://brookespublishing.com/product/cdi/
Picture Peabody Vocabulary Test–Revised (PPVT-R) (Dunn & Dunn, 1981)	The PPVT-R consists of 175 stimulus words and 175 corresponding image plates This assessment measures individual's receptive (hearing) vocabularies for American Standard English This test is standardized on a nationally representative sample of children and youth	All children	Ages 3–18	https://www.nlsinfo.org/content/cohorts/nlsy79-children/topical-guide/assessments/peabody-picture-vocabulary-test-revised
preLAS: Pre-Language Assessment Scale 2000 (Duncan & DeAvil, 1998)	Consists of an oral language component and a pre-literacy component Identify incoming students Place second language learners in appropriate classroom settings Monitor student progress along the stages of language acquisition Report language acquisition/skills in early childhood dual language programs Provides a standardized language proficiency measure for all students Access both English and Spanish editions	Spanish and English edition	Ages 3 to 6 years	https://laslinks.com/prelas/

(continued)

Table 10.1. *(continued)*

Assessment	Brief assessment description	Target audience	Age span	Contact information
Test of Early Reading Ability–Fourth Edition (TERA-4) (Reid et al., 2018)	Testing time: 30 minutes Administration: individual Scoring: manual or online This test assesses mastery of early-developing reading skills This test is standardized on a representative sample of 1,025 children representing 29 states and 271 different zip codes	All children	Ages 4–0 through 8–11	https://www.proedinc.com /Products/14635/tera4-test-of -early-reading-abilityfourth -edition.aspx
Woodcock Language Proficiency Battery– Revised (WLPB-R) English and Spanish Forms (Woodcock, 1991)	The WLPB-R provides an overall measure of language proficiency and greatly expanded measures of oral language, reading, and written language in both English and Spanish The WLPB-R English Form and Spanish Form are parallel versions that facilitate comparison between the languages Administration time: 20–60 minutes	All	Ages 2 to 90+ years	Richard W. Woodcock, Ana F. Muñoz-Sandoval (Spanish Form): https://www.worldcat.org /title/woodcock-language -proficiency-battery-revised -wlpb-r/oclc/39723305

Note: This table includes tests that were used in research related to bilingual learners and focused on language development of bilingual learners.

grandparents are often a child's primary caregiver. It may be common that grandparents tend to feed a toddler or preschooler to avoid messes in the dining area, resulting in the child not developing self-feeding skills or other fine motor skills compared to peers who started self-feeding at a young age.

Furthermore, the examiner should understand the language acquisition process. It is important to consider that young DLLs learning a new language can be a very complicated task. For example, learning a language includes many domains, including vocabulary, phonology, syntax, pragmatics, phonological awareness, alphabet knowledge, and print conventions. In addition to learning a new language, children are also learning new social rules, beliefs, and values that may be different from the practices in their home culture. Therefore, assessing young DLLs must include input from family members to effectively evaluate the child's level of conceptual knowledge in both English and their primary language (Ackerman & Tazi, 2015; Peña & Halle, 2011; Zepeda et al., 2011).

It is important that the examiner have a firm understanding of the types of grammatical, phonological, and discourse errors that DLLs or multilanguage learners typically make as well as the common errors made in interlanguage (Grassi & Barker, 2010). The term interlanguage refers to a made up linguistic system developed by a child who is learning a second language in which the child uses language transfer, overgeneralization, and simplification to approximate the target language while preserving features of the native language. When conducting the assessment, if it is not possible to find someone who is knowledgeable about the child's culture, who speaks the same language, or who understands the language acquisition process, the team should at the very least arrange for a one-on-one situation with an interactive adult, caregiver, or teacher. High-context situations, such as a one-on-one interaction, can enhance receptive language abilities as well as increase the likelihood of expressive speech (Ball & Lewis, 2011; Copenhaver-Johnson & Katz, 2009).

Interchangeable Cuing Systems

For children who are DLLs or multilanguage learners, assessments should be administered in the child's native language. Keep in mind, again, that translation is not always an exact science. Sometimes words or phrases can sound inappropriate and even offensive to another culture (Fabri & Freidel, 2008). If an English language assessment is translated into another language, the assessment should be carefully reviewed for linguistic and cultural appropriateness by someone who understands the language and culture and who is well versed in the complex issues of both assessment and translation (National Association for the Education of Young Children, 2009). When translation is not available, nonverbal cuing systems paired with multiple visual or gestural cues can support the assessment of young children who are DLLs or multilanguage learners.

Alternative, Flexible Materials

When assessing young children who are DLLs or multilanguage learners, teachers should use materials that align with the child's cultural or linguistic backgrounds. The National Association for the Education of Young Children (2009) recommends a systematic, observational assessment process incorporating culturally and linguistically appropriate tools as the primary source of guidance. In other words, when using multiple assessments, teachers should rely more heavily on those that are 1) observation based and 2) culturally and linguistically appropriate for the child (Espinosa, 2015). If the transdisciplinary team has enlisted the support of a cultural guide who knows and understands the child's language and culture, that person can help determine the appropriateness of assessment tools by examining them for cultural bias. Box 10.1 includes useful resources that teachers can use as a starting place in finding assessments that may be appropriate for children who are DLLs or multilanguage learners.

Alternative Responses

When allowing for alternative responses, teachers should consider the strengths of the child and attempt to align the response options with the child's unique set of skills (Neisworth & Bagnato, 2004). For example, incorporating materials that are familiar to the child, such as pictures, toys, or objects from the child's home, can encourage children who are from diverse cultural backgrounds or who are DLLs or multilanguage learners to narrate stories or role-play events to show what they know and can do (Copenhaver-Johnson & Katz, 2009; Hills, 1992). Allowing children to provide work samples as responses is an alternative option. Family observation, photographs, and videos can serve as documentation of children's behaviors in a culturally familiar context (Losardo & Syverson, 2011). Finally, DLL children or multilanguage learners should be given the option of a translator or cultural guide to accommodate their responses during the assessment process.

MEASURES

Regardless of a child's ability or the assessment purpose, federal law, state policies, and recommended practice repeatedly call for using measures that are technically sound, multifaceted, and nonbiased. These terms are defined more fully as follows.

- Technically sound: supports purposes for which the assessments or measures are valid and reliable; administered by trained and knowledgeable personnel, using only assessment materials that have been validated for the specific purpose for which they are used

- Multifaceted: uses more than one procedure or criterion for determining an appropriate educational program for a child; made by a multidisciplinary team or group of persons, including at least one teacher or specialist; develops partnerships with parents and families as essential stakeholders in the assessment process

- Nonbiased: administered so as not to be discriminatory on a racial or cultural basis, in the child's native language, and in the form most likely to yield accurate information; accurately reflects the child's aptitude or achievement level or whatever other factors the test purports to measure; uses assessment methods that are developmentally appropriate, culturally and linguistically responsive; provides individually, culturally, and linguistically appropriate assessment of all children's strengths

Unfortunately, as with many assessments available, used, or mandated in early childhood intervention, there is a dearth of appropriate assessment measures for young children with diverse abilities. Specifically, few assessments have been normed or validated for children from specific cultural populations. As noted in this chapter and elsewhere, assessments are of great concern when it comes to children from diverse cultural, and linguistic backgrounds in the standardization or normative group (Peña et al., 2006). Further, the use of standardized testing procedures or materials creates bias and a lack of fairness in the items, procedures, and interpretations have not been validated for children from different backgrounds (Ackerman & Tazi, 2015; Johnstone et al., 2008). Many of the prompts, settings, materials, procedures, and even items are biased or otherwise unfair and penalize children from diverse backgrounds. Additionally, many assessments were not designed with universality or equity in mind, and rarely are accommodations made for this group of children, instructions provided on how to make appropriate modifications, or little, if any, evidence available of the validity and reliability of scores or findings when modifications are made.

In addition, few assessments were designed with universality and equity in mind (Thurlow et al., 2001). Universality is defined as design procedures or built-in accommodations that enable all children to demonstrate their underlying and often-unrealized functional capabilities (i.e., universality identifies both strengths and limitations). Universality is increasingly being considered from an instructional perspective; however, little attention has been given to the need for universality of assessment measures. At the heart of universality is the notion of equity and leveling the playing field. Equity refers to assessment items and procedures, which are designed so that any child can demonstrate underlying competence. Equity in this sense emphasizes functional rather than topographical content (form) and adheres to universal design concepts. Few tests, however, are designed with equity in mind, and assessment items tend to emphasize topographical versus functional content. (See earlier discussion regarding form and function, as well as Box 10.3 for the characteristics of a universally designed assessment.)

Box 10.3.   Characteristics of Universally Designed Assessment

Are aimed at inclusive assessment populations
Measure what they intend to measure (precisely defined constructs)
Contains accessible items with minimal bias
Have simple, clear, and intuitive instructions and procedures
Are amenable to accommodations
Are readable and comprehensible
Are legible

Sources: Johnstone et al. (2008); Thompson & Thurlow (2002); Thurlow & Kopriva (2015).

Assessing the growing number of children who are from diverse cultural backgrounds can be especially challenging given the lack of appropriate tools available to teachers. As a result, some teachers have turned to alternative assessment practices (Losardo & Syverson, 2011). For example, Losardo and Syverson suggest naturalistic assessment that takes place during children's typical routines and addresses developmental and functional skills. This approach is ideal for assessing young children who are DLLs or multilanguage learners, as information can be gathered by observing family interactions. Ecobehavioral interview (Barnett et al., 1992) is one model of naturalistic assessment that is used to collect data on the child's abilities and areas of concern by observing family interactions. Similar to naturalistic assessment, play-based focused assessment where children are observed during play offers flexible, authentic, and individualized assessment context, material, and procedures for assessing all development areas. Some examples are Symbolic Play Scale (Nicolich, 1977) and Transdisciplinary Play-Based Assessment (TPBA; Linder, 2008). Both approaches use play as a context; Symbolic Play Scale specifically assesses children's play behaviors, and TPBA is used for assessing skills across developmental domains. Portfolio is another authentic individualized assessment type whereby educators seek information from family members and draw a whole picture of a child's performance across different settings. For example, two commonly adopted portfolio approaches, Ounce Scale (Meisels et al., 2003) and Work Sampling System (Dichtelmiller et al., 2013), help early childhood education programs develop individualized portfolio systems to identify and meet children's unique needs (Losardo & Syverson, 2011). Dynamic assessment refers to an assessment process that initially aims to evaluate a child's ability to learn and then retests the child after intervention is delivered. Dynamic assessment is often recommended for assessing DLLs or multilanguage learners because of its function of differentiating language differences from language impairment (Patterson et al., 2020; Peña et al., 2001). For example, Gutierrez-Clellen and Quinn (1993) described a dynamic approach that assesses narratives of DLLs or multilanguage learners. Assessors collect samples of narratives in various settings, explain the contextualization rules of different narrative contexts and offer specific examples to children, and scaffold children through the use of verbal cues and modeling (Losardo & Syverson, 2011, p. 152).

SUMMARY

The purpose of this chapter was to promote the use of recommended assessment practices discussed in Chapter 1 as they apply to children who are DLLs or multilanguage learners. First, the chapter included an overview of challenges that teachers face when assessing cultural and linguistic diverse children. Issues surrounding the biased content and method of traditional assessments were explored. Misinterpreted assessment outcomes that lead to an overrepresented DLL or multilanguage learner population in special education were discussed.

Specific recommendations for assessing young children who are DLLs or multilanguage learners were provided next, and readers were directed to consider what and how information should be gathered across purposes within the assessment process. Teachers were encouraged to gather information from families and focus on language skills and cultural practices, to consider the influences and biases created during the assessment process, to incorporate interchangeable cuing systems, and to utilize alternative, flexible materials and allow children to provide alternative responses. Finally, alternative measures available for assessing young children who are DLLs were discussed, and suggestions for selecting an appropriate assessment tool were provided to better serve these unique learners. For more information on how these strategies for gathering information contribute to the decision-making process, see Chapter 5. In brief, information gathered on DLLs is used for subsequent decisions as illustrated in that chapter.

REFERENCES

Ackerman, D. J., & Tazi, Z. (2015). Enhancing young Hispanic dual language learners' achievement: Exploring strategies and addressing challenges. *ETS Research Report Series*, *2015*(1), 1–39.

Artiles, A. J., Rueda, R., Salazar, J. J., & Higareda, I. (2005). Within-group diversity in minority disproportionate representation: Language learners in urban school districts. *Exceptional Children*, *71*(3), 283–300. https://doi.org/10.1177%2F001440290507100305

Ball, J., & Lewis, M. (2011). "An altogether different approach": Roles of speech-language pathologists in supporting Indigenous children's language development. *Canadian Journal of Speech-Language Pathology and Audiology*, *35*(2), 144–158.

Banerjee, R., & Guiberson, M. (2012). Evaluating young children from culturally and linguistically diverse backgrounds for special education services. *Young Exceptional Children*, *15*(1), 33–45. https://doi.org/10.1177%2F1096250611435368

Barnett, D. W., Macmann, G. M., & Carey, K. T. (1992). Early intervention and the assessment of developmental skills: Challenges and directions. *Topics in Early Childhood Special Education*, *12*(1), 21–43. https://doi.org/10.1177/027112149201200105

Barone, D. M., & Xu, S. H. (2008). *Literacy instruction for English language learners: Pre-K–2*. Guilford Press.

Bedore, L. M., Peña, E. D., Joyner, D., & Macken, C. (2011). Parent and teacher rating of bilingual language proficiency and language development concerns. *International Journal of Bilingual Education and Bilingualism*, *14*(5), 489–511. https://doi.org/10.1080/13670050.2010.529102

Bedore, L. M., Peña, E. D., Summers, C. L., Boerger, K. M., Resendiz, M. D., Greene, K., & Gillam, R. B. (2012). The measure matters: Language dominance profiles across measures in Spanish–English bilingual children, *Bilingualism, 15*(3), 616. https://doi.org/10.1017/S1366728912000090

California Department of Education. (2016). *Family partnerships and culture.* Author.

Clarke, P., & F. K. A. Multicultural Resource Centre. (1992). *English as a 2nd language in early childhood.* Free Kindergarten Association, Multicultural Resource Centre.

Copenhaver-Johnson, J., & Katz, L. (2009). *Supporting young English language learners and their families.* A Professional Development Module Supported by the Ohio Department of Education. Early Childhood Quality Network.

Counts, J., Katsiyannis, A., & Whitford, D. K. (2018). Culturally and linguistically diverse learners in special education: English learners. *NASSP Bulletin, 102*(1), 5–21.

De Feyter, J. J., & Winsler, A. (2009). The early developmental competencies and school readiness of low-income, immigrant children: Influences of generation, race/ethnicity, and national origins. *Early Childhood Research Quarterly, 24*(4), 411–431.

Dichtelmiller, M. L., Jablon, J. R., Marsden, D. B., & Meisels, S. J. (2013). *Omnibus guidelines: Preschool through third grade.* Pearson.

Drury, R. (2007). *Young bilingual learners at home and school: Researching multilingual voices.* Stoke-on-Trent Staffordshire.

Duncan, S. E., & DeAvila, E. A. (1998). *preLAS: Pre-Language Assessment Scale 2000.* CTB/McGraw-Hill.

Dunn, L. M., & Dunn, D. M. (1981). *Peabody Picture Vocabulary Test-Revised (PPVT-R).* American Guidance Service.

Espinosa, L. M. (2005). Curriculum and assessment considerations for young children from culturally, linguistically, and economically diverse backgrounds. *Psychology in the Schools, 42*(8), 837–853.

Espinosa, L. M. (2015). *Getting it right for young children from diverse backgrounds: Applying research to improve practice with a focus on dual language learners.* Pearson Higher Education.

Fabri, M. (2008). Cultural adaptation and translation of assessment instruments for diverse populations: The use of the Harvard Trauma Questionnaire in Rwanda. In L.A. Suzki & J. G. Ponterotto (Eds.), *Handbook of multicultural assessment: Clinical, psychological and educational applications* (3rd ed., pp. 195–219). John Wiley & Sons.

Farnsworth, M. (2018). Differentiating second language acquisition from specific learning disability: An observational tool assessing dual language learners' pragmatic competence. *Young Exceptional Children, 21*(2), 92–110. http://www.doi.org/10.1177/1096250615621356

Farver, J. A. M., Xu, Y., Lonigan, C. J., & Eppe, S. (2013). The home literacy environment and Latino head start children's emergent literacy skills. *Developmental Psychology, 49*(4), 775.

Fenson, L., Marchman, V. A., Thal, D. J., Dale, P. S., Reznick, J. S., & Bates, E. (2006). *MacArthur-Bates Communicative Development Inventories (CDIs).* Paul H. Brookes Publishing Co.

Goodz, N. S. (1994). Interactions between parents and children in bilingual families. In F. Genesee (Ed.), *Educating second language children: The whole child, the whole curriculum, the whole community* (pp. 61–81). Cambridge University Press.

Grassi, E., & Barker, H. B. (2010). *Culturally and linguistically diverse exceptional students: Strategies for teaching and assessment.* SAGE Publications, Inc.

Gutierrez-Clellen, V. F., & Quinn, R. (1993). Assessing narratives of children from diverse cultural/linguistic groups. *Language, Speech, and Hearing Services in Schools, 24*(1), 2–9.

Gutiérrez, K. D., & Rogoff, B. (2009). *3.1 Cultural ways of learning. Knowledge, values and educational policy: A critical perspective* (pp. 114).

Haynes, J. (2006). *Everything ESL.net.* http://www.everythingesl.net/inservices/language_stages.php

Guzman-Orth, D., Lopez, A. A., & Tolentino, F. (2017). *A Framework for the Dual Language Assessment of Young Dual Language Learners in the United States. Research Report. ETS RR-17-37.* Education Testing Service.

Hills, T. W. (1992). Reaching potentials through appropriate assessment. In S. Bredekamp & T. Rosegrant (Eds.), *Reaching potentials: Appropriate curriculum and assessment for young children* (pp. 43– 64). National Association for the Education of Young Children.

Individuals with Disabilities Education Improvement Act (IDEA) of 2004, PL 108–446, 20 U.S.C. §§ 1400 *et seq.*

Johnstone, C. J., Thompson, S. J., Bottsford-Miller, N. A., & Thurlow, M. L. (2008). Universal design and multimethod approaches to item review. *Educational Measurement: Issues and Practice, 27*(1), 25–36.

Lewis, K., & Ginsburg-Block, M. (2014). Early childhood literacy and language programs: Supporting involvement of DLLs and their families. *NHSA Dialog, 17*(2).

Linder, T. W. (2008). *Transdisciplinary Play-Based Assessment, Edition (TPBA2).* Paul H Brookes Publishing Co.

Losardo, A., & Syverson, A. N. (2011). *Alternative approaches to assessing young children.* Paul H. Brookes Publishing Co.

Martin, N. A. (2015). *Expressive One-Word Picture Vocabulary Test-4 (EOWPVT/EOWPVT-4 SBE, English and Spanish).* Academic Therapy Publications.

Mattes, L. J., & Santiago, G. (1985). *Bilingual Language Proficiency Questionnaire-English and Spanish.* Academic Communication Associates.

McLean, M. (2000). *Conducting child assessments: Culturally and linguistically appropriate services early childhood research institute* (Technical Report #2). University of Illinois at Urbana-Champaign.

Meisels, S. J., Dombro, A. L., Marsden, D., Weston, D., & Jewkes, A. (2003). *The Ounce Scale: Standards for the developmental profiles, birth-42 months.* Pearson Early Learning.

Menken, K. (2000). *What are the critical issues in wide-scale assessment of English language learners? NCBE Issue Brief No. 6,* 1–8. National Clearinghouse for Bilingual Education.

Menken, K. (2008). *English learners left behind: Standardized testing as language policy* (Vol. 65). Multilingual Matters.

Menken, K., Hudson, T., & Leung, C. (2014). Symposium: Language assessment in standards-based education reform. *Tesol Quarterly, 48*(3), 586–614.

Montenegro, E., & Jankowski, N. A. (2017). *Equity and assessment: Moving towards culturally responsive assessment* (Occasional Paper No. 29). University of Illinois and Indiana University, National Institute for Learning Outcomes Assessment (NILOA).

National Association for the Education of Young Children (NAEYC). (2005). *Screening and assessment of young English language learners. Supplement to the NAECS/SDE joint position statement on early childhood curriculum, assessment, and program evaluation.* https://www.naeyc.org/sites/default/files/globally-shared/downloads/PDFs/resources/position-statements/ELL_Supplement_Shorter_Version.pdf

National Association for the Education of Young Children (NAEYC). (2009). *Where we stand on assessing young English language learners.* http://www.naeyc.org/files/naeyc/file/positions/WWSEnglishLanguageLearnersWeb.pdf

Neisworth, J. T., & Bagnato, S. J. (2004). The mismeasure of young children: The authentic assessment alternative. *Infants & Young Children, 17,* 198–212. http://dx.doi.org/10.1097/00001163-200407000-00002

Nicolich, L. M. (1977). Beyond sensorimotor intelligence: Assessment of symbolic maturity through analysis of pretend play. *Merrill-Palmer Quarterly of Behavior and Development, 23*(2), 89–99.

Paradis, J., Genesee, F., & Crago, M. B. (2021). *Dual language development and disorders: A handbook on bilingualism and second language learning* (3rd ed.). Paul H. Brookes Publishing Co.

Park, M., Zong, J., & Batalova, J. (2018). *Growing superdiversity among young US dual language learners and its implications.* Migration Policy Institute.

Patterson, J. L., Rodriguez, B. L., & Dale, P. S. (2020). Dynamic assessment language tasks and the prediction of performance on year-end language skills in preschool dual language learners. *American Journal of Speech-Language Pathology, 29*(3), 1226–1240.

Pelletier, J., & Corter, C. (2005). Toronto first duty: Integrating kindergarten, childcare, and parenting support to help diverse families connect to schools. *Multicultural Education, 13*(2), 30–37.

Peña, E. D. (2016). Supporting the home language of bilingual children with developmental disabilities: From knowing to doing. *Journal of Communication Disorders, 63,* 85–92.

Peña, E. D., Gutiérrez-Clellen, V. F., Iglesias, A., Goldstein, B., & Bedore, L. M. (2018). *Bilingual English Spanish Assessment (BESA™).* Paul H. Brookes Publishing Co.

Peña, E. D., & Halle, T. G. (2011). Assessing preschool dual language learners: Traveling a multiforked road. *Child Development Perspectives, 5*(1), 28–32.

Peña, E., Iglesias, A., & Lidz, C. S. (2001). Reducing test bias through dynamic assessment of children's word learning ability. *American Journal of Speech-Language Pathology, 10,* 138–154.

Peña, E. D., Spaulding, T. J., & Plante, E. (2006). The comparison of normative groups and diagnostic decision making: Shooting ourselves in the foot. *American Journal of Speech-Language Pathology, 15,* 247–254.

Philips, S. U. (1983). *The invisible culture.* Longman Publishing.

Qi, C. H., Kaiser, A. P., Milan, S. E., Yzquierdo, Z., & Hancock, T. B. (2003). The performance of low income African American children on the Preschool Language Scale-3. *Journal of Speech, Language, and Hearing Research, 46,* 576–590.

Reid, K., Hresko, W. P., & Hammill, D. D. (2018). *Test Early Reading Ability (TERA-4).* PRO-ED.

Russakoff, D. (2011). *PreK-3rd: Raising the educational performance of English language learners (ELLs).* PreK-3rd Policy to Action (Brief. No. 6). Foundation for Child Development.

Schumann, J. H. (1978). *The pidginization process: A model for second language acquisition.* Newbury House.

Spinelli, C. G. (2008). Addressing the issue of cultural and linguistic diversity and assessment: Informal evaluation measures for English language learners. *Reading & Writing Quarterly, 24,* 101–118.

Squires, J., Bricker, D. D., & Twombly, E. (2009). *Ages & Stages Questionnaires®, Third Edition (ASQ®-3).* Paul H. Brookes Publishing Co.

Thompson, S., & Thurlow, M. (2002). *Universally designed assessments: Better tests for everyone!* (NCEO Policy Directions No. 14). National Center on Educational Outcomes, University of Minnesota.

Thurlow, M. L., & Kopriva, R. J. (2015). Advancing accessibility and accommodations in content assessments for students with disabilities and English learners. *Review of Research in Education, 39*(1), 331–369. http://dx.doi.org/10.3102/0091732X14556076

Thurlow, M., Quenemoen, R., Thompson, S., & Lehr, C. (2001). *Principles and characteristics of inclusive assessment and accountability systems* (Synthesis Report 40). National Center on Educational Outcomes.

Umansky, I. M., Thompson, K. D., & Díaz, G. (2017). Using an ever–English learner framework to examine disproportionality in special education. *Exceptional Children, 84*(1), 76–96.

Wackerle-Hollman, A., Durán, I., Rodriguez, M. C., Brunner, S., Kohlmeier, T., Callard, C., & Palma, J. (2018). *Individual Growth & Development Indicators-Español (IGDIs-E).* IGDILab.

Wagner, R., Torgesen, J., Rashotte, C., & Pearson, N. A. (2013). *Comprehensive Test of Phonological Processing–Second Edition (CTOPP-2).* Pearson.

Wiig, E. H., Semel, E., & Secord, W. A. (2013). *Clinical Evaluation of Language Fundamentals–Fifth Edition* (CELF-5). NCS Pearson.

Williams, P. (2007, January). *Disproportionality and overrepresentation (Module 5). Building the legacy: IDEA 2004 training curriculum.* National Dissemination Center for Children with Disabilities. https://www.parentcenterhub.org/wp-content/uploads/repo_items/legacy/5-trainerguide.pdf

Woodcock, R. W. (1991). *Woodcock Language Proficiency Battery-Revised: WLPB-R.* Riverside Publishing.

Woodcock, R. W., & Muñoz-Sandoval, A. F. (1995). *Woodcock Language Proficiency Battery–Revised Spanish (WLPB-RS).* Riverside Publishing.

Zepeda, M., Castro, D. C., & Cronin, S. (2011). Preparing early childhood teachers to work with young dual language learners. *Child Development Perspectives, 5*(1), 10–14.

CHAPTER 11

Recommended Practices for Assessing Children With Severe and Multiple Disabilities

Jennifer Grisham, Ashley Lyons-Picard, and Kristie Pretti-Frontczak

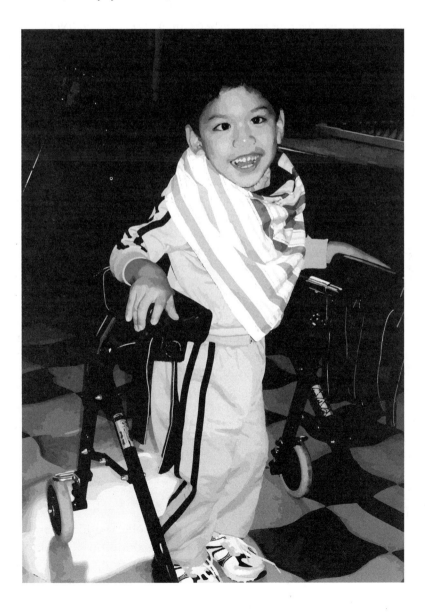

Delmy teaches preschool in a publicly funded preschool program that serves children who qualify for special education services and children who are at risk due to socioeconomic variables. Delmy has 15 children in her class, with seven of those children having IEPs and the remainder having no diagnosed disabilities. This is Delmy's third year of teaching; each year she has worked with children with a variety of disabilities, including children with Down syndrome, autism, and speech/ language delays. This year, however, Delmy has a new student in her class who has more challenges than any she has taught in the past. Carlos has cerebral palsy and moves around his environment in a wheelchair with the help of someone in the classroom. Carlos does not use speech to communicate but rather facial expressions and vocalizations. Delmy has been told that Carlos does not process visual and auditory information like other children. Delmy wants to provide Carlos with a positive experience in her inclusive classroom, yet she does not know where to begin. She realizes that the first thing she needs to do is a high-quality assessment to help her know what and how to teach Carlos. However, she knows she cannot do it alone.

The law, recommended practices, ethics, and research emphasize that young children with disabilities be included and taught in natural and least restrictive environments (LREs; Etscheidt, 2006; Sandall et al., 2005)—in other words, in places where, and activities in which, children without disabilities of the same age and their families would participate (Jackson et al., 2009; Raab & Dunst, 2004). As the number of children with disabilities who are served in community settings has increased, so has the overall diversity of the population of young children being served. As a result of demographic changes, the push for LRE and inclusion, and the growing need for out-of-the-home care, early childhood programs are increasingly faced with assessing and meeting the needs of children with progressively more severe and multiple disabilities (Copple & Bredekamp, 2009; Durand, 2008).

The purpose of this chapter is to promote the recommended assessment practices discussed in Chapter 1 as they apply to children with multiple disabilities. The text that follows is divided into four main sections. The first section illustrates the need to work as a member of a transdisciplinary team when assessing young children with multiple disabilities. The second section provides an overview of the challenges and general considerations for assessing these children. In the third section, specific recommendations and suggestions are made for the assessment process. Finally, the fourth section concludes the chapter with a discussion of the measures available for assessing young children with multiple disabilities.

TRANSDISCIPLINARY TEAMING

In a transdisciplinary approach to professional collaboration, teams (which always include the family) attempt to maximize communication and collaboration by crossing disciplinary boundaries and engaging in a simultaneous assessment process (King et al., 2009; Woodruff & McGonigel, 1988). Transdisciplinary teams are more necessary than ever when serving young children who have severe or multiple disabilities. Specifically, when assessing young children with multiple disabilities, a transdisciplinary approach allows the team to ensure much needed expertise in collaborative problem solving and joint decision making. For example, when determining how and when to transition a child who is tube fed to oral feeding, no single team member will possess all of the expertise or information necessary to make a decision regarding the initial feeding problem, the nutritional needs of the child, or the readiness of the child and family for the transition.

All of the team members need to understand that they represent or come from different philosophical or training orientations. Team members are likely to represent medical (e.g., neurologists, nurses, audiologists), educational (e.g., early interventionists, interpreters), or therapeutic (e.g., occupational and physical therapists, speech-language pathologists) models. In addition, teams serving young children with severe and multiple disabilities are likely to include specialists with expertise in particular disabilities or disorders (e.g., vision, hearing, dual language acquisition, autism). Therefore, team members must understand that individual training, philosophical beliefs, and past experiences will influence all aspects of working with a young child and their family. For example, some team members may feel that modifications or adaptations to the testing procedures are in order because standardized testing presents bias and does not provide an accurate picture of a child's performance. Others may think that standardized testing produces the most objective results—that when accommodations are made, standardization is broken, and the norms reported for the test no longer apply. The team is thus put into a situation where some members believe and trust in one set of assessment practices and other team members advocate for another. To work effectively, particularly with regard to assessment, team members need to recognize these differences and use open communication to reach consensus on how best to address various issues.

Effective transdisciplinary teams recognize that the most central participant is the child's family (Bruder & Bologna, 1993). As discussed in Chapter 3, family-centered practice is recommended in early childhood intervention within and across the provision of all services (Sandall et al., 2005). Families should be viewed as experts on their children. Particularly in the case of young children with severe and multiple disabilities, parents and other caregivers can provide valuable information about the children's functioning at home and in the community that would be extremely difficult, if not impossible, to gather by other means. Families are the team members who can best describe the children's capabilities, challenges, and developmental history. Given their clear understanding of the child's interests and abilities, families can also help make decisions about which assessments are most appropriate (McLean et al., 2004). Finally, family members can support the administration of assessments because they are best able to interact with the child and to elicit the child's optimal level of functioning (Bagnato & Simeonsson, 2007). During the assessment process, teams must share responsibilities and ensure that families are involved to the extent they desire in all aspects of assessment, including planning the assessment, administration of assessment measures, summarization and interpretation of findings, application of planning intervention, and identification of services. Chapter 6 provides additional information about how transdisciplinary teams participate in play-based assessments as a strategy for making the eligibility process more authentic.

In general, transdisciplinary teams need to understand that development 1) is interrelated (Allen & Marotz, 2010), 2) is heavily influenced by culture (Klingner et al., 2007; Shonkoff & Phillips, 2000), 3) is best understood when the child is viewed as a whole and within the context of his or her family and community (Bronfenbrenner, 1977; National Association for the Education of Young Children [NAEYC], 2020), and 4) often result in patterns of predictable responses that should be considered when drawing conclusions or making decisions (Ferrell, 1998). As teams adopt such a framework, they will find that their assessment practices will change in terms of which assessments are used, who administers the assessment, how assessment information is summarized, and how assessment information is used to make decisions. For example, a number of specialists, experts, caregivers, educators, and therapists may be involved in assessing children with severe and multiple disabilities. As a family moves through the assessment process, each assessor may ask similar questions regarding the child's developmental history, family concerns, and past treatments. It is unnecessary for a family to answer these common questions multiple times. Further, each assessor may generate their own report and set of recommendations. When team members write individual reports, they are unaware of whether their recommendations are in conflict or support the suggestions of others, often leaving families on their own to decipher what to do next. To maximize the benefits of a transdisciplinary team, particularly through the assessment process, members should develop and maintain a set of skills around their role and the role of other team members. Figure 11.1 depicts the cycle, or various aspects, of role release.

Although role release, enrichment, expansion, extension, and so forth can be overwhelming and a bit intimidating initially, the underlying notions are that no one team member is more important than another, that one can assess skills and abilities that fall outside one's traditional training (e.g., a physical therapist can help observe and document a child's performance as the child interacts and communicates with familiar adults), and that it is the collective and multiple lenses at which we view a child within the context of their family that provide the most accurate and comprehensive information. Given the complexity of issues and mediating factors that need to be considered when assessing children with severe and multiple disabilities, teachers can easily see how having more eyes is better.

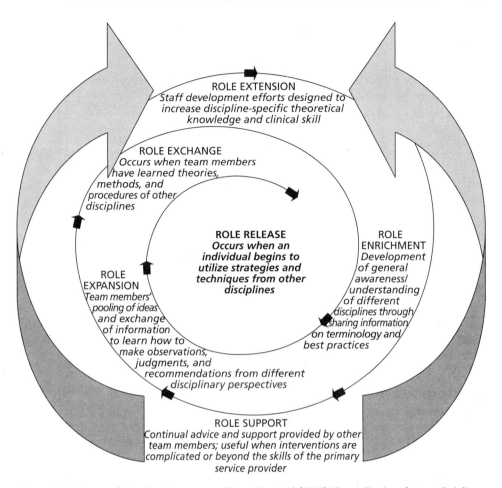

Figure 11.1. Aspects of the role release process. (From King et al. [2009], The application of a transdisciplinary model for early intervention services. *Infants & Young Children, 22*[3], 211–23; reprinted by permission.)

GENERAL CONSIDERATIONS FOR ASSESSING CHILDREN WITH SEVERE AND MULTIPLE DISABILITIES

This section provides general considerations for assessing children who have severe or multiple disabilities (including those who are medically complex). The section discusses some of the challenges teachers face when conducting assessments for children with severe and multiple disabilities and presents an overview of the general issues surrounding the measures teachers have available to them. Special considerations for assessing learners with complex medical needs will be highlighted.

Children with severe or multiple disabilities are often considered untestable (Rosário et al., 2019). In fact, a national study of eligibility practices of over 250 preschool psychologists with over 7,000 children found that nearly 60% of the children would have been deemed untestable if the psychologists had followed standardized procedures (Bagnato & Neisworth, 1995). The extremity of behaviors and skill levels characteristic of children with severe or multiple disabilities can make it difficult for teams to differentiate whether poor performance on an assessment is due to skill deficits or another issue directly related to the child's disability (e.g., lack of functional motor movements, language, attention; Neisworth & Bagnato, 1992). Often, the measures being used contribute to the challenge because they are generally inappropriate for children with severe or multiple disabilities (Neisworth & Bagnato, 2004). Specifically, the mismatch between the child and the assessment can be found within the content, the expected response, or the method for gathering assessment information associated with the measure.

Content of the assessment refers to what the test items are actually measuring. For children with severe or multiple disabilities, items measuring specific sets of skills are often beyond their capabilities (Snow & Van Hemel, 2008). For example, items measuring locomotor skills such as running, skipping, and riding a bike are typically beyond the scope of what a child with a severe motor impairment can or will be able to accomplish. Other early developmental assessments contain items that are beyond the scope of the abilities of a young child with sensory impairments. For example, a child with a visual impairment may have difficulty demonstrating competence on items that require a performance that is heavily dependent on vision (e.g., visually recognizes mother, eye–hand coordination in reaching).

In addition, content often measures specific responses to scripted items that do not exemplify the skills needed for participation in daily routines (McCormick & Nellis, 2004). In other words, assessment content leads to ableist practices by measuring form rather than function. *Form* refers to the specific skill the child is to perform, whereas *function* refers to the purpose of the skill. For example, a test item that examines a child's ability to use a spoon to transfer food from a bowl to their mouth is an item that measures a specific skill (i.e., form). The purpose of the skill (i.e., the function) is to feed oneself, not necessarily to use a spoon. In another example, a child with a hearing impairment may be unable to turn and look at a noise-producing object (i.e., form), but they are perfectly capable of attending to environmental stimuli (i.e., function). Formal assessment measures often include content that emphasizes form and does not allow for examination of true functions of skills or behaviors, making it easy to misinterpret an issue directly related to the child's disability as a skill deficit. (See Box 11.1 for more examples of assessment content that measures form versus function.)

Method refers to the process used to obtain the information about a child's performance and includes the cueing systems used to present test items as well as the response accepted from the child. Generally, standardized cuing systems such as verbal instructions paired with visual stimuli are a barrier for many children with severe or multiple disabilities. For instance, children with visual or hearing impairments will have difficulty seeing or hearing the stimuli being presented. Children with sensory impairments struggle with either hyper- or hyposensitivity to particular test stimuli involving sound, touch, movement, or positioning (Downing & Chen, 2003; Ermer & Dunn, 1998), which often leads to

---

Box 11.1.   What Is This Item Really Measuring? Examples of Assessment Content That Measures Form Versus Function

Form		Function
Picking up a towel to reveal a hidden object	→	Finding common objects in hidden and/or object usual locations
Jumping over an 8-inch hurdle	→	Navigating objects while moving
Saying noun/verb phrases	→	Getting wants and needs met
Lacing a 4- × 6-inch card with five holes	→	Manipulating objects
Walking 10 feet in a straight line	→	Getting from Point A to Point B
Fastening four buttons on a shirt or jacket	→	Putting on a front-opening garment using any functional means
Walking on a balance beam	→	Displaying balance when mobile
Putting together a four-piece inlaid puzzle	→	Solving problems
Saying name, age, and address	→	Providing personal information
Stringing beads	→	Following a sequence

---

avoidance behaviors such as shutting down or running away (Autism Speaks, 2008; Hirstein et al., 2001).

Concurrently, standardized responses such as labeling, pointing, and moving objects are barriers for many children with severe or multiple disabilities (Rowland, 2009). For instance, the child with a severe motor delay might have limited capacity for these standardized responses, whereas children with speech or language impairments may be unable to produce linguistic information (e.g., labeling objects) and, therefore, unable to communicate in the required response method.

More often than not, it is both the content and the method of an assessment that are mismatches for a child with severe or multiple disabilities. For example, the content and method of traditional intelligence tests are language dependent (Schum, 2004). A child with a language disorder would probably be unable to access a traditional intelligence test for multiple reasons. First, it is likely that the child would be unable to interpret the linguistic information provided within the test questions. Second, even if the child could interpret the test questions, he or she would probably be unable to communicate a response. Finally, even if the child could interpret the linguistics of the question and communicate a response, it is often the case that the information is beyond the scope of the understanding or experience of a preschool-age child. The use of measures with nonfunctional items outside the scope of children's capabilities, inflexible cuing systems, and required standardized responses plays an enormous role in the challenge of assessing young children who have severe or multiple disabilities (Schum, 2004).

Children With Complex Medical Needs

Children who are medically complex present a unique challenge to teachers and other professionals engaged in early childhood assessment. We often consider these children to have severe and/or multiple disabilities; however, this group requires special consideration because their needs are often overlooked or misunderstood. Although roughly 15% of U.S. children have special health needs of some kind, children with complex medical disabilities represent less than 1% of the total U.S. population of children (Murphy & Clark, 2016). In general, those with identified complex medical disabilities or rare diseases may more obviously be seen as in need of special assessment consideration and thought to be severely disabled.

Importantly, however, for some students with disabilities (especially those with autism), having a health impairment of any kind may present significant additional challenges when it comes to assessment that are not always obvious. For example, most school districts include students with a variety of health impairments, such as asthma, type 1 diabetes, epilepsy, cystic fibrosis, and more. For students without other disabilities, Section 504 of the Americans with Disabilities Act (ADA, 1991) is usually sufficient to ensure that consideration is given to how their health impairment affects participation in daily activities, including assessment. On the other hand, those students who have an eligible disability outside of their health impairment may be significantly affected in ways that are sometimes poorly understood by both the medical and educational communities.

Under IDEA (2004), students who undergo an educational evaluation for eligibility and who are found to qualify under one of 14 categories (including OHI, or Other Health Impairment) are entitled to appropriate accommodations and/or modifications, including considerations for assessment. These students are also protected by Section 504 of the Americans with Disabilities Act (ADA, 1991). Although there are numerous students in schools across the country who are protected by the ADA, those students who have health conditions that affect their access and participation in the general curriculum—and who therefore are eligible for special education services—require special consideration with respect to assessment provision and interpretation.

Not all children who are medically complex are outwardly considered to have severe disabilities. Although it is easy to see how a child who is paralyzed in some way needs special consideration when it comes to assessment, it is not always obvious to see how assessment procedures or interpretive practices may be biased or inaccurate for those who have a health impairment such as type 1 diabetes and a disability such as autism. For example, a student with these two diagnoses may have incidences of high or low blood sugar that heighten sensory differences or emotional regulation, and it may be difficult to determine how to adjust assessment procedures or interpretation in light of these fluctuating blood sugar levels. Thus, the interplay of many common disabilities with a variety of medical conditions is not well understood and caution must be taken when conducting assessment and interpreting results.

SPECIFIC RECOMMENDATIONS

This section provides specific recommendations for assessing children who have severe or multiple disabilities (including those who are medically complex). The section provides specific recommendations regarding what and how information is gathered across assessment purposes.

What to Assess

When assessing children with multiple or severe disabilities and those who are medically complex, teachers need to gather information about the general effects of the disability on typical development to support their interpretations of test results (i.e., determine whether a documented delay should be considered an area of need or if the delay is within the typical trajectory for same-age peers with the same disability). For most children with multiple or severe disabilities, or who are medically complex, the course of development is different, not necessarily slower (Ferrell, 1998). For example, research has shown that children with visual impairments learn things in a different sequence and at a different rate than children who are typically developing (see Box 11.2). As a general rule, teachers should avoid comparisons between children who are typically developing and children with a disability and should keep in mind that a disability in one area affects a child's abilities or developmental trajectories in other areas.

Gathering information about the child's use of functional skills is critical when assessing young children with multiple or severe disabilities as well as those who are medically complex (Browder, 2001). As previously mentioned, teachers should examine function rather than form. For example, an item that measures ability to get from Point A to Point B is a more appropriate assessment of a child's functioning than an item that focuses on specific locomotor skills, such as walking or running. Children may demonstrate the function of the skill by moving around in a wheelchair, crawling, or using a walker. Likewise, an open-ended item that measures a child's ability to communicate their wants and needs is more functional than focusing on specific verbal communication skills, such as speaking or pointing. Therefore, teachers should focus on developing comprehensive descriptions of a child's functioning on tasks or skills considered important to the child's present and future performance (Meisels & Atkins-Burnett, 2000).

In addition to gathering information about a child's functional skills, Malloy (2010) recommends that a child's vision and hearing should be considered during the assessment process, because many children who have severe

---

Box 11.2.   Executive Summary Conclusions About How Children With Visual Impairments Learn Things in a Different Sequence at a Different Rate

Research Question 1: Do children between birth and 5 years of age who are visually impaired attain developmental milestones at ages that differ from those of children who are typically developing?

Results:

- The age of acquisition for 12 milestones was delayed in comparison to typically developing children.

- For five milestones, median age of acquisition was within the range of attainment for typical children. All five milestones that fell within the range for typically developing children were behaviors that required expressive and receptive communication.

- Two milestones were acquired earlier by children in this study than by typical children (copying a circle; relating past experiences). Earlier acquisition is somewhat suspect, however, because data are available for less than 10% of the total sample.

Research Question 2: Do children between birth and 5 years of age who are visually impaired attain developmental skills in a sequence that differs from the sequence followed by children who are typically developing?

Results:

- Seven milestones were acquired in a different sequence for children in this study than for typically developing children.

- Searching for a dropped object, feeding self bite-size pieces of food, and moving 3 or more feet by crawling were generally acquired in a later sequence by all children, with and without additional disabilities.

- Walking without support, controlling bowel movements, and repeating two-digit sequences were acquired in a later sequence for children with additional impairments.

- Copying a circle occurred earlier in the sequence for children with additional impairments but later in the sequence for children without additional impairments. However, this, too, is suspect because of low numbers of children who had actually acquired the skill.

Adapted from a portion of the executive summary report from Project PRISM: A Longitudinal Study of Developmental Patterns of Children who are Visually Impaired. To access the complete executive summary and/or the full research report, please visit http://www.unco.edu/ncssd/research/PRISM /default.html and multiple disabilities also have sensory impairments. In addition, Malloy recommends that information about the child's likes and dislikes, along with information on times of day, people, or activities in which the child best functions, should be obtained. Finally, information about situations that are difficult for the child should be ascertained. Children with severe and multiple disabilities, including those who have medical conditions, may often be fatigued or overwhelmed by environmental stimuli. Understanding prime times of the day and preferred materials and activities in which to engage the child will assist the team in developing an instructional program in which the child will be successful.

How to Assess

The remainder of the section provides recommendations for how transdisciplinary teams should approach the assessment process for children with severe and multiple disabilities. Teachers need to consider the influences and biases inherent to the assessment process, integrate and use interchangeable cuing systems and alternative materials, and allow children to provide alternative responses.

Influences and Biases

When assessing young children with severe and multiple disabilities, teachers should consider influences and biases created by both the assessment setting or situation and those who are conducting the assessment. Using an authentic assessment approach (i.e., familiar adults in familiar settings) is critical to the success of the assessment process. Research has shown that when conducting assessments of young children who have severe or multiple disabilities in familiar settings, familiar adults are able to elicit better performance and more elaborate responses (Barkley, 1982; Copenhaver-Johnson & Katz, 2009; Fuchs & Fuchs, 1984).

Interchangeable Cuing Systems

Teachers should also try to incorporate interchangeable cuing systems when assessing children with severe and multiple disabilities. Assessments should be administered in the mode of communication most commonly used by the child (Espinosa, 2005). Often, the mode of communication used by children with severe and multiple disabilities is nonverbal. Teachers should incorporate the use of picture communication systems, augmentative communication devices, object and tactile cues, and gestures or sign language when appropriate. Nevertheless, teachers should beware of translating standardized verbal tests into any alternative mode of communication. For example, sign language is not a precise equivalent of spoken language, so translation can invalidate the standardization of test procedures (Schum, 2004).

In addition to using interchangeable cuing systems, the manner in which cues are represented should be adjusted to match the needs of the child. For example, children with receptive language deficits will benefit when test questions, instructions, and commands are short, concrete, and repeated (Zentall, 1988). For children with hearing impairments, teachers should ensure that the administration of any auditory information is within the child's acuity level. Pairing appropriate cues with reinforcement can help improve motivation and, therefore, test performance for children with behavioral disabilities (Singh et al., 2005). When using reinforcers, teachers should consider the interests and preferences of the child. For example, for children with autism, repetitive stimulation (e.g., strobe light, vibration, rocking) can be more motivating than typical primary reinforcers (e.g., food; Freeman et al., 1976; Margolies, 1977).

Alternative, Flexible Materials

When assessing young children with severe and multiple disabilities, teachers also need to utilize alternative and flexible materials. Choosing materials that are a match for the child's capabilities and that allow for flexibility in the assessment process will give children with severe and multiple disabilities multiple ways of accessing the test content. For example, when children have visual impairments, teachers should choose materials that provide tactile information or large, contrasting visual displays. For children with behavior disorders, instruments with more manipulative items and shorter duration of tasks are an appropriate choice (Shaw, 2008).

Alternative Responses

When allowing for alternative responses, teachers should consider the strengths of the child and attempt to align the response options with the child's unique set of skills (Neisworth & Bagnato, 2004). For example, instruments that emphasize nonverbal procedures, such as pointing to pictures or signaling choice with an eye gaze, are appropriate for children with communication disorders or who are nonverbal. For children with motor impairments, teachers should acknowledge and verify movement responses that are approximations of standard responses and appear to demonstrate intent (Robinson & Fieber, 1988). Allowing children to draw their responses is an alternative option. When children produce verbal responses, teachers should focus on the function or content of the response rather than the form. Finally, children with severe and multiple disabilities should be given the option of using adaptive equipment, augmentative communication devices, or other supportive technologies to accommodate their responses during the assessment process.

MEASURES

When selecting measures for assessing children with severe and multiple disabilities, the same considerations identified for assessing children who are DLLs should be acknowledged. Assessment tools should be technically sound, which in this case suggests that in order to be valid, those measures should be validated for children with severe and multiple disabilities. In addition, measures should be multifaceted, suggesting that groups of parents, along with children's families, should be involved in the assessment process. Finally, the measure must be unbiased, allowing children with severe and multiple disabilities to use any communication system to demonstrate their knowledge.

The best way to ensure that measures are appropriate for learners with severe and multiple disabilities is to select universally designed assessments. Assessments that meet this criteria are "are designed from the beginning, and continually refined, to allow participation of the widest possible range of students, resulting in more valid inferences about performance" (Thompson et al., 2005, p. 2). Similar to universal design for learning, which is applied to instruction, universally designed assessments are developed so that the needs of the entire population are considered at the time the assessment is developed and not adapted afterward. Often applied to the development of statewide accountability assessments (e.g., Johnstone et al., 2006), the idea of universally designed assessments has applicability when designing any measure for learners with severe and multiple disabilities. Examples include 1) ensuring that items measure what they intend to measure and not a specific behavior form (see discussion above about form versus function); 2) ensuring that materials can be used, regardless of a child's visual abilities; 3) using a variety of different ways of sharing information with the child beyond speech; and 4) allowing for the use of assistive technology.

There are some assessments that meet the necessary criteria for accurately assessing children with severe and multiple disabilities. For example, the Adaptive Behavior Assessment System–Third Edition (ABAS-III; Harrison & Oakland, 2015), the Behavior Assessment System for Children–Third Edition (BASC-3; Reynolds & Kamphaus, 2015), and the Pediatric Evaluation of Disability Inventory (PEDI; Haley et al., 1992) include children with disabilities in their normative sample. Further, the Assessment, Evaluation, and Programming System for Infants and Children (AEPS®)–Second Edition (Bricker, 2002), BASC-3, PEDI, and Transdisciplinary Play-Based Assessment, Second Edition (TPBA2; Linder, 2008) have been validated for particular populations, including children with disabilities. Last, AEPS and the Desired Results Developmental Profile (DRDP; California Department of Education, Early Education and Support Division and Special Education Division, 2015) are examples of assessments that emphasize universality and equity. (See Bagnato et al., 2010, for a complete review of 81 common early childhood intervention assessments.) Table 11.1 includes a summary of assessments that were specifically designed for children with severe or multiple disabilities. Although the assessments in Table 11.1 may not meet all recommended practice standards discussed here and throughout the book, they were, at a minimum, designed or validated for children with severe or multiple disabilities. See Box 11.3 for general considerations for selecting assessments when working with children with severe or multiple disabilities.

Table 11.1. Alphabetical listing of assessment measures designed for young children with severe/multiple disabilities

Assessment	Brief assessment description	Target audience	Age span	Contact information (authors, publisher, website)
The Callier-Azusa Scale (CAS)[a]	Developmental assessment with subscales that evaluate children's visual, auditory, and tactile development	Children who are deafblind, but also useful for any child with multiple or severe disabilities, particularly hearing and/or visual impairments	Children functioning below a developmental age of 6–7 years	Author: Stillman, R. D. Publisher: University of Texas at Dallas, Callier Center for Communication Disorders Website: https://calliercenter.utdallas.edu /evaluation-treatment/callier-azusa-scale/ Scale G, which assesses children's overall development (latest revision 1978), and Scale H, which assesses children's communicative development (latest revision 1984), can be ordered through the website.
Central Institute for the Deaf Preschool Performance Scale (CID–PPS)	Intelligence test yielding a deviation IQ that assesses nonverbal cognition	Children with hearing impairments	Children with a chronological age of 2–6 years	Authors: Geers, A. E., & Lane, H. S. Publisher: Stoelting Co. Website: https://www.stoeltingco.com/
Communication Matrix	Developmental assessment that evaluates communication skills and behavior and that assists users in identifying logical communication goals	Individuals who experience any type or degree of disability, including severe and multiple disabilities, intellectual limitations, and sensory or physical impairments	Individuals of all ages at the earliest stages of communication development; individuals with a communication developmental age of 0–24 months	Author: Rowland, C. Publisher: Design to Learn Projects of the Oregon Health & Science University Website: https://www.ohsu.edu/design-to -learn and/or https://www.communicationmatrix.org/

Table 11.1. (continued)

Assessment	Brief assessment description	Target audience	Age span	Contact information (authors, publisher, website)
The Dimension of Communication	A tool for assessing the developmental levels of learner, irrespective of age and/or disabilities	Children, adolescents, and young adults who have multiple disabilities, including severe or profound mental disability and deaf-blindness	There is no specific age, but it can be used to evaluate children to young adult	Authors: Mar, H. H., & Sall, N. M. Publisher: St. Joseph's Children's Hospital, U.S. Department of Education, Office of Educational Research and Improvement, Educational Resources Information Center Website: https://documents.nationaldb .org/products/dimensions-of -communication.pdf
DRDP Access[a]	A criterion-referenced assessment with domains that measure children's self-concept, social and interpersonal skills, self-regulation, language, learning, cognitive competence, math, literacy, motor skills, and safety and health	Young children with disabilities	Children birth to 5 years	Author: Desired Results Access Project, California Department of Education, Special Education Division Publisher: California Department of Education, Special Education Division Website: http://www.draccess.org
Every Move Counts[a]	Curriculum-based assessment using a functional hierarchy to evaluate sensory-based communication	Children with significant sensorimotor and developmental disabilities, including autism	Children functioning at a developmental age of 18 months or less	Authors: Korsten, J. E., Foss, T. V., & Berry, L. M. Publisher: EMC, Inc. Website: https://www.everymovecounts.net/

(continued)

Table 11.1. (continued)

Assessment	Brief assessment description	Target audience	Age span	Contact information (authors, publisher, website)
The Functional Schemes Assessment	Designed to assess people with multiple disabilities, including deafblindness Two parts: developing a communication profile and designing an intervention plan Uses observation, interview, and structured interaction Has six dimensions: symbol use, intent, complexity, social action, vocabulary used, comprehension Scored on 5-point scale with examples at each level Users are encouraged to add items to each subsection of things a child can do if nothing on the list illustrates the capacity a particular child demonstrates For teachers working with visually impaired children who have multiple disabilities Used in conjunction with the FIELA curriculum to make sure activities are at the appropriate level Many items are tied to having Dr. Nielson's equipment	Children with visually impaired and multiple disabilities	Birth to 48 months	Author: Nielsons, L. Publisher: Ministry of Social Affairs Website: https://www.lilliworks.org/
Infused Skills	Developmental assessment that analyzes social communicative interactions, emotional development, senses/motor skills, basic concepts, and representation and cognition	Children with visual impairments who may also have cognitive and behavioral challenges	No specific chronological or developmental age indicated; appropriate for children with no verbal skills to those with higher cognitive functioning but still in need of life skills instruction	Author: Texas School for the Blind and Visually Impaired Publisher: Texas School for the Blind and Visually Impaired (TSBVI) Website: https://www.tsbvi.edu/ and/or https://www.tsbvi.edu/handouts/oct06/infused-skills-assessment.pdf

Table 11.1. (continued)

Assessment	Brief assessment description	Target audience	Age span	Contact information (authors, publisher, website)
INSITE[a]	Developmental checklist designed for use by home-based programs and parents	Children with sensory and/or multiple impairments	Children with a chronological age of birth through 6 years	Author: The SKI-HI Institute, a Division of the College of Education's Department of Communicative Disorders and Deaf Education at Utah State University Publisher: HOPE, Inc. Website: https://ski-hi.mystrikingly.com/ and/or https://comdde.usu.edu/
Leiter-R	Nonverbal cognitive (intelligence) assessment that is administered in the manner of a game that assesses reasoning, visualization, memory, and attention	Children with speech impairments, autism, ADHD, hearing, vision, and/or motor impairments, traumatic brain injury, and other types of communication and/or sensory disabilities	Children and individuals with a chronological age of 2–20 years	Authors: Roid, G. H., & Miller, L. J. Publisher: Western Psychological Services (WPS) Website: https://www.wpspublish.com /leiter-3-leiter-international -performance-scale-third-edition
The Language Environment Analysis System (LENA)	Automatic, computerized language assessment that screens and diagnoses verbal language delays and disorders in children and adults	Children, but especially those with or at risk for disabilities, particularly autism	Children with a chronological age of 2–48 months	Authors: Paul, T. D., & Paul, J. A. Publisher: LENA Foundation Website: http://www.lenafoundation.org/ and/or http://www.lenababy.com/
Oregon Project[a]	Criterion-referenced assessment that measures child performance on cognitive, language, self-help, socialization, fine motor, and gross motor skills	Children who are blind or visually impaired	Children with a chronological age of birth through 6 years	Authors: Anderson, S., Boigon, S., Davis, K., & DeWaard, C. Publisher: Southern Oregon Education Service District Website: https://www.soesd.k12.or.us /or-project-order/

(continued)

Table 11.1. *(continued)*

Assessment	Brief assessment description	Target audience	Age span	Contact information (authors, publisher, website)
SKI-HI[a]	Curriculum-based language assessment that assists in developing individualized goals by evaluating receptive and expressive language	Children who are deaf or hard of hearing	Children with a chronological age of birth through 5 years	Author: Watkins, S. Publisher: HOPE, Inc. Website: http://www.hopepubl.com and/or http://www.skihi.org
School Inventory of Problem Solving Skills/Home Inventory of Problem Solving Skills (SIPSS/HIPSS)	Developmental assessment that gauges object interaction skills, including basic skills, ways to gain access to objects, and ways to use objects	Children who are nonverbal with multiple disabilities, including those with severe intellectual disability or sensory impairments such as deafblindness	No specific chronological or developmental age indicated	Author: Oregon Health and Science University Publisher: Design to Learn Projects of the Oregon Health and Science University Website: http://www.designtolearn.com/content/school-inventory-problem-solving-skills-sipss
Strategies for Teaching Based on Autism Research (STAR)	Curriculum-based assessment within an applied behavior analysis framework with a focus on receptive language, expressive language, spontaneous language, functional routines, academics, and play and social skills	Children with autism	Individuals of any age; the program and assessment are available at three distinct levels to meet the needs of all learners	Authors: Arick, J., Loos, L., Falco, R., Krug, D., & Gill, J. Publisher: STAR Autism Support, LLC Website: http://www.starautismprogram.com
Test of Early Communication and Emerging Language (TECEL)	A revision and standardization of the Nonspeech Test that assesses communication and language, gauges future language development, and explores early communication and emerging language	Typically developing young children and older individuals with moderate-to-severe language delays	2 weeks to 24 months; older children, adolescents, and adults who have language delays	Authors: Huer, M. B., & Miller, L. Publisher: PRO-ED Website: https://www.proedinc.com/Products/12640/tecel-test-of-early-communication-and-emerging-language.aspx

[a]Indicates the assessment was reviewed in Bagnato, S. J., Neisworth, J. T., & Pretti-Frontczak, K. (2010). *LINKing authentic assessment and early childhood intervention: Best measures for best practices* (2nd ed.). Paul H. Brookes Publishing Co.

> **Box 11.3.   General Considerations for Selecting an Assessment Instrument for Use With Children With Severe/Multiple Disabilities**
>
> - Do the items describe behaviors that a child with vision and hearing losses and/or motor impairments could be expected to show?
>
> - Are there sufficient items at the early developmental levels to clearly identify a child's current skills and measure progress in small steps?
>
> - Are the items appropriate to the child's chronological age, or do they describe behaviors one would expect to see only in infants and toddlers?
>
> - Are there sufficient examples to clarify the items and to determine how a particular skill might be observed in a child who is deafblind?
>
> - Does the assessment require information derived from observations in natural settings?
>
> - Do the results provide applicable information for program planning, or are they primarily numerical scores?
>
> - Does the instrument provide ideas about the next step for the child?
>
> - Are the results in a format that can be easily communicated to, and understood by, families?
>
> - Does the instrument require the user to possess specialized training or professional credentials?
>
> - Is there a parent version that a family member could complete, or a way for parents to provide their input and perspectives?
>
> From Rowland, C. (2009). *Assessing communication and learning in young children who are deafblind or who have multiple disabilities* (p. 9). Portland, OR: Design to Learn Projects; reprinted by permission.

SUMMARY

The purpose of this chapter was to promote the use of recommended assessment practices discussed in Chapter 1 as they apply to children with severe and multiple disabilities. First, the chapter illustrated the need for the teacher to work as a member of a transdisciplinary team when assessing young children with severe and multiple disabilities, highlighting the importance of role release. Next, general considerations for assessing young children with severe and multiple disabilities were described, and an overview of the challenges teachers face was included. Issues surrounding the content and method of traditional assessments were explored, and the inherent biases involved in the assessment process were discussed.

Specific recommendations for assessing young children with severe and multiple disabilities were provided next, and readers were directed to consider what and how information should be gathered across purposes within the assessment process. Teachers were encouraged to gather authentic assessment information from families, to focus on functional skills, to consider the influences and biases created during the assessment process, to incorporate interchangeable cuing systems, and to utilize alternative, flexible materials and allow children to provide alternative responses. Finally, issues around the measures available for assessing young children with severe and multiple disabilities were discussed, and suggestions for selecting an appropriate assessment tool were provided to better serve these unique learners.

REFERENCES

Allen, K. E., & Marotz, L. R. (2010). *Developmental profiles: Pre-birth through twelve*. Wadsworth Cengage Learning.

Americans with Disabilities Act of 1990, PL 101-336, 42 U.S.C. §§ 12101 *et seq.*

Anderson, S., Boigon, S., & Davis, K. DeWaard, C. (2007). *The Oregon Project for preschool children who are blind or visually impaired*. Southern Oregon Education Service. https://www.soesd.k12.or.us/or-project-order/

Arick, J., Loos, L., Falco, R., Krug, D., & Gil, J. (2004). *Strategies for Teaching Based on Autism Research* (STAR). STAR Autism Support, LLC. http://starautismprogram.com

Autism Speaks. (2008). *School community tool kit*. http://autismspeaks.org/docs/family_services_docs/sk/School_Community_Tool_Kit.pdf

Bagnato, S. J., & Neisworth, J. T. (1995). A national study of the social and treatment "invalidity" of intelligence testing for early intervention. *School Psychology Quarterly, 9*(2), 81–102.

Bagnato, S. J., Neisworth, J. T., & Pretti-Frontczak, K. (2010). *LINKing authentic assessment and early childhood intervention: Best measures for best practices* (2nd ed.). Paul H. Brookes Publishing Co.

Bagnato, S. J., & Simeonsson, R. J. (2007). *Authentic assessment for early childhood intervention: Best practices*. Guilford Press.

Barkley, R. A. (1982). Specific guidelines for defining hyperactivity in children (attention deficit disorder with hyperactivity). In B. Lahey & A. Kazdin (Eds.), *Advances in clinical child psychology* (Vol. 5, pp. 137–180). Plenum Press.

Bricker, D. (2002). *Assessment, Evaluation, and Programming System for Infants and Children* (2nd ed.). Vols. 1–4. Paul H. Brookes Publishing Co.

Bronfenbrenner, U. (1977). Toward an experimental ecology of human development. *American Psychologist, 32*, 513–531.

Browder, D. M. (2001). *Curriculum and assessment for students with moderate and severe disabilities*. Guilford Press.

Bruder, M. B., & Bologna, T. (1993). Collaboration and service coordination for effective early intervention. In W. Brown, S. K. Thurman, & L. F. Pearl (Eds.), *Family-centered early intervention with infants and toddlers* (pp. 103–128). Paul H. Brookes Publishing Co.

California Department of Education, Early Education and Support Division and Special Education Division. (2015). *Desired Results Developmental Profile (2015): A developmental continuum from early infancy to kindergarten entry*. Author.

Copenhaver-Johnson, J., & Katz, L. (2009). *Supporting young English language learners and their families*. A Professional Development Module supported by the Ohio Department of Education. Early Childhood Quality Network.

Copple, C., & Bredekamp, S. (Eds.). (2009). *Developmentally appropriate practice in early childhood programs serving children birth through eight* (3rd ed.). National Association for the Education of Young Children.

Desired Results Access Project. (2007). *Desired Results Developmental Profile (DRDP) Access*. Napa County Office of Education, California Department of Education, Special Education Division. http://draccess.org

Downing, J. E., & Chen, D. (2003). Using tactile strategies with students who are blind and have severe disabilities. *Teaching Exceptional Children, 36*(2), 56–60.

Durand, T. M. (2008). Celebrating diversity in early care and education settings: Moving beyond the margins. *Early Child Development and Care, 180*.(7), 835–848. http://doi.org /10.1080/03004430802466226

Ermer, J., & Dunn, W. (1998). The sensory profile: A discriminant analysis of children with and without disabilities. *The American Journal of Occupational Therapy, 52*(4), 283–290.

Espinosa, L. M. (2005). Curriculum and assessment considerations for young children from culturally, linguistically, and economically diverse backgrounds. *Psychology in the Schools, 42*(8), 837–853.

Etscheidt, S. (2006). Least restrictive and natural environments for young children with disabilities: A legal analysis of issues. *Topics in Early Childhood Special Education, 26*(3), 167–178. http://doi.org/10.1177/02711214060260030401

Ferrell, K. A. (1998). *Project PRISM: A longitudinal study of developmental patterns of children who are visually impaired.* University of Northern Colorado. http://unco.edu/ncssd/research /PRISM/default.html

Freeman, B. J., Frankel, B. J., & Ritvo, E. J. (1976). Effects of frequency of photic stimulation upon autistic and retarded children. *American Journal of Mental Deficiency, 81*, 32–40.

Fuchs, L. S., & Fuchs, D. (1984) Criterion-referenced assessment without measurement. *Remedial and Special Education, 5*(4), 29–32.

Geers, A. E., & Lane, H. S. (1984). *Central Institute for the Deaf Preschool Performance Scale* (CID-PPS). Stoelting Co. https://stoeltingco.com/

Haley, S. M., Coster, W. J., Ludlow, L. H., Haltiwanger, J. T., & Andrellos, P. J. (1992). *Pediatric Evaluation of Disability Inventory (PEDI).* New England Medical Center.

Harrison, P. L., & Oakland, T. (2015). *Adaptive Behavior Assessment System* (3rd ed.). Psychological Corporation.

Hirstein, W., Iversen P., & Ramachandran, V. S. (2001). Autonomic responses of autistic children to people and objects. *Proceedings of the Royal Society B, 268*, 1883–1888.

Huer, M. B., & Miller, L. (2011). *Test of Early Communication and Emerging Language (TECEL).* PRO-ED.

Individuals with Disabilities Education Improvement Act (IDEA) of 2004, PL 108-446, 20 U.S.C. §§ 1400 *et seq.*

Jackson, S., Pretti-Frontczak, K., Harjusola-Webb, S., Grisham-Brown, J., & Romani, J. M. (2009). Response to intervention: Implications for early childhood professionals. *Language, Speech, and Hearing Services in Schools, 40*, 424–434. http://doi.org/10.1044/0161-1461(2009/08-0027)

Johnstone, C., Altman, J., & Thurlow, M. (2006). *A state guide to the development of universally designed assessments.* National Center on Educational Outcomes, University of Minnesota.

King, G., Strachan, D., Tucker, M., Duwyn, B., Desserud, S., & Shillington, M. (2009). The application of a transdisciplinary model for early intervention services. *Infants & Young Children, 22*(3), 211–223.

Klingner, J. K., Blanchett, W. J., & Harry, B. (2007). Race, culture, and developmental disabilities. In S. L. Odom, R. H. Horner, M. E. Snell, & J. Blacher (Eds.), *Handbook of developmental disabilities.* Guilford Press.

Korsten, J., Foss, T., Berry, L. (1993). *Every Move Counts.* EMC, Inc. https://everymovecounts.net/

Linder, T. (2008). *Transdisciplinary Play-Based Assessment, Second Edition (TPBA2).* Paul H. Brookes Publishing Co.

Malloy, P. (2010). *Authentic assessment. Practice perspectives—Highlighting information on deaf-blindness. Number 6.* National Consortium on Deaf-Blindness.

Mar, H., & Sall, N. (1999). *Dimensions of communication: Assessing the communication skills of individuals with disabilities.* St. Joseph's Children's Hospital, United States Department of Education. https://documents.nationaldb.org/products/dimensions-of-communication.pdf

Margolies, P. J. (1977). Behavioral approaches to the treatment of early infantile autism: A review. *Psychological Bulletin, 84*, 249–264.

McCormick, K., & Nellis, L. (2004). Assessing cognitive development. In M. McLean, M. Wolery, & B. Bailey Jr. (Eds.), *Assessing infants and preschoolers with special needs* (3rd ed.). Pearson.

McLean, M., Wolery, M., & Bailey, D. B. (2004). *Assessing infants and preschoolers with special needs* (3rd ed.). Pearson Education Inc.

Meisels, S. J., & Atkins-Burnett, S. (2000). The elements of early childhood assessment. In J. P. Shonkoff & S. Meisels (Eds.), *Handbook of early childhood intervention* (2nd ed., pp. 231–257). Cambridge University Press.

Murphy, N. A., & Clark, E. B. (2016). Children with complex medical conditions: An under-recognized driver of the pediatric cost crisis. *Current Treatment Options in Pediatrics, 2*(4), 289–295. http://doi.org/10.1007/s40746-016-0071-7

National Association for the Education of Young Children (NAEYC). (2020). *Developmentally appropriate practice: A position statement of the National Association for the Education of Young Children.* Author.

Neisworth, J. T., & Bagnato, S. J. (1992). The case against intelligence testing in early intervention. *Topics in Early Childhood Special Education, 12*, 1–20.

Neisworth, J. T., & Bagnato, S. J. (2004). The mismeasure of young children: The authentic assessment alternative. *Infants and Young Children, 17*(3), 198–212. http://doi.org/10.1097/00001163-200407000-00002

Nielsons, L. (2000). *Functional Schemes: Functional Skills Assessment Learning Reassessment.* Ministry of Social Affairs. https://lilliworks.org/

Oregon Health and Science University. (1997). *School Inventory of Problem Solving Skills/Home Inventory of Problem Solving Skills* (SIPSS/HIPSS). Oregon Health and Sciences University. http://designtolearn.com/content/school-inventory-problem-solving-skills-sipss

Paul, T. D., & Paul, J. A. *The Language Environment Analysis System.* LENA Foundation. http://lenafoundation.org/

Raab, M., & Dunst, C. J. (2004). Early intervention practitioner approaches to natural environment interventions. *Journal of Early Intervention, 27*, 15–26.

Reynolds, C. R., & Kamphaus, R. W. (2015). *Behavior Assessment System for Children* (3rd ed.). American Guidance Service.

Robinson, C., & Fieber, N. (1988). Cognitive assessment of motorically impaired infants and preschoolers. In T. D. Wachs & R. Sheehan (Eds.), *Assessment of young developmentally disabled children* (pp. 127–152). Plenum Press.

Roid, G. H., & Miller, L. J. (2013). *Leiter-R.* Western Psychological Services (WPS). https://wpspublish.com/leiter-3-leiter-international-performance-scale-third-edition

Rosário, V. M., Gomes, C. M. A., & Loureiro, C. M. V. (2019). Systematic review of attention testing in allegedly "untestable" populations. *International Journal of Psychological Research and Reviews, 2*(19), 1–21. http://doi.org/10.28933/ijprr-2019-07-1905

Rowland, C. (2004). *Communication Matrix: A communication skills assessment.* Design to Learn Projects of the Oregon Health & Science University. https://communicationmatrix.org/

Rowland, C. (Ed.). (2009). *Assessing communication and learning in young children who are deaf-blind or who have multiple disabilities.* Design to Learn Projects.

Sandall, S., Hemmeter, M. L., Smith, B. J., & McLean, M. E. (2005). *DEC recommended practices: A comprehensive guide for practical application in early intervention/early childhood special education.* Sopris West.

Schum, R. (2004). Psychological assessment of children with multiple handicaps who have hearing loss. *The Volta Review, 104*, 237–255.

Shaw, S. R. (2008). An educational programming framework for a subset of students with diverse learning needs: Borderline intellectual functioning. *Intervention in School and Clinic, 43*(5), 291–299.

Shonkoff, J. P., & Phillips, D. A. (Eds.). (2000). *From neurons to neighborhoods: The science of early childhood development.* National Academies Press.

Singh, S., Barto, A. G., & Chentanez, N. (2005). Intrinsically motivated reinforcement learning. In *Advances in Neural Information Processing Systems 17 (NIPS).* The MIT Press.

SKI-HI Institute, a Division of the College of Education's Department of Communicative Disorders and Deaf Education at Utah State University. (1990) *Insite.* HOPE, Inc. https://ski-hi.mystrikingly.com/

Snow, C. E., & Van Hemel, S. B. (2008). *Early childhood assessment: Why, what, and how?* National Academies Press.

Stillman, R. (1978). *The Callier-Azusa Scale* (G-H eds.). South Central Regional Center for Services to Deaf-Blind Children and Callier Center for Communication Disorders, University of Texas at Dallas. https://calliercenter.utdallas.edu/evaluation-treatment/callier-azusa-scale

Texas School for the Blind and Visually Impaired. *Infused skills.* Author. https://www.tsbvi.edu/

Thompson, S. J., Johnstone, C. J., Anderson, M. E., & Miller, N. A. (2005). *Considerations for the development and review of universally designed assessments* (Technical Report 42). National Center on Educational Outcomes.

Watkins., S. *SKI-HI*. HOPE Inc. http://skihi.org.

Woodruff, G., & McGonigel, M. J. (1988). Early intervention team approaches: The transdisciplinary model. In J. Jordan, J. Gallaher, P. Huntinger, & M. Karns (Eds.), *Early childhood special education: Birth to three* (pp. 163–182). Council for Exceptional Children.

Zentall, S. S. (1988). Production deficiencies in elicited language but not in the spontaneous verbalizations of hyperactive children. *Journal of Abnormal Child Psychology, 16*, 657–673.

CHAPTER 12

Kindergarten Assessment

Julie Rutland, Jennifer Grisham, Lynn D. Sullivan, and Kristie Pretti-Frontczak

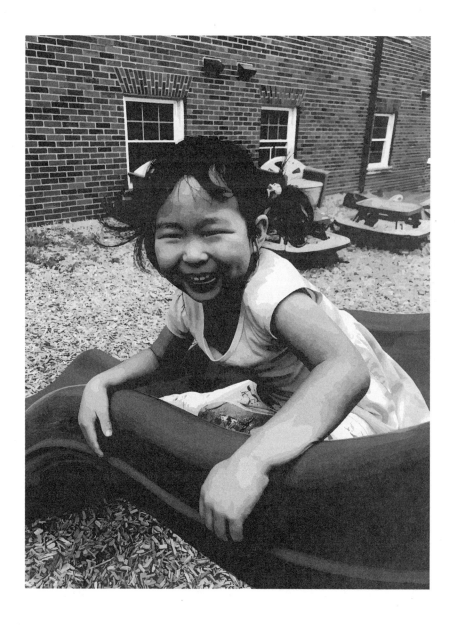

Chantei has been a kindergarten teacher for many years and has seen assessment change dramatically. When first teaching, there was flexibility in the methods and timing of assessments. Often, Chantei would develop assessments and evaluate children based on questions that emerged around each child's performance over time. The assessment practices were often informal and constructed by the teaching team. However, Chantei now faces kindergarten assessment expectations that seemingly leave little to no room for flexibility and have limited utility in making instructional decisions. Last week, which was the second week of the school year, Chantei was expected to assess the entire class of kindergarteners using a conventional, formal scripted assessment. For example, Chantei was expected to ask all children to identify English words, even children who were not yet identifying letters, those who were visually impaired, and those who were just beginning to learn English. The looks on students' faces confirmed Chantei's concerns—these assessments were inappropriate for many of her children and didn't allow her to use an equity lens of disability. So, later that day, Chantei met with other kindergarten teachers and started a conversation about how they could capture the strengths and abilities of the children in authentic ways. The goal of the grade level teachers was to find a way to advocate for assessment practices that allowed for student ability to take many forms and produce information they could use to plan meaningful lessons and experiences.

Standards-based education that stemmed from the No Child Left Behind (NCLB) Act of 2001 policies and regulations dramatically changed the way in which kindergarten looked. The main elements of NCLB were academic content standards, academic achievement standards, and state assessments. Each state defined academic achievement standards in reading/language arts, mathematics, and science. Such rigid kindergarten standards shifted the focus in kindergarten from teaching within a play-based, developmentally appropriate curriculum to emphasizing academics, specifically literacy and math. As the focus of instruction changed and instructional practices changed, so did kindergarten assessment. Whereas in past decades, kindergarten teachers' observations and self-made assessments were accepted as appropriate measures of child growth and development, more recently kindergarten assessment practices have become more formal and focused on specific academic skills, rather than looking at the whole child.

Following the NCLB Act, the Race to the Top–Early Learning Challenge (RTT-ELC) program was initiated as an effort to improve the quality of early learning and development and close what some refer to as the achievement gap. One of the intentions of RTT-ELC was to develop common standards within states and assessments that measure child outcomes. Prior to the RTT-ELC, only half of the United States required universal assessments of kindergarten students (Stedron & Berger, 2010). Of those states, there were varying definitions of the knowledge and skills measured. Only 11 states required schools to use instruments that addressed all five domains (physical well-being, social-emotional development, approaches to learning, language development, and cognition and general knowledge) of school readiness. And less than half of those states required instruments specifically for the evaluation of early literacy. Several of the states designed custom readiness measures based on teachers' observations of children's skills and abilities across multiple domains. Teachers had the flexibility to plan instruction independent of other classrooms or district mandates. This afforded children time and opportunity to learn concepts prior to assessment and permitted teachers to assess only what was appropriate for that unique child.

In 2015, replacing the NCLB act, the Every Student Succeeds Act (ESSA) furthered the desire of the federal government to provide equal opportunities for students disadvantaged by society and social constructs and to hold schools accountable for student learning and achievement. Under ESSA, there is much focus on kindergarten readiness and learning outcomes in the kindergarten year. In modern-day kindergarten classrooms, there are scripted tests, often conducted on computers, and implemented at predetermined intervals that are connected to not only child measures, but also teacher performance ratings. Teachers feel pressure to develop instructional activities that will directly link to the standards and affect children's scores in hopes of driving up the scores on mandated assessments. These assessments were developed by leaders who had good intentions but inadequate knowledge of developmentally appropriate assessment for young children. This paradigm shift has led to negative feelings toward assessment itself, but appropriate assessment is the ultimate guide for determining a child's developmental readiness and planning instruction.

The focus of this chapter is on key issues around how to implement authentic and developmentally appropriate assessment practices in kindergarten, while acknowledging the role of any required conventional assessment practices. In the first section, varying ideas of kindergarten readiness, what defines kindergarten readiness, and assessments often used to understand readiness are reviewed. The need for timely referrals and tiered instruction is described in the second section. The final section discusses the use of assessment to inform program planning in the kindergarten classroom.

KINDERGARTEN READINESS AND KINDERGARTEN ASSESSMENT

Kindergarten readiness is a topic of interest to a wide group of stakeholders, including families, teachers, communities, and both state and national policy makers (Aiona, 2005; DiBello & Neuharth-Pritchett, 2008; Fonseca, 2017; Maxwell & Clifford, 2004; Saluja et al., 2000). Over three decades ago, the topic became a focal point, as stakeholders were urged to address the readiness of young children transitioning into kindergarten (Kagan, 1990). The transition to kindergarten demonstrates the shift from early learning standards that address all domains to primary education standards that focus on academics. However, it is well documented that children who enter kindergarten ready to meet both the academic standards and social and emotional expectations are more likely to have success in both academics and life in later years (Snow, 2006). In the 1980s and 1990s, standardized tests and other assessment measures were used in preschool and kindergarten to determine if a child would be promoted or retained. We now understand that readiness is based on the whole child, which includes the following:

- Physical well-being (e.g., health, motor development)

- Social-emotional development (e.g., social skills, emotional regulation)

- Approaches to learning (e.g., ability and inclination to use skills)

- Language development

- Cognition and general knowledge (Kagan, 1992)

As such, assessment data is gathered to understand each child's ability to engage with and learn kindergarten content rather than a means to promote or retain a child.

In the years following the NCLB Act there was an increase in the number of states with kindergarten readiness definitions. Although we are making progress, there is yet to be a common definition of kindergarten readiness (Auck & Atchinson, 2016; Sabol & Pianta, 2017). What makes this even more daunting is that children are now being prepared for an increasingly rigorous, academically focused kindergarten experience (Bassok & Galdo, 2016; Brown, 2013; Stipek, 2006), which may cause teachers to narrow their instruction, leaving less time to focus on the whole child (e.g., social-emotional development). Pretti-Frontczak et al. (2016) offer three remedies for avoiding these practices: 1) recognizing that readiness is impacted by children's interactions with others and their experiences, 2) considering the interrelatedness of development when considering a child's readiness, and 3) accepting the diverse ways and rates at which children learn.

By the year 2006 great strides were noted in the appropriate use of assessments for kindergarteners. A growing number of states began tracking the readiness of children entering kindergarten using a variety of assessments including commercially developed tools, tools developed within the state, and a combination (Weisenfeld, 2017). Currently, many states have regulations for required kindergarten readiness assessments. For example, Delaware, Florida, Kentucky, Mississippi, New Mexico, North Carolina, and Rhode Island have statutes, rules, and/or regulations that require readiness assessment prior to or within the first 30 days of the kindergarten school year (Education Commission of the States, 2018). These types of assessments, known as kindergarten readiness assessments (KRAs), are valuable tools for leaders and teachers because they provide a picture of children's knowledge and skills and enhance teaching and learning. Specifically, KRAs can support the following:

- well-designed schools that meet the needs of their incoming kindergartners by informing them of the needs of the child and family.

- identification of child strengths and areas in need of improvement

- targeted instruction and strong transitions

- parent–teacher partnerships

- appropriate referral for evaluation (Regenstein et al., 2017)

However, there are precautions to avoid using KRAs. First, they are not intended for use in grouping children. Second, and most importantly, kindergarten readiness assessments are not designed to determine if a child can enter kindergarten. In most states, age determines when a child may enroll in kindergarten.

Similar to the KRA, kindergarten entry assessments (KEAs) are measures used to collect data on children within the first few months of kindergarten. KEA data provide a baseline for instruction and a means to measure future progress. Prior to the 2012 initial RTT-ELC grant, which required the implementation of a KEA, many states had no systematic method for collecting extensive data on kindergarteners. Specifically, the RTT-ELC suggested that, at a minimum, KEAs should cover language and literacy, cognition, approaches toward learning, physical well-being, and motor development. In response to such challenges, there was a need to accurately assess children's abilities and skills, and KEAs are now common in our school systems, serving a variety of purposes:

1. identifying developmental abilities of children as compared to benchmarks and standards,

2. informing instructional practices,

3. identifying needed resources for teachers, specialists, and students, and

4. informing program and early childhood initiatives (Shields et al., 2016)

States vary in the dimensions (e.g., reading, phonological awareness) and formats (e.g., checklists, rating scales, performance-based and direct assessments) that are used as KEAs (Connors-Tadros, 2014) as they work within the limitations of budget, reporting requirements, and needs of stakeholders. Furthermore, states may use widely recognized KEAs, whereas others have developed their own. Recommendations for such mandated entry assessments are that they be completed by someone who has a rapport with the child and over multiple points in time (Snow, 2011). Developmentally appropriate practice suggests that teachers collect data from multiple sources and that authentic assessment strategies be used. See Chapter 2 for more information on authentic assessment. This may include student work samples and observations. Teachers then rate a child's skill level as relative to research-based developmental expectations (National Association for the Education of Young Children [NAEYC], 2021).

There are many advantages to performance-based, authentic assessments. First, valuable instructional time is conserved when compared to lengthy administration of direct assessments (McAfee & Leong, 2011). It is also widely understood that authentic assessment is less intrusive, and students perform better when in a familiar setting, doing what they typically do, and with people with whom they are familiar. And, finally, these types of assessments provide more functional and relevant information that is captured across environments and in the context of daily activities (Atkins-Burnett, 2007; Snow & Van Hemel, 2008).

Most importantly, teachers, administrators, policy makers, and researchers should have a clear understanding of the purpose of the assessment. Research suggests that teachers' understanding of the purpose and use of KEAs is inconsistent (Harvey & Ohle, 2018). It is critical that kindergarten teachers are familiar with using formative, observation-based, assessment in natural contexts and environments (NAEYC, 2009) as described in Chapter 2. The North Carolina Office on Early Learning (2019) assembled a framework for collecting formative assessment data in kindergarten by collecting photos of children demonstrating skills, interviewing families, and collecting work samples (https://files.nc.gov /dpi/documents/earlylearning/kea/keaconstructprogressions_2.25.19.pdf).

TIMELY REFERRALS AND TIERED INSTRUCTION

In an effort to remove barriers that prohibit learning, frequent monitoring of student's responses to current strategies using a multitiered system of support (MTSS) model is employed in many kindergarten programs. The Division for Early Childhood (2021) provides guidance for implementing an MTSS model for young children. The paper describes a cyclical process of gathering assessment information, analyzing the data, developing a plan, implementing the plan, and monitoring progress to determine if the plan is working. The goal of this cycle of data collection is to determine if targeted and intensive instructional strategies are working or if another strategy is needed. There are many different models of MTSS, and there is no one particular model that is widely employed or researched. That said, many programs use a process called response to intervention (RTI), which uses a tiered system like those used in MTSS approaches to focus exclusively on supporting academic achievement in young children (whereas MTSS models in general are more comprehensive and include a focus on social-emotional support).

In particular, the use of RTI often includes three tiers of support: Tier 1, which involves providing all children in the classroom with high-quality scientifically based instruction to ensure that any learning difficulties are not the result of inadequate instruction; Tier 2, which provides targeted instruction to select children or groups of children that varies in intensity, duration, and frequency; and Tier 3, which is reserved for children who do not make adequate progress at Tier 2 and who therefore require more frequent, individualized, and intensive interventions that target specific areas of need.

Importantly, the Individuals with Disabilities Education Act (2004) makes clear that the use of RTI types of frameworks must not be used to justify a delay in referring a child for special education eligibility. Unfortunately, the danger seems to be that children receiving tiered support are often placed in classrooms and labeled RTI children, spending months waiting to get referred for special education. It is imperative that kindergarten teachers effectively collect data on individual children using the performance monitoring techniques discussed in Chapter 7 so that they can measure the effectiveness of tiered interventions. This practice guides instruction and allows the teacher to begin planning for next steps without delay. Similarly, it is crucial that school districts employ referral criteria that do not delay eligibility determination, thereby potentially preventing a child from receiving necessary special education services.

PROGRAM PLANNING IN KINDERGARTEN CLASSROOMS

Teachers, schools, districts, and states have varying purposes for collecting assessment information. Previously discussed KEAs or KRAs are often dictated by state or local education policies. In other words, those assessments are required. However, they fall short of providing information necessary for determining the developmental status of individual children in the classroom or the needs of small groups of children who might need additional intervention. Program planning assessment guides these instructional decisions. The most common purpose is to guide instruction. There are two types of tools that might be used for program planning purposes in kindergarten: curriculum-based measures and curriculum-based assessments.

Curriculum-Based Measures

Curriculum-based measures (CBMs) are designed to measure student academic growth as well as the effectiveness of instruction (Deno, 1985). Unlike traditional norm-referenced tests, CBMs align with scaffolded skills leading to larger goals. Norm-referenced tests occur less frequently, typically once or twice a year, and do not provide opportunities to catch small learning gaps before they become large. CBMs are used frequently, take very little time (e.g., a 3-minute reading probe), and enable teachers to identify students who are struggling on specific short-term learning skills. Additionally, CBMs help teachers determine which teaching strategies work. Data collected from CBMs are used to inform practice so that teachers can develop specific and realistic goals for their students. Box 12.1 includes examples of two CBMs often used in kindergarten.

Although CBMs are beneficial in determining if children need additional instruction in a given area, the tools are designed primarily to examine basic academics (e.g., math and literacy) and do not take into account the whole child and whether the absence of developmental skills might be adversely impacting a child's ability to learn early academic skills. Also given that assessment practices often guide the curriculum, tools that focus only on academics may result in a curriculum that overlooks other areas of development that impact school success (e.g., social-emotional development).

Box 12.1.   Two Examples of Curriculum-Based Measures Often Used in Kindergarten

The Dynamic Indicators of Basic Early Literacy Skills (DIBELS): The DIBELS is a measure of reading ability that is used nationally in many kindergartens. The purpose of the DIBELS is to measure a variety of reading skills and predict outcomes for individual students as related to benchmarks.

The Measure of Academic Progress (MAP testing): MAP testing is a computerized adaptive test, meaning every student will get a unique set of test questions based on their responses to previous questions. When a student answers correctly, the next question will be more challenging, and when a student answers a question incorrectly, the next question will be less challenging. The purpose of MAP testing is to determine what a child knows at a given point in time and what they are ready to learn next. The test allows student growth to be tracked over time and also measures growth between tests.

Curriculum-Based Assessments

A second way that program planning assessment can be conducted in kindergarten is by using a curriculum-based assessment (CBA). CBAs are described in Chapter 2, and their overall use with young children with and without disabilities is described in Chapter 6. The primary advantages of using a CBA with kindergarten-age children is that a CBA provides a holistic picture of young children's development. Instead of examining only narrow academic outcomes, the CBA addresses all developmental areas that are interrelated. This can aid in understanding why children may have difficulty learning particular academic content. For example, if children are having difficulty with reasoning and problem-solving skills, they are likely to have difficulty learning early math concepts. If children have poor fine motor skills, they are going to struggle with writing their name, identifying/labeling sight words, and drawing pictures.

A number of CBAs that are used in early intervention and preschool extend to kindergarten and even into primary grades. For example, the Teaching Strategies GOLD (Heroman et al., 2010) measures social-emotional, physical, language, cognitive, literacy, math, science and technology, social studies, the arts, and English acquisition. Students from birth to third grade are assessed on 38 objectives across these areas, with most objectives having dimensions that are assessed to clarify the objectives, resulting in about 90 items. The GOLD assessment is administered through observation of children during ongoing daily interactions and documented through anecdotal notes, photos, videos, and work samples (https://teachingstrategies.com/solutions/assess/gold/).

Another example of a CBA that documents children's development in kindergarten is the Assessment, Evaluation, and Programming System–Third Edition (AEPS®-3) (2022). The assessment includes items across the fine motor, gross motor, adaptive, cognitive, literacy, math, social communication, and social-emotional developmental and content areas. The assessment is administered through observing children during daily activities and routines, documenting observations, and then assigning a numerical score of 2 (mastered), 1 (emerging), or 0 (not ready) to each item.

The challenge for kindergarten teachers in administering a complete CBA with each child is a matter of time, resources, and competing demands. In many states, kindergarten teachers are the only adults working in the classroom. In addition, other assessment demands are often mandated by state and local education agencies (e.g., KEA). Despite these challenges, the aforementioned benefits of using a CBA remain. To address some of the challenges of administering an entire CBA, authors of the AEPS-3 (2022) developed a new tool that is part of their larger test, titled Ready-Set. The Ready-Set is a subset of 40 items derived from the larger test that specifically targets skills that young children in kindergarten need to learn. The test addresses all of the developmental areas from the larger tests and is administered using the same strategies (observations, documentation, scoring). The Ready-Set is accompanied by a family report document that families can complete to assist with data collection. Also included is a set of assessment activities, structured activities that can be implemented in the kindergarten classroom and that contain AEPS-3 Ready-Set items. Teachers can conduct the assessment activities while documenting/scoring items from the Ready-Set. Figure 12.1 illustrates an example of the book time assessment activity. Multiple children can be assessed at one time during assessment activities, increasing efficiency in data collection.

Ready-Set **aeps3**

Name: Emily Robinson

Score Key			Note Key
Mastery performance 2	Emerging performance 1A = Assistance 1I = Incomplete 1AI = Assistance/Incomplete	No performance 0	C = Conduct M = Modification Q = Quality R = Report

Test date:	9/28/2021					
Examiner(s):	Amanda Peters					

	Target	Score	Notes	Score	Notes	Score	Notes
1. Manipulates object with two hands, each performing different action FM.B3		2	C M Q R		C M Q R		C M Q R
2. Holds writing tool using three-finger grasp to write or draw FM.C1		1I	C M Q R		C M Q R		C M Q R
3. Jumps forward GM.B6		2	C M Q R		C M Q R		C M Q R
4. Skips GM.B7		2	C M Q R		C M Q R		C M Q R
5. Uses hands to hang on play equipment with bars GM.C2		1A	C M Q R		C M Q R		C M Q R
6. Uses culturally appropriate social dining skills AD.A5		2	C M Q R		C M Q R		C M Q R
7. Recognizes and reports information regarding safety AD.D4		1A	C M Q R		C M Q R		C M Q R
8. Maintains cooperative activity SE.C3		2	C M Q R		C M Q R		C M Q R
9. Interacts appropriately with others during small-group activities SE.D1		2	C M Q R		C M Q R		C M Q R
10. Interacts appropriately with others during large-group activities SE.D2		2	C M Q R		C M Q R		C M Q R

Figure 12.1. Example of the Book Time Assessment Activity Ready-Set. Multiple children can be assessed at one time during assessment activities, increasing efficiency in data collection. (From Bricker, D., Dionne, C., Grisham, J., Johnson, J., Macy, M., Slentz, K., & Waddell, M. [2022]. *Assessment, Evaluation, and Programming System for Infants and Children, Third Edition [AEPS®-3]*. Paul H. Brookes Publishing Co.; reprinted by permission.)

SUMMARY

Although many kindergarten teachers are feeling pressure to teach academic content to meet assessment standards by the end of each school year, ultimately, all children learn and grow uniquely. Therefore, we must use varying methods of assessment to determine the developmental level of each child so that we can plan to support their needs. The mandated assessments may provide information, but not all that is needed to develop lessons to support individual needs. Covering broad academic content through scripted academic curriculum leaves little time for free choice, recess, and other opportunities for authentic assessment in natural environments and discovering emergent learning. These natural learning environments provide opportunities for systematic observation without disrupting instruction. Teachers must be intentional about scheduling times that provide opportunities for gathering authentic assessment as an intentional part of instruction, as discussed in Chapter 2. Chapter 2 also provides additional information on the research base for authentic assessment in the classroom along with strategies for flipping the script on conventional assessment practices. In Chapter 5, step five specifically discusses the role of the teacher in making critical decisions to determine if additional testing and/or information is needed. It also provides additional information regarding organizing opportunities for authentic assessment.

Just as there is not a single approach to planning the curriculum, there is no single approach to assessment. However, the approach used should be relative to the overall framework of accountability within the school district and state. As has been discussed in earlier chapters, the challenge remains with kindergarten teachers to meet the professional guidance of organizations such as Division for Early Childhood and NAEYC while balancing classroom assessment practices with developmental, academic, and reporting purposes.

REFERENCES

Aiona, S. (2005). Assessing school readiness. *Educational Perspectives, 38*(1), 47–50.

Atkins-Burnett, S. (2007). *Measuring children's progress from preschool through third grade* (No. 2d7310d35a3e4a129792dde6d1f5107b). Mathematica Policy Research. https://www.mathematica-mpr.com/-/media/publications/pdfs/measchildprogress.pdf

Auck, A., & Atchison, B. (2016). *50-state comparison: K–3 quality.* Education Commission of the States.

Bassok, D., & Galdo, E. (2016). Inequality in preschool quality? Community-level disparities in access to high-quality learning environments. *Early Education and Development, 27,* 128–144. https://doi.org/10.1080/10409289.2015.1057463

Bricker, D., Dionne, C., Grisham, J., Johnson, J., Macy, M., Slentz, K., & Waddell, M. (2022). *Assessment, Evaluation, and Programming System for Infants and Children–Third Edition (AEPS®-3).* Paul H. Brookes Publishing Co.

Brown, C. P. (2013). Reforming preschool to ready children for academic achievement: A case study of the impact of pre-k reform on the issue of school readiness. *Early Education and Development, 24,* 554–573. https://doi.org/10.1080/10409289.2012.694352

Connors-Tadros, L. (2014). *Information and resources on developing state policy on kindergarten entry assessment (KEA) (CEELO FASTFacts).* Center on Enhancing Early Learning Outcomes. http://ceelo.org/wp-content/uploads/2014/02/KEA_Fast_Fact_Feb_11_2014_2.pdf

Deno, S. L. (1985). Curriculum-based measurement: The emerging alternative. *Exceptional Children, 52*(3), 219–232.

DiBello, L. C., & Neuharth-Pritchett, S. (2008). Perspectives on school readiness and prekindergarten programs: An introduction. *Childhood Education, 84*(5), 256–259.

Division for Early Childhood (DEC). (2021). *Multi-tiered system of support framework in early childhood: Description and implications.* Author.

Education Commission of the States. (2018). *School readiness and transitions: Are kindergarten entrance assessments required?* http://ecs.force.com/mbdata/MBQuest2RTanw?rep=KK3Q1811

Fonseca, M. (2017). *Smoothing out the bumps of transitioning to kindergarten.* AEM: Professional Development Grant: Preschool Development Grants Technical Assistance. https://files.eric.ed.gov/fulltext/ED583131.pdf

Harvey, H., & Ohle, K. (2018). What's the purpose? Educators' perceptions and use of a state-mandated kindergarten entry assessment. *Education Policy Analysis Archives, 26*(142).

Heroman, C., Burts, D. C., Berke, K. L., & Bickart, T. S. (2010). *Teaching Strategies GOLD: Objectives for development and learning: Birth through kindergarten.* Teaching Strategies, LLC.

Kagan, S. L. (1990). Readiness 2000: Rethinking rhetoric and responsibility. *Phi Delta Kappan, 72*(4), 272–279. http://policyforchildren.org/wp-content/uploads/2013/08/Readiness-2000-Rethinking-Rhetoric-and-Responsibility.pdf

Kagan, S. L. (1992). Readiness past, present, and future: Shaping the agenda. *Young Children, 48,* 48–53.

Maxwell, K., & Clifford, R. (2004). *School readiness assessment. Beyond the Journal: Young Children on the Web.* http://www.calstatela.edu/sites/default/files/groups/Anna%20Bing%20Arnold%20Children's%20Center/Docs/naeyc_school_readiness_article.pdf

McAfee, O. D., & Leong, D. J. (2011). *Assessing and guiding young children's development and learning.* Allyn & Bacon.

National Association for the Education of Young Children (NAEYC). (2009). *Where we stand on curriculum, assessment, and program evaluation.* http://www.naeyc.org/files/naeyc/file/positions/StandCurrAss.pdf

National Association for the Education of Young Children (NAEYC). (2021). *DAP: Observing, documenting, and assessing children's development and learning.* https://www.naeyc.org/resources/position-statements/dap/assessing-development

No Child Left Behind Act of 2001, PL 107-110, 115 Stat. 1425, 20 U.S.C. §§ 6301 et seq.

North Carolina Office of Early Learning. (2019). *NC construct progressions and situations.* Public Schools of North Carolina, State Board of Education, Department of Public Instruction. https://files.nc.gov/dpi/documents/earlylearning/kea/keaconstructprogressions_2.25.19.pdf

Pretti-Frontczak, K., Harjusola-Webb, S., Chin, M., Grisham-Brown, J., Acar, S., Heo, K., Corby, M., & Zeng, S. (2016). Three mistakes made worldwide in "getting children ready for school." *Young Exceptional Children, 19*(1), 48–51.

Regenstein, E., Connors, M. C., Romero-Jurado, R., & Wiener, J. (2017). Effective kindergarten readiness assessments: Influencing policy, informing instruction, and creating joyful classrooms. *Policy Conversation, 6.* https://www.startearly.org/app/uploads/pdf/PolicyConversationKRA2017.pdf

Sabol, T. J., & Pianta, R. C. (2017). The state of young children in the United States: School readiness. In E. Dearing & E. VotrubaDrzal (Eds.), *Handbook of early childhood programs, practices, and policies.* Blackwell. https://doi.org/10.1002/9781118937334.ch1

Saluja, G., Scott-Little, C., & Clifford, R. (2000). Readiness for school: A survey of state policies and definitions. *Early Childhood Research and Practices, 2*(2), 3–55.

Shields, K. A., Cook, K. D., & Greller, S. (2016). How kindergarten entry assessments are used in public schools and how they correlate with spring assessments (REL 2017-182). U.S. Department of Education, Institute of Education Sciences, National Center for Education Evaluation and Regional Assistance, Regional Educational Laboratory Northeast & Islands. http://ies.ed.gov/ncee/edlabs/regions/northeast/pdf/REL_2017182.pdf

Snow, C. E., & Van Hemel, S. B. (2008). *Early childhood assessment: Why, what, and how.* National Academies Press.

Snow, K. L. (2006). Measuring school readiness: Conceptual and practical considerations. *Early Education and Development, 17,* 7–41.

Snow, K. L. (2011). *Developing kindergarten readiness and other large-scale assessment systems: Necessary considerations in the assessment of young children.* National Association for the Education of Young Children.

Stedron, J. M., & Berger, A. (2010). *NCSL Technical Report: State approaches to school readiness assessment.* National Conference of State Legislatures.

Stipek, D. (2006). No Child Left Behind comes to preschool. *The Elementary School Journal, 106,* 455–466. https://doi.org/10.1086/505440

Weisenfeld, G. (2017). *Assessment tools used in kindergarten entry assessments (CEELO FastFact).* Center on Enhancing Early Learning Outcomes.

Index

Page numbers followed by *f*, *t*, and *b* indicate figures, tables, and boxes respectively